THE INSIDERS' GUIDE ®

TO

Mississippi

THE INSIDERS' GUIDE ®

TO

Mississippi

by
Sylvia Higginbotham
and
Lisa Monti

The Insiders' Guides®, Inc.

Co-published and marketed by:
Gulf Publishing Co., Inc.
205 DeBuys Rd.
(601) 896-2100

Co-published and distributed by:
The Insiders' Guides Inc.
The Waterfront • Suites 12 &13
P.O. 2057
Manteo, NC 27954
(919) 473-6100

•

SECOND EDITION
1st printing

•

Copyright ©1995
by Gulf Publishing Co., Inc.

•

Printed in the United States
of America

•

ISBN 0-912367-82-2

Gulf Publishing Co., Inc.

Project Coordination
Wanda Howell

Account Executives
Elaine Davenport
Becky Turnage
Ann French
Jana Brune
Phyllis Killegrew
Courtney Broyard
Judy Galloway
Ben Garraway

**Daryl Evans, Darrell Ross,
Michelle Evans,
Cheryl Fishman**, artists

The Insiders' Guides® Inc.

Publisher/Editor-in-Chief
Beth P. Storie

President/General Manager
Michael McOwen

Vice President/Advertising
Murray Kasmenn

Partnership Services Director
Giles Bissonnette

Creative Services Director
Mike Lay

Online Services Director
David Haynes

Sales and Marketing Director
Julie Ross

Managing Editor
Theresa Chavez

Project Artist
Mel Dorsey

Fulfillment Director
Gina Twiford

Controller
Claudette Forney

Preface

To say that much has been written about Mississippi is like saying that Mississippi has produced some pretty good writers, entertainers, athletes and entrepreneurs.

Unfortunately, what some people outside of the state remember most clearly are stories of injustices written decades ago. Accomplishments are not nearly as newsworthy, so the rest of the story has not always been told.

Those who know this state recognize that Mississippi has many stories to tell, partly because its people have been through so much and because they have so much to offer. Storytelling through words and music has carried many Mississippians to prominence, among them William Faulkner, Eudora Welty, Richard Wright, Elvis Presley, Jimmie Rodgers, Leontyne Price, Tammy Wynette, B.B. King, John Grisham and Oprah Winfrey.

Mississippi is a decidedly diverse place. This is home to excellence in the arts, history embodied in architecture, graciousness in manners, prosperity in commerce and advances in technology. From the hilly north to the southern shoreline, Mississippi's geography contains a varied accumulation of extraordinary natural beauty. Its communities and neighborhoods represent simple country living and the cosmopolitan mix of big-city life — with the amenities of both.

Visitors can easily experience this diversity and are encouraged to do so. Just listen to our world-class musicians play and sing the blues, jazz, country and bluegrass. Come celebrate the state's assorted ethnic backgrounds at a year-round succession of fairs, festivals and special events. Take a true taste of Mississippi in the simple pleasures of home cooking or the fine ethnic equivalents found in Creole, German and Lebanese restaurants. Tour the museums, workshops and art galleries where talented artisans create paintings, sculpture, pottery and jewelry. Enjoy the quiet beauty of the state's collection of parks, forests and waterways. Or take your chances, so to speak, in the glitzy dockside gaming houses along the river and coastline.

We think you'll find some common ingredients among Mississippi's diversity: a brand of genuine Southern hospitality that has reached legendary status; a colorful history respectfully played out in monuments and pageantry; a resilience to rebound from adversity, whether dealt by human or natural forces; and a keen appreciation for the arts.

A great deal has been documented and speculated and imagined about this sometimes misunderstood and often underestimated state. We're sure you'll see for yourself how distinct and wonderful our Mississippi is.

About the Authors

Sylvia Higginbotham, who has been a freelance writer for about 10 years now, says it's what she plans to do as long as she keeps her wits and a modicum of wisdom. Before she began a freelance writing/communications company, Higginbotham worked for newspapers, television stations and advertising/public relations firms in Shreveport and Lafayette, Louisiana and in Mississippi. She's also been a rep for a market research firm, executive director of a historic foundation and public relations specialist for a utility company.

Her work appears in various newspapers, magazines and guidebooks — under her own name — and she writes award-winning videos for municipalities and businesses. Higginbotham says that women of a certain age get bored with business suits and begin to think about exercising other options. She did, and she's glad, even though the hours are often long, the pay is sometimes inconsistent and there's an investment to be made in computers, copiers, fax machines and offices. She's also thankful for her years of sales experience, for she believes that selling is essential to what she does today. Sylvia makes her home in Columbus with husband Joe, who is also self-employed. They have two daughters, Saxonie and Shaye, who live with their families in Louisville, Kentucky, and Denver, Colorado. Higginbotham won the Mississippi Travel Media Award in recognition of her contributions to and promotion of Mississippi.

Lisa Monti is editor of *Coast Business*, an award-winning biweekly publication that covers business news, people and issues. She also is associate editor of *Coast Magazine*, the lifestyle magazine of the Mississippi Coast. Both are based in Gulfport.

Lisa worked previously as a freelance writer/editor for several years. She wrote newspaper and magazine articles and columns and published newsletters, brochures and other works in her home office. Her clients included economic development agencies.

Before undertaking the challenge of self employment, Lisa worked for government agencies and in private industry. She studied journalism and English at the University of Southern Mississippi in Hattiesburg.

Her interests include travel, computers and gardening. She plans to do more writing for more regional and national publications.

Photo: Tim Isbell, The Sun Herald

One balloon lands safely near a cotton field in Canton during a hot air balloon festival.

Acknowledgments

Thanks to all the fine people who bought the first book then told us they liked it. Again this year, thanks to the outstanding people in the tourism industry in Mississippi who are always so helpful — from the State Division of Tourism to local CVBs, chambers of commerce staffers and the Mississippi Travel Promotion Association. It's a pleasure to work with pros who know that the more information we have, the better the book about our Mississippi will be. Thanks, especially, to Carolyn Denton, Columbus CVB. Thanks to my family and friends for support and encouragement, especially Joe Higginbotham and my mother, Mrs. Floye Robbins, and special thanks to Project Coordinator Wanda Howell of Gulf Publishing Co., Inc./The Sun Herald; Beth Storie, the publisher at Insider's Guides Inc.; Theresa Chavez, our patient editor at Insiders' Guides® in Manteo, North Carolina, and coauthor Lisa Monti, who wrote about the Gulf Coast, the River Cities of Natchez and Vicksburg and the Heartland south of Interstate 20, except for Jackson; my areas were Jackson and north of I-20.

We appreciate so much all the coverage we've had in the press, especially the nice color pieces by Lea Anne Brandon for the *Clarion-Ledger* and Kat Bergeron with the *Sun Herald*. Thank you, and again, thanks to readers, bookstores and advertisers.

— Sylvia

Needless to say, tracking down and verifying the thousands of details contained in this guide took the help of people too numerous to count and name individually. To all of them, I am grateful. Special thanks for their generous assistance go to: freelance writer and researcher Susan Bosco, who helped gather and check some of those details; Ann Briggs and Leisa French of The Meridian/Lauderdale County Partnership; the Tourism Development Division of the Mississippi Department of Economic and Community Development; Anne Mohon of the Natchez Convention and Visitors' Bureau; Lenore Barkley of the Vicksburg Convention and Visitors Bureau; Biloxi Visitors Center; Mississippi Beach Convention and Visitors Bureau; Lisa Ingram of Mississippi Wildlife, Fisheries and Parks Department; the reference librarians at the Bay St. Louis-Hancock County Library; Judy Scruggs of the Port Gibson/Claiborne County Chamber of Commerce; the Hattiesburg Convention & Visitors Bureau; Hancock County Chamber of Commerce; the Mississippi Gaming Commission; the Brookhaven/Lin-

Photo: Sylvia Higginbotham

You'll see a beautiful view of the Gulf Coast shoreline from the lawn of the Beauvoir, the last home of CSA President Jefferson Davis.

coln County Chamber of Commerce; the Clarke County Chamber of Commerce; the Magee Chamber of Commerce; the Hazlehurst Area Chamber of Commerce; Crystal Springs Chamber of Commerce; Pike County Chamber of Commerce; Jefferson Davis County Chamber of Commerce; the Wayne County Chamber of Commerce; George County Eco- nomic Development Foundation; and the Covington County Chamber of Commerce. Thanks also go to Wanda Howell of The Sun Herald, cowriter Sylvia Higginbotham and Insiders' Beth Storie and Theresa Chavez for their support in this endeavor.

— Lisa

Table of Contents

Directory of Maps

Mississippi

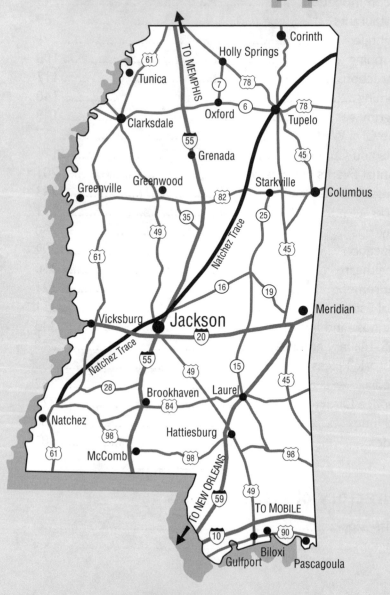

Regions

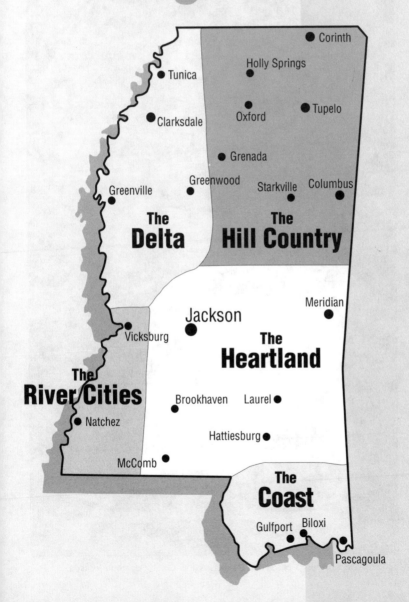

Corinth

Holly Springs

Tunica

Oxford   Tupelo

Clarksdale

Grenada

Greenwood   Starkville   Columbus

Greenville

The
Delta

The
Hill Country

Meridian

Jackson

Vicksburg

The
Heartland

The
River Cities

Brookhaven   Laurel

Natchez

Hattiesburg

McComb

The
Coast

Gulfport   Biloxi

Pascagoula

Photo: Herb Welch, The Sun Herald

The Governor's office and the Mississippi Capitol dome in Jackson.

How to Use This Book

This book is the first in The Insiders' Guide® series to cover an entire state. Whereas other guides provide an inside look at cities and regions, this statewide approach provides in-depth coverage from the hills in north Mississippi to the southern coastline.

We've divided the state into regions of fairly equal size, starting at the top and carving out five sections. Then we concentrate our coverage on the major cities and groups of towns in each of those regions.

The northernmost section is the Hill Country, followed by the Delta, the central Heartland, the River Cities of Vicksburg, Natchez and Port Gibson along the Mississippi to the southernmost region, the Coast. (A map is included to illustrate how we've dissected the state.)

It's evident just by these regional names how diversified a state Mississippi is, and readers will notice the variety that's packed into 82 counties reaching from the Tennessee border to the Gulf of Mexico. Mississippians enjoy sharing their heritage and other prized possessions with visitors, and it's our hope that this book will help you take advantage of everything here.

Each chapter follows the regional approach, from north to south, so that if you want to find a casino in Biloxi, a fishing spot around Meridian, a blues festi-val in Greenville, antique stores in Natchez or antebellum homes in Columbus, you can easily locate the information under the appropriate regional headings. The same is true for shopping, accommodations, restaurants and all other topics.

For orientation purposes, we've included overviews of all the areas we've covered. You'll find some special chapters on the Civil War, pilgrimages, daytrips and gaming that help portray Mississippi in its completeness. Some special Insider tips are scattered throughout the guide to help you make the most of your visit. Our first tip: Mississippi has one statewide area code, 601, so all of the entries in this book list the telephone number only. Remember to dial 601 for all long distance calls made within the state.

We don't guarantee that we've included every single bit of information about Mississippi, but we can promise that these pages will reveal many surprising things to its readers. It's been a learning process for all of us involved in the publication of this guide, and we're pleased to offer this second edition with our new and updated findings. We hope y'all will share your own discoveries with us as well. Please write to us at The Insiders' Guides®, Inc., P.O. Box 2057, Manteo, North Carolina 27954.

Photo: Kat Bergeron, The Sun Herald

Backyards, porches, swings and giant oak trees are part of many memories forever etched into the minds of native Mississippians.

My Mississippi

By Sylvia Higginbotham

Back in the 1960s, when I was a young and impressionable Mississippian who considered Ayn Rand the intellectual guru of the day, the thing to do was leave the Magnolia State to seek adventure and see how people lived in the real world. At the first opportunity, I left college and rural Jones County, Mississippi, in search of the bright lights and big city.

New York City-bound, I arrived at Penn Station full of expectation and excitement, knowing that I was finally close to Broadway plays, quaint bookstores, wonderful museums and Central Park. I found the flash and dash and glitz and glitter as well as the decadence and dilettantes that give the City its unique ambiance.

I had no idea that rent would be higher than the high-rise I expected to live in near Central Park. Nor did I realize that so few of the 8 million or so New Yorkers live anywhere near the Park. Many live in the surrounding boroughs, which is where I found an affordable place. Brooklyn is a far cry from Manhattan, though in the mid-'60s, Prospect Park was not so bad.

After a whirlwind first few weeks of seeing the basic sights, conquering the subway system, ferreting out the best cheap restaurants and learning the names of the people who ran the neighborhood vegetable stands, I was homesick. I missed the great towering green trees of Mississippi, even the red clay hills I'd found so unappealing a few months prior. We frequented a very old neighborhood cemetery, for it was the only place with beautiful trees, except for the park. I missed the white porch swings and wicker furniture so prominent back home. The concrete stoop or the fire escape just could not compare. I missed the fragrance of honeysuckle and magnolia in the spring and the sweet perfume of a chinaberry tree in full bloom. The scents and sounds in my Brooklyn neighborhood were olive oil and garlic emanating from Greek and Italian neighbors who spoke languages I could not understand.

How I craved the scent of a sweet potato pie baking in my Big Mama's (grandmother's) kitchen. I desperately longed to hear the soft and delicate sounds of the South as my mother and her friends talked about the garden club and flowers in the most mellifluous Mississippi voices.

Books kept reminding me of what I was missing. I traded Ayn Rand and others like her for William Faulkner and James Agee and as many Southern writers as I could find at the local library. I memorized certain descriptions and said them to myself quite often, especially a passage from Faulkner's *Wedding in the Rain*:

It was a summer of wisterias. The twilight was full of it and the smell of his father's cigar as they sat on the front gallery after supper, while in the deep, shaggy lawn below the veranda the fireflies blew and drifted in soft random.

I would have sacrificed my library card for one quick glimpse of the lush woods and foliage surrounding our house in the country, back home, and for a chance to sit on the porch after supper and watch the fireflies. The library had a copy of Harper Lee's *To Kill a Mockingbird*, which made me cry profusely all five times I read it.

Even though the people in my neighborhood were kind and friendly and we communicated with smiles when we couldn't understand each other's words, after seven months of unadulterated homesickness, I headed down South to the Magnolia State. Back to the land of Dixie's dew and Dorothy's daisies, where kin folk waited to welcome me home. When my train, the *Southerner*, pulled into the depot in Laurel on a bright sunny afternoon, I finally understood the majesty of Mississippi. It has wondrous scenic beauty to rival any state, and in it live the best people on earth.

There are still a few pockets of the state relatively untouched by time, where a grand and glorious heritage prevails. People appear to be kinder and gentler in these special places, where racial conflicts have not been reinforced, and street crime is not a factor.

This is not to say that we haven't had problems in some of our towns and cities. We have. Inhumanity rears its ugly head on occasion here too. But not as often and not as senselessly. We try to find ways to overcome adversity. Sometimes we have to stop and remember that we're Mississippians, one and all, and that we've always been people who talk and listen and share.

I've been back home, after detours in several other states besides New York, for more than a dozen years now. And it is a pleasure to be back to what Mississippi novelist James Street called "the promised land." Here's an excerpt from Street's book, *Oh, Promised Land*:

I've found a new land — a greener land — even the birds are friendly. The land is warm and lush. And Great God, what trees! They just stand there and look way down at you. Ay, Chock, that's the Promised Land.

Indeed, Mississippi has the potential of being the promised land for many of us who've chosen to return here. Perhaps we come back expecting to make a difference — now that we're mature and wise — or maybe we come to partake of our state's own special brand of homegrown civilization.

Inside
Area Overviews

Part of Mississippi's diversity lies in its geography, which, as reflected in this book, extends from the hilly north through the state's rolling, wooded midsection to the flat, sandy counties in the south.

There is a diversity in how each area developed over the generations and how each has recovered from hard times. More diversity is found in the ways Mississippians live and make their living and how they celebrate what makes them unique. In some corners of the state, history grabs much of the spotlight; in others, technology takes center stage.

Mississippi is a collection of land, rivers, monuments, festivals, farms, industries, works of art and much more spread throughout an assortment of communities, cities and towns.

We've divided the state into five distinct sections: The Hill Country, The Delta, The Heartland, The River Cities and The Coast. Each contains a description of the general area and some specifics about the major cities and towns therein. For complete descriptions of specific events, attractions and other points of interest mentioned in this overview, please see the Annual Events and Festivals, Attractions, The Arts and other chapters in this book.

Photo: Slyvia Higginbotham

Bridges over the "Mighty Mississippi" in Vicksburg.

The Hill Country

The Hill Country is what most outsiders expect Mississippi to be: clean and green, slow and sultry and steeped in tradition and front-porch stories, thanks to more than a few notable Mississippians who've introduced this part of the Magnolia State to the world.

Meandering along the back roads, following the routes of Indians, settlers and soldiers, one can easily imagine the way things were a couple of centuries ago when early Mississippians inhabited the land. To the Chickasaw Indians, it was a region rich in game and unspoiled by civilization. It was their home; the place they must have hated to leave. To settlers, it was the promised land, the place they planned never to leave. To soldiers of the War Between the States, it was a place to die for. Some died defending a way of life; others died destroying it. Still others from the Hill Country — William Faulkner, Elvis Presley and Tennessee Williams — helped put the region on the map. Add current bestselling author John Grisham to the list of notables, and understand the appeal of north Mississippi.

About the best way to experience the beauty of the Hill Country is to drive along the Natchez Trace Parkway, an old route used for thousands of years by Indians and others who came before us. The Trace is a 440-mile long, narrow strip of outstanding scenery that connects Nashville, Tennessee; and Natchez, Mississippi. It cuts diagonally across Mississippi for about 310 miles, from the upper northeast corner to the lower southwest corner. The Trace is indeed a parkway, and it is administered and maintained by the National Park Service. The speed limit is a strictly enforced 50 mph. It's best to drive slowly so as not to miss nature and wildlife along the way. Keep your eyes open, for you could spot deer frolicking and feeding on the green grass bordering the Trace. Except for historical markers, the pristine setting is undisturbed by signs, commercial vehicles and the Styrofoam clutter of fast food. Towns just off the parkway offer food, gas and lodging, though the only gas station directly on the parkway is at milepost 193.9. The Natchez Trace Parkway Visitors Center at Tupelo offers a wealth of information on the Parkway and its development, as well as books and gift items.

Whether traveling on the Natchez Trace or along a major highway or back road, the Hill Country encompasses a varied terrain: the rocky foothills of the Appalachian Mountains; the lush, rolling hills of Oxford; the hills and rich prairie land that border Columbus. And in between lie small towns, several colleges, a military base, major manufacturing facilities and thousands of people who are proud to call the Hill Country home.

Columbus

This quintessentially Southern town about 10 miles from the Alabama line in northeast Mississippi is well-known to history lovers, for history literally lives here. The streets are lined with magnificent pre-Civil War mansions, most are Greek Revival in architectural style, though it's not uncommon to see Italianate, Gothic, Federal or an eclectic combination of two or more styles. The houses are dressed to the nines and ready to greet guests during the annual spring Pilgrimage, a two-week event held around the first of April.

The grand old homes of Columbus are privately owned residences of local folks, and they've been lovingly preserved or expensively restored, or both. Two homes, Liberty Hall (1832) and Amzi Love (1848), have remained in the same families since they were built. And sixth- or seventh-generation anything in this still-new USA is quite a coup.

Columbus was incorporated in 1821, after about 125 people settled in the area. Originally called "Possum Town" because of the opossum-like features of trader Spirus Roach, the official town was given the more dignified name of Columbus. Planters and yeoman farmers from the eastern coastal area had seen their cotton-producing land exhausted by the plantation system, so they came westward seeking better soil. After cotton crops came in and when the river was high, steamboats transported cotton down the Tombigbee River to Mobile, Alabama. On the return trip, the steamboats were laden with fine furnishings and accessories for the opulent homes that cotton built in the 1830s through 1850s. Some of those homes are now bed and breakfast inns, complete with fine period antiques and Southern hospitality. Good restaurants are available, and so are chain hotels.

The golden years of cotton culture were short-lived, for the nation was struggling with the issues of slavery and states' rights. The young nation was divided; Abraham Lincoln was elected president, and the War Between the States lasted four long and arduous years. During the Civil War, Columbus was never invaded by Federal troops, though the town served the Confederate cause in countless ways. After the bloody battle of Shiloh, approximately 3,000 wounded soldiers were housed in Columbus homes and churches. The women of Columbus tirelessly and silently tended the wounded. And after the war, some of those same women honored the dead from both armies with flowers, earning Columbus the moniker, "The town where flowers healed a nation." This generous deed, originally called 'Decoration Day' back in 1866, is the event that fostered the nation's Memorial Day.

Women have long been significant to Columbus' history — or herstory. Along with the Memorial Day observance begun by women, Columbus is the home of the nation's first state-supported college for women, Mississippi University for Women, which has had several name changes over the years. Since 1884, "The W" as it is affectionately called, has provided quality education for women, and since 1982, smart men too. It is recognized nationally for scholastic excellence and leadership opportunities for those who choose The W.

Today, Columbus, population 30,000, is a festive town where annual events and celebrations flourish, from the Mardi Gras-like krewes that parade during Pilgrimage, to an annual barbecue cookoff contest called the Pigfest. The town is not short on culture, either, with an active Arts Council that brings in top talent from Broadway to L.A. Speaking of the performing arts, one of the world's best-known playwrights was born in Columbus and lived in a gracious Victorian house that now serves as the official Columbus Welcome Center. The late playwright is Tennessee Williams, who won prestigious awards for *A Streetcar Named Desire*, *Cat on a Hot Tin Roof* and *The Glass Menagerie*, among others.

A nice cultural mix comes from the local university and Columbus Air Force Base, one of the four pilot-training facilities for the USAF. The base brings in some of America's best and brightest, for Air Force pilots are handpicked. Pilots, and others from the base and local industry, enjoy sporting events that are plentiful in the area. Choices include: Southeastern Conference college sports, fishing and hunting along the Tennessee-Tombigbee Waterway, year-round golf and tennis opportunities and more.

Industry thrives here too, thanks to aggressive leadership and attractive incentives. Columbus/Lowndes County is recognized throughout the state as an area rich in a varied industrial base and in organizations that encourage industry, among them Columbus-Lowndes Economic Development Association and the Chamber of Commerce.

Those who come here temporarily and return to retire say that Columbus offers the best of both worlds: an old-fashioned sense of community and a very progressive attitude. The Convention and Visitors Bureau has information and brochures. Contact the CVB at P.O. Box 789, Columbus 39703; (800) 327-2686 or 329-1191.

Starkville

It's easy to feel hopeful in Starkville, the home of Mississippi State University, for the promise of youth is everywhere. One also notices the sense of well-being that comes from the knowledge that others care. Starkville is filled with folks who care enough to get their doctorates so that they can teach others or find solutions to problems through extensive research. In fact, MSU consistently ranks among the top-100 universities in the nation in obtaining research grants and funding. Private-sector research at the Mississippi Research & Technology Park is a boon to industry in the region too. Opportunity abounds in Starkville for anyone interested in education, research and technology.

The town and the university have shared many long and happy years. Starkville has been a town since 1835; MSU came about in 1878. Originally called Boardtown because a nearby mill provided the clapboard to construct the town's buildings, the name was soon changed in honor of Revolutionary War hero John Stark. Locals still refer to the name Boardtown in festivals and other activities.

In 1863, Starkville was invaded, and raided, by Union troops. Before it could completely recover from the war's devastation, a fire in 1875 destroyed most of downtown. Once again, Starkville rebuilt and emerged bigger and stronger than ever, her people even more determined that Starkville prosper.

The Starkville of today is home to about 17,000 citizens who say their town exemplifies the quality of life to which most towns aspire. It has the friendliness of a small Southern town as well as other amenities one would expect of a city. Theater, concerts, and symphony performances are all available in Starkville. And quite astounding for a town this size, five museums tout heritage and happenstance. Visitors to the area are encouraged to take informative tours of the campus; these tours include dairy manufacturing, food science and enology (where Mississippi wines are researched and developed) and the outstanding Mississippi State University Arboretum.

As one might expect, the most popular activities in this college town are sporting events: basketball, baseball and especially football. MSU Bulldog fans come from across the South, with kids, parents and picnic baskets in tow. Tailgate par-

Photo: Harrison County Tourism Commission

*The Mississippi Gulf Coast's 26-mile expanse of man-made beach
is said to be the longest of its kind in the world.*

ties commence on the morning of the game and last well into the night.

The nearby Noxubee National Wildlife Refuge offers the outdoor sports of regulated hunting, fishing, hiking, wildlife observation points and outstanding bird-watching opportunities. It's a picturesque place, too, and great for photographing nature.

Though Starkville has a limited number of white-cloth and candles restaurants, a good meal is not hard to find. Casual dining is the norm, and po' boy sandwiches, a great Dixie delicacy, are abundant throughout the town. Lodging is abundant too, though it's best to make reservations well in advance of football weekends. Expect the usual chain motels, and a very nice 40-room restored 1920s hotel now called The State House. The Visitors & Convention Council has complete information and maps; contact them at 322 University Drive, Starkville 39759; 323-3322.

Aberdeen

This river town has been called "a Mississippi treasure" because it is quiet, quaint and boasts friendly, locally owned retail stores bordering the wide main street. Aberdeen is a town where leisurely strolls downtown or along the adjoining residential streets offer unexpected pleasures. Maier's Jewelry and Gift Shop on Commerce Street (the main thoroughfare, also Highway 45) is the oldest family-owned and operated jewelry store in Mississippi; it's been open since 1889.

Across the street from Maier's and down about a block, see St. John's Episcopal Church, a handsome edifice dating back to 1852. Don't miss the bell made of silver coin sitting atop the tower. The engraving on the bell says that it was presented to the church in Aberdeen, Mississippi, by "A.D. Bownam and 35 New York merchants. 1853." From all accounts, there may have been a clergy connection, as in a New York clergyman who came to the South and then told his former parishioners or friends of the new little church in Aberdeen. This is reliable speculation but cannot be documented.

The town was young (incorporated in 1837) when the Episcopal church was built, and the townspeople were in awe of the magnificent stained-glass windows in the Anglican church. Aberdeen was a prosperous town even back then, for by 1850, the population was more than 5,000, a greater population than that of older Mississippi towns. Aberdeen was, and is, in the center of a rich cotton-producing soil.

Lovely old antebellum and Victorian houses remain as evidence of the wealth of early Aberdeen, and one former home, The Magnolias (1850) now houses the Chamber of Commerce. Visits to the homes of history throughout Aberdeen and to the Evans Memorial Library & Museum will acquaint you with the area. The library has a good collection of genealogical research material and interesting local history. Perhaps those interested will learn about the section of Aberdeen called "Silk Stocking Avenue," now Franklin Street. Some say the name came about because of the affluence of the neighborhood; others say times were tough back then, and only one pair of silk stockings were to be found in Aberdeen, and they were on that street.

The Aberdeen/Monroe Chamber of Commerce invites inquiries. Contact them at P.O. Box 727, Aberdeen 39730; 369-6488.

Amory

Amory is the next-door neighbor to Aberdeen, also in Monroe County, and also accessible to the Tennessee-Tombigbee Waterway. It's a town of less than 8,000, and it still has an ambiance of old Mississippi. Amory is a relatively new town by some standards, for it was founded in 1887 by the K.C.M.& B. Railroad. The new town site was chosen because it's a halfway point between Memphis and Birmingham, both of which were major depot cities for the railroad. The town was named for railroad stockholder Harcourt Amory.

The town of Amory was carefully planned, from its wide streets to an orderly arrangement of business and residential areas. The new railroad town took the place of the old Cotton Gin Port, once located about 3 miles west of Amory and at one time a busy trade area for the Tombigbee River and the Chickasaw Indian villages along the west side of the river. Once the railroad and its employees — along with churches and schools — came to Amory, the merchants and traders from Cotton Gin Port followed, and the old port town ceased to exist.

By the early 1950s, the railroad changed and so did the towns dependent upon it. The leaders of Amory began looking for and recruiting industry to fill the gap left by the railroad, and they found textiles. Garment industries came, and Amory became known as the "Pants Capital of the World." Now, the town is also home to other than manufacturers, including those who make sports equipment, valves and more.

The Amory Regional Museum is an interesting stop for visitors, among them the 25,000 or more who come to the big Amory Railroad Festival each April. Another big event that is gaining in popularity is Stars Over Amory held every other year. A native of the town, now a talent agent in L.A., brings some of his clients to Amory for a talent show extraordinaire, with proceeds from the performance funding an educational scholarship. The next 'Stars' event is scheduled for the fall of 1996. The last event was hosted by former Miss Mississippi Mary Ann Mobley and her husband Gary Collins; among the performers were Susan Anton, Nell Carter, Sela Ward, and many more. For additional information about Amory, contact the Economic Development Partnership of Monroe County, P.O. Box 128, Amory 38821, 256-7194.

West Point

West Point, a town of about 8,500, has garnered much deserved recognition for its preservation/restoration efforts. West Point has an exemplary Main Street program, the results of which are obvious in the downtown area. It's obvious in more ways than one that this northeast Mississippi prairie town is innovative and community-minded. Residents are now enjoying the Rails to Trails Parkway, which came about when organized action on the part of citizens encouraged the railroad that ran through downtown to move outside the city. The former rail tracks are now trails, and scenic things are springing up along the way. There's an "arbor of memories" that features bricks purchased in memory of lost loved ones; and nearby is the Sally Kate Winters Park. It features a gazebo, park benches, band stands, playground equipment and lots of room for joggers and walkers.

Photo: Tim Isbell, The Sun Herald

Driving through the Vietnamese community in Biloxi, one can see the practice of Vietnamese skill, culture and tradition. This woman is growing rice for her family.

The Winters Park is also the site of the big Prairie Arts Festival, held each year the Saturday before Labor Day. Thousands of people come from far and wide to shop the wares of artists and craftsmen from several states. Exhibitors booths fill the park, and shoppers take up the remaining space. It's a much-anticipated fun and festive event.

Another project that involved major restoration in downtown West Point is the old Henry Clay Hotel. It's a marvelous turn-of-the-century structure that houses 30 apartments for the healthy elderly. The Henry Clay provides a secure environment and close proximity to numerous amenities. It's one of the best addresses in town. More apartments are in downtown buildings.

West Point is proud to be the home of something old and something new, both with similar names. Waverley Mansion, the 1852 plantation near West Point, is a major tourist attraction and one of the most popular historic homes in the South. Four circular staircases connect cantilevered balconies that lead to an octagonal observatory 65 feet above the ground floor. It is a private residence, but open every day of the year for tours. It is a Southern showplace, inside and outside.

Also near West Point and Waverley Mansion is the new Old Waverly Golf Club and residential community. An 18-hole championship golf course designed by Jerry Pate and Bob Cupp has been rated by the PGA as Mississippi's Most Challenging and one of the top 100 clubs in the United States. The course winds through the home sites and meanders among native forests and dogwood trees.

For more information on all that West Point has to offer, contact the Clay County Economic Development Corporation, 510 E. Broad Street, West Point 39773; 494-5121.

Tupelo

Tupelo is a town that appeals to families who want good schools, a strong business environment and the kind of values that can be found in a place where community is an important word. Across the state, people say that Tupelo has character and that folks who live here work together to get things done. There are no Old South vestiges in Tupelo, no antebellum mansions in this town where people are proud of their "poor backgrounds," according to one business leader. This all-American city has a go-for-it image not unlike that of its most famous son, Elvis Presley.

Tupelo, a city of about 31,000, lies 100 miles southeast of Memphis, Tennessee, where the famous rocker moved after his first 12 formative years in Tupelo. An old Southern saying is that the apple never falls far from the tree, and indeed, neither did Elvis. He kept up with his Tupelo roots and came back for concerts in the early years of his fame. Proceeds from a 1957 concert were donated to the City of Tupelo for the development of a park, just one indication of Presley's generous nature.

Elvis Aaron and Jesse Garon were twins born in 1935 to Vernon and Gladys Presley of Tupelo, though Jesse died at birth. The twins were born at the Presley's small home, a two-room shotgun style house that Vernon built with borrowed money, actually $180. By the time Elvis was 3, times were hard, and the little white frame house had been repossessed. The Presleys lived in several other homes in Tupelo before moving to Memphis in 1948, and the rest is history: The musically inclined young man who wore his hair much longer than the crew-cuts of the day and chose clothing colors and styles unlike the other boys his age, changed the world of popular music.

His legend lives in Tupelo, where the Elvis Presley Center and the new Elvis Presley Museum feature his birthplace, a meditation chapel, a gift shop, a lake and camping and picnicking facilities.

Tupelo is also home to the Natchez Trace Parkway Visitors Center, just north of Tupelo directly on the Trace. The visitors center offers a video of the modern-day development of the Natchez Trace and touches upon its early history. Maps, exhibits, books and items for sale make this a popular stop in Tupelo.

Tupelo serves northeast Mississippi as a regional shopping area, where malls, downtown shops and a selection of restaurants add to the city's popularity. A big furniture market draws people from everywhere, for Tupelo has become one of the South's leading furniture producing cities. Approximately 200 companies manufacture upholstered furniture and components within a 50-mile radius of Tupelo. Plentiful hotel rooms add to the city's appeal as a marketplace.

Museums, art galleries, exemplary schools, a city ballet, theater groups, a big new 10,000-seat convention center and several annual festivals make Tupelo a good choice for young Mississippians who look for quality-of-life opportunities, or those who just wish to visit for a day or two. The Tupelo Convention & Visitors Bureau, P.O. Box 1485, Tupelo 38802; 841-6521 or (800) 533-0611, will be pleased to provide more information.

Corinth

Corinth is a town steeped in Civil War history, for it hosted major battles and had thousands of soldiers, of both armies, trekking through the streets from 1861 to 1865. This quaint, quiet community in upper northeast Mississippi's gently rolling hills saw more military action during the War Between the States than did any other in the Confederate West. War historians know it well.

Nearby Shiloh National Military Park, just across the state line in Tennessee, is a 3,872-acre cemetery that contains about 3,900 gravesites of soldiers from eight different wars. A museum displays Civil War military equipment and facts about the soldiers who fought at Shiloh; a movie and audio tape are available as well as other historical documentation. For more information call (901) 689-5275.

Many of the houses the Federals commandeered or those used by the Confederates through invitation, still line the streets of this town of 13,000. The houses built before 1860 and the later Victorian structures have names that suggest roots in other countries: Kimmonwych, Dillingham, Tweddle and one purely American — the Fish Pond House. Built in 1856, the Fish Pond House features a decorative wooden railing surrounding a tin container that was once used to collect rainwater. These private residents are not open for daily tours, though the Curlee House is open limited hours or by appointment.

The Northeast Mississippi Museum houses war relics and artifacts. Antique shops offer a few fine antiques and many fun pieces; a theater arts group tackles ambitious productions; an Arts Council presents jazz and other concerts; annual festivals keep locals and visitors interested and active.

Here's an interesting business fact: the internationally known and respected *National Geographic* magazine is printed each month in Corinth at Ringier America and shipped worldwide. Also, *The New York Times* owns Corinth's daily newspaper.

For additional information, contact the Tourism Promotion Council, P.O. Box 1988, Corinth 38834; 287-5269 or (800) 748-9048.

Oxford

Oxford is a place known well to Southern writers and lovers of books about the South, for it is the home of numerous critically-acclaimed Southern authors. Though not many have achieved the critical success of Oxford native and Pulitzer and Nobel Prize-winner William Faulkner, or the financial success of another Oxford-based writer, John Grisham, the town has spawned a plethora of novelists.

Noted literary scholars and aspiring writers gather for a week each summer at the Faulkner and Yoknapatawpha Conference held at the University of Mississippi (Ole Miss) campus. Each year features a different theme; in 1994, it was Faulkner and gender. This year's theme examines Faulkner and cultural contexts.

In Oxford, you're never too far from University-related activities, either those of a cultural nature or anything pertaining to Ole Miss sports. Rebel fans are totally loyal men and women of all ages, many of whom can be found at tailgate parties in the Grove on campus. Some come to the Grove before or after football games with gourmet foods intact, complete with elaborate settings and floral centerpieces.

The town of Oxford is in itself an attraction. It has just enough small-town charm to be inviting and enough sophistication to be interesting. *USA Today* called Oxford "A thriving New South arts mecca." Indeed it is, set amicably among the lovely old homes and tree-lined streets. Surely, it would not be difficult to write in such idyllic surroundings.

Don't miss the place mentioned in many of Faulkner's books — the Oxford Square — the center of the downtown

Mississippi's Intriguing Town Names

Native Americans are responsible for some of the more difficult names to pronounce, among them Shuqualak (shu-ga-lock), Toccopola (ta-ka-po-la) and Pascagoula (pas-ca-goo-la), but many other states also lay claim to tribal names. Let's talk about the real glitz and grits names unique to Mississippi, such as Soso. There is such a town in Smith County, west of Laurel — in the same general vicinity as Cracker's Neck, Sullivan's Hollow and a community known simply as Greasy Spoon. Hot Coffee, also in south central Mississippi, not too far from Jackson, is said to be the home of actor Stella Stevens. It's not too far from D'Lo. Midnight, in the Delta, is another memorable town name. It's in Humphreys County and is home to about 200 people. Midnight is just north of the unforgettable Yazoo City.

The Delta sports other such names as Panther Burn, Alligator, Rolling Fork, Coldwater and Friar's Point, to name a few. North Mississippi claims Byhalia (said By-hay-ya by locals), Potts Camp, Water Valley — not so odd a name but most unusual when one can't readily find a body of water nor a valley. Out from Amory, there's a place called Becker Bottoms. Probably the two most mispronounced cities in the state are Tupelo, which outsiders call Tue-pe-low, though it's actually To-pill-oh. The Coast boasts Biloxi, or as Yankees are wont to say, By-Lox-eye. Locals know it as Ba-lux-e. Add such town names as Eastabutchie, Pelahatchie, Shubuta and Itta Bena, and see a few reasons why Mississippi is such a colorful a state.

business district and the hub of activity since the town was founded in 1837. The Square is a prime spot from which to view the comings and goings of this town of 10,000. Good shopping, offering everything from antiques to apparel, is within a few feet of the Square. Good restaurants are close by, and so is a wonderful bookstore that serves cappuccino on a gallery overlooking the Square.

Faulkner's home, Rowan Oak, is just on the outskirts of town. It's a columned, two-story planter's home that sits at the end of a cedar-lined drive. Rowan Oak was the beloved place from which Faulkner wrote many of his best works. Today, it is staffed by curators from University Museums. Rowan Oak is open for tours year round, except holidays.

There's lots to see and do in Oxford, any time of the year. For complete details, contact the Oxford Tourism Council, P.O. Box 965, Oxford 38655, 234-4651.

Holly Springs

It is surprising to find a small town

that is so characteristic of the old South in close proximity to a major city. Holly Springs, a town of about 7,000, sits 30 minutes southeast of Memphis, Tennessee. And the differences are far greater than the distance.

During the War Between the States, Union Army Gen. U.S. Grant took a personal interest in Holly Springs and saved it from destruction, so naturally it is rife with Civil War history and antebellum mansions. Some Southerners — those of the planter persuasion — lived well back in those days, and that lifestyle is still evident in Holly Springs.

Hillcrest Cemetery is the final resting place of 13 Confederate generals and many locals who didn't survive the yellow-fever epidemic of 1878. The creativity represented in the cast-iron and wrought-iron fencing merits a trip to the cemetery.

The Marshall County Historical Museum includes Chickasaw Indian artifacts, early farm tools, costumes, textiles, a physician's office equipment, and old quilts. The museum is also a good place to pick up souvenirs.

One of Holly Springs' most interesting sites is the Kate Freeman Clark Art Gallery, which has an admission fee and is open by appointment only, though this inconvenience takes nothing away from the works inside. Holly Springs native Kate Clark, at a very young age, painted more than 1,000 paintings prior to 1914; she died in 1957. When Kate was only 16, her mother took her to New York City and enrolled her in the New York School of Art, where her professor was noted artist William Merritt Chase. She refused to sell even one of her paintings, and few had even seen them until her death.

For additional information on Holly Springs, or Montrose, the 1858 Greek Revival mansion, contact the Chamber of Commerce at 154 S. Memphis Street, Holly Springs 38635, 252-2943.

Southaven

Southaven, in the upper northwest corner of the state near Memphis, is the newest and fastest growing town in Mississippi and one of the fastest growing in the Southeast. Though it is still technically in what locals call the Hill Country, the Delta almost claims it too, for some say that the Mississippi Delta begins in the lobby of the Peabody Hotel in Memphis. Desoto County, home of Southaven and sister city Horn Lake, has grown from a population of 53,930 in 1980 to 76,572 in 1993. According to projections, the county will have reached a population of more than 90,000 by 1998. Some of the growth is attributed to a close proximity to Memphis, the casino industry in nearby Tunica County and progressive local leadership who saw to the upgrading of infrastructure and community services. Unemployment is almost nonexistent, and Southaven prides itself on being "a good, clean community with good housing," according to the Chamber of Commerce.

To date, Southaven's most famous native son is John Grisham, the lawyer/state legislator turned author whose books make best-seller lists almost immediately after their release. Grisham grew up on Staunton Street, graduated from Southaven High and later practiced law on Stateline Road. Indeed, Southaven is a bright spot in Mississippi's successful economic development profile. For information on Southaven, contact the Southaven/Horn Lake Chamber of Commerce, 210 Goodman Road, Southaven 38671, 349-2545.

The Delta

If one region of Mississippi stands out as the most controversial and the most intriguing, it must be the Delta. It's a place where, at certain times of the year, the mind's eye creates fanciful cotton-related images. One Delta daddy's darlin' recalls that as a child, her eyes followed the cotton rows, full of fluffy white bolls, all the way to the sky where the bolls touched the puffy white clouds. In her young mind, the world was soft and white and filled with sunny days and quiet nights. Others view it differently. They talk about the harshness, the endlessly long hot summers, the prevailing attitude of indifference. But that's part of the controversy that surrounds the Delta and enhances its mystique.

The forever flat and mysterious land inspires artistic leanings quite common in the Delta. The pace is slow and languid; people take the time to tell a story or two or write a song about Delta days. And there's always something to write about and sing about in Delta-land, good or bad, it generates commentary.

The Mississippi Delta — folks here just say The Delta — is indeed a place one never forgets. Greenville is the biggest city in the Delta, and it's directly on the Mississippi River. To further stake its river claim, the Welcome Center is a replica of an old paddlewheeler riverboat. Nearby in Leland, Jim Henson's boyhood was spent on the banks of Deer Creek, where the irrepressible Kermit the Frog and other Muppets were created.

The Delta is called the "Cradle of the Blues" for good reason: It spawned such blues legends as Sonny Boy Williams, Robert Johnson, B.B. King, Son Thomas, Howlin' Wolf, and John Lee Hooker. Other entertainers who hail from the area include Ike Turner of the Ike and Tina duo, Charley Pride and Morgan Freeman, who gained national recognition while *Driving Miss Daisy*. Rumor has it that Freeman makes his home in the Delta when he's not off shooting a film or appearing in a Broadway play.

The blues, a music of the struggles of a people and a region, is enjoying a resurgence. Blues aficionados from as far away as Europe come to the blues clubs of Greenville and Clarksdale, and they pass through such towns as Tutwiler, where they pay tribute at the grave of Sonny Boy Williamson.

Tutwiler is also the place where W.C. Handy, best known for creating "St. Louis Blues," is said to have heard the blues for the first time. Reports of the day say he thought the "field holler" music weird. Later, however, on a long wait for a train in Tutwiler, Handy sat beside a man who, though shabbily dressed, created wonderful music by gently massaging his pocket knife against his guitar strings and by wailing unusual lyrics. Handy's interest was piqued, and he later attributed "Yellow Dog Blues" to the man in the train station in tiny Tutwiler.

Clarksdale is the home of the Delta Blues Museum, helped on its way to recognition by the band ZZ Top who, in

Some local chambers of commerce can provide information on self-guided tours that showcase history and other special features.

Insiders' Tips

conjunction with New York City's Hard Rock Cafe, waged a campaign to help fund the blues museum. It's the best place to begin a study of blues music, which has become so much a part of The Delta. Another Clarksdale event that gets attention from the entertainment industry is the annual Tennessee Williams Festival, held each fall. It's a new festival and already one of the state's best. Though the playwright who wrote such favorites as *A Streetcar Named Desire* and *Cat on a Hot Tin Roof* was born in Columbus, he was in Clarksdale often visiting his grandparents, and he lived there for a time in his younger years.

Among the other typical Delta towns are Inverness, Belzoni — where the Catfish Center shows how Mississippi produces 80 percent of the world's catfish — Itta Bena, Leland and the uniquely named Panther Burn and Midnight. Larger towns, with populations in the 10,000 range, include the memorable Yazoo City and Indianola, also typically Delta in manner and mind-set. In the right circles, Delta manners are *de rigueur* if one is to advance and make the right connections. It helps tremendously to have an old Delta name and a few thousand acres of prime farm land. After all, the Delta boasts the nation's richest farmland, and those who manage and nurture the land must feel its importance.

The small upper Delta town of Tunica, population 1,800, once known for its cotton and soybean production, is quickly becoming known for its casinos on the Mississippi River and the newfound prosperity they've brought. There's a resurgence going on in downtown Tunica, from the renovation of an old hotel, to updated stores and buildings that now house gaming-related industries. Countywide, the 4 percent of gross gaming revenue that goes into county coffers averages about $1.2 million a month to date, and that pays for a lot of infrastructure improvements. In fact, U.S. 61, the main artery between Tunica and nearby Memphis, is being expanded to four lanes to accommodate the increased traffic coming into the casinos, which at last count numbered 8. Amidst the flurry of activity, though, the people of Tunica appear to be determined to preserve their small-town values. Churches are flourishing, schools are better than ever and the quality of life is improving.

Even with the new gaming money and the changes it's bringing to some Delta towns, there's still a sense of timelessness here that helps keep this region so special. The Delta is a place like no other, and it is inimitable.

Greenville

This busy town on the Mississippi River is called the Crown Jewel of the Delta and with its crown comes a strong sense of place, a confidence in its importance to the scheme of things along the mighty river. Mississippian Eudora Welty said in *Some Notes on River Country*, "Perhaps it is the sense of place that gives us the belief that passionate things, in some essence, endure." Welty also wrote the outstanding book, *A Delta Wedding*.

There's a mythical, magical quality in Greenville that makes you want to linger longer and learn more. Maybe it's the close proximity of the mysterious, unpredictable river; perhaps it's the rich soil that is so fertile bumper crops emerge, year after year. Whatever the reason, the Delta has been called the "most Southern place on earth," and it's that Southern-ness that is sure to generate interest from writers, artists and film producers. This part of the Delta has a culture all its own — a culture created in the all-important African-American churches, in fields where workers toiled before the advent of high-tech farming and in juke joints where troubles are forgotten and camaraderie reigns supreme.

Those who study the blues as an art form remind us that the roots of the blues are deep in religion. Though it's not always visible to the untrained eye, most true blues singers are fundamentally religious. Listen to the lyrics, you'll notice religious references.

About 30,000 people come into Greenville each September for a glimpse of the culture that spawned Delta Blues music and to hear greats and near-greats perform the sounds that know no bounds. Blues lovers come in vans and travel trailers, cars and on motorcycles, to sit under awnings or beach umbrellas in the sweltering Delta sun. It's a gathering of all peoples who share a common bond: an appreciation for the music of a region.

Greenville boasts more published writers than any other town its size in America. Among those best known are Shelby Foote, William Alexander Percy, Walker Percy, Ellen Douglas, Beverly Lowry, travel writers/photojournalists Bern and Franke Keating and Hodding Carter, among many. Find out more at the Greenville Writer's Exhibit, at the public library.

There's much more to Greenville than blues music and renown writers. A famous restaurant or two boasts patrons from the late Elvis Presley to those high in current political circles; one such eatery is the legendary Doe's Eat Place. It's not much to look at from the outside, and the inside won't win a prize for stunning decor, either, but this place is completely unique, and we hope it never changes. Once the food is served, all else is forgotten.

Shopping is good in this river town. The Stein Mart stores originated in Greenville, so expect bargains. Nearby towns have bargains too, and unexpected findings. In Leland, there's a museum on Deer Creek that features the Muppets, Kermit the Frog and other creations from the fertile mind of Delta native Jim Henson. Also near Deer Creek in the little town of Stoneville sits the largest USDA research facility east of the Mississippi. In fact, it's an international farm research complex known as the Silicon Valley of agriculture.

Three miles north of Greenville, find Winterville Mounds, one of the largest groups of Indian mounds in the Mississippi Valley. Predecessors of the Chickasaw and Choctaw Indian tribes constructed the mounds between 1000 and 1400 A.D. Note the 55-foot-high Great Temple Mound. Since Winterville Mounds is a state park, park rangers are available to conduct tours. There's also a museum and gift shop on the premises. The Washington County CVB has information on all the area attractions; contact them at 410 Washington Avenue, Greenville 38701, (800) 467-3582 or 334-2711.

Greenwood

Greenwood is where the Delta mystique begins. Perched peacefully on the famous Yazoo River and surrounded by thousands of acres of prime cotton-producing land, Greenwood is known as the "Cotton Capital of the World." In fact, not only does Greenwood harvest some of the world's best cotton, it also celebrates it with an annual festival.

Called C.R.O.P. Day, which is an acronym for Cotton Row on Parade, this major festival takes place in downtown Greenwood where cotton factor offices are located. "Factors" are cotton buyers and sellers who occupy 24 of the 57 buildings in the historic district. The entire district, which borders the Yazoo River and includes Front Street and Ram Cat Alley, is listed on the National Register of Historic Places. Other big events in the Delta include the Mississippi International Balloon Classic and the Crossroads Blues Festival.

Cottonlandia Museum tells the Delta story, while nearby Florewood River Plantation, a state park, recreates 1850s plantation life as a living history museum. In Greenwood, one notes a definite carry-over from earlier times; a planter society still exists. If the cotton crops are good, so are the moods of those who harvest it, and parties will flourish. During a bad year, the mood is almost morose.

Rambling old homes along tree-canopied Grand Boulevard and River Road were designed for entertaining, and entertain they do in Greenwood. Some parties last all weekend and involve several host families. People here enjoy good times and good friends. They're cooperative too. Tourism industry leaders have formed the Mississippi Delta Tourism Association, a first for the region. It is comprised of the towns of Greenwood, Greenville, Clarksdale and the Delta border towns of Yazoo City and Grenada. They pool resources and funds to bring tourists into this special region of the state.

Greenwood is the shopping and cultural center for the eastern Delta, and it is known for good restaurants too. It's a popular site for antique shopping and an excellent place from which to base antiquing expeditions into other Delta towns. Nearby Indianola is home to the Crown Restaurant and Antique Mall, where smoked catfish paté, is a great delicacy and winner of impressive culinary awards.

All around Greenwood, it's easy to see that the Delta's money crop, right up there with cotton and soy beans, is catfish farming. Farm-raised catfish is a major industry here, and this Delta product is in demand across the United States. For more information on Greenwood, contact the Convention & Visitors Bureau, P.O. Box 739, Greenwood 38930, 453-9197 or (800) 748-9064.

Cleveland

"... The hills suddenly come to an end and there is one long, final descent. Out in the distance, as far as the eye can see, the land is flat, dark, and unbroken, sweeping away in a faint misty haze to the limits of the horizon. This is the great delta. Once it was the very floor under the sea; later knee-deep in waters and covered with primordial forests — a dark shadowy swampland, fetid and rich." — Willie Morris, *North Toward Home*.

Mississippi writer Willie Morris describes the Delta so beautifully, his words must be used in close proximity to Cleve-

Photo: Harrison County Tourism Commission

Visitors and locals alike appreciate the unusually colorful sunsets on the waters of the Gulf.

land, for Cleveland typifies the Delta. Pretty and peaceful, strong and secure, a bit of a paradox, but a place where hospitality is a way of life. Cleveland is a college town, home of Delta State University.

With Cleveland as a base, venture into interesting towns nearby, such as Merigold, where McCarty Pottery is an excellent site from which to look and learn. The McCartys are Mississippi artists famous for creating outstanding pottery from Mississippi clay.

Back in Cleveland proper, you'll find an active downtown, nice residential areas and about 15,400 friendly people. For additional information, contact the Cleveland-Bolivar County Chamber of Commerce, P.O. Drawer 490, Cleveland 38732, 843-2712.

Clarksdale

This thriving Delta town is home to almost 20,000 people who enjoy the fruits of the land: fishing, hunting and entertaining Delta-style, which means seasonal events and subsequent parties. Deltans love a good time and good food, all year long.

The attraction that brings tourists to town is the Delta Blues Museum. It promotes and protects the musical heritage of a region and gives folks a reason to come calling. Delta Blues is a unique form of Southern music germane to African Americans who toiled in the Delta cotton fields long before the days of mechanization and agribusiness. Blues music influenced jazz, rock 'n' roll and current country. Delta Blues is considered an introduction to a culture that is still evident in deep Delta-land.

Another popular attraction is the relatively new Tennessee Williams Festival, held each October. The playwright visited Clarksdale often as a child (his grandfather was the rector of the Episcopal church) and later used local places and people in his plays. The Tennessee Williams Festival features films and plays, lectures, discussions and a walking tour of his old neighborhood. The Sunflower River Blues Festival is up and coming, another celebration of blues music.

For additional information about Clarksdale events and activities, contact the Clarksdale/Coahoma Chamber of Commerce at P.O. Box 160, Clarksdale 38614, (800) 626-3764 or 627-7337.

The Heartland

If the Delta is the soul of Mississippi, then the Heartland is aptly named, for it's the big and bold heart of the state. There are no mountains, and the only beaches are small strips of sand along the Ross Barnett Reservoir, but it's an area much-loved by residents of the state. Pineywoods and gently rolling hills typify the terrain of the Heartland, where rivers and streams meander through the region. The Heartland includes the state capital of Jackson, which means that things are a bit more official in these parts, and there's obviously more opportunities for travelers and newcomers.

Jackson is a New South city where the best of the past is honored, such as hospitality and common courtesy, but the future is what Jacksonians are banking on. It's where many of the state's best and brightest from the major universities locate to make their mark in law, medicine and banking. And once they arrive, they take full advantage of all the city has to offer. Throughout the year, Jacksonians find plenty to do and many things to support, from any one of the 400 churches, various civic organizations or two opera companies. This mecca for diehard Mississippians is a busy town where locals say "there's one good time after another."

Jackson's northern neighbor, Canton, is a pretty place with a lively town square and a school that specializes in arts and crafts. It's also the place where a gigantic flea market is held twice a year. Nice and quiet Clinton, Jackson's neighbor to the west, is home to Mississippi College, which was founded in 1826. A well-planned walking tour shows the best Clinton has to offer. Both towns are bedroom communities for Jackson.

The popular town of Madison is growing in leaps and bounds just north of Jackson. It's clean and green and very appealing to young families. Up the Natchez Trace from Jackson, find the town of Kosciusko, named for a Revolutionary War hero from Poland. There's a museum, funded and staffed by volunteers, where information is available, along with a wax figure of the town's namesake. Kosciusko is a good place to stop along the Natchez Trace Parkway, and while there, drive through the Victorian neighborhoods and see the stately old homes.

Elsewhere in the Heartland, the town of Philadelphia, trying very hard to overcome a negative image stemming from the Civil Rights movement of the 1960s, is actually a quiet and friendly place. (Most of the locals wouldn't mind if such films as *Mississippi Burning* went elsewhere.) For the most part, give or take one or two bad apples in any barrel, there are kind and decent people here, many of whom have never engaged in cruel, racially motivated activities and disapprove of those who have.

Philadelphia probably has produced more noteworthy personalities, per capita, than any town its size. The late Turner Catledge, popular editor of *The New York Times*, claimed Philadelphia as home, and there's country star Marty Stuart, a host of pro football players, plus a list of about 20 more prominent Americans who hailed from this town of less than 7,000.

Locals attribute this to a strong sense of community and excellent role models.

Philadelphia is the home of the Neshoba County Fair, Mississippi's giant house party where camptown houses are coveted possessions, and the Choctaw Indian Fair, an annual tribute to Choctaw-Indian culture. Both events take place in summer, and both are major events for locals and visitors. Local, regional and national politicians "stump" at the Neshoba fairs. Stumping became a phrase when politicians of old stood on tree stumps to see all who were listening to them. Neshoba County is also home of Mississippi's only land-based casino, owned by the Mississippi Band of Choctaw Indians. The Silver Star Hotel and Casino is 3 miles west of Philadelphia. For information about Philadelphia, contact the Chamber of Commerce, P.O. Box 51, Philadelphia, 656-1742.

Jackson

For a town that was originally named Le Fleur's Bluff and was still considered "a little town in the wilderness" as late as the mid 1820s, Jackson has indeed come a long way. Slavery and states' rights were issues in Jackson for years before the outbreak of the Civil War in 1861. During the war, Jackson became known as "Chimneyville" because Gen. William Tecumseh Sherman ordered the wholesale burning of the town. Jackson courageously recovered from the Civil War and Reconstruction, yellow-fever epidemics and until the turn of the century, a slow growth rate. Since then, it has been full of vim and vigor and hard to hold back.

Today, this city of 396,400 (metro) is bold and aggressive, finding and claiming its niche in the changing American South. Jackson is a sprawling, friendly city that has managed to maintain a small-town quality. People are busy but never too busy for a smile and cordial greeting. And they are absolutely loyal to their city. Those who were born here hope to stay forever; those who've come from elsewhere in the state quickly claim Jackson as their own, often declining job promotions and advancements that require relocating.

As with any city in the United States today, the crime rate is higher than Jacksonians would like, but most crime activity is drug-related and in isolated areas. It is apparently not a factor to those who wish to enjoy Jackson's many amenities.

Jackson is an outdoor town where more than 3,000 acres of parks and recreation areas, including LeFleur's Bluff State Park, provide various outdoor opportunities for the city's residents. As if that weren't enough, the Ross Barnett Reservoir is just north of town, and it boasts 50 square miles of water and adjoining picnic areas. Golf courses and tennis courts are plentiful, both private and public, and the weather allows year-round play. As a matter of fact, Rand McNally's

---

Jackson got the nickname "Chimneyville" because not much was left but brick chimneys after Union troops burned the town in 1863. Union Gen. Sherman said to General Grant, "Jackson will no longer be a point of danger. The land is devastated." They should see it now.

Insiders' Tips

• **23**

Places Rated Almanac says that Metro Jackson is No. 1 in the nation in accessibility to golf courses.

There's plenty for the nonathletic, too; indoor events keep Jacksonians as busy as they want to be. The performing arts have a home in Jackson, and they include New Stage Theatre, Ballet Mississippi, the Christian ballet company Ballet Magnificat, Mississippi Symphony, the Modern Dance Collective and many programs provided by the active Arts Alliance of Jackson.

Jackson is very proud to be this country's host city for the International Ballet Competition. The IBC rotates annually between Jackson; Moscow; Varna, Bulgaria; and Helsinki, Finland. Jackson hosts IBC every four years. It's the only IBC host city to offer the prestigious International Dance School, which provides instruction by world-class dancers. The next IBC to be held in Jackson will be in 1998.

Indeed, Jackson is a city of culture and style — but it has also made a name for itself as a leader in business, industry, law and medicine. Innovative medical research is ongoing and recognized throughout the South. Jackson enjoys an excellent business climate and has one of the lowest unemployment rates in the southeast. Talented young people call Jackson "the New South's new city of opportunity".

Restaurants in Jackson, about 300 in all, run the gamut of specialties. Expect a smattering of continental cuisine and a lot of regional seafood and Southern favorites. Guests to the city welcome the restaurant choices and the 5,500 hotel rooms. For information on conventions, festivals or other Jackson specifics, contact the Metro Jackson CVB, P.O. Box 1450, Jackson 39215, (800) 354-7695 or 960-1891.

Meridian

Meridian was incorporated only four years before Gen. Sherman burned it in 1864 and declared that the city no longer existed. A few years later Meridian's population was rebuilding and reestablishing a city that would become crucial to the eastern part of Mississippi's midsection.

The first train arrived in 1855, heralding the city's role as a junction for railroads. During the 1890s, Meridian enjoyed great progress, thanks to the booming lumber industry. Census figures from 1910 to 1930 show that Meridian was the largest city in the state, until the capital city of Jackson gained that distinction. Today Meridian has a population of 41,000.

Aviation is a major element in Meridian's past and present. Back in 1935, brothers Al and Fred Key set an endurance record by staying aloft in *Ole Miss* for 653 hours and 34 minutes. During World War II the Army Air Force Base was established in Meridian, and today the Naval Air Station is the city's largest employer, with more than 2,000 personnel.

Meridian is also home to Peavey Electronics Corp., the world's largest manufacturer of power amplifiers and a familiar name in the music industry.

Residents of Meridian support a broad range of cultural and recreational events and opportunities. It is, after all, the hometown of Jimmie Rodgers, who is recognized as the father of Country music. Rodgers is honored with a museum of his own in Highland Park (19th Street and 41st Avenue) and an annual festival in May. Blues, jazz and other types of music are showcased at a number of festivals and by several local musical groups. The city boasts a symphony orchestra, a little theater and a museum of art.

Support for education has been evident throughout the city's history, starting in 1865 with the establishment of Meridian Female College. Its public education system dates back to 1885. Meridian Junior College, now known as Meridian Community College, was founded in 1937. In recent years Meridian schools have been recognized for their excellence.

Among the fine examples of architectural styles found in Meridian is the venerable Grand Opera House of Mississippi, built in 1890 and located at 2206 Fifth Street. Citizens are slowly restoring the only second-floor opera house in the South, where Sarah Bernhardt and Helen Hayes, among notable others, once performed.

Additional information about the area is available from the Meridian/Lauderdale County Partnership, P.O. Box 790, 721 Front Street Extension, Meridian 39302, 693-1306 or (800) 748-9970.

Hattiesburg

Hattiesburg calls itself "the Other Mississippi" to distinguish itself from older cities and those located along the Mississippi River and Gulf Coast.

Here in the piney woods is a city that was established nearly two decades after the Civil War and soon became the fourth largest in the state, thanks to the railroad and the timber industry. Today the surrounding two-county area has a population of nearly 100,000. Hattiesburg (population 42,000) is home to the University of Southern Mississippi, William Carey College and all the associated collegiate sports and cultural activities. Accommodations, restaurants and shopping are extensive, thanks in large part to the student population. The city's medical facilities are top notch.

Outdoor recreation is available at the city's expansive park system in the form of golf, camping, hiking, boating, fishing, baseball, tennis, swimming, horseback riding, canoeing and more.

Hattiesburg's past is preserved in its historic districts, including one of the largest in southeast Mississippi — 115 acres with intact structures spanning architectural styles from 1884 to 1930. A few years ago, the U.S. Conference of Mayors bestowed its Livability Award to Hattiesburg, marking the first time a city with a population less than 50,000 received the honor.

The Hattiesburg Convention and Visitors Bureau has more information. The address is P.O. Box 16122, 6443 U.S. 49, Hattiesburg, 39401, 268-3220 or (800) 63-TOURS.

Laurel

The lumber industry and the developing railroad system gave sleepy Jones County a shove toward development in the late 1800s that resulted in rapid development and in the establishment of the city of Laurel in 1881.

Early in 1900, Laurel was called "the lumber capital of the world," and mills there shipped more yellow pine than any other place.

Laurel got another economic boost in 1926 when William Mason developed the process of turning the lumber industry's wood waste into what we know today as Masonite. The Laurel-based Masonite Corporation is the world's largest hardboard manufacturer.

The end of the lumber boom in the 1930s was followed by the discovery of oil in 1942. As a result, Jones County's economic base has expanded to include more than 20 companies serving the oil industry today. Poultry and metal fabrication are other top industries.

Laurel is home to the first art museum in Mississippi. The Lauren Rogers Museum of Art at Fifth Avenue at Seventh Street opened in 1923. Here, in the quiet of the prettiest street in the city's attractive historic district, you'll find an outstanding collection of paintings, prints, silver pieces, Native-American baskets and rotating exhibits. In addition to its more than 10,000 square feet of exhibit space, this impressive museum houses an extensive reference library.

Laurel is the home town of Leontyne Price, the Juilliard-trained star of the New York Metropolitan Opera. She was the first African American to attain international celebrity as an opera singer.

Laurel, with 18,800 residents, is the largest city in Jones County, population 62,000.

For more information, contact the Jones County Chamber of Commerce, P.O. Box 527, 153 Base Drive, Laurel 39441, 428-0574.

McComb

About an hour away from Hattiesburg is McComb in Pike County. This area was built in part by the lumber and petroleum industries. McComb has 12,000 residents, and the county has nearly 37,000.

There are approximately 35 industries that provide a diversified base for the local economy. Products range from aluminum windows and doors to clothes, corrugated containers and parts for mobile homes and recreational vehicles. Goods are shipped and received via an excellent transportation network consisting of highways, railways, waterways and airways.

In addition to its public and private school systems, Pike County students can attend Southwest Mississippi Junior College in Summit and the University of Southern Mississippi in Hattiesburg.

McComb has five municipal parks, amateur theater groups, golf, tennis, swimming pools and easy access to Percy Quin State Park and Bogue Chitto Water Park. Contact the Pike County Chamber of Commerce and Economic Development District, P.O. Box 83, 202 Third Street, McComb, 39648, or call 684-2291 for more information.

Brookhaven

This is "Homeseeker's Paradise," according to Brookhaven's nearly 100-year-old nickname. Situated in the piney woods of southwestern Mississippi, Brookhaven, population 10,200, is 55 miles south of Jackson in Lincoln County (population 30,300).

The city was founded in 1818 and takes its name from the Long Island hometown of founder Samuel Jayne.

Brookhaven considers itself one of the best places to live for a number of reasons, one of which is education. Its outstanding schools include nearby Copiah-Lincoln Community College and Southwest Mississippi Community College. The parks and recreation program is comprehensive, and there is a new recreational complex that's considered one of the best in the state. The community theater group is, in terms of longevity, second only to Meridian's. Health-care services include those provided by the recently expanded King's Daughter's Hospital plus mental health, physical therapy, home health, hospice, dental and nursing homes.

The 40 manufacturing companies located in Brookhaven/Lincoln County include a Fortune 500 company (Packard Electric with 500 employees) and a Fortune 500 service company (Wal-Mart Distribution Center with 1,200 employees).

For maps, listings, tourism information and other data, contact the Brookhaven-Lincoln County Chamber of Commerce, P.O. Box 978, 230 S. Whitworth Avenue, Brookhaven 39601, 833-1411.

Throughout the Heartland are a number of smaller cities that have distinct histories and flavors. One of them is **Hazlehurst**, located north of Brookhaven. It was the setting for the movie version of *Crimes of the Heart*, based on the Pulitzer Prize-winning play by Mississippian Beth Henley. For fans of Delta blues, Hazlehurst is known as the birth place of the legendary Robert Johnson. For more information contact the Hazlehurst Chamber of Commerce, P.O. Box 446, Hazlehurst 39083, 894-3752.

Just north of Hazlehurst is **Crystal Springs**, known in the early 1900s as the "tomato capital of the world." At that time the city was the largest tomato shipping center in the country. The city's Chautauqua Arboretum and Botanic Gardens is a major attraction. For more information contact the Crystal Springs Chamber of Commerce, P.O. Box 519, Crystal Springs 39059, 892-2711.

The River Cities

It's impossible to ignore the Civil War history in which Natchez, Vicksburg and Port Gibson are so steeped. History drives the tourism industry, which is important to the economy in the River Cities. In Natchez alone, tourism employs more than 2,000 people and has an economic impact estimated to be $35 million. Recently Natchez and Vicksburg began experiencing the growth of a new Mississippi industry — dockside gaming, increasing employment and revenues.

Many reminders of historic events and a gracious way of life remain in the cities and towns along the river. They are preserved in the architecture and monuments and are proudly displayed during the popular Pilgrimages, which are major tourist draws.

Natchez

Natchez and the antebellum South are synonymous, but the city actually dates back to 1716, making it one of the oldest in North America. Natchez played some important roles during the ensuing years, when possession changed hands from the French to the British and then the Spanish. The Natchez river port, the only one between New Orleans and the mouth of the Ohio River, brought great wealth to the area, as did the steamboat river commerce. Plantation owners spent some of their fortunes on lavish homes, beautiful gardens and elegant entertainment.

It was that opulent period that organizers of the first Spring Pilgrimage back in 1932 wanted to showcase. Their idea was a resounding success, and eventually a fall version of the popular open house began. Thirty historic homes and gardens welcome visitors to take an enjoyable look into the past. For information and reservations, call Natchez Pilgrimage Tours, (800) 647-6742.

Today, the people in Natchez (population 19,500) still know how to enjoy themselves, and they take their celebrations seriously. Mardi Gras here is a full-blown series of parades, balls and parties. The Opera Festival, for lovers of various kinds of music, entertains appreciative audiences, as does the annual Floozie

Contest during which the *Mississippi Queen* and *Delta Queen* steamboats pause in Natchez in late June during their yearly race to St. Louis. The passengers and crews compete as floozies, and a panel of local dignitaries judge who's best in this raucous contest. The Great Mississippi River Balloon Race is another popular event, held in October, that brings together music, food, rides and a grand time for its participants.

In addition to the large number of historic sites, there are other significant attractions, including Natchez-Under-The-Hill, once Mississippi's equivalent to the infamous Barbary Coast, which now hosts restaurants, shops, bars and casino gaming. The 440-mile Natchez Trace, originally a foot path used by Indians, starts here and makes its way across Mississippi up to Nashville.

For more information about Natchez, contact the Convention and Visitors Bureau, P.O. Box 1485, 422 Main Street, Natchez 39121-1485, (800) 647-6724 or (800) 99-NATCHEZ.

Vicksburg

While Natchez received little damage during the Civil War, Vicksburg suffered enormously because of its strategic location on the river. Gen. Grant's 1863 assault on the "Gibraltar of the Confederacy" is recounted in the 1,858-acre Vicksburg National Military Park, considered the best preserved Civil War battlefield in the nation.

History is also preserved in the grand homes, a dozen of which are open all year for inspection. More open their doors to the public during the Spring Pilgrimage. Museums in this city of 21,000 present an interesting look into the city's past, showcasing local history, boats, toys, dolls

and even a soft drink. The Old Court House Museum on Cherry Street is where Jefferson Davis began his career in politics and where Grant reviewed his troops. At the Gray and Blue Naval Museum, 638-6500, a fleet of Civil War gunboat models are among the featured items. Toys and soldiers have their own museum south of the court house. Yesterday's Children Antique Doll and Toy Museum has more than 1,000 dolls, antique and new, on display. The Biedenharn Museum of Coca-Cola Memorabilia pays homage to the fact that Coke was bottled there for the first time in 1894.

Visitors are welcome to tour the Waterways Experiment Station on Halls Ferry Road. This is the Army Corps of Engineers' largest research and development facility, where engineers and scientists work with scale models of rivers and other waterways.

For those who prefer being on the river to studying one, there are Hydro-Jet Boat Tours that offer daily 20-mile tours covering 500 years of history.

For information about Vicksburg attractions and events, see our Attractions and Annual Events chapters. You may also get in touch with the Convention and Visitors Bureau, P.O. Box 110, Clay Street and Old Miss. Highway 27, Vicksburg 39181. Call 636-9421 or (800) 221-3536.

Port Gibson

Port Gibson, in 1811, was the third city to be incorporated in the state, but at that time, the Claiborne County area had already been settled by the Choctaw Indians. Life in this typical frontier town, where saloons and a race track provided entertainment, changed dramatically with the arrival of the Presbyterians and the

Methodists. Now Port Gibson (population 1,800) is known for its many churches, the most famous of which has the gilded hand atop the steeple pointing upward.

Today this is an attractive, quiet place that Gen. Grant declared back in 1863 was "too beautiful to burn." Residents are proud of the fact that their city had the first library in the state, the second newspaper and the third Masonic Lodge.

There's plenty of history in and around Port Gibson and a number of ways to take it all in. One way is the annual Spring Pilgrimage, a two-day event that includes home tours and festivities celebrating local heritage. Another way is to take a self-guided walking tour of historic homes, churches and cemeteries, many of which have special identification markers out front. Driving tours are more practical for taking in the sights around the area, including the 23 mansion columns known as the Ruins of Windsor, 12 miles southwest of town; the Grand Gulf State Park with a Civil War museum and picnic areas; and Grand Gulf Nuclear Station on Waterloo Road.

To get maps for self-guided tours and other information, contact the Port Gibson-Claiborne County Chamber of Commerce, P. O. Box 491, U.S. 61 S., Port Gibson 39150, 437-4351.

The Coast

The Coast is made up of a string of cities and towns in three counties from the Louisiana state line across to Alabama. Most municipalities are very old — including some of the oldest in the state — but two were incorporated in the last few years. This is considered the most diversified area in the state, thanks in good measure to its distinct cultural mix. To underscore their unique coastal sense of community, some residents believe there are actually two Mississippis — the Coast and North Mississippi. The dividing line, it is said with tongue in cheek, is I-10 — just a few miles from the sand beaches.

Bay St. Louis

In 1818, Bay St. Louis, then called Shieldsborough, was incorporated, making it the oldest established community on the Coast. The name was changed to Bay St. Louis in 1882 by popular demand. By then the town was already known as a resort for the wealthy planters and aristocrats of New Orleans and Natchez. Today, Bay St. Louis (population 8,000) draws visitors to its historic downtown where more than 100 buildings are on the National Register of Historic Places. Antiques and works of art are among the local shop specialties. The city was recently named one of the best small towns for art lovers (along with Ocean Springs) by author John Vallani in his book, *100 Best Small Art Towns in America*. A newer attraction in the city is one of the county's two dockside casinos. The city is revitalizing its historic downtown to attract even more visitors and shoppers. Murals are being painted on the exterior walls of some businesses and government offices, and fresh flowers will soon be placed on light posts. Additional lighting is being added around Main Street, and the sidewalks will have freshly painted sailboats to guide pedestrians to various points of interests and shops.

There has been a great deal of construction activity; among the more significant projects have been the expansions of the main branch of the library system and the hospital. Plans call for the restoration of the old L&N railroad depot, now used by Amtrak. *This Property is Con-*

demned, starring Natalie Wood and Robert Redford, was filmed around the depot district. The area north of Bay St. Louis remains rural, except for the upscale residential development of Diamondhead located just off I-10. Also nearby is NASA's John C. Stennis Space Center, the largest employer in Hancock County. To find out more about Bay St. Louis and Waveland, contact the Hancock County Chamber on U.S. 90, 467-9048.

Waveland

The town of Waveland was a part of Shieldsborough when it applied for a charter in 1888. Here, in the land of waves, city dwellers from nearby New Orleans set up summer retreats among the permanent homes of residents who, for the most part, were the descendants of earlier French and Spanish settlers. Waveland (5,400) is home to Buccaneer State Park, one of the most popular in the state and located right on the beach. Buccaneer features a water park in addition to campgrounds and picnic areas. This small city is host to popular St. Patrick's Day and Mardi Gras parades. In fact, Waveland boosts the Coast's only all-female Carnival krewe, the group that puts on the colorful parade and festive, formal Mardi Gras ball.

For other outdoor recreation, Waveland offers plenty of options, including the Garfield Ladner Memorial Fishing Pier on Beach Boulevard. In the works is an 8-mile bike path that will wind its way through Waveland and Bay St. Louis. Many of the homes along the beach in Waveland and Bay St. Louis were destroyed in Hurricane Camille in 1969. There are still some vacant lots where houses stood before the storm. While the tiny downtown area around Coleman

Avenue still has some activity, the real shopping action is out on U.S. 90. Waveland is home to some of the county's largest stores, including two major discount department stores and the large Sav-A-Center grocery story chain. There are also fast-food and seafood restaurants and some antique and specialty stores on the highway.

Pass Christian

Pass Christian is a quaint town (incorporated in 1838, 5,560 people) where wealthy New Orleanians built their summer homes. Along the beach, and especially on Scenic Drive, are many beautiful homes with manicured lawns. The picturesque harbor in the Pass is the site of what is popularly believed to be the second-oldest yacht club in the country. The Chamber of Commerce office is nearby. Beauty and history are proudly preserved here, thanks to a very active Historical Society. A special treat is the tour of homes and Pilgrimage stops at some of the prettiest homes and gardens to be found anywhere. Visitors can appreciate the beauty and community spirit here even more when they realize that in 1969, Pass Christian suffered enormous devastation during Hurricane Camille. In addition to the loss of life, many historical and architectural treasures were destroyed, making the surviving structures even more precious.

The small downtown offers some great shopping at such stores as Parkers for fine jewelry and the Hillyer House for all kinds of jewelry, art and more. Good food is also readily available at such restaurants as the charming Blue Rose near the harbor and at casual Pirate's Cove on the beach for some of the best po' boys to be found anywhere. New to

Azaleas are a favorite springtime shrub of Mississippi gardeners and visitors alike.

the downtown is Morning Market for tasty food items including gourmet specialties and fresh bread from a New Orleans bakery. Contact the Pass Christian Chamber of Commerce on U.S. 90 at 452-2252.

Long Beach

Long Beach (population 15,800) is a bedroom community of quiet neighborhoods and good seafood restaurants that is situated between Pass Christian and Gulfport. Perhaps the best-known landmark in Long Beach is the Friendship Oak on the beautiful beachfront campus of the University of Southern Mississippi. The giant oak has been dated to the late 1400s and today has a trunk that measures 17 feet and limbs that extend more than seven feet. USM is at the former site of the all-female Gulf Park College. Adding to the commerce of the city is the Long Beach Industrial Park. The city's schools are noted for academic excellence.

Long Beach is the site of Boggsdale, a collection of homes dating back to the late 1800s. It was here that Hale Boggs,

who served in the U.S. Congress representing Louisiana for 18 years, was born in the family home. Boggs, the House Majority leader, disappeared in a plane crash in 1972. The location of Boggsdale on U.S. 90 is noted with a historical marker.

Many visitors make a trip to Long Beach to try the fresh seafood at such popular restaurants as The Chimneys and Chappy's, both are along U.S. 90. Contact the Long Beach Chamber of Commerce at the Small Craft Harbor, 863-6666.

Gulfport

Situated at the spot where U.S. 90 running west to east and U.S. 49 running north to south connect is Gulfport, the business center of Harrison County. It's also the largest city on the Coast in population (63,400) and size after its annexation of an area to the north. Gulfport shares the county seat distinction with neighboring Biloxi. The thriving Mississippi State Port is at this former railroad town, and its major customers are Dole,

Chiquita and Dupont. The port has been operating for nearly 100 years. The city's two casinos — the Copa and the Grand Casino Gulfport — are situated in the port, contributing about half of the port's revenue.

Here too is the regional airport and the Naval Construction Battalion Center. Rice Pavilion is the site of the famous Mississippi Deep Sea Fishing Rodeo, held every Fourth of July. Other festivities include Mardi Gras balls and parades during the Carnival season. Fans of boxing will note that John L. Sullivan beat Paddy Ryan in a bare-knuckle match in 1882 to become the undefeated world heavyweight champion. The fight took place near Courthouse Road and is duly noted with a historical marker.

Besides the shopping opportunities downtown and along busy Pass Road, Gulfport will soon be home to a major outlet mall near I-10. William Carey College has its Coast campus in Gulfport at the site of the former Gulf Coast Military Academy. Next door is the U.S. Naval Home for retirees. For more information, contact the Mississippi Gulf Coast Chamber of Commerce at 1401 20th Avenue, 863-2933.

Biloxi

French settlers arrived in Biloxi in 1699, and it has been welcoming visitors ever since. At one time the city was known as the "seafood capital of the world." Today, Biloxi (population 46,300) is home to the largest concentration of the Coast's 8,000 Vietnamese. Biloxi is also home to Keesler Air Force Base, one of the largest technical training centers in the Air Force with a population of 26,000. It's here that the famous Hurricane Hunters are sta-

tioned. At this writing, Biloxi was home to eight of the Coast's 12 dockside casinos are operating in Biloxi. Visitors will also enjoy the many other attractions, restaurants, nightclubs, shops and stores that make Biloxi a favorite destination. Highlights include the George E. Ohr Arts and Cultural Center, the Coast Coliseum, Edgewater Mall, Beauvoir, the Biloxi Lighthouse, the Seafood and Maritime Museum and much more. And Mardi Gras here is a full-blown celebration. For more information contact the Biloxi Bay Chamber of Commerce, 119 Rue Magnolia, 435-6149, or the Mississippi Gulf Coast Chamber of Commerce, 1048 Beach Boulevard, 374-2717.

D'Iberville

The newest city in Harrison County (and on the Coast) is D'Iberville, which was incorporated in 1988. This city north of Biloxi has a population of 7,000. It takes its name from the French explorer who established the area in 1699. To find out more about this city and area, contact the North Bay Area Chamber of Commerce at 10491 Lemoyne Boulevard, D'Iberville, 392-2293.

Ocean Springs

Across the bridge from Biloxi in Jackson County is Ocean Springs, with an art community that's centered around the Walter Anderson Museum of Art and the Anderson family compound called Shearwater Pottery. You could spend lots of enjoyable time strolling down tree-lined Washington Avenue, stopping by specialty shops and restaurants along the way. History lives in the architecture and in the celebrations, including the reenactment of the landing of D'Iberville, the French explorer, and a living history weekend at the replica of Fort Maurepas.

The headquarters of the Gulf Islands National Seashore is in Ocean Springs, as is Gulf Coast Research Laboratory. The Ocean Springs Chamber of Commerce can provide more details. It's at 1000 Washington Avenue, 875-4424.

Pascagoula

Pascagoula (population 25,900) and neighboring Moss Point make up the industrialized hub of Jackson County. Pascagoula is home to Ingalls Shipbuilding, the largest employer in the state, and to Naval Station Pascagoula. These two facilities have an enormous impact on the area and have brought in new residents to the city. Pascagoula has a good number of parks, including I.G. Levy Park, Beach Park and River Park and Pier on the west bank of the Pascagoula River. The city's name, by the way, came from the Indian tribe that lived along the banks of the river, also known as the Singing River. The area's history is on display at the Old Spanish Fort and Museum and at the floating Scranton Museum. The Jackson County Chamber, 825 U.S. 90, 762-3391, has up-to-date information on Pascagoula, Moss Point and Gautier. For more information call the Jackson County Chamber of Commerce, 762-3391.

Gautier

Gautier (population 10,000) is another new city, incorporated in 1986. It's between Ocean Springs and Pascagoula/Moss Point. Gautier is home to the Jackson County Campus of the Mississippi Gulf Coast Community College, Singing River Mall and the Mississippi Sandhill Crane National Wildlife Refuge. The city celebrates a favorite local catch at the annual Mullet Festival. For more information call the Jackson County Chamber of Commerce, 762-3391.

Moss Point

North of Pascagoula is the smaller city of Moss Point (population 17,800), which calls itself "A Friendly Place." Moss Point hosts large industries such as International Paper Co. and First Chemical Corp., as well as shipyards and related businesses. The city is revitalizing the downtown area by widening roads and making other infrastructure improvements. Community groups are adding nice touches to the appearance of the city and sponsoring special events for residents. For more information call the Jackson County Chamber of Commerce, 762-3391.

*Trolleys shuttle locals and guests along oak-lined Highway 90
at Mississippi Beach.*

Photo: Coast Transit Authority

Inside
Getting Around

Modes of transportation for getting to Mississippi and traveling about the state represent an unusual pairing of nostalgia and modern convenience. For example, visitors may arrive by commercial jet and then tour historic sites from a horse-drawn carriage or steamboat. Pilots can fly in to any of nearly 80 airports. Drivers will find a network of modern highways as well as the scenic Natchez Trace Parkway, whose origins are an Indian trail. For those who want someone else to do the driving, popular destinations areas offer taxis, limos, tour buses and even tour boats. In the larger cities, local transit service and rental cars are readily available. Whatever method you choose, we hope you'll find all means of getting here and getting around enjoyable.

Highways

The interstate highway system in Mississippi spans the state from all borders and totals approximately 700 miles. These interstate highways include I-10, which extends along the Mississippi Gulf Coast; I-20, which runs across the center of the state east and west; I-55, which runs north and south through the center of the state; and I-59, which runs through the southeastern portion. I-220 in the Jackson area connects I-20 W. and I-55 N. as well as U.S. 49 and U.S. 51.

A series of well-maintained state highways complements the interstate system. According to a recent study by the University of North Carolina at Charlotte, Mississippi's highways are the best in the South and fourth-best in the nation. And things are getting even better for drivers. By the year 2000, Mississippi will have completed a $1.5 billion expansion, adding 1,000 miles to its multi-lane highway system.

The speed limit on the interstate highways is 65 mph unless otherwise stated; other U.S. highways have a speed limit of 55 mph unless otherwise posted.

Seat belts are mandatory for drivers and front seat passengers.

Children younger than 4 must be in a child passenger restraint device. Violation of this law can result in a $25 fine.

Rental Cars

Rental cars are available at most commercial airports in Mississippi. If you need to know before you go, these toll-free numbers should help: Avis, (800) 831-2847; Enterprise, (800) 325-8007; Hertz, (800) 654-3131; and National, (800) 227-7368.

The Hill Country

COLUMBUS

Avis	328-1636
Enterprise	328-7610
Hertz	328-3293
National Car Rental	327-8183

STARKVILLE

Starkville Buses	324-0474, (800) 499-0474
Enterprise	323-3389

TUPELO

Hertz	844-9148
Budget	840-3710
Enterprise	842-2237

OXFORD

Callahan Bus Lines	236-3548
McCullough Car Rentals	234-4231

WEST POINT

Hannah Tours	494-5038

CORINTH

Hertz	286-3385

The Delta

GREENVILLE

Avis	378-3873
Hertz	335-6076

GREENWOOD

Mike Turner Auto Sales	453-7136

CLARKSDALE

Nabors Chevrolet	624-2585
Greg Coker Autos	624-2571

GRENADA

Kirk Auto Co.	226-3632
Grenada Carriers	226-4816

The Heartland

JACKSON

Capital Charters/ Grayline of Jackson	939-0519, (800) 841-6817
Corrigan Travel/ Cline Tours	981-6969, (800) 233-5307
Avis	939-5853
Auto & Truck Rental	948-3391
Enterprise	825-2840
Hertz	939-5312
LeFleur's Limousine	956-LIMO

MERIDIAN

Avis	483-7144
Hertz	485-4774

The River Cities

NATCHEZ

A-B Motor Co.	442-2847
Natchez Ford-Lincoln-Mercury	445-0060
U-Save Auto Rental	445-8910
Enterprise	442-4600

VICKSBURG

George Carr Buick Pontiac	636-7777

The Coast

BAY ST. LOUIS

Enterprise	466-4319

Insiders' Tips

Seasoned travelers say that it is highly advisable to have confirmed hotel reservations before arriving in towns where casinos operate. It is difficult, at best, to find impromptu overnight accommodations in casino towns along the Mississippi River and the Gulf Coast. Call in advance!

Biloxi

U-Save Auto Rental	436-9248
Budget Car & Truck Rental	388-1017
Sears Car & Truck Rental	388-2561

Gulfport

Avis	864-7182
Hertz	863-2761
Thrifty Car Rental	863-8642

Ocean Springs

U-Save Auto Rental	875-7500

Pascagoula

Enterprise	762-6431

Charter Buses

The Hill Country

STARKVILLE BUSES
P.O. Box 359 or 214 S. Jackson
Starkville   *324-0474, (800) 499-0474*

This company arranges group transportation for all occasions, including family reunions and trips to area Pilgrimages and outlet malls. Starkville Buses also offers accommodation packages and regularly scheduled tours. Tell them your needs, and they'll quote a price.

HANNAH TOURS, INC.
852 Meade
West Point   494-5038, (800) 526-6507

If your group needs transportation while in the area, or if you want to have a complete package arranged, Hannah says "anywhere, anyplace, anytime." Prices are given on request.

TOMBIGBEE TOURS & TRAVEL
1372 Ridge Rd., Columbus   328-8282

Tombigbee arranges tours and transportation for 46 passengers per bus. Name your destination and needs, and they'll handle the rest for a prearranged price.

The Delta

No charter bus or receptive tour companies are listed for the Delta, however; any tour company in Jackson or elsewhere in the state will be pleased to help; see below.

The Heartland

CAPITAL CHARTER/GRAYLINE OF JACKSON
451 U.S. Hwy. 49 S.
Richland   939-0519, (800) 841-6817

Complete tour arrangements and tour bus service are offered by this company with more than 30 years experience. They're fully insured.

CORRIGAN TRAVEL/CLINE TOURS
4864 I-55 N.
Jackson   981-6969, (800) 233-5307

This Mississippi-owned and operated motorcoach charter company plans complete transportation arrangements for all types of groups, including churches, schools and clubs. They'll provide prices based on your needs and requests.

JACKSON TOUR & TRAVEL
1801 Crane Ridge Dr.
Jackson   981-8415, (800)873-8572

This locally owned primary-tour operator offers independent departures to Natchez, the River Road of Louisiana and other destinations in the South. Call for itineraries and rates.

The River Cities

NATCHEZ PILGRIMAGE TOURS
State and Canal Sts.
Natchez   446-6631, (800) 647-6742

Tours of the city's historic sights are available year round aboard an authentic London double-decker bus. One-hour tours cost $10. Horse-drawn carriage tours, lasting about 45 minutes, cost $8 for adults. Passengers see the historic downtown area.

The Coast

COASTING INC.

Gulfport   864-2044

Custom-planned group tours of local attractions for children and adults are provided by this company. On every tour, the last stop means "lagniappe," which consists of refreshments such as wine and cheese or soft drinks. Costs vary, depending on the number in the group and type of tour. Step-on guides are available. Enjoy all-inclusive tours, with transportation and admissions averaging about $25 a person.

MAGNOLIA TOURS AND TRANSPORTATION INC.

111 Rue Magnolia   374-7423
Biloxi   (800) 642-4684

Magnolia Tours offers guided tours of the Coast and New Orleans aboard a motor coach. Cost of the Coast tour is $15 per person; the New Orleans city tour costs $30 a person.

CASINO ACTION TOURS

1884 Beach Blvd.
Biloxi   388-2834, (800) 557-3483

This is a new company that shuttles guests daily from Gulfport and Biloxi hotels and motels to the Coast casinos. Locals are welcome as well. For $6 you get minibus transportation to two casinos plus meals, souvenirs and other freebies, including coins and match play. Ask about their New Orleans tours that start at $29 for a 2.5-hour city tour.

HOTARD/GRAYLINE MISSISSIPPI BEACH

(800) 565-8913

This new charter service, based in New Orleans, offers a Mississippi Beach Tour that departs from the main entrance of Isle of Capri Casino in Biloxi. The 2-hour tour takes visitors to the Tullis-Toledano Home, the Church of the Redeemer, the Biloxi Lighthouse and the Port of Gulfport. Tours are at 10 AM on

Photo: The Sun Herald

Amtrak passenger trains serve several communities in Mississippi.

Tuesday, Thursday and Saturday, and the cost is $17 for adults and $8 for children. There's also an 8-hour New Orleans tour that includes a 2-hour tour of the city and concludes with a 1.5-hour swamp tour by boat. It departs the Isle of Capri at 8:30 AM on Wednesday, Friday and Sunday. The price is $43 for adults and $21 for children. Plans call for the tour schedule to be expanded.

Air Service

Mississippi has some 75 public and private airports serving the aviation requirements of private pilots and businesses. Twenty of the public airports have a minimum of 5,000-foot, hard surfaced and lighted runways. Commercial-airline service is available in seven key areas around the state: Tupelo, Columbus, Greenville, Jackson, Meridian, Hattiesburg/Laurel and Gulfport/Biloxi.

The Hill Country

GOLDEN TRIANGLE REGIONAL AIRPORT
2080 Airport Rd., Columbus   327-4422

GTRA was jointly built by the cities of Columbus, Starkville and West Point, and Lowndes County. It is almost equidistant between the three cities, and it is 12 miles west of Columbus, off U.S. Highway12/82. GTRA is served by American Eagle, (800) 433-7300, Atlantic Southeast, (800) 282-3424, and Northwest Airlink, (800) 225-2525, for connecting flights in Memphis, Nashville and Atlanta. Thirteen flights daily bring passengers into and out of northeast Mississippi.

The first thing incoming passengers see is the new, major renovation of the airport. It is now bigger and better than ever, and ever functionally state of the art.

Ratliff Air Services, 328-9312, is the fixed-base operator adjacent to GTRA;

flying lessons are available here. A Congressional Field Office is also located at the regional airport. Ground transportation is available through Airport Limousine Service, 328-1334; Avis, 328-1636; Hertz 328-3292; Enterprise, 328-7610; and National, 327-8183.

TUPELO MUNICIPAL AIRPORT
631 Jackson Ext., Tupelo   841-6571

The Municipal Airport in Tupelo is served by American Eagle, (800) 433-7300, and Northwest Airlink, (800) 225-2525. Ten flights daily arrive and depart Tupelo. The airport is owned by the city. Two fixed-base operators are on the premises: Southernaire, 842-6918, and Tupelo Aero, 844-9112. Ground transportation is available through Budget, 840-3710; Enterprise, 842-2237; and Hertz, 844-9148.

The Delta

GREENVILLE MUNICIPAL AIRPORT
Rt. 1 Box AB300
Greenville   334-3121

Northwest Airlink, (800) 225-2525, serves this Delta town with three incoming and three departing flights per day to Memphis. A fixed-base operator is on the premises to service private aircraft. Two parking lots are available for passengers who require extended parking. Ground transportation is available through Avis, 378-3873, or Hertz, 335-6076.

The Heartland

JACKSON INTERNATIONAL/
ALLEN C. THOMPSON FIELD
Airport Rd.
Jackson   939-5631

The state's only 100-flight-per-day international airport is served by American, (800) 433-7300; Delta, (800) 221-1212;

Northwest, (800) 225-2525; USAir, (800) 428-4322; and Continental Express, (800) 525-0280. Delta averages 32 flights daily; American, 22; Northwest, 22; USAir, 16; and Continental Express, 8. Destinations for the 50 outgoing flights daily include Atlanta, Dallas/Ft. Worth, Washington, D.C., New York City, Chicago, Nashville, Orlando and Cincinnati. Jet aircraft land and take off on two parallel runways. JIA's major renovations include 20 additional ticket counters with a waiting area and a new baggage claim area. Passengers from throughout Mississippi use this airport for departures and arrivals. A new four-lane drive makes access easier.

The Jackson airport also owns and operates Hawkins Field in West Jackson. It's a general aviation facility that also serves air travelers to the Jackson area. Ground transportation in Jackson is available through Avis, 939-5853; Hertz, 939-5312; Budget, 932-2126; LeFleur's Limousine, 956-LIMO; and others.

HATTIESBURG/LAUREL REGIONAL AIRPORT
1602 Terminal Dr.
Moselle   *545-3111*

Hattiesburg/Laurel Regional Airport Authority owns this airport, which is funded by Forrest and Jones counties. The airport serves the eight-county Pine Belt region and is 9 miles north of Hattiesburg and 18 miles south of Laurel on I-59, Exit 76. The terminal has a passenger-waiting area, lounge and snack bar. One airline serves the airport: Northwest Airlink, (800) 225-2525, with three flights daily to Memphis. Ground transportation is available from Hertz, 544-4914, and Budget, 545-2620. The fixed-base operator is U.S. Aviation, 544-0951. There is 24-hour police and fire protection.

MERIDIAN REGIONAL AIRPORT
Key Field, Meridian   *482-0364*

Meridian's airport is 5 miles southeast of the city center, on U.S. 11 S. Air service is provided by Atlantic Southeast and Northwest Airlink. Atlantic Southeast, 485-3165, (800) 282-3424, has three daily flights to Atlanta; Northwest Airlink, (800) 225-2525, has five flights a day to Memphis. The terminal is newly renovated, but the only food service is from vending machines. Hertz, 485-4774, and Avis, 483-7144, offer ground transportation, as does Meridian Cab Co., 693-6338. Parking in the daytime is free, but if you park overnight, you'll be expected to pay $1 on the honor system. The fixed-base operator is Meridian Aviation Inc., 693-7282, whose pilots offer flying lessons. Aircraft maintenance is provided by a contractor to the FBO.

The Coast

GULFPORT/BILOXI REGIONAL AIRPORT
U.S. 49 S., Gulfport   *863-5951*

Four carriers serve this regional airport, providing service to Atlanta, Dallas/Fort Worth, Nashville, Houston and Memphis. There are 50 daily arrivals and departures and more than 1,450 seats available daily. The airlines are: ASA/Delta, 863-1688, (800) 282-3424; American Eagle, 863-5377, (800) 433-7300; Northwest Airlink, 864-5514, (800) 225-2525; and Continental Express, 863-6280, (800) 525-0280.

The three-story terminal was constructed in 1981 and contains a restaurant/lounge, gift shop/newsstand, visitors hospitality (information) booth and ATM. Ground transportation includes courtesy vans, taxis, limousines and charter services; rental cars are available from

Avis, 864-7182; Hertz, 863-2761; Budget, 864-5181; and National, 863-5548.

For private pilots there is a transient aircraft hangar and parking area available at the full-service general aviation terminal operated by U.S. Aviation Corp., 863-2570, the fixed-base operator at the airport.

Railways

Mississippi has a total of 20 rail systems, 2,986 miles of mainline railroads and six key distribution yards located around the state, including one yard in Columbus on the Tennessee-Tombigbee Waterway, one in Greenwood on the Yazoo River and another in Gulfport on the Gulf of Mexico.

Amtrak serves the following cities, listed alphabetically: Batesville, Biloxi, Brookhaven, Canton, Durant, Grenada, Gulfport, Hattiesburg, Hazlehurst, Jackson, Laurel, Meridian, McComb, Pascagoula, Picayune and Winona.

For Amtrak ticket information and schedules, call (800) 872-7245.

The Hill Country

The only Hill Country town served by Amtrak is Batesville with trains 58 (north from New Orleans to Chicago) and 59 (south from Chicago to New Orleans) passing five days per week. The southbound *City of New Orleans* train arrives in Batesville at 7:36 AM daily; the northbound departs at 8:55 PM.

The Heartland

Grenada is a border town, close to the Delta and on the border of the Heartland. The outbound *City of New Orleans* arrives every day but Tuesday and Wednesday in Grenada at 8:19 AM; the northbound train 58 departs at 8:12 PM. The same train arrives in Winona, in the upper Heartland, at 8:42 AM; northbound departure from Winona is 7:47 PM.

Durant, close to the geographic center of the state, also is served by Amtrak trains 58 and 59. The southbound train arrives at 9:07 AM; the northbound train departs at 7:21 PM.

Jackson's Amtrak service southbound to New Orleans arrives at 10:20 AM; northbound departure to Chicago is at 6:21 PM.

Meridian, Laurel and Hattiesburg are served by Amtrak's *Crescent* route between New York and New Orleans. The train has daily arrivals and departures. For Meridian the arrival is 3:10 PM, and departure is 3:15 PM on the southbound run; northbound route arrival is 11 AM, and departure is 11:05 AM. Southbound time for Laurel is 4:14 PM and 4:45 PM in Hattiesburg. On the return, arrival in Hattiesburg is 9:21 AM and 9:52 AM in Laurel.

"Only Positive Mississippi Spoken Here" was the theme for the 1995 Mississippi Governor's Conference on Tourism. The state, once the recipient of negative reportage, wants to do its part to negate the negativism. From all accounts, the campaign is working, along with the slogan, "The South's Warmest Welcome."

Insiders' Tips

The Coast

Amtrak's *Sunset Limited* serves Bay St. Louis, Gulfport, Biloxi and Pascagoula on its Los Angeles-Miami transcontinental route. On Tuesday, Thursday and Sunday, the eastbound train departs at the following times: Bay St. Louis, 12:07 AM; Gulfport 12:25 AM; Biloxi 12:40 AM; and Pascagoula 1:10 AM. The westbound route on Monday, Wednesday and Saturday arrives in Pascagoula at 9:10 AM, Biloxi at 9:35 AM, Gulfport at 9:52 AM and Bay St. Louis at 10:15 AM.

Waterways

Mississippi is a state bordered on two sides by water, and it is touched by water on the upper east border. The Gulf of Mexico is on the southern tip of the state; the Mississippi River runs along the western boundary; and the Tennessee-Tombigbee Waterway runs along the upper northeast. Inland, the commercially navigable Yazoo River runs from Vicksburg to Greenwood. The state has 11 major ports, three of which accept ocean vessel and barge loads, including the Port of Vicksburg on the Mississippi River. The Tennessee-Tombigbee Waterway connects with 14 navigable rivers in the central United States. It provides essential barge transportation to business and industry located along its 234-mile inland course; it's quickly becoming known throughout the region as a mecca for fishermen and outdoor recreation enthusiasts. The safe and scenic Tennessee-Tombigbee Waterway connects middle America with the Gulf of Mexico at Mobile, Alabama, by utilizing inland rivers. For information on prime industrial development opportunities and sites along the Tenn-Tom Waterway, call the TTW Development Authority in Columbus, 328-3286. They have studies, brochures and other pertinent information.

The major ports on the Gulf of Mexico include the state's two deep-water ports at Gulfport and Pascagoula, both U.S. Customs ports of entry. Nearby in Pearlington is Port Bienville at the Pearl River's mouth. The ports at Gulfport and Pascagoula are served by trucking and shipping lines and rail. The state has two foreign trade zones, covering the Coast and Vicksburg/Jackson.

Mississippi has nearly 800 miles of commercially navigable waterways. Along the Mississippi River, there are inland ports at Natchez, Vicksburg, Greenville and Rosedale.

The 234-mile Tennessee-Tombigbee, which runs from the Gulf of Mexico to Tennessee and connects middle America to the world, represents the largest and most ambitious project ever undertaken by the U.S. Army Corps of Engineers. The project began in 1972 and was completed in 1984, making the Tenn-Tom "America's Newest River," one completely safe and scenic for commercial traffic and pleasure boaters.

Inside
Accommodations

Playing host to visitors is something Mississippi has done well for a very long time. This is, after all, the Hospitality State and home to the highly popular pilgrimages during which historic homes throw open their doors and warmly welcome guests.

Just about any kind of accommodation is available, from the mom-and-pop establishments to the newest versions of hotel and motel chains. Of particular interest to history buffs and those with a desire to be pampered are bed and breakfasts, whose growing numbers reflect their popularity. For the thrifty traveler, modest accommodations are plentiful throughout the state. Those with a bigger budget can find rooms and suites with views and many extras. Choices, of course, are more plentiful in the larger cities and tourist areas, such as the Coast, Natchez and Jackson. The following is a partial listing of some of the state's accommodations, starting with bed and breakfasts and followed by hotel and motels.

Bed and Breakfasts

Travelers are discovering the pleasures of staying in bed and breakfast inns, and as a result, Mississippi's bed and breakfast business is booming. Most of the folks who graciously invite overnight guests are those who live in historic homes, primarily antebellum, some Victorian. A few of Mississippi's bed and breakfasts have been passed down from generation to generation; they are very special indeed. Others were purchased because the owners loved the architecture, or perhaps they wished to combine a love of architecture, history and additional income. Additional income, whether through tax credits or bed and breakfast revenue, is helpful when it comes to maintaining a rambling multistory house that was built in the mid 1800s. Painting alone costs well into the thousands, and it must be done periodically. Aluminum siding is not an option, for most of the historic homeowners are serious about keeping the structure as close as possible to the period of construction, and in those days, folks probably didn't even imagine siding.

It is "of the period" dedication that distinguishes Mississippi's bed and breakfast inns. One overnight guest was heard to say, "It's like spending a weekend at Tara," which is a *Gone With the Wind* reference often used to describe these hallowed homes of history. You'll find some of the most hospitable people at bed and breakfast inns, for the majority of these owner/managers are pros at the art of Southern hospitality.

As a rule, historic inns have a few restrictions: adherence to check in-check out times, no children younger than 12, no smoking except in designated areas if

Photo: The Sun Herald

A spectacular view from the Eola Hotel in Natchez.

at all and no pets. Most bed and breakfasts are not handicapped accessible because of the high porches and steps. Of course, there are exceptions, but if any of these categories applies, ask before making reservations.

At last count, there were about 100 bed and breakfasts in Mississippi, with the largest concentration, 33 or so, in Natchez.

Throughout the state, other bed and breakfasts are waiting for guests to arrive to share the history and hospitality of Mississippi's finest homes. Rates vary according to locale, room size and amenities, but plan on paying anywhere from $60 to $160, double or single occupancy; breakfast and tour are included. Most bed and breakfasts accept major credit cards; some accept personal checks with ID.

The bed and breakfast price code is:

$	Less than $60
$$	$61 to $85
$$$	More than $85

See below a regional breakdown in which we've listed some of our favorites in each region. For a complete listing of Mississippi bed and breakfasts, call the Mississippi Division of Tourism, (800) WARMEST. Also, Lincoln, Ltd. Bed and Breakfast Reservation Service in Meridian can help; call them at 482-5483 or (800) 633-6477.

The Hill Country

The following five bed and breakfasts are members of the Columbus Historic Foundation, sponsors of the Columbus Pilgrimage. All these homes are antebellum (built prior to 1860), and they are all listed on the National Register of Historic Places. Rates at press time were $85, double or single occupancy, with a house tour and breakfast included. Additional meals in the house may be arranged for an extra fee. For reservations, call the Columbus Historic Foundation, 329-3533. Other bed and breakfasts in Columbus are not booked through the Historic Foundation, but they are fine properties just the same. The Columbus Convention and Visitors Bureau has information on all bed and breakfasts, though they do not do booking, 329-1191 or (800) 327-2686.

AMZI LOVE HOME

305 Seventh St. S.
Columbus   328-5413, 329-3533
$$

At the A. Love Home, guests feel as though they're stepping back into the mid-1800s because this bed and breakfast inn is so unchanged from its early days. We know that it is unchanged, for it has been in the same family all this time — the eighth generation is in residence now — and they've made a concentrated effort to preserve the home.

Amzi Love was the bridegroom who built this Italianate-style villa for his bride Edith nearly 150 years ago. The furnishings, some original to the house, are smaller in scale than other furnishings of the day. It appears that the furniture was designed to be more compatible with the cottage-style architecture. Sid Caradine, the present occupant/descendant, greets guests and tells them of his family's history. He also serves a great cup of cappuccino and provides guests with extras, such as the use of thick terry-cloth robes. Ask about the love stories at the A. Love Home, built in 1848. A full breakfast is served.

CARTNEY-HUNT HOUSE
408 Seventh St. S.
Columbus   329-3856, 329-3533
$$

From its tree-shaded site on the historic Southside, the Cartney-Hunt House stands guard over Seventh Street like a strong and sturdy fortress, tall and proud. And this marvelous old Federal-style structure has reason to be proud; it is the oldest brick house in north Mississippi. It was built around 1828. It can be proud, too, because its extensive restoration a few years back won prestigious restoration awards. Improvements made did not alter the architectural integrity of the house, they just made it compatible with this century. Current colors and wall coverings were chosen because it's what research determined was the style of the day. Today, appropriate antiques add to the historic significance of this house. Even though it boasts documented period restoration, the house is comfortable and very livable. Guest rooms are completely private, beautifully appointed and contain all the conveniences one would expect in a luxury hotel.

Owners Vicki Hicks Hardy and husband Kirk Hardy are pleased to share their home with guests, and it shows. "Having company" is a way of life for the Hardys, for Vicki's family home is Rosewood Manor, one of the area's best-known antebellum mansions and the house that greets many official guests of the city. Kirk is a CPA; Vicki's a teacher. Guests keep coming back to stay at the Cartney-Hunt House bed and breakfast, and that speaks well of the proprietors.

LIBERTY HALL
Miss. 69 to Yorkville Rd. to Armstrong Rd.
Columbus   328-4110, 329-3533
$$

As guests from cities are quick to say, there's no more perfect a country retreat in these parts than Liberty Hall. It's an authentic planter's home built in 1832. From its vantage point on a tree-canopied ridge, it reigns supreme over a massive lawn, a narrow, winding drive bordered by a split rail fence and a quiet little brook that meanders through the wooded property. It's the way country places were meant to be.

Once inside, you'll pass through the foyer and its black-and-white tiled floor; see fine period antiques in the formal living room to the right and the casual, everyday living room to the left. You won't want to miss the wonderful portraits on the walls, for Liberty Hall is still inhabited by descendants of the planter who built the rambling old house. Actually, the seventh generation is in residence now. It's truly a cherished family home where traditions are still honored. Four generations of family members gather every week for Sunday dinner that consists of such Southern favorites as roasts, fried chicken and lots of fresh garden vegetables.

Guests have the upstairs rooms, which have managed to remain country comfortable yet "citified" in amenities. A full breakfast can be served in your bedroom or in the formal dining room. Liberty Hall and its occupants, the W.S. Fowler family, very well represent the old-fashioned Southern hospitality we hear so much about.

TEMPLE HEIGHTS
515 Ninth St. N.
Columbus   328-0599, 329-3533
$$

Temple Heights (1837) is aptly named, for it resembles a temple of sorts, and it sits high atop a hill. So high, in fact, it is said that Alabama, about 10 miles to the east, can be seen from the top floor. The architectural style is a combination of Federal and Greek Revival, with 14 tall Doric columns on three sides of the house. These styles were prominent at the time Temple Heights was built in 1837. The house has four stories with a hall and two large rooms on each floor.

The owners, Carl and Dixie Butler, are historians and educators who have thoroughly researched all aspects of their home and its furnishings. Their house is furnished predominantly with Empire and Restoration pieces appropriate to the age and style of the house. The vibrant colors in some areas are appropriate to the period, as well. Guests enjoy a fine selection of antiques and the big breakfast served at Temple Heights, which usually features homemade biscuits and jams. If you're interested in local history, the Butlers are among those who know it best. There's an original outdoor kitchen on the grounds, no longer in use as a kitchen, but now almost museum-quality in its new focus as part of the house tour.

WHITE ARCHES
122 Seventh Ave. S.
Columbus   328-4568, 329-3533
$$

White Arches is one of the most unique of Columbus' antebellum bed and breakfasts, for it has a style all its own. This lovely home, built in 1857, is a combination of several architectural styles of the day, which included Greek Revival, Gothic and Italianate. The result of this combination gives it the look of an ornate villa one might see overlooking a vineyard in Europe. From its perch on a corner in Columbus, White Arches always elicits accolades from passersby.

The interior reflects the grandiose age and time in which the house was built. The handsome mahogany stairway, the decorative molding and plasterwork, the original silvered doorknobs, and the library's built-in floor-to-ceiling walnut bookcases are truly grand. The guest rooms are beautifully appointed with antiques and nice decorative accessories. Owners Sarah and Ned Hardin are gracious people by nature, and it shows in the attention to detail they give to their home and its overnight guests.

Insiders' Tips

When in Natchez, pick up a free Tourist Guide to Historic Natchez, printed and distributed monthly by the *Natchez Democrat*. It is a thorough and helpful guide to the best of Natchez and is available in many locations.

THE FOURTH AVENUE COTTAGE
403 Ninth St. S.
Columbus   328-9575
$$

This sunny, comfortable cottage behind the antebellum Max Andrews Home is completely private and impeccably furnished in antiques, yet it has many modern conveniences too, from a microwave and indoor grill to current best-sellers lining the bookcase. Grand, colorful flower arrangements give it a touch of home, as do other design elements carefully selected by owner Fran Andrews Brown and friends. Fran grew up on the premises and knows all the interesting stories regarding her home and the cottage. Fran is also an antiques dealer and a teacher. She and her family recently moved back to the Max Andrews Home.

The Cottage is in the historic Southside, near the Mississippi University for Women campus. Rates are $70 per night, though special rates apply for extended stays.

HIGHLAND HOUSE
810 Highland Cir.
Columbus   327-5577
$$$

This lovely old home gets lots of attention, for it sits in a prime spot in Columbus. It's on the corner of Seventh Street N. and Highland Circle, highly visible to all who drive through this very pretty part of town. The massive house was built in 1909 at the site of an antebellum home that had supposedly been burned by a jealous housekeeper. Known for years as Lindamood, the new owners named it Highland House, which fits well with the tall white columns and pilasters of this red brick mansion. The new owners also updated the interior so that is now features elegant French furniture and design. The physician and his family who

now live at Highland House offer four bedrooms, each complete with a TV and VCR, plus use of a video library that boasts more than 2,000 titles. The exercise room and its state-of-the-art equipment is also available to guests, as well as a fax and copier. Breakfast consists of a brunch menu featuring croissant, a breakfast casserole, marinated fruit and special fruit jams. All four guest rooms have private baths, and they are indeed grand. Rates are $100 per night, single or double occupancy; tour included.

THE CARPENTER PLACE
1280 Miss. 25
Starkville   323-4669
$$-$$$

The Carpenter Place is Oktibbeha County's oldest home extant; it was built in 1835. Drive onto the property via a long and narrow road bordered by a pecan orchard, then arrive at this gracious home. It's what most folks imagine a country place to be: warm, inviting and a welcome respite from the busy world. The back of the house adjoins an English-style brick courtyard, complete with seasonal flowers in bloom. From there, enjoy views of the fields and woods nearby.

Guests to the home are encouraged to enjoy the family treasures in this two-story, impeccably restored planter's home. They are welcome to see and explore the 140 acres of woods and wildlife surrounding the home. The present owners are descendants of the original owners. Rates are $65 for the main house; $150 for the Carriage House suite, which is away from the main house and totally private.

THE MOCKINGBIRD INN
305 N. Gloster
Tupelo   841-0286
$$-$$$

Owners Jim and Sandy Gilmer of the

Mockingbird Inn are world travelers, and their bed and breakfast inn reflects their preferences in world cities. Each room has a different theme, among them Venice, Paris, Athens, Bavaria and, here in the United States, Sanibel Island and Mackinac Island.

The Gilmers spent years collecting special decorative accessories for the bed and breakfast they hoped to someday have. Someday is here, and the Bavarian Room, for instance, recalls an Alpine ski lodge, complete with old sled and ski equipment. In the Venice room, you almost expect to look out and see the canal, complete with gondolas. The Mockingbird Inn affords plenty of space for work or rest and is a favorite of business people in town for the big Tupelo furniture market. Some folks like to know that this house, built around 1925, is directly across the street from the school Tupelo native Elvis Presley attended as a child. Rates range from $65 to $ 95 per night.

OLIVER-BRITT HOUSE
512 Van Buren Ave.
Oxford 234-8043
$

The Oliver-Britt House, named for owners and sisters Mary Ann Britt and Glynn Oliver, was once a physicians' clinic. The two-story brick structure built around 1905 is decorated in a happy, homey style that makes bed and breakfast guests feel as though they've come home. Some of the five rooms are more chintz-patterned and romantic than others, but most are so comfortable you'd like to linger longer. Antiques are interspersed with contemporary furniture, though it's a pleasant blend. A nice feature: French doors open onto a gallery upstairs. A full breakfast is served. Rates are $45 to $55, depending on the room.

PUDDIN PLACE
1008 University Ave.
Oxford 234-1250
$$

Puddin Place is a Victorian House with a big back porch complete with a swing and ceiling fan. It offers a leisurely look at the way things were at the turn of the century and is a perfect place from which to stroll around Oxford. Expect to find some antiques and a warm, friendly atmosphere that is reminiscent of visiting in the comfortable home of an old friend. All accommodations are suites; rates are $85 per night, double or single occupancy, including tax and a very nice breakfast.

THE GENERAL'S QUARTERS
924 Fillmore St.
Corinth 286-3325
$$

The shady lawn leads to a rambling old house built around 1870 that has created its niche in the historic district of Corinth. Civil War buffs who visit Corinth and surrounding area will want to know that this is 22 miles from Shiloh National Military Park. The lovely streets of Corinth invite a nice stroll too. Guest rooms feature canopy beds, brass beds and an eclectic mixture of antiques. A wonderful Southern breakfast is served. Rates are $75, single or double; suites are $85.

The Delta

UNCLE HENRY'S PLACE
5860 Moon Lake Rd.
Dundee 337-2757
$$

Fans of both William Faulkner and Tennessee Williams may recognize the Moon Lake Club, for they both mentioned it often in their writings. Back then, it was known far and wide as a casino that offered the finest foods, memorable nightlife and the kind of gambling that lost more than one Delta fortune. Now, it's a bed and breakfast inn complete with restaurant and a picture-book setting on Moon Lake. Patrons say the restaurant's food is the best around. Uncle Henry's Place, built in 1926, is between Clarksdale and Tunica, a mile off U.S. 49 near where U.S. 61 intersects. It is now owned and managed by the daughter and grandson of Uncle Henry, who purchased the property in 1946. Rates are $65 per night, per room, and the price includes a big breakfast.

THE RIVERS' INN

1109 River Rd., Greenwood   *453-5432*
$-$$

This is a New Orleans-style home built in the early 1900s. It has undergone a bit of a design change since it was built and is now considered an architectural mixture, which means that it's not of a pure style, but pretty and comfortable nevertheless. There are five bedrooms in all; the two upstairs have shared baths as do two downstairs. Guests enjoy the swimming pool and a full breakfast of such specialties as eggs with mushroom sauce and pecan muffins, secret recipes of proprietor Mrs. Rosemarie Kennedy. Upstairs rooms are $58.50; downstairs are $62 per room, per night.

MOUNT HOLLY

Miss. 1
Chatham   *827-2652*
$$-$$$

It is most unusual to find a grand Italianate mansion sitting in the middle of the flat Mississippi Delta, but that is exactly what you'll find just west of Rolling Fork on historic Miss. 1, also known as the Great River Road. Mount Holly was built around 1856, and today it sits regally near the beautiful Lake Washing-ton, remaining a fine example of antebellum architecture. Mount Holly is listed on the National Register of Historic Places.

Because of its prime location in the heart of Delta wildlife land, many serious hunters and fishermen have enjoyed the hospitality of Mount Holly, which includes the huge plantation breakfast that gets them on their way to the surrounding sportsman's paradise. There are five guest rooms, though they recommend only three for the view. Rates range from $75 to $95 per night.

MISS LOIS' VICTORIAN INN

331 S. Washington Ave.
Greenville   *335-6000*
$$

This Victorian structure features antiques throughout the main house and the "shotgun house" on the premises, which by itself accommodates up to four people. It is nicely appointed. Miss Lois' is a pleasant and comfortable place from which to enjoy the Delta's many offerings. The comfortable Victorian home gets many return guests; some have standing reservations each month. A continental breakfast is available at the guests' convenience. Rates are $65 double or single.

NO MISTAKE PLANTATION

5602 Miss. 3, Satartia   *746-6579*
$$$

No Mistake Plantation, built around 1838, is surely a little piece of heaven, for it is far from the frustrations of the real world. Set amid seven acres of lush foliage and a lake, it's quiet, clean and very green. Guest rooms are spacious and lovely and contain fine antiques and interesting artifacts pertinent to the house. Dinner is included in the price of the bed and breakfast, and it features Southern favorites deliciously prepared and elegantly presented.

There's also a completely furnished log cabin on the premises, which may be rented. No Mistake Plantation is between Vicksburg and Yazoo City, on Highway 3. You may recognize it upon arrival, for this picturesque plantation, with the lake in front, has appeared in many magazines. Rates are $110 without tax, and remember, this includes a wonderful candlelight dinner and full Southern breakfast.

The Heartland

MILLSAPS BUIE HOUSE
628 N. State St.
Jackson   352-0221
$$-$$$

This impressive property is one of only 10 in Mississippi to have won AAA's Four-Diamond award, and those who know the Millsaps Buie House say it's an honor well deserved. Built in 1888, this elegant Victorian bed and breakfast boasts 11 bedrooms and a downtown Jackson location. It is furnished with antiques and very good reproductions, including tester or canopy beds, rosewood chairs and marble-top tables. Guests enjoy the run of the house, which includes a grand piano and courting bench in the parlor and a library.

Almost out of place in this Victorian mansion are computer dataports for the business people who prefer an elegant setting. Rates range from $85 to $170; there are separate prices for single and double occupancy.

FAIRVIEW
734 Fairview St., Jackson   948-3429
$$$

This Colonial Revival house, built in 1908, is listed on the National Register of Historic Places, and it is a popular site for weddings, receptions, dinners and more. Fairview can accommodate up to 200 for a sit-down dinner, with a full-time chef and staff available to handle all preparations and service. It offers three suites and two bedrooms on two floors, each with private bath, phone and cable TV. The lovely manicured lawn is an asset to the rambling white house that looks picture perfect and has been featured in *Country Inns* magazine. In fact, it was selected as one of the top-10 inns for 1994, according to the magazine. The breakfast menu varies, and they always prepare foods according to the preference and needs of the guests. Rooms are $95 and suites are $165; breakfast is included.

REDBUD INN
121 N. Wells St.
Kosciusko   289-5086
$$-$$$

Easily accessible from the Natchez Trace, this 1885 Victorian house holds a bed and breakfast as well as a restaurant on the first floor. It is obvious that the Redbud Inn has been lovingly preserved. The multicolored two-story house features a wide center hall, heart-pine wainscoting, ornate mantels, original interior blinds and a grand staircase. It's a Queen Anne style and is listed on the National Register of Historic Places. It's within walking distance of the town square. Better still, the antique furnishings are for sale, if the guest takes a particular liking to them. A downstairs guest room is handicapped accessible. Room rates are $75 to $100.

THE HAMMOND-ROUTT HOUSE

109 S. Natchez, Kosciusko   *289-4131*
$$-$$$

As the home of pioneers to the area, this rambling house got its start as a dog-trot style back in the late 1830s, but it has evolved over the years and now has an eclectic facade. For instance, in the 1920s, a Colonial-style gallery was added, which once again changed its look. American and French antiques are used throughout the house, which is known more for its significant history than its grandiose style. Guests have access to the entire house, for the folks who own it live in a lovely three-story Victorian nearby. It also boasts a meeting room and a memorabilia room, which exhibits early historical documents and interesting anecdotes about the former residents. The owner's Victorian may be toured, by appointment, and they offer a guided tour to include the Redbud Inn plus a meal at the Redbud, for $17 per person. The Hammond-Routt House is within walking distance of the downtown Courthouse Square. Two rooms are available for bed and breakfast at $60 each; the inclusion of an adjoining room is $90.

FRENCH CAMP ACADEMY INN B&B

Hwy. 413
McCool   *547-6835*
$

This is the only inn in close proximity to the scenic Natchez Trace Parkway, which is only a block away. French Camp is approximately 85 miles north of Jackson and 80 miles south of Tupelo. The inn is appropriately and pleasantly rustic with rich woods and country decor. It boasts "old fashioned comfort," and clean, country air scented with pine and cypress. It is also known for the hospitality of the innkeepers.

French Camp Academy Inn is constructed of two log cabins, each more than 100 years old. Chinked log walls and a country setting are a perfect backdrop for the homemade jams and jellies and full Southern breakfast, which consists of such favorites as sorghum-soaked biscuits, creamy grits and fresh eggs. Innkeepers are Ed and Sallie Williford, both of whom teach at nearby French Camp Academy. Rates are $60 per room, double or single.

TALLY HOUSE

402 Rebecca Ave.
Hattiesburg   *582-3467*
$$

Guests at this restored house in the historic neighborhood district will find four rooms with private and semiprivate baths. The beautiful garden areas on the expansive grounds include statuary. There's an inviting two-story porch for relaxing outdoors and interesting antiques and artifacts throughout the house. Rates range from $50 to $75 nightly.

THE MOURNING DOVE
BED AND BREAKFAST

556 N. Sixth Ave.
Laurel   *425-2561, (800) 863-DOVE*
$$$

This new bed and breakfast in Laurel's

historic district near the Lauren Rogers Museum is the only one in Jones County. The house, built in 1907, is an American four-square. Guests stay in the two one-bedroom cottages behind the house. The former servants' quarters has 12-foot ceilings and heart pine floors. Both have a private bath, cable TV/VCR and kitchen area with refrigerator, microwave and coffee maker. A "Southern Gourmet" breakfast is served in the kitchen. Rates are $95 a night for the servants' quarters cottage.

The River Cities

Natchez is full of bed and breakfasts nearly 30 in all — guests will be treated to a full breakfast and tour of the homes as part of their stay. These historic homes have private baths, air conditioning and heating. All listed bed and breakfasts accept major credit cards. Many can be booked through the Natchez Pilgrimage Tours, 446-6631 or (800) 647-6742.

MONMOUTH
36 Melrose Ave.
Natchez   442-5852, (800) 828-4531
$$$

Monmouth (1818), known for its beauty and history, contains belongings of its more famous owner, Gen. John Anthony Quitman, a soldier and governor of Mississippi. Monmouth's striking facade features huge white square columns. There are six bedrooms and one suite in the main house, three bedrooms and one suite in the servants quarters, four bedrooms each in the garden cottages and carriage house and six plantation suites. Rates are $105 to $185. Monmouth's 25 guest rooms and suites are designer perfect and antique proud. Monmouth has also won the prestigious designation of

membership in "Small Luxury Hotels of the World."

THE BURN
712 N. Union St.
Natchez   442-1344, (800) 654-8859
$$$

This historic three-story inn was used by Federal soldiers as a headquarters and a hospital. The semi-spiral stairway, beautiful gardens, antiques and columns are some of its special features. There are three bedrooms in the main house in addition to four bedrooms in another section, where school-age children are welcome. Rates range from $99 to $135.

DUNLEITH
84 Homochitto St.
Natchez   446-8500, (800) 433-2445
$$$-$$$$

This National Historic Landmark is unique among Mississippi's historic homes thanks to the colonnaded galleries and Tuscan columns that surround the two-story structure. Dunleith's architecture and antique furnishings are superb. Tours of the home and gardens and full breakfasts are included in the room or suite rate range of $85 to $175 for these two properties. Dunleith is furnished with 18th- and 19th-century antiques and sits on 40 landscaped acres. An antebellum bathroom is in the three-story service wing attached to the rear of the Greek Revival house. The main house has three bedrooms, and the courtyard wing has eight bedrooms. Guests pay from $85 to $130.

GOVERNOR HOLMES HOUSE
207 S. Wall St.
Natchez   442-2366
$$$

This beautifully decorated home of Mississippi's first elected governor was named best in the state by a recent

Clarion-Ledger readers poll. This is one of the oldest and most historic homes in the Old Spanish Quarter, and it is decorated beautifully with period paintings and furnishings, porcelain and Oriental carpets. All suites have private baths. A delicious plantation breakfast is served in the formal dining room. The house is listed on the National Register of Historic Places. There are four rooms, two of which can accommodate three people. Rooms are $85 a night; a third person is $30 extra.

THE BRIARS

31 Irving Ln.
Natchez   446-9654, (800) 634-1818
$$$

This historic house is on 19 acres in a private setting overlooking the Mississippi River. It was here that Varina Howell Davis married Jefferson Davis in the parlor in 1845. There are 13 rooms in the mansion and four more plus a suite in buildings close to the mansion. Guests can enjoy the gorgeous gardens and the pool. Room rates range from $130 to $145; the suite is $335. A Southern breakfast is included. The Briars is behind the Ramada Inn.

THE DUFF GREEN MANSION

1114 First East St.
Vicksburg   636-6968, (800) 992-0037
$$$

Duff Green, named for the wealthy merchant who had the mansion built, was the site of many festive parties during the antebellum era. During the war the 12,000-square-foot mansion was turned into a hospital where soldiers from the Union and the Confederacy were treated. Newly restored, Duff Green hosts guests in seven rooms. The mansion is in Vicksburg's Historic District. Per night cost is $65 to $160.

CEDAR GROVE MANSION INN

2300 Washington St.
Vicksburg   636-1000, (800) 862-1300
$$$

Cedar Grove is one of the South's largest historic mansions and is home to one of its largest antique collections. A Union cannonball remains lodged in the parlor wall of the exquisitely furnished inn. Enjoy fine dining in the courtyard room and cocktails in the piano bar. Guests can stay in one of 35 luxurious rooms or suites. The grounds boast formal gardens, gazebos, fountains, a courtyard, pool, spa, tennis and lawn croquet. The rates are $90 to $165.

ANCHUCA

1010 First East St.
Vicksburg   631-6800, (800) 469-2597
$$$

This Greek Revival home is the site of a speech by Jefferson Davis, President of the Confederacy. Anchuca is noted for its period antiques and beautiful gas-burning chandeliers. Guests stay in the original slave quarters or the guest cottage at a cost of $75 to $190.

CANEMOUNT PLANTATION

Miss. 552 W.
Lorman   877-3784, (800) 423-0684
$$$

Near Port Gibson, Canemount is a 6,000-acre plantation and wildlife sanctuary that offers three suites to guests. Within the grounds are the Windsor Ruins, the 23 columns left after fire destroyed the Windsor plantation house. Canemount guests stay in three historic cottages equipped with wood-burning fireplaces or stoves. There are guided tours for guests looking for wildlife and birds, or they can take a stroll along the nature trail. For $145 to $165 per night, guests receive a tour of the grounds, cocktails, hors d'oeuvres, dinner and wine in addition to breakfast.

OAK SQUARE

1207 Church St.
Port Gibson 437-4350, (800) 729-0240
$$$-$$$$

This is a fully restored Greek Revival Mansion where guests stay in 11 rooms in guest houses, slave quarters and a carriage house. Oak Square features a rare collection of memorabilia from the Civil War. Prices range from $85 to $95, and family discounts are available.

GIBSON'S LANDING

1002 Church St.
Port Gibson 437-3432
$$$

This historic inn contains five rooms in the main house that are furnished with period antiques. All rooms have private baths, phone, cable TV and refrigerators. Rates range from $75 to $105 for rooms and suites.

The Coast

THE FATHER RYAN HOUSE

1196 Beach Blvd.
Biloxi 435-1189, (800) 295-1189
$$$

There's a wonderful view of the Mississippi Sound from the 60-foot porch in front of this house that's named for the poet laureate of the Confederacy. This bed and breakfast offers nine rooms, all of which are luxuriously furnished in classic antiques. The beach houses have more primitive antiques and an island theme. One house has two bedrooms, one has three bedrooms; both have living and dining rooms and plenty of space for four to six people. The house is in a historic residential area close to beach rentals and a mile from the nearest casino. Rates are $80 to $125.

RED CREEK COLONIAL INN BED & BREAKFAST

7416 Red Creek Rd.
Long Beach 452-3080, (800) 729-9670
$$

This is a three-story, raised French cottage with a 64-foot porch, complete with swings.

Each of the three guest rooms has its own style — Country, French and Victorian — and all are furnished with antiques and double beds. There's also a bunk room with two single beds but no bath to accommodate older kids. The beautiful 11-acre grounds feature large scenic and shade-providing magnolia trees and huge live oaks that are more than three centuries old. Plans call for stables and a vineyard. The beach is about 5 miles away from the inn. The rates are $49 to $69 for double occupancy for the three rooms, each of which has a private bath. The bunk room costs $15 nightly. To reach Red Creek, take Exit 28 off I-10, then travel south for 1.5 miles. Credit cards are not accepted. Call for group rates and extended stay rates.

HARBOUR OAKS INN

126 W. Scenic Dr.
Pass Christian 452-9399
$$$

This three-story antebellum home looks out over Pass Christian's scenic boat harbor, one of the prettiest settings on the beach, and nearby yacht club. This historic inn is an old hand at hosting guests in style. It is, after all, the former Crescent Hotel, the only resort hotel in town left over from the 19th century when the Pass was a popular retreat for the wealthy from New Orleans and Natchez. The first floor was recently renovated and has five rooms, three of which face the beach. All have private baths and are decorated with antiques from the owners' families. There's a billiard room for guests as well as a kitchen stocked with beverages and wine for guests' pleasure. The proprietors are eager to introduce guests to the calming effect of watching the sun set over the Gulf of Mexico while sipping a beverage on the porch. A full breakfast is served in a formal setting. Rates range from $78 to $98.

BAY TOWN INN

208 N. Beach Blvd.
Bay St. Louis   466-5870, (800) 467-8466
$$$

Guests have a wonderful view of the Bay of St. Louis from this turn-of-the-century planter's home with an inviting veranda. There are seven guest rooms with private baths, a downstairs parlor and dining room and an upstairs sitting room. Each room is named and has its own personality. The Papa Rowland, for example, is the large corner room facing the bay. It's decorated in deep greens and burgundy and is furnished with a queen-size bed and writing table in the sitting area. The bath is equipped with a claw-foot tub and antique sink. Guests can relax in the swing under the magnolia tree or in the front porch rockers. Next door is the quaint historic downtown district, with restaurants and antique stores within easy walking distance. Children older than 14 are welcome, but pets aren't. Rates are $75 for the five upstairs rooms and $85 for the two downstairs rooms. Call for corporate rates.

Hotels and Motels

This is a partial listing of overnight accommodations in each geographic area. The range to expect for most motel rooms in the state is $40 to $50 in smaller towns; $50 to $135 in Jackson and the Gulf Coast. For a complete listing of all properties in each town in Mississippi, contact local chambers of commerce; see chamber listings elsewhere in this book, or the local convention and visitors bureau, also listed elsewhere. All hotels and motels accept most major credit cards unless otherwise noted.

Here's an explanation of the rates for double occupancy rooms (tax is not included):

$30 to $40	*$*
$41 to $60	*$$*
$61 to $85	*$$$*
More than $85	*$$$$*

The Hill Country

BEST WESTERN ABERDEEN INN

U.S. Hwy. 45 N.
Aberdeen   369-4343, (800) 528-1234
$$

This new property is on the outskirts of Aberdeen, within walking distance of the Tennessee-Tombigbee Waterway. The restaurant, on the premises, serves three meals and features Southern cooking at its best. This Best Western offers 50 rooms, complete with room service. There's a nice pool too.

The wonderful Revolving Tables Restaurant in Mendenhall is thought to have been the setting for Eudora Welty's novel, *The Ponder Heart*. Welty attended Mississippi University for Women with the owner's mother. Built in 1915, the present owners are the third generation to run the old hotel, now restaurant only, which serves delicious Southern food boardinghouse style.

Insiders' Tips

COMFORT INN

1210 U.S. Hwy. 45 N.
Columbus   329-2422
$$

This motel is adjacent to a shopping mall and restaurants, and it serves a nice continental breakfast each morning. The 106 rooms are comfortably furnished and spacious. It's near the Highway 12/82 bypass and within three blocks of downtown.

HAMPTON INN

2015 Military Rd.
Columbus   328-6720 , (800) HAMPTON
$$

A new motel, this Hampton Inn is near all Columbus shopping and attractions. Restaurants are close by. This 60-room motel is just off the Highway 12/82 bypass. Enjoy the warm Mississippi sun while using the new pool.

COLUMBUS HOLIDAY INN

506 U.S. 45 N.
Columbus   328-5202, (800) HOLIDAY
$$

This 153-room property is locally owned, and it boasts a restaurant, lounge and conference facilities. It's also within two blocks of downtown Columbus. The restaurant, Annabelle's Courtyard, is popular with locals who come for breakfast and lunch buffets. This Holiday Inn offers a big pool, room service, Showtime and a daily happy hour in the lounge.

GILMER INN

321 Main St./U.S. 82
Columbus   328-0070
$$

The 74-room Gilmer has the most convenient downtown location, and it's near lots of antique shops. Some of the guests enjoy strolling through the historic district, which begins across the street from the Gilmer. Also across the street is a restaurant, and several others are in the vicinity. A small pool is available for hotel guests. The Gilmer Inn faces the new Columbus Welcome Center, the former home of playwright Tennessee Williams.

RAMADA INN

1200 U.S. Hwy. 45 N.
Columbus   327-7077, (800) 228-2828
$$

The Ramada has a restaurant, a lounge called Montana's, live entertainment and an atrium bar for after-work relaxation. Some of 119 guest rooms overlook the atrium lobby. This Ramada offers an outdoor pool, room service, cable TV that includes free HBO and ESPN.

REGENCY PARK

2218 U.S. 45 N.
Columbus   327-2251
$$

This 100-room hotel is locally owned, and personal service is emphasized by the owners. Rooms are clean and comfortable; restaurants and shopping are close by on Highway 45. Guests enjoy a nice outdoor pool and cable TV in rooms.

EXECUTIVE INN

U.S. 72 W. and U.S. 45
Corinth   286-6071
$$

This conveniently located property has a restaurant, an outdoor pool and business services for travelers. It has in excess of 100 rooms. Room service is available.

BEST WESTERN/OXFORD INN

1101 Frontage Rd.
Oxford   234-9500, (800) 528-1234
$$

Close proximity to Ole Miss and William Faulkner's home makes this a good choice for overnight in Oxford. It has a restaurant, lounge and pool on the premises. Banquet facilities accommodate up to 100 people. It has 100 rooms.

HOLIDAY INN

400 N. Lamar Ave.
Oxford   234-3031, (800) HOLIDAY
$$

This 100-room Holiday Inn serves some of the best Southern cookin' you'll find in a hotel restaurant. It's within walking distance of the Square, and it has an outdoor pool, banquet facilities for 200, room service, cable TV and a travel agency on the premises.

RAMADA INN/UNIVERSITY

2201 Jackson Ave.
Oxford   234-7013
$$

The Ole Miss campus and tourist attractions are within a mile of this motel. It has three suites and 116 rooms, an outdoor pool, banquet facilities for 300 and a free continental breakfast. Most days, a manager's reception includes a complimentary cocktail.

HOLIDAY INN

Miss. Hwy. 12 and S. Montgomery St.
Starkville   323-6161, (800) HOLIDAY
$$

Expect a good restaurant, lounge, and satellite hi-net conference capabilities. The management staff here makes an all-out effort to assure that guests' needs are met. They provide room service, suites, HBO, Showtime and meeting rooms. It has 173 rooms and a nice outdoor pool.

THE STATEHOUSE HOTEL

Corner Main and Jackson St.
Starkville   323-2000
$$-$$$ (800) 722-1903

This small hotel, now listed on the National Register of Historic Places, began back in 1925 as the Hotel Chester. A major renovation in 1985 gave it an up-

scale new look and a new name, the Ivy Guest House. It's a far more elegant hotel than guests expect to find in a small Southern town. The hotel's luxury rooms are furnished with excellent antique reproductions, and so are the junior suites, executive suites and Presidential suite. Since 1993, the Ivy has been The Statehouse Hotel. In downtown Starkville, the Statehouse boasts a wonderful lounge (the Library) with lots of rich wood on the bar and tables, a restaurant (the Waverly), small conference facilities and 43 rooms. Guests can expect room service, a complimentary drink in the lounge and a 10-percent discount on restaurant food.

BEST WESTERN/STARKVILLE INN

119 Miss. 12 N.
Starkville   324-5555
$$ (800) 528-1234

All beds are queen and king size. There's an outdoor pool and complimentary coffee. There's also a fax machine, copier, an executive suite and HBO. Small pets are accepted.

REGAL INN

Miss. Hwy. 82 E.
Starkville   323-8251
$$

Newly renovated rooms give this motel added appeal. It has a restaurant and lounge, outdoor pool, at-door parking and is only minutes from the MSU campus. Weekly rates, AARP and government rates are available too. Room service is offered.

UNIVERSITY INN

Miss. 12 and Spring St.
Starkville   323-9550
$$ (800) 475-UNIV

Parents of students are welcome guests at this property near the MSU campus.

Tennessee Williams: A Southern Playwright

Tennessee Williams was a native Mississippian whose life and works have inspired a major fall festival in the Delta town of Clarksdale, a Welcome Center in Columbus and a big literary festival in New Orleans. Indeed, this playwright may have begun gathering material for his future works at a very early age, perhaps through osmosis. He lived with his grandparents in Columbus and Clarksdale when his grandfather The Rev. Walter Dakin was an Episcopal priest in these towns, and Tennessee accompanied the Rev. Dakin on parish calls.

The young Tom Williams must have sat quietly, listened carefully, and remembered colorful stories, for they were told with great skill and talent in such plays as *A Streetcar Named Desire*, *Cat on a Hot Tin Roof*, *The Glass Menagerie*, *Summer and Smoke* and many others. The first two men-

Much of the work of Mississippi playwright Tennessee Williams was drawn from his Southern roots.

tioned won Pulitzer Prizes. The playwright, born in Columbus in 1911, died in 1983. Someone said at his funeral that, "During half of his career, Williams produced a body of work that did and still does give our theater one of the few claims to greatness." It was the role of Stanley Kowalski in the film version of *Streetcar* that catapulted young Marlon Brando to fame. Paul Newman and Elizabeth Taylor portrayed Brick and Maggie in the film *Cat on a Hot Tin Roof*, and Newman and Joanne Woodward worked together in *The Long, Hot, Summer*. Richard Burton and Ava Gardner made *The Night of the Iguana*, and the list could go on. Also while eulogizing Williams, Frank Rich of The New York Times News Service said, "If there is a literate person who has not encountered Amanda and Laura Wingfield, Blanche DuBois and Stanley Kowalski, or Maggie the Cat and Big Daddy, his life is poorer for it." Learn more about the critically acclaimed playwright at the Tennessee Williams Festival, the second weekend in October, in Clarksdale. The three-day event includes performances of plays, a literary conference, tours of his childhood home and haunts and blues music. For information on the festival, call 624-4461 or (800) 626-3764.

This motel has a restaurant, lounge, outdoor pool, complimentary coffee, fax, copier, room service, meeting facilities and 118 rooms.

COMFORT INN
1190 N. Gloster St.
Tupelo   842-5100, (800) 221-2222
$$

This 83-room Comfort Inn is near all Tupelo attractions. It has a weight room, complimentary breakfast and two meeting rooms. Comfort Inn will accept personal checks with ID, and they are prepared for business travelers, with meeting rooms, fax and copier. Parking is available in front of most rooms.

ECONO LODGE
1500 McCullough Blvd.
Tupelo   844-1904, (800) 55-ECONO
$$

The 100-room motel, at the intersection of U.S. 78 Business and Highway 45 Business, has meeting rooms, suites, airport transportation, fax and an outdoor pool. Handicap parking spaces are available, and so is HBO. A continental breakfast is included.

HOLIDAY INN EXPRESS
923 N. Gloster St.
Tupelo   842-8811, (800) 465-4329
$$

This is a 124-room Holiday Inn Express, known for good value. There isn't a restaurant on the premises, though several are nearby. Special services include a meeting room, outdoor pool, coin laundry, babysitting, cable TV and Satellite Cinema. There's also a fax and copier and a free Continental breakfast.

EXECUTIVE INN
1011 N. Gloster St. at U.S. 45 and 78
Tupelo   841-2222, (800) 533-3220
$$

A heated indoor pool, sauna, garden atrium lobby, restaurant and lounge are available. Additionally, special services include coffeemakers in all rooms, complimentary newspapers, banquet and business conference facilities, safe deposit boxes, notary public and fax. There are 115 rooms, and special group accommodations are available upon request.

RAMADA INN
854 N. Gloster St. at U.S. 45 and 78
Tupelo   844-4111, (800) 228-2828
$$

This is the home of the Cafe Bravo, where guests and local folks go for gourmet dining. Tupelo's 230-room Ramada offers business services such as 10 meeting rooms and a conference room, fax, copier, valet/laundry, limo service, a sauna, exercise room, gameroom and a hair salon for men and women. Bogart's Lounge offers free hors d'oeuvres and live entertainment most nights. There's a pool and an exercise room on request, and group rates are available.

TRACE INN
3400 W. Main, Tupelo   842-5555
$$

Just off the scenic Natchez Trace

Parkway, this 134-room property sits on 15 acres and has a restaurant on the premises, an outdoor pool plus other amenities, including direct billing with references. Parking at drive-up rooms is appreciated too. Big meeting rooms are available. It's three minutes from the airport, and an airport courtesy car is available.

The Delta

BEST WESTERN REGENCY INN
2428 U.S. Hwy. 82 E.
Greenville   334-6900, (800) 528-1234
$$

A continental breakfast is available at this property, and several restaurants are nearby. Also, there's a racquetball court, an exercise room, an indoor heated pool and refrigerators in rooms. This is a good address for those doing business in the Delta.

HAMPTON INN
2701 Hwy. 82 E.
Greenville   334-1818, (800) HAMPTON
$$

This conveniently located inn appeals to business travelers and has a restaurant next door. There's also a health club, sauna and a continental breakfast available.

RAMADA INN
2700 U.S. Hwy. 82 E.   (800) 228-2828
Greenville   332-4411
$$

A restaurant is on the premises of this Ramada. A lounge features live entertainment most nights. It's a good place to meet locals or to relax after a day on the road. There's a heated indoor pool and an exercise room available on request.

HAMPTON INN
U.S. 82   455-5777
Greenwood   (800) HAMPTON
$$

This 100-room property appeals to business travelers, perhaps because of the business services offered and the free waffle breakfast. There's a refrigerator in every room, a heated indoor/outdoor pool, a sports court and a whirlpool. This motel, formerly a Best Western, has been newly renovated. There isn't a restaurant on the premises, but a Shoney's is next door.

RAMADA INN
900 W. Park Ave. at U.S. 49 and 82
Greenwood   455-2321, (800) 228-2828
$$

All you need for a comfortable stay in Greenwood is here, complete with a full-service restaurant and lounge. Expect a fitness room, hot tub and outdoor pool. It has 138 rooms plus room service and cable TV.

CLEVELAND INN
U.S. 61 S., Cleveland   846-1411
$$

This 119-room inn is near the college, and it is has a restaurant on the premises. This locally owned property offers room service, an outdoor pool, a lounge, HBO and a dedicated long-term staff.

HOLIDAY INN
Miss. 8 and I-55
Grenada   226-2851, (800) HOLIDAY
$$

This inn is known for its good restaurant, a cafe, lounge and live entertainment. There's also a pool and outdoor playground equipment. They provide tourist information and fax/copier services for business people. It's near Grenada

Lake and has 129 rooms, complete with cable TV and room service.

COMFORT INN

910 U.S. 82 E.
Indianola   887-6611, (800) 228-5150
$$

This is a comfortable place to stay in this part of the Delta. The 50-room property is AAA rated, and it offers a free continental breakfast. It's a good central location for Delta doins'.

CLARKSDALE COMFORT INN

710 S. State St.
Clarksdale   627-9292, (800) 228-5150
$$

This Comfort Inn has 93 rooms, with banquet meeting rooms, an exercise room and a sports court, a heated indoor-outdoor pool and a whirlpool, fax and voice mail services, valet services, a complimentary continental breakfast and paper. Restaurants are nearby.

DAYS INN

1910 State St.
Clarksdale   624-4391
$$

A conference center is available for up to 200 persons; the manager will make arrangements for you. Managers and staff will also make special arrangements for flowers, cards, gift baskets and champagne to be delivered to rooms or in the city limits. A pool is on the property, and a continental breakfast is prepared each morning.

SAM'S TOWN
HOTEL & GAMBLING HALL

North of Tunica, Robinsonville Rd.   363-0700
Commerce Landing   (800) 456-0711
$$$

This hotel is a part of Sam's Town, the first casino hotel in Tunica County. It's a western-themed hotel and casino complex, complete with five restaurants, nine bars and lounges, the area's largest western retail store, a dance hall and casino gaming. The 200 initial rooms have now increased to 500. Amenities include cable TV, in-room movies, suites, meeting and conference rooms and an exercise room with sauna.

HORSESHOE CASINO & HOTEL

Off U.S. 61   357-5500
Tunica   (800) 303-SHOE
$$-$$$

The 200-room hotel at this casino overlooks a courtyard and an outdoor swimming pool. The Horseshoe is nestled among a 220-acre Casino Center, which also includes the Sheraton Casino and Circus Circus. Three restaurants and two lounges are in the hotel and casino complex.

The Heartland

CABOT LODGE NORTH

Jackson I-55 N. at E. County Line Rd.
Ridgeland   957-0757, (800) 342-2268
$$$

This pleasant 208-room motel near Northpark Mall offers a complimentary arrival cocktail and deluxe continental breakfast. A pool, cable TV and special weekend rates are attractive for weekend trips to Jackson. Cabot Lodge also has a location near Milsaps College.

HOLIDAY INN DOWNTOWN

200 E. Amite St.
Jackson   969-5100, (800) HOLIDAY
$$

This one is near the Capitol, Trademart, Governor's Mansion and more, with Bentley's full-service restaurant and Fitzroy's lounge on the premises. Special amenities include a weekend lunch buffet and Sunday brunch buffet.

There are 18 meeting rooms and banquet facilities for 1,000. Included in the 358 rooms are an executive parlor and suites. There's an outdoor pool, an exercise room and HBO. Small pets are allowed in rooms.

CABOT LODGE MILLSAPS
2375 N. State St.
Jackson   948-8650, (800) 874-4737
$$$

A great room with fireplace makes this property look amazingly like a lodge. It features a complimentary welcoming cocktail and deluxe Continental breakfast. It has 205 rooms, a pool and a lending library. Business travelers love the convenience of the sixth floor business center, where they find a free fax, copier and more. Executive accommodations include robes in the rooms and use of a nearby fitness center.

EDISON WALTHALL
225 E. Capitol St.
Jackson   948-6161, (800) 932-6161
$$$

This hotel, one of Mississippi's finest, is right downtown, near the Governor's Mansion, State Capitol and museums. It's an AAA Four-Diamond Hotel with a Mobil Three-Star restaurant. It offers an outdoor heated pool with a hot tub and a fitness center, plus meeting rooms, airport transportation and true Old-World charm. It has 208 rooms and three suites. A refurbished Edison Walthall was built in 1928. Also expect room service, a gift shop, fax, copier

and a courtesy van for trips within 3 miles of the hotel.

MARRIOTT RESIDENCE INN
881 E. River Pl.
Jackson   355-3599, (800) 331-3131
$$$-$$$$

If it's necessary to be away from home, the 120-room Residence Inn is the next best place. The kitchen facilities, comfortable furniture and pleasant surroundings make it a place you want to return to after a busy day. Continental breakfast is served.

RAMADA COLISEUM
400 Greymont St.
Jackson   969-2141, (800) 228-2828
$$$

This motel is across from the Coliseum, and it has a restaurant, lounge with live entertainment and complimentary shuttle service to the airport. This one's also a convention center with 400 rooms.

RAMADA PLAZA HOTEL
I-55 at 1001 E. County Line Rd.
Jackson   957-2800, (800) 228-2828
$$$

This hotel, formerly called the Ramada Renaissance, rises high above its neighbors and can be easily spotted from I-55 N. It is one of the best addresses in town for business travelers, and this Ramada is prepared to meet their needs with business services. Enjoy two restaurants, two lounges with live entertainment and full convention facilities. If you're there through the weekend, take advantage of the fabulous Sunday lunch buffet. It has 300 rooms.

QUALITY INN NORTH
4641 I-55 N.
Jackson 982-1044
$$

The newly remodeled guest rooms are a plus, so are the special weekend rates and 10 percent AARP discount. Expect an outdoor pool, meeting rooms, airport transportation, a restaurant and a lounge. This motel is also near two shopping centers.

WILSON INN
310 Greymont Ave., I-55 at High St.
Jackson 948-4466
$$

It's across the street from the Coliseum and Fairgrounds; restaurants are nearby. The Wilson provides complimentary popcorn and punch at check-in. There's a refrigerator in every room and microwaves in many rooms. Kids stay free with parents. It has 110 rooms.

BEST WESTERN MERIDIAN
2219 S. Frontage Rd.
Meridian 693-3210
$$

This 120-room motel is at I-20/59. Its amenities include free local telephone service, cable TV with HBO, an outdoor pool and patio and meeting rooms. There's live entertainment nightly in the lounge, and The Depot Restaurant is open daily starting at 6 AM.

HAMPTON INN
618 U.S. 80 and 11
Meridian 483-3000
$$

One- and two-bedroom suites are among the 116 rooms at this motel, which also offers airport transportation. There's a swimming pool and exercise rooms with

a whirlpool. Guests receive a free continental breakfast.

HOLIDAY INN NORTHEAST
610 U.S. 80 and 11
Meridian 485-5101
$$$

This Holiday Inn has 191 rooms, plus meeting rooms for up to 200 people, a swimming pool, tennis courts and airport transportation. There's entertainment in the La Veranda Lounge, and Denny's Family Restaurant is open 24 hours a day.

HOLIDAY INN SOUTH
U.S. 45, Meridian 693-4521
$$

This newly remodeled, 174-room motel offers a swimming pool, children's playground, free local calls, laundry facilities, cable and pay-per-view movies. It also has the Patio Restaurant and Copper Door Lounge. Take Exit 153 off I-20/59.

HOWARD JOHNSON'S
1613 U.S. 80 and 11
Meridian 483-8281
$$

Accommodations include 142 rooms, a lounge with nightly entertainment, the Greenbriar Restaurant, a heated swimming pool, a Jacuzzi and a convention center for 400 people.

The River Cities

BEST WESTERN RIVER PARK HOTEL
645 S. Canal St.
Natchez 446-6688, (800) 274-5532
$$$

The old and the new blend together here in an elegant fashion. Besides 145 rooms, this hotel offers a lounge, an outdoor pool, a Jacuzzi, a gift shop, meeting rooms and The Cafe, a full service restaurant (room service is available).

HOLIDAY INN

271 D'Evereux Dr.
Natchez   442-3686, (800) HOLIDAY
$$

The 139 rooms here are newly remodeled. Guests will find Diamond Jim's lounge, an outdoor pool, meeting rooms and The Rain Tree, a full-service restaurant. This Holiday Inn offers AAA and AARP discounts.

HOWARD JOHNSON LODGE

U.S. 61 S.
Natchez   442-1691, (800) 541-1720
$$$

This property has 131 rooms with free local calls and cable, plus a full-service restaurant and The Small Bar on the premises. You'll also find an outdoor pool, banquet facilities and meeting rooms.

NATCHEZ EOLA HOTEL

110 N. Pearl St.
Natchez   445-6000, (800) 888-9140
$$$

This downtown landmark, built in 1927, has 125 rooms, fine dining in Cafe La Salle, Julep's restaurant for casual dining, the Moonflower Lounge overlooking the Mississippi River, a lounge, gift shop and lots of history. The most distinguished feature of the small, beautifully decorated lobby is the manually operated elevator. The Eola is the only hotel in Mississippi to be included among the prestigious National Trust for Historic Preservation's "Historic Hotels of America." It's one of 60, and it is listed on the National Register of Historic Places. Rooms aren't fancy, but the hospitality shines. The Eola is very convenient to some of the city's antebellum homes and antique shops.

RAMADA INN HILLTOP

130 John R. Junkin Dr.
Natchez   446-6311, (800) 256-6311
$$-$$$

This 172-room inn overlooks the Mississippi and is five minutes from downtown. There's a dining room, lounge and pool and perhaps the best river view in the state.

HARRAH'S CASINO & HOTEL

1310 Mulberry St.
Vicksburg   (800) HARRAHS
$$$$

Harrah's seven-story hotel, adjacent to the casino with its shops and restaurants, offers free continental breakfast to its guests. There are 117 rooms with 16 suites, plus covered parking and child-care facilities.

The Coast

The Coast has approximately 8,000 rooms in more than 68 hotels and motels. Casinos are now a major player in the accommodations pictures; several are building, or planning to build, large hotels at dockside sites. Others have purchased established properties and are renovating them. More information about hotel, motel and condo rentals, campgrounds and RV parks is available from

Insiders' Tips

Watch for more Coast casinos to open hotels in 1995 and 1996.

the Mississippi Beach Convention & Visitors Bureau, P.O. Box 6128, Gulfport 39506, (800) 237-9493 or 896-6699.

SHONEY'S INN
9375 U.S.49
Gulfport   *868-8500, (800) 222-2222*
$$$

Shoney's has 110 rooms, a Shoney's restaurant next door and is near the Gulfport/Biloxi Regional Airport. Nonsmoking rooms are available.

BEST WESTERN BEACH VIEW INN
2922 W. Beach Blvd.
Gulfport 864-4650, (800) 748-8969
$$$

This 150-room inn is located near the State Port, which has two casinos. Guests may use the complimentary limousine to travel to the casinos. There's a lounge with live entertainment, a steak restaurant and pool. Some rooms have a view of the Gulf. The inn is near downtown and the sand beach.

HOLIDAY INN BEACHFRONT GULFPORT
1600 E. Beach Blvd., Gulfport   *864-4310*
$$$

Guests choose from 229 rooms at this property, which is convenient to beach attractions and casinos. Enjoy a restaurant, pool, meeting facilities, golf packages and entertainment in the lounge.

HOLIDAY INN GULFPORT AIRPORT
9415 U.S. 49 N.
Gulfport   *868-8200*
$$$

This Holiday Inn has 152 rooms and

is near the Gulfport/Biloxi Regional Airport. Relax in the pool and enjoy entertainment in the lounge. This hotel is an easy drive from the beach and other attractions in and around Gulfport.

HOLIDAY INN BEACHFRONT COLISEUM
2400 Beach Blvd.
Biloxi   *388-3551, (800) 441-0882*
$$$

This property has 268 rooms, an Olympic-size pool, live entertainment in the lounge, hot tub suites and airport transportation on request. It's next door to the Coast Coliseum and across the street from a very popular strip of the beach.

BROADWATER BEACH RESORT HOTEL
2110 Beach Blvd.
Biloxi   *388-2211, (800) 647-3964*
$$$$

Adjacent to The President Casino, the Broadwater has 332 rooms, three restaurants, the largest covered marina in the world, two golf courses, a lounge, two pools and lighted tennis courts. The hotel is also affiliated with Broadwater Tower and Broadwater Inn, both on the Biloxi beach. Casino shuttles pick up and deliver passengers to nearby dockside establishments at no charge.

BROADWATER TOWER
2060 Beach Blvd.
Biloxi   *388-7000, (800) 325-9384*
$$$$

This beach property has 284 rooms, a lounge, a restaurant, a pool, tennis courts and is situated a block from The President Casino and its sister hotel, the Broadwater Resort.

A third facility, the Broadwater Inn, has 218 rooms and is nearby on Beach Boulevard.

Hampton Inn

9445 U.S. 49	868-3300
Gulfport	(800) 426-7866
$$$	

The Hampton Inn has 158 rooms, including 69 brand new ones. Guests have use of the swimming pool and receive a complimentary continental breakfast from 6 to 10 AM. The suite here has a hot tub. Rates are slightly higher on weekends.

Edgewater Inn

1936 Beach Blvd.	
Biloxi	388-1100, (800) 323-9676
$$$$	

This newly expanded locally owned property has 62 deluxe rooms, junior suites and suites located across from the beach and near the casinos and shopping. All rooms have a refrigerator and microwave. There's an indoor spa, sauna, gym, large outdoor pool and Waffle House restaurant that is open 24 hours.

Quality Inn Emerald Beach

1865 Beach Blvd.	
Biloxi	388-3212, (800) 342-7519
$$$	

This Quality Inn has 62 rooms, a heated pool and a full-service restaurant, all at a beach front location. Prices vary according to room location. The restaurant is known for very good seafood dishes.

Gulf Beach Resort

2428 Beach Blvd.	
Biloxi	385-5555, (800) 323-9164
$$$	

This seven-story hotel has 228 rooms, a restaurant, three lounges including a sports bar and one with live entertainment and pools for adults and kids. Guests have access to free casino shuttle service.

Paradise Beach Resort

220 W. Beach Blvd.	
Long Beach	864-8811, (800) 538-7752
$$$	

This motel, on the beach and near downtown Long Beach, has 101 rooms, a restaurant, lounge, pool, tennis court and putting green.

La Font Inn

U.S. 90 E.	
Pascagoula	762-7111, (800) 647-6077
$$-$$$	

This locally owned inn has 192 rooms and lots of amenities, among them a restaurant, lounge, Olympic-size pool, lighted tennis courts, a playground, exercise room, steam baths and guest laundry.

Diamondhead Days Inn

103 Live Oak Dr.	
Diamondhead	255-1300, (800) 497-3685
$$$	

Guests can enjoy the indoor heated pool, restaurant and lounge in the resort community. There's an indoor heated pool, hot tub, shuttle transportation to local casinos and meeting facilities.

Grand Casino Hotel-Biloxi

245 Beach Blvd.	432-2500
Biloxi	(800) 354-2450
$$$$	

This luxury hotel opened in early 1995 offering guests 500 rooms and lots of amenities, including a full-service spa, a retail shopping arcade and a swimming pool overlooking the gulf. This hotel also has Kids Quest, a supervised activity center for children and an arcade for teens.

COMFORT INN
1648 Beach Blvd.
Biloxi   432-1993
$$$-$$$$

This new 68-room inn has a number of different types of accommodations for guests. Some rooms have two double beds, and some have a king-size bed. Three rooms have Jacuzzis, and several have kitchenettes. Free continental breakfast is included in the price. The motel is served by the casino shuttles upon request. Rates increase slightly on weekends.

DAYS INN
26350 West Beach Blvd.
Pass Christian   452-4301
$$$

This new beachfront property has 59 comfortable rooms and offers free continental breakfast, a pool and free local calls. Golf packages are available.

KEY WEST INN
1000 U.S. 90
Bay St. Louis   466-0444, (800) 833-0555
$$

This new motel has 44 rooms, 40 of which have two double beds. The four King Deluxe rooms have king size beds, a wet bar, microwave and refrigerator. There is no restaurant on the property, but a new Waffle House is adjacent to the inn.

Key West offers free shuttle service to the two local casinos.

CASINO MAGIC INN
711 Casino Magic Dr.
Bay St. Louis   466-0891, (800) 5MAGIC5
$$-$$$$

Casino Magic's new inn has 200 rooms in two four-story buildings near the casino action. Most rooms have two queen size beds; others have one king-size bed or two full size beds. Each of the 20 junior suites has a coffeemaker, refrigerator and microwave. The deluxe suite has a big-screen TV, wet bar and balcony overlooking the pool and Jacuzzi. All rooms have beverage service and bellman service. Casino Magic's Players Club members receive a discount.

MAGNOLIA PLANTATION HOTEL
16391 Robinson Rd.
Gulfport   832-8400, (800) 700-7858
$$$$

This new hotel, a former country estate, has 20 rooms and 12 suites plus a pool, Jacuzzi and conference center. Rates include a full breakfast buffet served in the dining room. The beautiful grounds feature a lake and fountains, all in a secluded setting 7 miles from U.S. 90. Golf and casino packages are available.

Photo: BRAVO!

The open kitchen at BRAVO! Italian Restaurant is one of Jackson's favorite dining experiences. Chef Dan Blumenthal serves his creations to the delight of diners.

Inside
Restaurants

You'll find some of the country's best food — Southern and otherwise — in Mississippi restaurants. Enjoy a quick bite at a neighborhood restaurant or dine at an elegant restaurant with a full gourmet menu with an international flavor. Specialties abound, and the choices are all yours. Sample outstanding barbecue, the freshest seafood and vegetables and expertly prepared home-cooked meals and ethnic delights. Try the sophisticated taste of New South Cuisine, or go for the hearty Mediterranean, Middle Eastern, Italian, French and New Orleans-style dishes with a Mississippi twist. Dig into hushpuppies, fried green tomatoes, golden-fried chicken and deep-fried catfish. Order the just-caught crabs and shrimp boiled hot and spicy, or select delectable broiled trout, plump oysters on the half-shell and tender steaks fixed just the way you like. Now you're getting the idea.

Whether you have an educated palate or just a healthy appetite, you'll find something to satisfy your hunger because Mississippi kitchens are turning out some very tasty fare indeed.

Of course, with all these choices, there's no way we can list all the wonderful restaurants we'd love to tell you about. If we've missed one of your favorites or new discoveries, write us at the addresses listed in the front of this book. We'll consider your suggestions when we update this information. In the meantime, we'll list a few restaurants in every region. The average cost of a dinner for two in most of the restaurants mentioned is less than $30; slightly more in Jackson and on the Gulf Coast. Our price code doesn't include appetizers, alcoholic beverages, taxes or tips. All restaurants accept major credit cards unless otherwise noted. Enjoy!

Less than $20	$
$21 to $35	$$
$36 to $50	$$$
More than $50	$$$$

The Hill Country

BROWNE'S DOWNTOWN
509 Main St., Columbus   327-8880
$

Browne's is a good restaurant to walk to if you're downtown. It's in an old brick building and still has much of the interesting architecture intact, though it has been upscaled to a contemporary decor. It has booths and tables with white cloths and white napkins. The walls and ceiling are deep green. The food is California-like, featuring a variety of fluffy green salads, pastas, creative sandwiches and soups. A bar and big glass windows face Main Street. Browne's is open Monday through Saturday for lunch and dinner.

HARVEY'S

200 Main St., Columbus   327-6982
$-$$

At the foot of River Hill, Harvey's is a contemporary restaurant that uses lots of green plants and old brick and woodwork as decorative elements, and it's a great favorite of locals. Harvey's menu features seafood, chicken, pasta and steak. Most dishes have a Cajun flavor because Johnny Wooten, chef/manager, trained and worked in south Louisiana. He's also working on a cook book, which will emphasize health-conscious dishes. Harvey's serves great salads, which are filling and festive enough for an entire meal. The Southland Salad is nothing short of outstanding, and Harvey's creates its own array of salad dressings. A bar runs the length of the right side of Harvey's, and it is a busy place after work weekdays. At Harvey's, you always know the quality and service will be consistent. The Columbus Harvey's is the first of four in a chain.

RUBEN'S

On the river, just off Hwy. 82
Columbus   328-9880
$

You'll be hard pressed to find better catfish and other seafood than Ruben's serves. The steaks are superb too. The fish is broiled or fried golden brown. If steak is your preference, you can watch owner/chef Steve Heinz grill it for you. A salad bar, choice of potato and hushpuppies come with your meal. This has great atmosphere for a river restaurant. It can get crowded on weekends, but those who have to wait a few minutes pass the time reading hundreds of business cards attached to the wall in the foyer. Ruben's serves dinner only.

WOODY'S

2420 Military Rd., Columbus   327-7869
$$

The menu at Woody's offers a wide choice of seafood and beef specialties, served with a big crisp salad, soup and a vegetable du jour. Homemade bread is brought out with the soup, which is a choice of gumbo or clam chowder. The interior is rather dark and not too intimate unless you ask for a booth. In the winter, a table by the big brick fireplace is a treat. Enjoy a good selection of wines. There's also a Woody's in Tupelo that has an excellent reputation. Woody's serves dinner only, Monday through Saturday.

PROFFITT'S PORCH

Officer's Lake Rd., Columbus   327-4485
$

This was once a camphouse overlooking Officer's Lake; now it's a popular restaurant that specializes in red beans and rice and po' boy sandwiches. Slow-cooked and well-seasoned red beans are served in big bowls with garlic bread. Salads are good too, and the sandwiches will fill you up. In nice weather most people prefer to sit on the porch because the view is lovely, but the lake and woods can also be seen from inside. There are lots of windows and unpretentious decor that makes Proffitt's Porch comfortable and fun. Proffitt's is a favorite with military personnel. The desserts are homemade and delicious and available for lunch or dinner. It's closed on Mondays.

APPLEBEE'S

Miss. 12 E., Starkville   324-3459
$

Folks in Starkville are pleased to have this chain restaurant in their midst. Its Southwestern specialties are particularly popular with MSU students and faculty. Baskets of hot and tasty barbecue ribs are popular items too. Applebee's serves lunch and dinner every day. There's also an Applebee's in Columbus, on Highway 45 N. with the same menu and decor.

HARVEY'S
406 Hwy. 12, Starkville   323-1639
$

This is the same Harvey's as in Columbus and Tupelo, with the same quality and great food. See our Columbus listing for details.

OBY'S
Academy Rd., Starkville   323-0444
$

This looks like a college place, complete with posters, kegs and very casual decor. Oby's serves masterful sandwiches and burgers, and it is a favorite stop for Mississippi State University students and faculty.

RICHEY'S RESTAURANT
513 Academy Rd., Starkville   324-2737
$$

People from throughout the region come to Richey's for their steaks, though seafood and all the menu items are superb. It's not a place where you see a lot of young children, just adults enjoying their food. Entrees are served with a vegetable and salad. The interior is dark wood, and subdued lighting is used. Richey's is open for dinner only Monday through Saturday.

GLOSTER 205 RESTAURANT
205 N. Gloster St., Tupelo   842-7205
$$

This restaurant is in a spiffed-up old house, and it serves steaks, fresh seafood, prime rib, pasta dishes and salads. The atmosphere here is more formal than in most Tupelo establishments, but this is a very casual town. Expect good food in an upscale and trendy atmosphere. Complete with lots of green plants, nice woodwork and white tablecloths and napkins

JEFFERSON PLACE
823 Jefferson St., Tupelo   844-8696
$

In a residential neighborhood, this regional favorite restaurant is known to serve hand-trimmed beef, seafood and great sandwiches. Jefferson Place has a bar and a sometimes-enthusiastic crowd. The old house it calls home has dark wood paneling, which is brightened up by open windows and light table clothes. It is casual and is open for lunch and dinner six days; it's open for lunch only on Sunday.

THE FRONT PORCH
2827 Cliff Gookin, Tupelo   842-1591
$

This casual atmosphere is the perfect place for the house specialties: catfish and steaks, both of which come with potato and salad. It has a front porch, complete with rockers. The interior design aims for the rustic, with light wood and windows galore. The lunch schedule varies, so call ahead first to make sure they'll be open.

VANELLI'S
1302 N. Gloster St., Tupelo   844-4410
$

Papa Vanelli started this place, and now a Sports Bar within the restaurant bears his name. The restaurant proper is in a building that features Greek statues and other Mediterranean decor. With this Italian name, expect Italian-American food and a few Greek specialties too. They feature a popular pasta buffet that includes fettuccine with crabmeat, manicotti and a Grecian spaghetti. Locals end the meal with Vanelli's special baklava. Vanelli's serves lunch and dinner daily.

THE RIB CAGE

206 Troy St., Tupelo   *840-5400*
$

Enter this old building with its polished wood floors and you'll see that it's an appropriate setting for a local favorite that specializes in barbecue ribs, chicken plates and sandwiches. They serve great salads too. It's open for lunch and dinner six days a week and brunch/lunch only on Sunday.

CITY GROCERY

118 Van Buren Ave., Oxford   *232-8080*
$$

Out-of-towners are surprised to find continental flavor in a Southern town, especially in a place with such an unassuming name. The menu here is the most sophisticated in town. Specialties vary. Be sure and try the most memorable shrimp and grits. Expect a bit of classic French, Italian and Thai too. The talented chef changes the menu often. City Grocery serves lunch and dinner Monday through Saturday and enjoys a reputation as one of the state's finest restaurants..

DOWNTOWN GRILL

1115 Jackson Ave., Oxford   *234-2659*
$

This restaurant is in a prime location, for it overlooks the Square. The casually sophisticated Downtown Grill serves beef, chicken and seafood specials well prepared and presented with a Southern touch. It is owned by Ole Miss alums and features a piano bar overlooking the square. This restaurant is operated in the gracious tradition of the university. It's closed on Sunday.

SMITTY'S

208 S. Lamar Blvd., Oxford   *234-9111*
$

The late William Faulkner frequented this place, and it probably looks the same now as it did in the 1950s. Smitty's serves great vegetable plates and burgers, and they serve up a superior bowl of homemade soup with cornbread. It's a popular site for breakfast too. Smitty's is just south of the Square. Smitty's serves three meals everyday, and coffee and such anytime.

Photo: David Purdy, The Sun Herald

Insiders know where to congregate for good food and a lot of comaraderie.

THE HOKA CAFE

304 S. 14th St., Oxford   234-3057
$

Whatever is doin' at the Hoka is completely casual, whether it's a vintage art film or a spur-of-the-moment concert with a musician that might appear in town. Its decor is typically college. It offers nachos, stir-fry, Italian, Mexican and more. It's open in the late afternoon and evening only.

VICTOR'S RISTORANTE

106 S. Lamar Blvd., Oxford   234-3700
$

Victor's is on the Square, so it has the Square ambiance of old-world charm and upscale shops situated around the historic courthouse. The businesses on the square are popular places. At Victor's, expect a luncheon buffet weekdays, and for dinner. Victor's prides itself on its homemade sauces that complement their dishes. Baked chicken Parmesan is a favorite, but do try whatever the nightly special happens to be. It's always good. Victor's is open for lunch and dinner daily.

PHILLIPS GROCERY

541-A Van Dorn Ave.
Holly Springs   252-4671
$

If you're in the interesting town of Holly Springs during the day Monday through Saturday, walk into Phillips Grocery, across from the railroad depot. Order a hamburger; chances are you'll have the best hamburger you've ever sunk your teeth into. A few years back, *USA Today* named Phillips' hamburgers one of the three most perfect burger renditions in the United States. Phillips also offers onion rings, crunchy fried okra, french fries and sandwiches. Phillips Grocery has been in business since 1948.

COMO STEAK HOUSE

201-203 Main St., Como   526-9529
$$

Steak lovers from Memphis to Jackson know about Como Steak House where USDA choice corn-fed beef is the house favorite. It's cooked over an open pit with real charcoal, according to owner John Bradley Wells, and it's cooked to perfection. Wells says that the grilled chicken and grilled catfish are equally as good. The restaurant is in a rustic old building with original tin ceiling and other interesting architectural details. It serves dinner only Tuesday through Saturday. Reservations are advised. Como is north of Batesville just off I-55.

The Delta

CHAMOUN'S
REST HAVEN RESTAURANT

U.S. Hwy. 61, Clarksdale   624-8601
$

The Mediterranean countries are well-represented here in the Delta in this restaurant known far and wide for its delicious food. Kibbie is a house specialty, along with cabbage rolls, fresh pita bread and a wonderful baklava. Chamoun's has become a dining tradition that's suddenly getting lots of attention as a must-do. Chamoun's serves three meals a day Monday through Saturday.

THE RANCHERO RESTAURANT

1907 State St. Clarksdale   624-9768
$-$$

Townspeople are proud of this restaurant, and the smoked loin baby-back ribs keep 'em coming back for more. Lobster tail and choice top sirloin, or catfish or gumbo, fill the bill too. The Ranchero is a family-owned restaurant that's been in Clarksdale since 1959. Desserts include homemade cheesecake and lemon icebox pie. As well as great food, those who frequent the Ranchero enjoy seeing the antiques and wall to wall memorabilia.

KC's

U.S. 61, Cleveland	843-5301
$$-$$$	

The great food prepared by the Joe family of Cleveland has received rave reviews from the local media and diners too. Both Chinese and American cuisine is served at KCs. From the appetizer (try the Tureen of Duck made with pistachio nuts and black truffle served with a zesty mustard on the side) to the Seared Sea Scallops served on a bed of chèvre cream sauce, or Grilled Tenderloin or Rack of Lamb, everything is a delight. For a memorable meal, top it off with butterscotch creme brulée, and look forward to your next trip to KCs.

LAFITTE'S FEAST

1 Treasure Dr.	
Robinsonville	363-6600
Commerce Landing	(800) 727-7684
$-$$	

Follow the signs in and around Tunica to Treasure Bay Casino, and arrive at Lafitte's Feast, Treasure Bay's buffet restaurant. Following the casino's pirate theme, the restaurant is named for notorious pirate Jean Lafitte. The buffet features Cajun and Creole entrees that include étoufée, jambalaya, blackened fish and an array of other buffet items. Lafitte's Feast serves lunch and dinner daily and breakfast on weekends, plus an all-you-can-eat seafood buffet on Friday and Saturday nights. Go 5 miles west on Miss. 304 from U.S. 61.

SAM'S TOWN

North of Tunica	
Robinsonville Rd. at Commerce Landing	
Robinsonville	363-0700,(800) 456-0711
$-$$	

Four restaurants are part of the Sam's Town Hotel and Gambling Hall, which is the biggest casino entertainment complex in the South. The restaurants follow the Old West theme around which Sam's is developed. Billy Bob's, a tablecloth restaurant, is the place to go for steaks; Corky's Bar-B-Q serves up great barbecue and ribs in a pub environment; the Uptown Buffet is an array of limitless food and a weekend brunch; and Smokey Joe's offers cook-to-order favorites and daily specials. Calamity Jane's is an ice-cream parlor that also serves hamburgers and such. From U.S. Hwy. 61, take Miss. 304 W. for 5 miles.

UNCLE HENRY'S PLACE

5860 Moon Lake Rd.	
Dundee (near Lula)	337-2757
$$	

Follow U.S. 61 to U.S. 49 W. and see the signs to Moon Lake Road, which is one mile left of 49. This restaurant, formerly known as the Moon Lake Club, is said to have been a backdrop for some of playwright Tennessee Williams' works. Dinner (no lunch) consists of gourmet seafood, Cajun and Creole specialties and char-grilled steaks. Uncle Henry's is also a bed and breakfast. The restaurant is closed Monday.

DOE'S EAT PLACE

502 Nelson St., Greenville   334-3315
$$

This popular, quaint restaurant in a rundown old store has been serving great steaks and hot tamales to Deltans and others for more than 50 years. Rumor has it that Elvis Presley sent his plane from Memphis to Doe's at least once a month to get hot tamales. National politicians and entertainers have added Doe's to their must-do list as well. Doe's steaks literally hang off the plate, and they're served with potato and salad. Doe's serves dinner only Monday through Saturday.

THE SHELTON HOUSE

217 S. Washington Ave.
Greenville   334-3083
$

Plan to be in Greenville around lunch time Monday through Saturday, and don't miss the Shelton House. It's in a residential neighborhood, in an older house that has a big glassed-in front porch and several other rooms where elegant lunches are served. Our favorite is the chicken and artichoke casserole, but that's just one of many. The Shelton House has made desserts its specialty, and here's a sampling of what's in store: strawberry trifle, blackberry cobbler with homemade ice cream, hot brownie pudding with homemade ice cream and eight cheesecakes, all homemade. It's open for lunch only, but will serve dinner for private parties.

ANNA CASEY'S

2525 Hwy. 82 E., Greenville   332-3799
$

Try the étouffée here, or a Mexican or Italian specialty, and you'll see why Anna Casey's is a popular Delta restaurant. Beefeaters say the steaks are superb too. Enjoy dinner in this quiet and pleasant atmosphere, Monday through Saturday.

C&G RESTAURANT

205 Central St., Greenville   335-6294
$$

This restaurant serves up a good steak and standard accompaniments from its authentic old railroad depot, where old brick walls add atmosphere. C&G is also next to the levee and is now a part of the Las Vegas Casino. The bar at this depot cum restaurant is where locals gather. Lunch and dinner are served daily.

HOW JOY

Hwy. 82 E., Greenville   335-1920
$

Meaning "good luck" in Cantonese, How Joy is one of the state's oldest and most respected Chinese restaurants. Customers know to expect good food and good service, and they are never disappointed. Plump butterfly shrimp is reason enough to keep coming back. How Joy is open for lunch and dinner seven days a week.

CICERO'S

Old Leland Rd.
Stoneville (just east of Greenville)   686-4854
$

What a surprise to find Cicero's in so small a town. They do great things with catfish and other fish. Red snapper and salmon are special treats. They're known for their steaks and for the friendly folks who serve them up. The atmosphere is not elegant — the table tops are Formica with paper place mats — but the food is what draws people to this casual country place for lunch Monday through Friday or dinner every night but Sunday.

LILO'S

Hwy. 82, Leland   *686-4401*
$

This Italian restaurant has been in the same family for generations. They serve dinner only, and the food is very good. Spaghetti and lasagna are sure bets, and the salads are crisp and full. Bluesman Bougaloo Ames performs on Thursday, and it is usually pretty crowded when he plays. Remember, this is the Delta — blues country.

THE CRYSTAL GRILL

423 Carrollton Ave., Greenwood   *453-6530*
$

It's been in the same spot since 1913, and the food keeps getting better. Luncheons include daily specials such as short ribs of beef, veal cutlets, soup and salad and two vegetables. (The vegetables are cooked just the way Southerners like them.) Expect very good steaks and seafood as well as the best homemade desserts around. The meringue looks to be three-inches high. The Crystal is open for breakfast, lunch and dinner six days a week, and it's one of those Delta institutions that makes this region so special. It's closed Monday.

LUSCO'S

722 Carrollton Ave., Greenwood   *453-5365*
$$

This is another Delta tradition and has occupied the old store building since 1933. The only meal is dinner, and it is a delight, whether you order steak, seafood, gumbo (it tastes more like a seafood bisque) or a big salad. Once inside, the area is more private than it looks from the entryway — partitions separate groups of diners. The house specialty is broiled pompano. It's open Tuesday through Saturday.

WEBSTER'S

216 W. Claiborne, Greenwood   *455-1215*
$$

Many Deltans eat here because of its upscale decor. Webster's is open for dinner only, and the menu items include steaks, seafood and some lighter pasta offerings. There's a full bar, which is also a popular place. It's open Monday through Saturday.

YIANNI'S

506 Yalobusha, Greenwood   *455-6789*
$-$$

This open, airy restaurant serves up wonderful fresh fish and lighter fare, as well as filet mignon and outstanding angel hair pasta. The chicken salad is the best around. Yianni's is contemporary and casual. It's relatively new by Delta standards, but it's making a name for itself. The bar is a good place to be after work if you want to chat with locals. Saturday, dinner only is served. It's closed Sunday. Lunch is served Monday through Friday. It's closed Sunday.

Insiders' Tips

Ole Country Bakery, on U.S. 45 at Brooksville, south of Columbus, has expanded and remodeled, and the Mennonite women who run the bakery continue to bake the best poppy seed bread and desserts in this part of the country. It now serves sandwiches and salads for lunch. It's closed Sunday and Monday.

THE ANTIQUE MALL AND CROWN RESTAURANT, LTD.

Off State Hwy. 448
5 miles north of Indianola   887-2522
$

This is a totally unexpected experience. Driving to the Antique Mall and Crown Restaurant through fields and Delta land, you wonder what kind of restaurant could be at the end of this long and narrow road. Upon arrival you know. It's an exceptional restaurant where the luncheon menu includes a choice of two entrees, usually a chicken or catfish delicacy, plus salad, vegetables and delicious desserts. Antiques are everywhere, and it is not unusual for patrons to buy the table on which they've just finished lunch. This makes a very nice shopping and luncheon experience in the deep Delta, and it is open for lunch only Tuesday through Saturday.

THE MAIN EVENT

310 S. Main St., Yazoo City   746-4171
$

Daily luncheon specials are very good and very fast, which says something nice about the efficiency of this downtown restaurant housed in an old store building. Steak, ribs, seafood, chicken, and South-of-the-Border specialties are well-prepared and courteously presented. A glass storefront window overlooks the comings and goings of Yazoo City. The Main Event serves lunch Monday through Friday; it serves dinner Monday through Saturday and is closed Sunday.

The Heartland

AMERIGO

6592 Old Canton Rd.
Ridgeland (northeast Jackson)   977-0563
$-$$

Jacksonians love Amerigo. It is upscale and casual but not stuffy, and, of course, it specializes in Italian food. The American offerings are outstanding too. The house favorite is shrimp scampi, which is incomparable. Amerigo presents fresh fish specials, pastas and veal each night. Tiramisu is particularly good here. Lunch and dinner are served daily.

BRAVO!

4500 I-55 N.
Highland Village, Ste. 244
Jackson   982-8111
$-$$

This Italian restaurant just opened in 1994 and has already earned the exclamation after its name. Walk into its sophisticated Tuscan decor with muted colors and natural woods, and smell the creations of Chef Dan Blumenthal, a California Culinary Academy grad. He came from a San Francisco restaurant to start Bravo! with brother David Blumenthal and friend Jeff Good. Favorites are veal Marsala and calzone primavera, a wood-fired vegetarian folded pizza. For pasta, try the spaghetti and gulf shrimp. One of our favorites is the grilled yellowfin tuna, lightly grilled and topped with a zesty sun-dried tomato pesto. With espresso, cappuccino and tiramisu served most anytime, this restaurant can only get better. Bravo! serves lunch and dinner; it's closed Monday.

GRADY'S

1169 E. County Line Rd.
Jackson   957-3326

This popular restaurant has won approval from health-conscious Jacksonians, for along with the Grady's specialties on the menu, among which are slow-roasted prime rib, Southern-style quail, and mesquite-seared baby back ribs, you'll find healthy lighter fare. Among the healthy foods are citrus shrimp, mesquite lite chicken and spring vegetable pasta. Grady's American Grill offers a casual atmosphere that one would expect with such menu items as a Mile High Blues Burger, and the service is good. Grady's serves lunch and dinner.

DENNERY'S
I-55 at High St., Jackson   354-2527
$$

This one specializes in Greek food, though prime rib and fresh seafood are ordered as often. It has been a popular place for Jacksonians since 1948; Dennery's has been in the same family for three generations. The Greek goddess of love adorns the interior fountain, and the table settings are enhanced by candlelight. A nice way to end the meal is with baklava or galaktoboureko. Dennery's serves lunch weekdays and dinner everyday night but Sunday.

THE ELITE
141 E. Capitol St., Jackson   352-5606
$

Not only is this one of Jackson's oldest restaurants, it's a favorite among downtown workers. The Elite has been a fixture in the heart of Jackson for 47 years, consistently serving good food and offering quick service. A house specialty, somewhat unexpected for a Greek-owned restaurant, is the enchilada plate. Another great favorite is the veal cutlet. Expect

Southern-style vegetables, delicious desserts and made-from-scratch dinner rolls (they're the best around.) Breakfast features homemade biscuits along with other standard breakfast items. Locals and visitors appreciate the warm, friendly atmosphere. The Elite serves breakfast, lunch and dinner daily.

BILL'S GREEK TAVERN
4760 McWillie Dr., Jackson   982-9295
$

Bill's is a most unusual restaurant, where "God Bless America" rings throughout the restaurant from time to time. A taste of the islands is what you'll get at Bill's, for the owner appears to be as proud to be Greek as he is to be in America. Among the entrees are the gyro, with slices of lamb and beef served with a Greek sauce. The fresh red snapper broiled in lemon and butter and Greek spices is outstanding and is served with a fresh Greek salad and Greek bread. Bill's serves lunch weekdays and dinner only on Saturday and Sunday.

GRIDLEY'S FINE BARBECUE
1428 Old Square Rd.
Jackson   362-8600
$

This confident restaurant says, "Forget what you thought you knew about barbecue and try ours." With such an attitude, no wonder they're becoming famous for barbecue ribs, pork, beef, shrimp and chicken. Gridley's boasts a fun family atmosphere. It serves lunch and dinner daily.

HAL AND MAL'S

200 S. Commerce St.
Jackson   948-0888
$

This restaurant in the old commercial district offers a varied menu and lots of activity. They serve seafood, burgers and sometimes a bit of Italian fare. It's a popular Jackson nightspot too, though it's a little hard to find. Most folks call for directions and entertainment listings, which may be blues, Cajun, jazz or country. Lunch and dinner are served daily except Sunday, when it's closed.

THE IRON HORSE BAR & GRILL

320 W. Pearl, Jackson   355-8419
$$

In the old Armour Smokehouse listed on the National Register of Historic Places, this three-story restaurant uses the thick, exposed brick walls and cast-iron hanging brackets from the old days as decorative elements. The Iron Horse Grill specializes in Tex-Mex and mesquite-grilled American steaks, prime rib and seafood; it serves great salads and pastas. The appetizers — great quesadillas and nachos — are as good as meals. Expect lunch and dinner Monday through Saturday.

MAYFLOWER RESTAURANT

123 W. Capitol St., Jackson   355-4122
$

The Mayflower has been feeding Jacksonians since 1935. Owner Mike Kontouris has a philosophy: Treat the customers well, serve them good food at a good price, and they'll come back. He does, and they do. The Mayflower has been featured in American Airlines' inflight magazine and other publications, but the important thing at the Mayflower is the food, which they serve 18 hours every day. A favorite is the Greek salad with lump crabmeat. They also serve up seafood specials, including speckled trout and redfish, and lots of pastas too.

NICK'S

1501 Lakeland Dr., Jackson   981-8017
$$-$$$

Not only does Nick's serve outstanding steaks, seafood and pastas, they also have the most impressive wine list in the state. Desserts are scrumptious too. Owner Nick Apostle was voted Mississippi Restaurateur of the Year for 1993; he attended the American Culinary Institute at Hyde Park and is the mastermind behind the restaurant's specialties. We think Nick's is one of the best. Nick's serves lunch and dinner weekdays and dinner only on Saturday; it's closed Sunday.

OLDE TYME DELICATESSEN & BAKERY

1305 E. Northside Dr.
Jackson   362-2565
$

Since 1961 this deli's specialties include the Reuben sandwich, stuffed cabbage, kosher beef ribs, plus other great deli food, gourmet foods and baked goods. Olde Tyme is in Highland Village; it's open til 9 PM Tuesday through Sunday; it's closed Monday.

PRIMOS RESTAURANT AND LOUNGE

4330 N. State St., Jackson   982-2064
$$

Primos has been a tradition in Jackson for many years. At Primos expect soft lights, casual elegance, fresh seafood and prime rib cooked to perfection. You'll enjoy terrific salads too. Piano music

A variety of ethnic restaurants can be found throughout Mississippi. Many dining experiences are entertaining as well as delicious.

complements the atmosphere on weekends. It's open for lunch Monday through Sunday and dinner Monday through Saturday.

RALPH & KACOO'S

100 Dyess Rd., Jackson   957-0702
$$

Whether it's located off E. County Line Road in Jackson, as this one is, or Toulouse Street in the French Quarter, count on Ralph & Kacoo's for the best in Cajun and Creole. This authentic Cajun establishment came from south Louisiana and brought with it wonderful native dishes. Expect authentic etouffee and gumbo, seafood platters, boiled crawfish, soft-shell crabs and so much more. It's all good . . . take your pick. It is open for lunch and dinner seven days a week.

RED HOT AND BLUE

1623 E. County Line Rd.
Jackson   956-3313
$

Slow-smoked Southern barbecue is what customers come for, and it is served up with Memphis-style rhythm 'n' blues. The barbecue tastes a lot like Memphis pit barbecue. Customers may eat in or take out, and they may specify wet or dry ribs. Wet ribs traditionally prepared with thick BBQ sauce; dry ribs feature very little sauce, but a blend of dry spices. Lunch and dinner are served seven days a week.

RUTH'S CHRIS STEAK HOUSE

1200 E. County Line Rd.
Northpark Mall, Jackson   957-2474
$$$$

This restaurant caters to serious steak lovers, for Ruth's Chris is famous in several states for serving cooked-to-perfection, corn-fed, U.S. Prime beef, custom-aged but never frozen, still sizzling when it's served at the table. Also find tasty Maine lobster, Northwestern salmon and a selection of other menu items. Ruth's serves dinner only everyday.

STOCKYARD STEAKS/RODEO'S

6107 Ridgewood Rd.
Jackson   957-9300
$$

Enjoy steak, of course, and seafood, at Stockyard Steaks. After dinner head to Rodeo's and enjoy western dance music. Red-and-white-checked tablecloths are perfect for the wood walls and floors. It's open for dinner only every day but Sunday.

YANNI'S RISTORANTE

5834 Ridgewood Rd., Jackson   957-1551
$

Yanni's invites you to taste the magic of Italy and other parts of the Mediterranean from their location on Ridgewood Road. The decor is Mediterranean, for sure, and the seafood Alfredo over tricolored tortellini is almost as good as being there. This restaurant already has a reputation to uphold, and it's less than 2 years old. Yanni's serves lunch and dinner.

VIRGILIO'S

2060 Main St., Madison   853-4010
$$

This new restaurant in Madison has loyal patrons from nearby Jackson who sing its praises. They know to expect elegant continental cuisine and fine wines, and they especially appreciate the valet parking. Virgilio's is in an old home, which only adds to its upscale appeal. Steaks, seafood, pasta and wild game also get rave reviews. Virgilio's is open for lunch Monday through Friday and dinner Monday through Sunday.

LAKE TIAK O'KHATA RESTAURANT

MS. Hwy. 15 S., Louisville   773-7853
$

A surprising array of well-prepared food is served at a big buffet every day, and folks come from all over to partake. It's in the lodge of a privately owned resort and lake; breakfast, lunch and dinner are served daily.

WEIDMANN'S

210 22nd Ave., Meridian   693-1751
$-$$

This place is an institution, with one of the biggest selections you'll find on any menu. It's been around since 1870 and packs in locals and tourists who come by the busloads. Weidmann's food is home-cooked, and it's all good. A local favorite is the vegetable plate. Save room for dessert; the restaurant is also known for its black bottom pie. Each table has a crock of peanut butter for starters, and you can take some home in your very own crock — ask at the cash register. Check out the walls lined with historic and homey photographs. Weidmann's open for breakfast, lunch and dinner.

HOLLYBROOK FINE DINING

1200 22nd Ave., Meridian   693-7584
$$

Enjoy fine dining in a historic setting. Choose from chicken, seafood and other dishes, and follow each meal with a wonderful homemade dessert. Hollybrook is open from 11 AM to 2 PM and 5 to 9 PM Monday through Friday and from 5 to 9 PM only on Saturday. Reservations are requested.

THREEFOOT DELI

22nd Ave. and Sixth St.
Meridian   693-9952
$

The deli is in the historic Threefoot Building and serves a hearty breakfast, hot lunches, sandwiches and homemade desserts. It's open 7 AM to 3 PM Monday through Friday.

THE DINNER BELL

229 Fifth Ave., McComb   684-4883
$ *Cash only*

The Dinner Bell has been serving good country Southern cooking for 50 years. There's lots of fresh home-cooked vegetables served in a round table buffet. The house special is fried eggplant, but other winners include fried chicken, yams and dumplings. The Dinner Bell is open from 11 AM to 2 PM daily except Monday and from 5:30 to 8 PM on Friday and Saturday.

THE REVOLVING TABLES

100 William Gerald Morgan Memorial Dr.
Mendenhall   847-3113
$ Cash and traveler's checks only

This is the original buffet offering traditional Southern family-style dishes, and three generations of the Morgan family have been serving customers here since 1915. There's a dozen or more fresh vegetables, five to seven entrees, a half-dozen salads, cornbread and biscuits made from scratch, relishes and desserts to choose from and enjoy. The Revolving Tables is open from 11 AM to 2 PM daily. However, after Labor Day the owners take a day off each week. The restaurant is in downtown Mendenhall at the corner of S. Main. The town is 30 miles south of Jackson and 50 miles north of Hattiesburg, a mile off U.S. 49.

WILD MAGNOLIA

1311 Hardy St., Hattiesburg   543-0908
$$-$$$

This is a first-rate Italian restaurant where Chef Charles Angelillo uses imported ingredients to prepare dishes according to his mother's and grandmother's recipes. He also does rack of lamb, lobster, steak, fresh tuna, swordfish and red fish. It's open Monday through Saturday from 5 to 10 PM; it's closed on Sunday.

CHESTERFIELD'S

2507 Hardy St.
Hattiesburg   582-2778
$$

Chesterfield's has an extensive menu, filled with burgers, steaks, seafood, sandwiches and salads in a casual to semiformal atmosphere. Hours are Monday

through Saturday 11 AM to 11 PM and Sunday from 11 AM to 10 PM.

The River Cities

COCK-OF-THE-WALK

200 N. Broadway
Natchez   446-8920
$

Delicious catfish fillets are the specialty here, along with Downriver Chicken, served with fried dill pickles and a pot-o-greens. Catfish also comes blackened and char-grilled. Try the delicious shrimp and oysters dishes too. All dinners are served with hot skillet bread. This is a fun place for good food: The costumed waitstaff ceremoniously flips hot skillet bread at your table. It's open Monday through Thursday from 5 to 9 PM, Friday and Saturday 5 to 10 PM and Sunday 11:30 AM to 1:30 PM and again from 5 to 8 PM.

THE FARE CAFE

109 N. Pearl, Natchez   442-5299
$

The Fare offers lots of local color as well as specialty sandwiches, soups, salads and a great selection of homemade desserts. A full breakfast is served from 7:30 AM until 10 AM. Hours are 7:30 AM to 3 PM Monday through Saturday.

PEARL STREET PASTA

105 S. Pearl St., Natchez   442-9284
$$

Italian specialties here include fettuccine Alfredo, lasagna and pasta primavera. If you prefer American, try the filet of beef. Specials are prepared daily. All entrees are served with a fresh green salad and hot garlic bread. Pearl Street Pasta is open Monday through Saturday from 11: 30 AM to 2 PM for lunch and 6 to 10 PM nightly for dinner. The atmo-

MISSISSIPPI

has it all . . .

Attractions...

Shopping...

Fine Dining...

"Hot" Seats!
Cool events!

MISSISSIPPI COAST COLISEUM & CONVENTION CENTER

- 11,500 "hot seats"
- Southeast's largest beachfront complex
- 100,000 sq. ft. convention meeting/exhibit space

2350 Beach Blvd., Biloxi, MS 39531
(601) 388-8010 • FAX (601) 385-2412

eading down the Natchez Trace with a full tank of cheese grits.

It was getting late. The sky had changed from blue to orange, and the Mississippi moon was signaling us to pull over and rest.

But we kept our car at a leisurely pace.  After all, our century-old bed and breakfast wasn't going anywhere.

As we stepped through the tall doors of the majestic antebellum home, I noticed how the small chandelier hanging in the foyer highlighted the old paintings lining the wide circular stairway. The window offered a view of a garden lit with fireflies.

Yes, this house *did* feel like home. This morning, my hunch was confirmed: Southerners like huge breakfasts. Our hosts made cheese grits, eggs, toast, country sausage and cinnamon apples. I suppose we'll need it. There are a lot of stops along the Natchez Trace between here and the casinos. And we're not going to miss any of them.

For your free Mississippi Bed & Breakfast Guide, call 1-800-WARMEST.

The South's Warmest Welcome

The Mississippi
Museum of Natural Science

Experience Mississippi's Natural Environment In All Its Rich Diversity

- Dramatically Staged Dioramas
- Massive Aquarium System
- Native Plant Garden
- Graphic and Hands-On Exhibits

Free Admission
Hours: 8:00 - 5:00 M-F, 9:30 - 4:30 Sat.
Take I-55, Pearl Street Exit near Fairgrounds
111 N. Jefferson St., Jackson, MS 39202 601/354-7303

Mississippi Department of Wildlife, Fisheries and Parks

CASINO STRIP-THE MOST OF EVERYTHIN

- More than 650 hotel rooms
- Over 5,400 slots
- Over 250 table games, including live poker and live keno
- 10 restaurants
- Pool, jacuzzi, sauna and workout room
- 2 video arcades
- 5 banquet facilities
- Live entertainment
- Just south of Memphis

Faster, more convenient—
NEWLY **expanded**
Hwy. 304

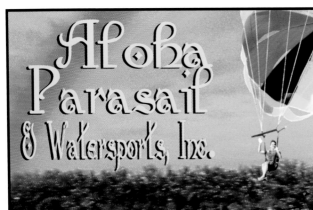

ALOHA

Welcome to the most versatile watersports facility on the Gulf Coast. Come spend a few hours or the entire day with our professional staff enjoying the water and white sand beaches of Mississippi.

FREE TRANSPORTATION PROVIDED
PARASAILING (6 PERSON MAXIMUM)
WAVERUNNERS (500 & 650 YAMAHAS)
HOBIE CATS - LESSONS AVAILABLE
WINDSURFERS - LESSONS AVAILABLE
WATER BOGAN
UMBRELLAS & CHAIRS
T-SHIRTS, CAPS, MUGS, ETC.
OWNER-OPERATED WITH OVER 20 YEARS COMBINED EXPERIENCE

ON THE BEACH • HOLIDAY INN GULFPORT
8:00 A.M. till Dark

Call for 24 hour reservations
Cellular: 601-341-DOIT • Office: 601-452-0299

Much more than history . . .

. . . we're biscuits in the oven and chickens under the porch, mules out in the field and the smell of fresh mown hay. The history is there too, the story of a people tied to the land, self-sufficient and proud.

In the middle of Jackson, Mississippi is an oasis of rural life, just off the interstate and nearly a century back in time. Call today for more information about our convention facilities.

Find it at the

Ag Museum

Jim Buck Ross Mississippi Agriculture and Forestry/National Agricultural Aviation Museum • Jackson, Mississippi

1-800-844-TOUR

This ad paid for by a grant from the Jackson Convention and Visitor's Bureau.

OPTIONS.

NORTHPARK

Dillard's, Gayfers, JCPenney,
McRae's, plus more than 120
other dazzling stores.

Open Monday-Saturday
10:00 a.m.-9:00 p.m.
Sunday 12:30 p.m.-6:00 p.m.
Exit I-55. County Line,
Ridgeland.

Savings to 75%

on name brands like Bass, Florsheim, Libbey Glass, L'eggs/Hanes/Bali/Platex, Bon Worth, Van Heusen, Farah, Sunsations Sunglass, Welcome Home, The Paper Factory, and many more! You'll also find great food at places like Main Street Eatery.

↑ to Memphis

← to Clarksdale I-55

↓ to Jackson

→ to Oxford

Batesville Exit 243B

Mon. - Sat. 9 a.m. - 9 p.m.
Sunday Noon - 6 p.m.
Call 1-800-361-7406
Group tours & RV's welcome

The Biggest Deals on I-55

• 10 Casinos an hour away • Fishing/outdoor recreation within minutes • Area museums and attractions.

REDEFINING ITALIAN COOKING.

ITALIAN RESTAURANT & BAR

B·R·A·V·O·!

SEAFOOD . VEAL . DUCK . STEAK
PASTA . WOOD-FIRED PIZZAS
OPEN TUESDAY-SUNDAY ALL DAY

HIGHLAND VILLAGE
JACKSON, MS
982.8111

Photo: Herb Welch, The Sun Herald

The Revolving Tables Restaurant has long been a favorite spot of locals and tourists alike. Guests share family-style, home-cooked meals served from a revolving base in the table's center.

sphere here is casual. If you like, you can take out orders.

LIZA'S CONTEMPORARY CUISINE
657 S. Canal St., Natchez   *446-6368*
$$

Liza's specializes in contemporary regional cuisine made with the freshest of ingredients. The menu changes every three weeks, with the chef making the most of meats, seafood, vegetables and pasta. Try the vegetarian and seafood dishes or the pork tenderloin. Liza's is open from 6 to 9 PM Tuesday through Thursday and 6 to 10 PM on Friday and Saturday.

BEECHWOOD RESTAURANT & LOUNGE
4451 E. Clay St., Vicksburg   *636-3761*
$$

Beechwood's menu features delicious steaks, seafood and po' boys. There's a lunch special Sunday through Friday. Try the popular Beechwood Classic, a filet with shrimp. The restaurant is open daily from 11 AM to 10:30 PM (to 12:30 AM on Friday and Saturday).

MAXWELL'S RESTAURANT & LOUNGE
4702 Clay St., Vicksburg   *636-1344*
$$

The most famous item on Maxwell's extensive menu is prime rib of beef au jus. Other dishes include stuffed flounder, steak and lobster, Veal Oscar and oysters galore. Kids have their own menu. It's casual and informal here. Maxwell's is open Monday through Saturday from 11 AM until 10 PM.

DELTA POINT RIVER RESTAURANT
4144 Washington St.
Vicksburg   *636-5317*
$$

The menu is continental, with veal, steaks and seafood, and the view of the Mississippi River is exceptional. Dinner is served from 5 to 10 PM daily. It's open an hour later on Friday and Saturday.

EDDIE MONSOUR'S
1903G Mission 66, Vicksburg   *638-1571*
$$

Specialties at this popular restaurant and lounge include Lebanese dishes, fresh seafood and steaks. It's open daily except Sunday from 11 AM to 2 PM for lunch and from 5:30 to 10 PM for dinner.

JACQUES CAFE IN THE PARK
4137 I-20 Frontage Rd.
Vicksburg   *638-5811*
$$

This restaurant, inside the Park Inn International Hotel, specializes in delicious steaks and fresh seafood dishes. Menu items range from $5 to $13. The owner was named the top restaurateur in the state last year. Jacques is open daily from 6 to 9:30 AM and 5 to 9 PM.

TAVERN IN THE PARK
3327 Clay St., Vicksburg   *638-4759*
$$

Adjacent to the Vicksburg National Military Park, Tavern features New Orleans dishes such as gumbo, po' boys and Southern cooking. Dinner prices range from $5.95 to $16. There is a country lunch buffet Monday through Friday for $4.95. The restaurant is open daily from 11 AM to 10 PM. If you're planning a picnic in the adjacent the park; you can order lunches to go right off the menu.

WALNUT HILLS
1214 Adams St., Vicksburg   *638-4910*
$$

Walnut Hills' round tables filled with down-home cooking are well known and for good reason. A typical menu features some of the best fried chicken found anywhere, plus country-fried steak, fried corn, snap beans, okra and tomatoes, cornbread and blackberry cobbler. The restaurant is open Monday through Friday starting at 11 AM. Service from the round tables is available until 2 PM; a la carte is available until 9 PM.

TUMINELLO'S
500 Speed St., Vicksburg   634-0507
$$

This restaurant dates back to 1899. Today its specialties include manicotti and stuffed veal. You can also try steaks cut to order, oysters on the half shell and lots of fresh seafood. There's also a cappuccino and espresso bar. Tuminello's is open from 5:30 to 10:30 PM Tuesday through Sunday. It's closed on Monday.

THE OLD DEPOT
RESTAURANT AND LOUNGE
South Market St., Port Gibson   437-4711
$-$$

This interesting restaurant is housed in an 1822 depot. In spite of the old-time setting right down to the ceiling fans, wooden floors and adjacent train tracks, the menu here is cosmopolitan, with steaks, seafood, pasta, po' boys and burgers available. There are daily lunch specials. It's open Monday through Saturday from 11 AM to 9 PM.

The Coast

ALBERTI'S
U.S. 90, near Broadwater Tower
Biloxi   388-9507
$$

Italian specialties and steaks are the crowd-pleasers here. Alberti's offers delicious veal parmesan, eggplant parmesan, spaghetti and chicken picata. The char-grilled steaks are outstanding. It's open Tuesday through Thursday from 2 to 10:30 PM, Friday and Saturday from 2 PM till 11:30 PM, and Sunday 2 to 10:30 PM.

FISHERMAN'S WHARF
315 E. Beach Blvd., Biloxi   436-4513
$$

Broiled, fried and blackened seafood specialties are offered here. The dessert of choice is Fisherman's Wharf pie, a secret recipe that keeps customers guessing and coming back. The Wharf is open from 11 AM until 11 PM on Friday and Saturday and 11 AM to 10 PM Sunday through Thursday.

THE FRENCH CONNECTION
1891 Pass Rd., Biloxi   388-6367
$$

Here you'll find continental cuisine, seafood and red meats perfectly cooked in an open hearth. A popular favorite specialty is Tar Babies, bacon-wrapped boneless chicken. This popular family-owned restaurant consistently gets raves for its food and relaxed atmosphere. The restaurant is open Monday through Saturday starting at 5:30 PM for dinner. Reservations are recommended.

MARY MAHONEY'S
OLD FRENCH HOUSE AND CAFE
138 Rue Magnolia, Biloxi   374-0163
$$

This is a Coast landmark and long-time favorite. In one of the oldest houses in the country, built in 1737, the restaurant has served presidents, entertainers and dignitaries with such dishes as lobster, fresh fish, shrimp and lump crabmeat. The cafe offers po' boys and sandwiches 24 hours a day, seven days a week. The restaurant hours are Monday through Saturday from 11 AM to 10 PM. Reservations are recommended.

KEPPNER'S GASTHAUS

1798 Beach Blvd. Biloxi   436-4878
$$

Keppner's offers authentic German food in a beer garden setting that welcomes families. It's open from 4 to 9 PM on Tuesday through Thursday, 4 to 10 PM on Friday, 11 AM to 10 PM on Saturday and 11 AM to 2 PM on Sunday.

THE CRAB HOUSE

Grand Hotel
U.S. 90, Biloxi   435-8940
$$

In spite of the name, The Crab House offers all kinds of seafood including local catches and deliveries from across the country. This family restaurant also serves steaks and chicken, and it has a kids menu. Breakfast, lunch and dinner are served daily.

TRAPANI'S EATERY

116 N. Beach Blvd.
Bay St. Louis   467-8570
$$

Trapani's is a popular eatery (formerly Mary's Eatery) with plenty of fresh seafood from the nearby Louisiana marshes transported straight to your plate. Have it fried, grilled or broiled. Trapani's is also a sure bet if you're looking for delicious po' boys and grilled steaks. House specialties are recommended and range from grilled yellow fin tuna to the New Orleans-style muffalleta sandwich piled high with meat and cheese and topped with homemade olive salad. Ask about the tasty daily specials. And try the homemade bread pudding for dessert.

VRAZEL'S FINE FOOD RESTAURANT

3206 W. Beach Blvd., Gulfport   863-2229
$$

Chef Vrazel specializes in French, Italian and Cajun cuisine. Vrazel's serves some of the most delicious food on the Coast, and the service is very good too. It's open Monday through Friday from 11 AM to 2 PM for lunch and Monday through Saturday from 5 to 10 PM for dinner.

WHITE CAP SEAFOOD RESTAURANT

Gulfport Small Craft Harbor   863-4652
$$

Choose from steaks, po' boys and seafood at this restaurant at the Gulfport Small Craft Harbor. Relax in the casual nautical atmosphere, and take a few minutes to pick up souvenirs in the gift shop.

Insiders' Tips

Taylor Grocery, out from Oxford, is more than a grocery store. It serves short-order food too and is a popular gathering place for those who know the area or happen to be with those who do. An Australian television crew from Sydney was in Mississippi earlier this year taping footage for a *Southern Belle Olympic Tour* to air in Australia. While they were at Taylor Grocery in Taylor, they ran into a couple from Sydney who recognized them from being on TV back home. When people from Sydney, Australia, meet their townspeople in a small store in Taylor, Mississippi, we know that the world is truly becoming a global community.

Mississippi Firsts

- Mississippi College in Clinton was the first coeducational college in the United States to grant a degree to a woman.
- The Mississippi Legislature in 1839 passed one of the first laws specifically to protect the property rights of married women.
- Mississippi University for Women in Columbus, established in 1884, was the nation's first state-supported college for women.
- Women of Columbus, back in 1866, helped the nation heal after the Civil War by placing flowers on the graves of Confederate and Union soldiers. As a result of this deed, Memorial Day is an annual observance.
- The first human lung transplant was performed in Mississippi by Mississippi physicians in 1963, at the University of Mississippi Medical Center in Jackson. The first human heart transplant was performed in Mississippi by Mississippi physicians in 1964, at the University of Mississippi Medical Center in Jackson. This operation occurred five years before Dr. Christian Barnard's historic heart transplant surgery.
- The most widely used medical textbook (physiology) in the world was researched and written by Dr. Authur Guyton of the University of Mississippi Medical School faculty.
- Brothers Fred and Al Key of Meridian broke the official world endurance flight record after 653 hours and 34 minutes aloft in their monoplane, *Ole Miss*.
- MTV (Music Television Network) was founded by Brookhaven native Bob Pittman when he was 32. MTV now has more than 30 million subscribers.
- The first football player to be pictured on a Wheaties cereal box was Columbia's Walter Payton.
- Hat maker John B. Stetson first learned his craft in the now-extinct town of Dunn's Falls near Meridian.
- Kosciusko, on the Natchez Trace, is the birthplace of TV talk show celebrity Oprah Winfrey, the first African-American woman to host a major talk show on national TV.
- Laurel native Leontyne Price was the first black woman to become a celebrated opera diva with the Metropolitan Opera.
- Mississippi is the only state to have produced four Miss Americas: Mary Ann Mobley, 1959; Lynda Lee Mead, 1960 (Mobley

Oprah Winfrey

and Mead were sorority sisters at Ole Miss); Cheryl Prewitt, 1980; and Susan Akin, 1986.

• The world's first transoceanic flight was performed in 1928 by H.T. Merrill from Iuka. The flight to England was made in a plane loaded with Ping-Pong balls.

• The national Parent-Teachers Association (PTA) was founded in Mississippi in 1909.

• The country's 4-H Club movement originated in Mississippi in 1907 under the guidance of William Hall "Corn Club" Smith, Superintendent of Schools in Holmes County.

BLUE ROSE
120 W. Scenic Dr., Pass Christian 452-9402
$$$

Dine overlooking the local harbor and the Gulf while you enjoy New Orleans entrees with a French flair. There's seafood, pasta, daily specials and gourmet desserts brought in from New Orleans. The restaurant is among an antique store and everything is for sale, even the dishes. Champagne brunch is on Sunday from 11 AM to 3 PM. The Blue Rose is open Wednesday through Sunday from 11 AM to 2:30 PM for lunch. It reopens at 5:30 PM until closing for dinner.

GERMAINE'S
1203 Bienville Blvd.
Ocean Springs   875-4426
$$

Gulf Coast and Creole cuisine are on the menu at this popular restaurant. Besides fine dining, you'll enjoy the elelgant and comfortable atmosphere. Germaine's is open Tuesday through Sunday from 11:30 AM to 2 PM for lunch and opens at 6 PM for dinner on Tuesday through Saturday.

JOCELYN'S
1608 Bienville Blvd.
Ocean Springs   875-1925
$$

Jocelyn's specializes in seafood. And if you like crab, they'll serve it to your liking with one of their specialty sauces. Jocelyn's has been family-owned and - operated for the last 12 years and is in a small, cozy, bright pink building — you can't miss it. The restaurant is open from 5 to 10 PM Monday through Saturday. Reservations are recommended.

MARTHA'S TEA ROOM
715 Washington Ave.
Ocean Springs   872-2554
$

For the best of Southern light fare in an English Tea Room setting, come to Martha's Tea Room. Your lunch sandwich can be served on fresh homemade bread, a croissant or pita bread. Choose from a tasty offering of salad plates, quiches and specialty dishes. Martha's is open for lunch only.

AUNT JENNY'S CATFISH RESTAURANT
1217 Washington Ave.
Ocean Springs   875-9201
$

Come hungry to this all-you-care-to-eat family-style restaurant. Enjoy catfish, chicken and shrimp in a well-decorated country atmosphere.

ANTHONY'S UNDER THE OAKS
1217 Washington Ave.
Ocean Springs   872-4564
$$

Nestled under massive 500-year-old

oaks, Anthony's offers a spectacular view of the bayou with a casual dining atmosphere. Enjoy fresh seafood, beef, veal, chicken and pasta dishes. Reservations are accepted.

ARMAND'S
141 Hwy. 90, Waveland   467-8255
$$

Chef Armand Jonte brought his New Orleans restaurant training to Waveland and opened a restaurant. Customers from "the city" and along the Coast have followed for his Creole cuisine. The menu changes daily. Special dishes include veal, turtle soup and corn-and-crabmeat bisque. It's open for lunch Wednesday through Friday and Sunday brunch from 11:30 AM to 2:30 PM. Dinner is served Wednesday through Sunday 6 to 9:30 PM. The place is well decorated but small, so reservations are requested.

JACK'S STEAK HOUSE
324 Coleman Ave., Waveland   467-3065
$$

Jack's is tiny, informal restaurant looks unassuming, but it offers some of the best steaks anywhere, and the seafood is great too. It's open seven days a week 5 PM to 9:30 PM. Reservations recommended for Friday and Saturday.

MARGUERITE'S ITALIAN VILLAGE
2318 Ingalls Ave. and 14th St.
Pascagoula   762-7464
$$

This local favorite specializes in Italian dishes, plus American and seafood entrees. Try the delicious veal. This small restaurant has a cozy atmosphere where it seems most everybody knows each other. Marguerite's is open Monday through Saturday from 5 to 10 PM.

RIVER DOCKS SEAFOOD PIER
525 Denny Ave., Pascagoula   762-0570
$$

River Docks is a local favorite that offers tasty seafood specials daily. At the foot of a drawbridge, the restaurant overlooks the Pascagoula River. Hours are 11 AM to 10 PM Monday through Friday and 5 to 10 PM on Saturday.

CHAPPY'S SEAFOOD RESTAURANT
624 Beach Blvd., Long Beach   865-9755
$$

For lunch and dinner daily, Chappy serves up fresh seafood and delicious desserts at its beachfront location. The restaurant opens at 11 AM and closes around 10 PM.

Photo: David Purdy, The Sun Herald

Country-and-Western music and line dancing are popular in night clubs throughout the state. Some clubs set aside special nights for dancing and instruction.

Inside
Nightlife

Ask Mississippians about nightlife, and you'll likely get a different answer from every person you ask. Depending on the location, nightlife means making the rounds of casinos. Casino choices are plentiful along the Gulf Coast, in the River Cities and in the Delta towns of Greenville and Tunica. Inland, there's only one. Near Philadelphia, it's the Silver Star, located on the Native American land of the Choctaw nation. In these parts, casinos are popular places to go for good food and recognizable entertainment, whether or not gambling is on the agenda. See our Gaming chapter for details about the state's casinos.

Elsewhere in the state, nightlife means gathering at a local bar to discuss the day's events or the latest Southeastern Conference game — north Mississippi is a hot spot for SEC sports, with both Mississippi State University and the University of Mississippi (Ole Miss) in the vicinity. Both these schools and their fans thoroughly entertain themselves at tailgate parties. The infamous tailgate parties begin before the game and sometimes continue long into the night, usually at private homes.

In the bigger towns, local nightspots offer theme nights along with the cocktail buffet and happy hour. At least one theme night is usually devoted to country and western music, where line dancing is the rage. Not all nightlife in the Magnolia State centers around bars, for churches offer a selection too. Many have active singles groups that sponsor cookouts, socials, evenings at the theater and other activities far removed from where alcoholic beverages are consumed.

Private parties are big here too, and some are glamorous and glitzy with no expense spared. Perhaps the best dress-up parties are sponsored by Mardi Gras-type krewes, or groups of local people who officially band together to celebrate Pilgrimages or other such events just as New Orleans krewes celebrate Mardi Gras. Other than krewes, there are such gatherings as Folderol in Columbus or the No-name Club in the Delta. In these towns, 50 or so couples get together annually to plan and implement a "big do" to which each member couple invites two other couples; dinner and dancing are part of the evening. Another important part, however, is the table decoration. Each sponsors' table of six or eight couples uses a different theme and decorates accordingly. The result borders on works of art. These parties are by invitation only, and they are usually followed by brunch on Sunday at a country place.

Except for the formal parties mentioned above or anything that requires an invitation, nightlife here is usually casual.

We'll list a sampling of what's available in each region.

Here are a few things you'll want to know about liquor laws in the state. Mississippi is a legally dry state concerning alcoholic beverages. The sale and consumption of liquor is made legal through local referendum, which means that throughout the state, expect a patchwork of wet and dry counties. State law also says — and strictly enforces — that liquor sold on the premises of a lounge or restaurant must be consumed there. The hours that the state recognizes for liquor store sales are 10 AM to 10 PM Monday through Saturday. Deliveries are not allowed, and liquor stores are not open on Sundays. Lounge hours may vary according to local laws, but the state mandates that lounges may be open from 10 AM to midnight except in areas that operate under a resort status, or in areas, such as Jackson, where local law provides for lounges to remain open until 1 AM. Resort areas have 24-hour liquor sales; all casinos in the state are in areas that have resort status.

We strongly urge that those who drink do not drive. If you do drink away from home, please appoint a designated driver.

The Heartland

APPLEBEE'S
NEIGHBORHOOD BAR AND GRILL
2332 Hwy. 45 N., Columbus   327-3348
Barnes Crossing Mall, Tupelo   840-4009

Locals gather round the bar to chat it up at this chain establishment while enjoying appetizers or meals. There's no entertainment, it's open daily.

C.J.'S SOCIAL CLUB
441 Wilkins Wise Rd.
Off Hwy. 45 N. Columbus   329-1711

This is a hot spot for the up-and-coming younger-than-30-or-so crowd in Columbus. Expect a dark bar and live music on certain nights. There's also a larger restaurant specializing in Italian food; it's open daily.

Photo: Vernon Matthews

Regulars gather each weekday or evening in neighborhood bars such as this one for relaxation. This group plays along with the TV game show "Jeopardy".

CLASSIX

201-D Alabama St. (Gateway Center)
Columbus   329-4819

Each night brings a special music and dance theme, from western music and line dancing, to rock 'n' roll. It's open Tuesday through Saturday from 5 PM till 1 AM; they offer complimentary buffet and some live entertainment.

HARVEY'S

Main St., Columbus   327-1639
Hwy. 12, Starkville   323-1639
S. Gloster, Tupelo   842-8763

Happy hour at Harvey's bar — any of the locations — is the place to see and be seen after work or after dinner. There's often talk of local politics interspersed with team talk. Count on Harvey's for tasty appetizers to accompany beverages. It's closed Sunday.

MAIN STREET BAR & GRILL

1302 Main St., Columbus   328-4340

This is a new bar and grill in an old building, actually an old railroad depot. Lots of stained glass and brick walls give it an historic feel, though it's very modern in its clientele and music, which consists of live bands most weekends. It's near the local college.

MONTANA'S AT THE RAMADA

Hwy. 45 N., Columbus   327-7077

A cozy atmosphere and live music attracts business travelers and locals. It's closed Sunday and Monday.

RICK'S CAFE AMERICAIN

319-B U.S. 82 E., Starkville   323-0782

This Starkville favorite brings in name bands, among them Pearl River, Quiet Riot and more. On non-live entertainment nights, DJs spin the mix, complete with a light show. Rick's also has three bars, seven pool tables, seven video games

and food. The Blue Parrot Sports Pub is in the same building and under the same ownership, and indeed, sports fans gather here.

CHEERS

La Galerie Shopping Center
500 Russell St., Starkville   324-2129

Billed as "the home of the Comedy Zone," two professional comedians perform each Wednesday at 9 PM. Happy hour follows the performance. Other nights, DJs appear with their music shows. Pool is popular here too.

MULLIGAN'S

U.S. 12, Starkville   324-3095

Local talent performs here along with some bands traveling through such as Catfish Jenkins. This bar seats 1,000, with a large dance floor and four bars. Pool tables and menu items such as fried shrimp and hamburgers make this a favorite stop.

THE DISTRICT CAFE

Hwy. 12, Starkville   323-9696

This bar and cafe offers food as well as spirits and usually lots of activity; it's open daily and often filled with students and staff from nearby Mississippi State U.

JEFFERSON PLACE

823 Jefferson St., Tupelo   844-8698

Casual, lively and usually a good place to meet locals, Jefferson Place offers food and spirits and live entertainment some evenings. Menu favorites include seafood and fancy sandwiches. It's in a rambling old house and is open daily.

THE RIB CAGE

206 Troy St., Tupelo   840-5400

It is most unusual to find "Tropical Tuesday" entertainment in a place known for great Southern barbecue ribs, but that's the deal at The Rib Cage. Hear live music each Tuesday, from 7 til 11 PM. Enjoy fine foods and spirits from morning til midnight.

BOGART'S

Ramada Inn
854 N. Gloster St., Tupelo　　　*844-5371*

Bogart's is known locally as an authentic nightclub, for live entertainment and dancing are offered nightly. Complimentary hors d'oeuvres are served from 6:30 to 8 PM each week night and Saturday.

JIM'S SHRIMP & OYSTER BAR

1721 N. Gloster St., Tupelo　　　*844-4326*

This local favorite offers live entertainment on Friday and Saturday from 8:30 to midnight. Along with beverages, seafood and steaks are high on the priority list. It's open each Monday through Saturday from 5 to 10 PM.

THE CITY GROCERY

1118 Van Buren Ave., Oxford　　　*232-8080*

Though this is a fine establishment that serves European cuisine, it's also a good place for a drink while overlooking the Oxford Square. It's in an old grocery store, complete with brick walls and hardwood floors, but thereafter the resemblance ends.

THE HOKA

304 S. 14th St., Oxford　　　*234-3057*

This old warehouse building houses an establishment about as Bohemian as it gets in Mississippi. The decor is most unusual. Drinks flow fairly freely, and food includes nachos, stirfry, Italian, chicken, salads and more. It's open daily till 2 AM.

THE GIN

Harrison Ave. at 14th St.
Oxford　　　*234-0024*

A restaurant and lounge, this one has a varied burger menu, apparently a favorite food to accompany beer. The Gin features live entertainment, some of national renown; it's closed Sunday.

PROUD LARRY'S

211 S. Lamar St., Oxford　　　*236-0050*

Live music is often on the agenda here as well as good times for all who enter. The management suggests pasta, salads, pizza, burgers or sandwiches for those who want food with their beverages.

The Delta

The nightlife in the Delta centers around private functions, the casinos in Greenville and Tunica and a few blues clubs if you're lucky enough to be there when the blues are being played. Greenville's Cotton Club Casino is a replica of an elegant 1920s luxury liner, and the Las Vegas is equally as interesting decor-wise. Tunica now boasts nine casinos, the first of which was the Splash. Sam's Town is billed as "the biggest and best," though Circus Circus and Harrah's may differ. The Tunica casinos, perhaps because of their close proximity to Memphis, attract top talent for shows. Recently, Willie

---

Insiders' Tips

Jerry Fisher, former lead singer of Blood, Sweat and Tears, owns Dock of the Bay in Bay St. Louis.

Nelson and Barbara Mandrell performed on the permanently-docked vessels.

PERRY'S FLOWING FOUNTAIN
816 Nelson St., Greenville   *335-9836*

Sometimes on weekends, local blues musicians gather here for a set or two. If they're playing, you'll hear them before you enter. If blues musicians aren't there in person, you'll hear their tapes.

ONE BLOCK EAST
240 Washington Ave., Greenville   *332-3800*

This new club is the revival of an old tradition, for years ago, One Block East was at this same site, which is one block east of the levee. Enjoy live blues music every weekend, which is sometimes interspersed with rock 'n' roll.

THE COTTON CLUB CASINO
Downtown on the Levee
Greenville   *378-8953, (800) 946-6673*

Locals say there's a whole lotta shakin' goin' on, and indeed there is if you're on one of the two casinos on Lake Ferguson, near downtown. Lounges, restaurants and occasional live entertainment make the river the place to be for after hours.

THE LEVEE LOUNGE
U.S. 49 and 82, Greenwood   *455-2321*

In the Ramada Inn, this is a popular place for locals who want to relax after hours and for guests of the Ramada. Entertainment, dancing and cocktails are what brings them in. A full-service restaurant is nearby.

WEBSTER'S
216 W. Claiborne St.
Greenwood   *455-1215*

This full bar provides a nice environment in an older home, all the amenities and fine food.

YIANNI'S
506 Yalobusha St.
Greenwood   *455-6789*

This restaurant and bar is owned by members of a well-established Delta restaurateur family. It offers a full bar in a romantic French country atmosphere.

The Heartland

Jackson has a plethora of places known as nightclubs and lounges, but we concentrate on those with wider appeal than neighborhood-type establishments. We've included those mentioned when we asked, "What's doin' in Jackson?" Here are the results of our queries and informal research on nightlife in the state's biggest city.

HAL & MAL'S
200 S. Commerce St., Jackson   *948-0888*

This converted 1920s warehouse in downtown Jackson is the place to be to hear good blues and other live music. It's best to call for an entertainment lineup for each specific month. Once there, fresh seafood and authentic Deep South cooking is a definite plus.

IRON HORSE BAR & GRILL
320 W. Pearl St., Jackson   *355-8419*

Locals looking for fun and food come

Watch for big-name entertainers at Mississippi's casinos.

Insiders' Tips

to this historic building, the former Armour Smokehouse. A piano bar draws downtown's after-work crowd and visitors in the know.

1001 BAR & SANTA FE GRILL
1001 E. County Line Rd. at I-55
Jackson   *956-1001*
   This bar and grill features live entertainment six days a week, plus food and spirits. It's one of Jackson's favorites; it opens at 5:30 PM Monday through Saturday.

POET'S
1855 Lakeland Dr., Jackson   982-9711
   You'll find live entertainment and dancing nightly in this Old World atmosphere. Good food and drinks add to its popularity.

RODEO'S
6107 Ridgewood Rd., Jackson   957-1400
   The delicious happy-hour buffet is usually busy, and so are the nights when Rodeo's offers free western dance lessons. Wednesday is ladies night; Thursday offers dance lessons for couples, and general good times are to be had on weekends. Call for specifics.

CAROLINE'S
712 23rd Ave., Meridian   693-6575
   This popular sports bar and grill is a hit with the 25-to-40 crowd and for lots of reasons. Caroline's has billiard tables, 10 TVs plus a big screen and a state-of-the-art jukebox filled with CDs. Another draw is the pub-style Southern menu,

with good and affordable fare such as barbecue, hamburgers, sandwiches, salads and typical bar appetizers. There's live jazz and rock a couple of nights a week. Caroline's is open 4 PM to 1 AM every day except Sunday.

HOWARD JOHNSON LODGE'S GREENBRIAR LOUNGE
110 Hwy. 11 and 80
Meridian   *483-8281*
   This place offers live entertainment Monday through Saturday from 8 PM to 1 AM. The music is mainly a mix of country and rock 'n' roll. The lounge hours are 3 PM to 1 AM.

CHESTERFIELD'S
2507 Hardy St., Hattiesburg   582-2778
   Chesterfield's lounge is open Monday through Saturday from 11 AM until closing, and from noon to 10 PM on Sunday. Food is available from the full lunch and dinner menu. A favorite is the appetizer specials. This is a popular spot located across from the University of Southern Mississippi, and customers here range in age from early 20s to mid-40s.

The River Cities

THE NEW ORLEANS CAFE
1100 Washington St., Vicksburg   638-8182
   This is a fun bar — two, actually — in a great historic location. The crowd is mixed, and on weekends there's music, mostly live, plus a jukebox anytime. There's also a game room here. The cafe is on a street that predates the Civil War

and in a building that since 1865 has housed a bank, two newspapers, a department store, the Knights of Pythias Hall and the Uneeda Biscuit Co. Service is available in the lounge and restaurant seven days a week from 11 AM until the 2 AM closing.

RIVER ROAD MILLER'S STILL
1101 Washington St., Vicksburg   638-8661

You can enjoy live music on the back patio every Sunday starting at 5 PM. The type of music depends on which musician drops by to play and who joins in. You can also order food from the restaurant that's served on the back patio until 2 AM. Lounge hours are 11 AM to 2 AM, and the restaurant is open from 11 AM to 10 PM except Monday.

PEARL STREET CELLAR
211 N. Pearl St., Natchez   446-5022

Two blocks off Main Street in a nice old building, Pearl Street Cellar serves customers downstairs and upstairs, where you can have a drink on the porch. Live bands perform on weekends, playing all kinds of music. Pearl Street Cellar is open Monday through Saturday from 4:30 PM until closing.

SCROOGE'S
315 Main St., Natchez   446-9922

Scrooge's is a restaurant, but it also has a full-service bar. You can order from its full-service menu that includes burgers, appetizers and salads. It's open 11 AM to 11 PM daily except Sunday.

UNDER THE HILL
25 Silver St., Natchez   446-8023

This is an old-time riverfront saloon at Natchez that attracts locals and tourists and ages from 21 to 61. There's live entertainment every weekend; expect to enjoy anything from classic rock to country and Cajun.

The Coast

The Coast has plenty in the way of live entertainment at lounges, restaurants, hotels and clubs. And with the casinos in full swing, there's more than ever to keep things lively. Some casino shows start as early as noon and feature local talent as well as big names, often free of charge. Coast hotels and motels have lounges where live entertainment can be found. Stereo music is also on tap at a number of local nightclubs, from Bay St. Louis to Ocean Springs. Several square-dance clubs get together weekly and welcome visitors. Here is a sampling of some of the local favorite spots for nighttime entertainment.

Check Friday's "Marquee" in *The Sun Herald* for complete listings of casino entertainment for the week.

DOCK OF THE BAY
119 N. Beach Blvd.
Bay St. Louis   467-9940

Dock of the Bay's owner, Jerry Fisher, is a former lead singer with Blood, Sweat and Tears. He performs here with his popular R&B band, the Music Company. Other top quality entertainers take the

Members of the Gulf Coast Jazz Society entertain patrons at a nightspot on the Coast.

stage as well at this favorite spot for music, drinks and food.

BOMBAY BICYCLE CLUB
830 Beach Blvd., Biloxi   374-4101

You'll find a little of everything here — from DJs on Thursday, Friday and Saturday to karaoke on Friday and Saturday.

THE COMEDY ZONE AT TREASURE BAY CASINO AND RESORT HOTEL
Hwy. 90, Biloxi   388-8489

Here, you'll find stand-up comics entertaining the crowds every weekend.

MALLINI'S POINT LOUNGE
Henderson Point
118 W. Bayview Ave.   452-2497

This lounge has live entertainment on weekends, mainly during the summer. More than 30 bands from nine states perform at this popular Pass Christian area club. The music is mainly alternative and rock. The early crowd is in the 30-and-older range, and after 10 PM the college-age crowd starts arriving. Mallini's opens at 4 PM and closes at 6 AM.

MICHAEL'S COUNTRY CLUB
9745 Hwy. 49, Gulfport   867-6322

Disc jockeys play new country favorites and some oldies every night starting at 7 PM. This is a popular spot for the 30-something crowd. Patrons enjoy a happy hour buffet served from 5 to 8 PM Tuesday, Wednesday, Thursday, Friday and Sunday. Happy hour is noon to 8 PM Monday through Friday. Wednesdays and Fridays are ladies nights. Sunday evenings from 7:30 to 11 PM are reserved for teens.

LARRY'S ON THE BEACH
614 Beach Blvd., Gulfport   896-8828

Larry's is a new favorite for those looking for an adult atmosphere, live music of the contemporary variety and food of major proportions. There are band concerts every weekend outside on the patio, which has seating for 110. Monday through Thursday the music moves inside. The restaurant serves large portions of chicken dishes, pizza, burgers and other great food. Larry's also has five large TVs, six pool tables, dart boards and a complete game room. It's open 24 hours a day.

AMERICAN SUPERSTARS PALACE CASINO

158 Howard Ave., Biloxi   432-8888

See Elvis, Madonna, Charlie Daniels and other superstar imitators in this tribute to some of the top names in entertainment. Locals enjoy this dinner buffet and show as much as casino visitors. Matinees are at 2 PM on Tuesday through Thursday and Saturday and Sunday. The evening shows are at 8 PM Tuesday through Sunday and 10 PM on Friday and Saturday.

AMERICA LIVE!

Grand Casino Gulfport, U.S. 90
Gulfport   870-1901

This brand-new 45,000-square-foot entertainment complex features fun on three floors. There's America's Original Grandstand sports bar, America's Showroom and Club with DJs and live entertainment, Knuckleheads comedy club and Lil' Ditty's with sing alongs and dueling baby grand pianos.

Inside
Shopping

Nothing happens, economically, until something is sold. We know many people who make things happen, for they keep the shops in a selling mode. Shopping is serious business in Mississippi, whether it's ferreting out the latest antique shops or loading up a van full of friends and heading to Birmingham or New Orleans to spend a weekend looking for sales and bargains.

As a rule, however, serious shoppers don't have to leave the state, for there's a multitude of shopping experiences right here in our own backyard. There's Stein Mart, the Mississippi-based family chain known for high value and low price; another Mississippi-based retail giant, McRae's, has good sales and bargains too. And there is a plethora of special apparel shops, such as Maison Weiss in Jackson, Ruth's in Columbus, Collections in Columbus and Tupelo, and Roberts in Laurel. Those who like the feel of an old-fashioned quality department store — and there aren't many such stores left — know about Neilson's, on the Square in Oxford. It's the state's oldest department store extant, and it has a little bit of everything. Benoist's in Natchez has been around since 1881, which brings to mind another quality shopping treat in Natchez: Brown Barnett Dixon's, where the sparkle of crystal and sterling always adds to the allure. The Gulf Coast is lit-erally lined with specialty shops that sell everything from handmade jewelry and crafts to expensive designer clothing, and more shops are springing up with the advent of the glittering casinos. Up from the Coast, Hattiesburg lays claim to a big new mall called Turtle Creek, which attracts shoppers from south and central Mississippi.

Shoppers who look for special items made by the hands of local artisans have a good selection too. A good place to begin is the Craftsmen's Guild of Mississippi. Talented artists who make up the guild display and sell their creations at various locations across the state.

The shopping possibilities in Mississippi are endless, but unfortunately the pages in this book aren't. Because we are covering the entire state, we may fail to list a few of your favorite discoveries. Let us know if we have inadvertently omitted a shop you think merits special mention, then look for it in the next updated book. Happy shopping!

The Hill Country

Antiques

Antique lovers across the South have discovered Columbus. They know that within a few downtown blocks at least

eight shops are waiting for browsers and buyers. Start on what locals call "River Hill," about a half block off Main Street/Highway 82, where **Riverhill Antiques**, 122 Third Street S., began with a big Victorian house filled with treasures. Owner Frank Loftis tours the country finding the best estate sales, then brings furniture, accessories, fine china, accent pieces and art back to River Hill. And there's more — next door. **Riverhill House**, another pretty Victorian, holds yet more antiques and special finds. Walk across the street to Riverhill's third and latest location, 309 Main Street, and you'll want to spend the day. This restored old Elks Club holds new mahogany and teak furniture and accessories, plus antiques too. Shoppers get lots of ideas here, for this location houses a couple of antiques and art dealers who sell gift items.

Still on Main Street, the next block east from Riverhill Antiques, both sides of the street are lined with shops you'll want to see. On the north side, **Dee's Interiors**, 411 Main Street, has a few antiques and lots of decorative accessories and gifts. If it's for the home, and if it's a quality item and currently popular, Dee's will have it. People come from as far away as Atlanta to shop at Dee's.

Down the street a few doors is **Stonegate Galleries**, 415 Main Street, where rare antique prints share space with original art and accessories. Great gifts, too, and truly unique and wonderful framing is done at Stonegate.

Cross the street and check out the antique furniture treasures at **Carriedale**, 422 Main Street, and at the **Columbus Antique Mall**, 418 Main Street. Decorative arts experts and collectors have found inexpensive items here that later sold at New York auction houses for big bucks. Down the street (west) from the Antique Mall, is a new shop that's painted deep gold and dark magenta on the outside, with a striped awning that emphasizes the colors. It's the **Market Place**, 408 Main, where interior designers are in residence. They sell a few antiques and lots of decorative accessories. Next, **Mad Horse Antiques**, 404 Main Street, has a grand selection of all styles of furniture. Prices for quality pieces are less than one would expect. The owner, Carolyn Neault, is a local historian.

Also within a couple of blocks is Eugenia Talbott's **Gallery and Antiques**, 116 Fifth Street N., where this local artist sells her work, including wonderful hand-painted room divider screens that feature handsome animals, as well as antiques and accessories. There are other dealers who don't have shops open on a regular basis, but they have merchandise on hand for most tastes. Mary Alice Stewart of **Stewart's Antiques**, 925 Third Avenue N., is a good example.

Twenty minutes west in Starkville, British-born Doris Watson, owner of **Watson's Village Antiques**, Highway 82 E., at the end of the four-lane, knows antiques and has direct sources in England for art glass and china. Unusual, hard-to-find furnishings may be waiting at Watson's. She specializes in early-American and English furniture. **Gini's Attic Antiques**, 1221 Old Highway 82 E., Clayton Village, near Starkville might just be the place to find an unexpected treasure, for the owner has a variety of items, "from junk to antiques" and a price range from $2 to $3,000. The **Artist & Crafter's Gallery**, 102 Main Street, in Starkville, across from the Courthouse, houses some antiques, plus

hand-crafted items, ceramics and country decorative accents.

Tupelo has a good selection of antiques and collectibles at the **Red Door Antique Mall** and **Collectibles Emporium**, 1001 Coley Road. This mall, at 10,000 square feet, is Tupelo's largest, with more than 35 dealers selling their wares. **Murphey's Antiques, Ltd.**, 1120 W. Main, specializes in English furniture and accessories and will open by special appointment if shoppers can't make it during regular hours. Also in Tupelo, the **Downtown Antique Mall**, 624 Main Street, is a small mall with antiques and interesting items — more 'old' than antique — next door to Goodyear. **P.A.M. Antiques**, 2229 W. Main, sells fine antiques and decorative gifts. Those who seek vintage clothing will find **The Main Attraction**, 210 W. Main, in Tupelo, for it's where those in the know go for treasures. **George Watson Antiques**, 628 W. Main, has antiques and unusual vintage pieces.

The historic town of Corinth is a wonderful place to shop for antiques. The **Crossroads Antiques Mall**, 714 Taylor, is a good place to start, for it's a big building full of furniture, glassware, Civil War relics and merchandise from estate sales. This won't be a quick trip if you want to see it all.

Oxford is a town antique shoppers love, and though some of the shops have new merchandise as well as antiques, it is still a place where treasures are found. **The Weather Vane**, on the Square, has a few antiques and outstanding decorative accessories. Also in Oxford, the **Bird in the Bush**, 1415 University Avenue, has antiques, gifts, furniture, crystal and accessories for the home. **The Kangaroo Pouch**, 613 S. Lamar Boulevard, is an excellent place to stop and shop for an-

Credit: Vernon Matthews, The Sun Herald

Wherever they might be in Mississippi, antique lovers are never far from a collection of antique shops.

tiques or other things. **Bea's Antiques**, 1315 N. Lamar, is the shop in Oxford that specializes in oak pieces, such as armoires, wardrobes, dressers, library tables and mantels. "Mostly American" antiques is what you'll find at Bea's. East of Oxford, on Miss. 6 E., **Tommy's Antiques**, Route 6, Box 210 A, has 9,200 square feet of French, English and Victorian antiques. Tommy's has 20 years experience selling antiques.

From Oxford, head on out Highway 7 to Holly Springs, and find **Antiques Mississippi**, 201 S. Center Street, with fine porcelain, Civil War artifacts and consignment items.

Specialty Shops

We mentioned this shop in the Antiques section, but it must be included as a specialty shop too, for **Dee's Interiors**, 411 Main Street, in Columbus has one of the largest selections of gifts and accessories in the entire Hill Country. **Tom Clark's Cairn Collection** is a big favorite. Also in Columbus, this shop has a new name, but the same people who pre-viously had Caldwell's Gifts own it; it's **Gifts, Etc.**, 917 Main Street, where distinctive gifts are sure to be found. Gifts, Etc. stocks such names as Gail Pittman, Pat Gavin, Vicki Carroll and more. **Old Main Books**, 423 Main Street, is a great place to shop for reading material if you care to discuss the authors or subject matter with someone quite knowledgeable. Owner Steve Pieschel is a former English professor, and his inventory reflects his taste in books, which is excellent.

Party & Paper, 218 Fifth Street S., in Columbus is more than a place to buy quality paper products for any occasion; it's a complete gift shop with a popular line of Mississippi gourmet products. You'll find great games and toys for kids as well as a vast selection of greeting cards. **The Stained Glassworks, Inc.**, 122 Fifth Street N., is a good place to find custom glass designs and unusual gift items.

The Bath Station, Highway 45, University Mall, in Columbus is so filled with wonderful items and accessories for the bath, you could spend hours here. They have a grand selection of general gifts and home accessories too.

East Columbus is the place to go if you're an artist or someone who wants to frame the work of an artist. **The Grapevine**, 204 N. McCrary Road, has prints, arts and craft supplies, baskets and brass. They do custom framing. **Jubilations Cheesecake**, 1536 Gardner Boulevard, 328-9210, is a business that got its start in Columbus, and though it is not a gift shop per se, folks buy one of the 25 flavors of delicious cheesecake as gifts, and Jubilations ships anywhere. Starkville's **Etc. Gifts**, 504 A Academy Road, sells gifts and accessories, furniture, fudge and other things for the home. **Giggleswick**, 220 Main Street, in Starkville has the type of merchandise normally found in gift shops in addition to much more. They sell fine gifts and interiors and have a personal shopping service, jewelry and Mississippi-made products.

Main Attractions, 214 W. Main, in Tupelo is just plain fun. It's a shop that has a little bit of everything, from vintage clothing, jewelry and gifts to shoes. Even if you aren't shopping for a particular item, chances are you'll find something you need or want here. **The Basket Case**, 491 S. Gloster, is a shop that has much more than baskets. Their gourmet foods and coffees are much in demand, as well as their wonderful pottery. It is in a mini mall that also incudes the specialty shops of **Collections**, an upscale women's apparel shop, and **Fragments**, where well-dressed women go for accessories and costume jewelry.

Our Children's Closet, 2303 W. Main Street, in Tupelo is a specialty shop that caters to children, newborn through size 14. It's so special, in fact, that customers here find handmade heirloom clothing, including Mississippi-made dresses from the Ashford Collection. Also in Tupelo, **The Velveteen Rabbit**, 348 S. Gloster, is another children's specialty shop that happens to be one of the largest in the South. Exquisite clothing and Victorian jewelry for the little people are plentiful.

The big **Barnes Crossing Mall**, 1001 Barnes Crossing Road, has a well-stocked **Bookland**. Back on W. Main Street in Tupelo, find **Gumtree Books**, 129-131 W. Main, the bookstore housed in **Reed's Department Store**. This store is frequented by Mississippi author John Grisham, who comes here to sign his numerous bestsellers. Also in Tupelo, the **Village Green Bookstore**, 1181 W. Main Shopping Center, has bestsellers and a good Mississippi section for those who appreciate homegrown material.

Head on out to Oxford, where you'll discover that the Square is the place to shop; it's where you'll find **The Frame Up/Basement Gallery** and their limited or open-edition prints and posters. They offer some originals and pottery too.

The Weather Vane, on the Square, has gifts for most occasions and lovely decorating touches for the home. Find them among a few English imports and antiques.

Overlook the Oxford Square, and enjoy a good cup of cappuccino at the inimitable **Square Books**, 1126 Van Buren Avenue, where two floors of books await

Insiders' Tips

Many of the state's specialty shops are closed on Sunday. Call before you go.

your perusal. Square Books has fans from everywhere, and it is a winner of the Haslam Award for Excellence in Bookselling. There's also **Waldenbooks** in **Oxford Mall**, 1111 W. Jackson Avenue, with quite a good travel section.

Shopping Malls

Leigh Mall, Highway 45, just north of downtown Columbus was the first mall in town. It's anchored on either end by **Sears** and **JCPenney**. In between, you'll find **Morrison's Cafeteria**, a theater, many clothing stores, including the upscale **Reed's** and **Smith & Byar's**, a bookstore, a health store, shoe stores, boutiques, a hair salon and more. Also on Highway 45 N. in Columbus, **University Mall**, 327-1491, holds a big **McRae's** store as its anchor. **Burchwood Books** is the mall's bookstore. It has a good selection of current bestsellers and a grand selection of regional books. University Mall also has clothing, card stores and more. Just across from University Mall is a smaller strip mall, **Littlewoods Mall**, home of **LeGrande's** gift and bridal shop, **Collection's** apparel for women and **CJ's Italian Restaurant**. Other shopping areas line the north end of U.S. 45, where the discount retailers and food chains congregate. Bargain shoppers galore flock to **Wall's**, on old Highway 82, just east of town. They buy fire and flood sale items from throughout the country.

There are no malls in Starkville, but it has its share of shopping centers — nine in fact. The best known, Starkville's **Le Galerie Shopping Center**, 500 Louisville Street, has boutiques, a printer, a travel agent and more.

Tupelo is home to one of the South's largest malls, the **Mall at Barnes Crossing**, 1001 Barnes Crossing, where shoppers from north Mississippi and north Alabama find most things on their shopping lists. **Belk's**, **McRaes**, **Sears** and **JCPenney** anchor this mall, and inside, there are specialty shops for clothing, sportswear, jewelry, gifts and accessories, books and shoes. Take time out for a bite in the big food court in the atrium, where there's also a carousel for kids.

Also in Tupelo, factory outlet stores — some as large as malls — attract big crowds. The **VF Factory Outlet** (for Vanity Fair), 423 Eason Boulevard, outlet shares space with an outlet for Bass shoes, cosmetics and other clothing stores. On the other side of town, **Warehouse Liquidators**, west on Cliff Gookin, sells clothing for the entire family, silk flowers, housewares and many treasures.

Oxford Mall, 1111 Jackson Avenue W., is anchored by a **Wal-Mart** and a **JCPenney**. **Beall-Ladymon** also sells clothing for the family here.

Factory Stores of Mississippi, I-55 and Miss. 6, Batesville, on the border as our regions are defined. (Batesville, a town of about 6,400 in Panola County, could classify as either The Hill Country or The Delta, and both are pleased to claim it.) The Factory Stores of Mississippi recently opened for business, with more stores continuing to open for an eventual grand total of 40 stores encompassing 133,000 square feet. Among the stores are Bass, Libby Glass, National Book Warehouse, and at least one or more stores for men's, ladies and children's clothing. It's the only factory outlet mall between Memphis and the Gulf Coast on I-55. Easy access of I-55 at Exit 243-B makes this a good stop for travelers as well as locals. Travelers will find a tourist and information center with lots of brochures on what's available in the area.

The Delta

Antiques

One of the Delta's best known antique shops is **The Fireside Shop**, 109 North Street, in Cleveland. Fireside prides itself on being a direct importer of English and Scottish antiques, but they also carry American furniture and more, including porcelain. This shop has a reputation for quality.

A big favorite in these parts is the **Antique Mall Ltd.**, Sunflower Road, out from Indianola. It's a surprise from the minute you arrive. Drive along a country road bordered by fields then enter a large building that also houses the Crown Restaurant. Actually, luncheon guests eat on the antique tables that are for sale. Browse among the fine antiques, English and American, and be treated to samples of the Crown Restaurant's marvelous catfish pâté from their line of specialty food items. The owners lived in the United Kingdom for a number of years, so there's a bit of a British flavor here.

Greenwood should be your next stop. A good place to visit is **Warehouse Antiques**, 229 Carrollton Avenue, where high demand items are estate silver and antique jewelry. Also, lots of furniture and glassware is housed in this old building, where other dealers shop. **Heritage House Antiques**, 311 E. Market, features English formal and country antiques — some French country pieces, some American — but not primitive. There's a good selection at Heritage House and plentiful ideas for decorating. **Patsy's Hodgepodge**, 511 Lamar Street, across from Greenwood's popular Crystal Grill, is just plain fun and offers a chance to find unusual things. **Fincher's Antiques**, 512 W.

Park Avenue, in Greenwood has a good selection of Empire pieces and upper-end country. It also has estate silver and gifts.

U.S. 82 W. leads to Greenville and more antique shops. On the edge of town, stop at the **Town & Country Antique Barn**, U.S. 82 E., and spend a while browsing. The Greenville shop **Select Antiques**, 533 U.S. 82 E., has English furniture, porcelain, glassware and more. In downtown Greenville, **The Decorative Touch**, 827 S. Main, has English furniture, porcelain, glassware and many special finds.

Lina's Interiors, Inc., 525 S. Main, in Greenville has one of the region's best selections of 18th- and 19th-century English antiques. If you're looking for mahogany pieces, this may be the place. Owner Lina Karlson is usually on the premises.

The town of Itta Bena, translated to "home in the woods" in Native American, has a shop downtown in the old First National Bank building; it's named **1919 Antiques**, where French, English, western European and Oriental antiques are prominently displayed and ready for sale. You'll find furniture and accessories here.

On the edge of the Delta, Yazoo City's **Main Street Antiques**, 211 N. Main Street, has furniture, glassware, collectibles and estate silver.

Specialty Shops

Mississippi Madness in Clarksdale, 1540 DeSoto, specializes in Mississippi's culinary delights, including such delicacies as black-eyed pea pâté. Better still, each item in the company's dry-mix products comes complete with a Southern story under the label. These products are available in specialty shops across the state, and they ship anywhere from the Clarksdale location.

You'll find home-grown produce in abundance along Mississippi's roads at either individual stands or large farmer's markets.

Credit: Herb Welch, The Sun Herald

In Indianola, the **Indianola Pecan House, Inc.**, U.S. 82 E., 887-5420, sells a plethora of pecans, which they have in gift packs and in a gourmet food line. They ship nationwide. Five miles north of Indianola, the **Antique Mall & Crown Restaurant**, 36 Sunflower Road, ships Mississippi products constantly, such as the cookbook, *Classic Catfish*. A Mississippi mousse that's called Catfish & Capers and the Smoked Catfish Pâté have won awards and make great gourmet gifts. Ask and they'll send a brochure. Their products are also available in gift shops and specialty stores.

No other Mississippi business claims more Mississippi products than **Little Bales of Cotton**, Old Leland Road, just outside the tiny town of Stoneville. They make and ship bales of cotton of all sizes and other gift/souvenir items with a Mississippi connection. It's an amazing place, one you won't soon forget.

In Greenville, the **Shelton House**, 217 S. Washington, serves as a specialty shop, antiques shop and restaurant. You may be enticed to enjoy a wonderful luncheon downstairs on an antique table that's for sale before heading upstairs to see the Christmas shop. Expect to find more Christmas ornaments and decorations than you can imagine in addition to great ideas for decorating trees.

McCormick Book Inn, 825 S. Main Street, is the place to purchase the works of the plethora of Delta writers who hail from the area, and **Bookland** at Greenville Mall, 1651 Highway 1 S., has bestsellers and bargain books.

Shopping Malls

Greenwood has two shopping centers, and though one is called a mall, there are no indoor malls. The centers are **Greenwood Mall**, Park Avenue, which has a **JCPenney** as the major retailer, and **Highland Park Shopping Center**, which has **Abide's** women's apparel, **Phil's Squire Shop** for men and **Youngland** for children.

The **Greenville Mall**, 1651 Highway 1 S., has **McRae's** and **JCPenney** as anchor stores, also **Sears** and specialty shops including **The Country Gentleman** and **Back in Time**. Shopping centers include **Village Shopping Center**, S. Main and Reed Road, and **Delta Plaza Shopping Center**, 800 U.S. 1 S. Expert shoppers know that bargains are to be had in downtown Greenville, for it's the home of **Stein Mart**, 219 Washington Avenue. As a matter of fact, Stein Mart's company-clearance center is downtown, 410 Washington; locals call it "Saks 5th Avenue Clearance Center." Prepare yourself: You'll encounter serious shoppers here.

The Heartland

Antiques

The **Fairground Antique Flea Market**, 900 High Street, in Jackson draws folks from across the state who come to have some semblance of a treasure hunt. Whether it is a real treasure or something fun or frivolous, it's the hunt that's the challenge. Dealers from throughout the state display their merchandise here. The Fairground Flea Market is open on weekends only.

This next one has a Ridgeland address, but Jackson claims it too, because it's hard to tell when Jackson stops and Ridgeland starts. It's the **Antique Mall of the South**, 367 Highway 51, a mile north of County Line Road. You're likely to find the unexpected here; 60 dealers are involved in the 14,000-square-foot facility. **Stately Home Antiques**, 737 N. State Street, sells fine antiques, including English and French furniture and accessories, Oriental pieces, porcelain and an extensive collection of lamp shades. This is a fun and new place to shop, and 40 dealers keep items replenished. It's **Interior Spaces**, Maywood Mart, I-55 at Northside Drive, where shoppers find good selections of antiques, art, accessories and gifts. Mary Ann Hughes is the owner. Another place that sells antiques, art, accessories and more is **Interiors Market** in Woodland Hills Shopping Center, Duling Street, off Old Canton Road. Nearby Madison, generating interest as an antiques mecca, is proud of the shops in their lovely town. They are in close proximity, either in the Madison Depot or nearby, so plan to spend leisurely time antiquing in this charming town. Some of the shops are closed on Monday, so if that's the day you plan to shop, call first. **Uptown Antiques, Etc.**, 111 Depot Drive, is where Sherrye LaCour sells fine French and American furniture, a good selection of sterling and other estate silver, vintage linens, glassware and much more. This is a favorite of many locals and neighbors from Jackson.

Alene's Antiques and Collectibles, 126 Depot Drive, in Madison is where those who seek pieces of unquestionable quality shop. See 18th-century and early American furniture and accessories and many other treasures. It's easy to remember this name, **Anne-Tiques**, also in Madison, 118 Depot Drive, where country and formal antiques include furniture, glassware, quilts, old toys and more. In the same vicinity, **Talk of the Town Antiques**, 120 Depot Drive, has treasured heirlooms including furniture and glassware and restored lamps and pictures. **The Inside Story**, 2081 Main Street, in the historic district, is fun and eclectic. Expect antiques, fine home accessories, the popular Jeep Collins handcrafted jewelry and much more. **Madison Antiques Market**, 100 Post Oak Road, has a large selection of American and English antiques, plus glassware, paintings and more.

On the historic Court Square in Kosciusko, off the Natchez Trace, is the

Peeler House and its very good selection of quality antiques — French, English and American — plus glassware, silver, porcelain, prints and other great finds. Also in Kosciusko, the **Redbud Inn**, 121 N. Wells, serves up the best lunch in town, serves as a bed and breakfast and sells antiques. In fact, if you like the table your lunch is served on, you can buy it.

There are a good number of antique stores in and around Meridian. **Cabin Antiques** has 18th- and 19th-century furniture and accessories and is just off U.S. 45 N. outside of town. In the **Wayside Shop** at 5523 Poplar Springs Drive, look for antiques, gifts and accessories. The **Old South Antique Mall** at 2101 Fifth Street is a two-story collection of booths. **Z's Fleas**, is another good bet at 1607 24th Avenue. Here you'll find country and formal furniture, baskets and other accessories in a small seven-room house. At 1300 25th Avenue, **Tapestry** offers crystal, linen, china, rattan and Victorian furniture and will special order sterling silver. **Bookers Antiques** outside of town on Miss. 19 S. sells antiques and bric-a-brac.

Specialty Shops

About the best-known specialty shop in Jackson is the **Chimneyville Crafts Gallery**, 1150 Lakeland Drive, in the two-story log building at the Ag Museum. The Gallery is a sales center for the **Craftsmen's Guild of Mississippi, Inc.**, a nonprofit organization of craftspeople and others interested in preserving and promoting the folk, traditional and contemporary crafts associated with the state. Jewelry, prints, wood carvings, quilts and pottery (and sometimes demonstrations) are available at the Chimneyville Crafts Gallery. It's closed Sunday.

The **Mississippi Crafts Center** at Ridgeland, on the Natchez Trace Parkway north of Jackson, is also a sales shop, and it sponsors a nationally recognized program of crafts demonstrations, classes and festivals. Works available for purchase include highly prized and perfect Choctaw cane baskets. It's open seven days a week.

Near Jackson, in Madison, **The Inside Story**, 2081 Main Street, sells antiques, gifts and special items, including the much-in-demand Jeep Collins Collection of crosses, hearts and handcrafted sterling and brass heirloom jewelry.

The **Madison Depot Bookstop**, 180 Main Street, advocates cordial, helpful service and a large selection of books, from classics to contemporary. Also find an array of bestsellers and books by Southern authors.

The **Earth Traders**, 1060 E. County Line Road, Centre Park, in Jackson/Ridgeland features masks, exotic pottery, art glass and more from Brazil, Santa Fe, Africa, the Himalayas and other places around the globe. Many of the items are handcrafted. **Jazzy Dancer**, Centre Park, off County Road, is Jackson's only dance specialty shop. With the IBC, Jackson Ballet and Ballet Magnificat, this shop is much in demand. Jazzy Dancer carries Danskin, Sade, Gilda Marx, Capezio, Blochs and more.

Fridge's, Center Courtyard, Highland Village, in Jackson has a reputation for having the most outstanding and imaginative gifts and distinctive home accessories in these parts. They're also the exclusive dealer for Baccarat crystal. Expect Limoges boxes and limited artwork from the state's top artists. Booklovers in the Magnolia State know about **Lemuria Book Store**, 202 Banner Hall, for it's where the best-known authors come to sign their books. The owner has hit upon something that works well-Lemuria is a popular place. Also find a children's bookstore called **OZ**, which offers an array of interesting books and other things.

Indeed, Jackson is a city that reads. **Cover to Cover Bookstore**, 238 Highland Village, has books in most any category, and they specialize in electronic title search. Special orders are welcome. The **Old Capitol Shop**, 100 S. State Street, is located in the Old Capitol Museum, which surely gives it an edge as an outstanding place to find Mississippi books, Southern history and a fine selection of general books and literature. **Books-a-Million** at Jacksonian Plaza, 4950 I-55 N., has what one has come to expect of this chain bookstore, a more than generous selection of hardback and paperback books. A favorite section is bargain books, here and at **Waldenbooks**, 1165 Metrocenter, another chain bookstore that never disappoints. **B Dalton Bookseller**, 1200 E. County Line Road, has a Ridgeland address, but Jackson claims it too, for it is in the big Northpark Mall. B Dalton has more than 25,000 book titles and other things to delight readers, such as books on tape and gift items. **Choctaw Books**, 926 North Street, has access to rare and out-of-print books and offers a good selection of used books.

The **Everyday Gourmet**, 2905 Old Canton Road, has much more than great gourmet foods and coffees; they also carry a vast collection of cookbooks, Mississippi products, Gail Pittman pottery — everything for the well-outfitted kitchen.

Taylor Maid, 1667 Lakeland Drive, in Jackson is a popular place for gourmet foods and coffees and a quick lunch. There's nothing better than their pasta salad. Once you visit, you may find yourself ordering one of their beautifully packaged gift baskets filled with Mississippi food products. Expect a variety of merchandise, including the latest *New York Times*. Deli take-out is a special treat.

The **Early Settler**, Highland Village, I-55 at Northside Drive, has great pewter and brass. They can special order Habersham furniture because they are the exclusive Habersham Plantation dealer in Jackson. The Early Settler is a good place to pick up gift items for any occasion.

Children's specialty shops are big in Mississippi, and **Hugs & Kisses**, School Street Crossing, Miss. 51, in Ridgeland sells a custom line of special-occasion apparel for girls from infants to preteen; boys infants to 7. These precious clothes are to be cherished.

The Polkadot Pony, 1060 E. County Line Road, at Centre Park is a dress-down dress-up store for children. It features play clothes as well as party clothes. **Me and Mom**, LeFleur's Gallery, Piccadilly at I-55 N., coordinates little brother and sister clothes, and sometimes Mom's too. It also sells maternity clothes. Some moms say there's reason to celebrate at **Celebrations** in Highland Village, for it's where they find heirloom designs for boys and girls and custom designs by Sandra Ashford. You'll enjoy a selection of accessories, shoes and more. Those who shop in Canton appreciate **Fairy Tales,** On the Square, which is a children's boutique that carries more than 150 lines of clothing for the little ones.

There are several nice gift shops around Meridian, including **All Through the House,** 4518 Poplar Springs Drive, which carries prints, watercolors, bird cages, candles, lamps and other gift items. **Hart-Hall Ltd.,** 1521 24th Avenue, sells jewelry, pottery, gourmet coffee and foods, among other gift items. Better women's apparel, including sportswear, is sold at **Kay's** at 2400 North Hills Street. **The Liberty Shop** at 404 22nd Avenue sells better junior and misses clothing, Crabtree & Evelyn bath items and Aramotique fragrances plus home accessories.

Aardvark Books and Cafe recently doubled its size and moved to its new location, 2932 North Hills Street, in the north end of town. This independently owned bookstore sells general interest titles, including best-sellers, and has a large science fiction section. There's also a small used section for sci-fi buffs. Aardvark carries the Sunday *New York Times.* The newly added cafe sells delicious cheesecakes (made by Jubilations in Columbus) and espresso plus other coffee favorites.

Another good place to find books is the gift shop in the **Lauren Rogers Museum of Art** in Laurel. There are books on the city itself, the state and the region, covering such topics as history and gardening. There are also books for children here as well as a nice selection of gifts including baskets made by the Choctaw Indians and jewelry made by local, national and international crafters. **Waldenbooks,** 910 Sawmill Road, is in the center of **Laurel's Sawmill Square Mall,** and is known to have a very good inventory on Southern travel and literature. They have several tables of bargain books too, which is always a plus for book lovers.

Shopping Malls

Jackson has more little nook-and-cranny shopping areas than you can imagine and several major malls too. The newest and the busiest is **Northpark Mall,** 1200 E. County Line Road, 957-3744, a massive two-story mall that is in the center of one of Jackson's fastest-growing residential and commercial areas. The major department stores are **Dillard's, Gayfers, McRae's** and **JCPenney.** There are also 125 specialty shops and stores. Enjoy a food court and a 10-screen cinema at Northpark. **Metrocenter Mall,** 3645 Highway 80 W., boasts 145 stores and specialty shops such as women's apparel, shoe stores, etc. **Centre Park,** 1060 E. County Line Road, is small enough to see all the shops and large enough to find what you need. Browse through children's shops, women's clothing stores and more. **Highland Village,** 4500 I-55 N., is where Jacksonians know they'll find upscale goods and services as well as such shops as **Maison Weiss Women's Specialty Shop** and the **Early Settler** accessory and gift shop.

Village Fair Mall, on 22nd Avenue S. off I-20/59, in Meridian is an enclosed mall that contains a variety of stores and restaurants. The hours of operation are Monday through Saturday from 10 AM to 9 PM and Sunday from 1 to 6 PM. The anchor stores are **McRae's** and **JCPenney. Goody's Family Clothing** is also located in the mall.

Hattiesburg's new **Turtle Creek Mall,** has four anchor stores: **Gayfers, Dillard's, McRae's** and **Goody's Family Clothing.** The mall also has a nine-theater cinema, a food court and a variety of specialty stores. Plans call for the addition of **Sears** and **JCPenney**. Turtle Creek is open 10 AM to 9 PM Monday through Saturday and noon to 6 PM on Sunday. It's at 1000 Turtle Creek Drive.

In Laurel, **Sawmill Square Mall**, has around 50 shops, including **JCPenney** and **McRae's**, plus smaller shops for apparel, cards, gifts, jewelry, shows, women's accessories and more. The mall, 910 Sawmill Road, is open Monday through Saturday from 10 AM to 9 PM and from 1 to 5 PM on Sunday. Hours are extended in December.

The River Cities

This is tourist territory, and that means lots of good shops, especially if you're looking for antiques. Shopping in Natchez could be an attraction in itself because there are many fine stores here, and those looking for antiques and specialty items will be particularly pleased with what they can find.

Antiques

Antique lovers will find more than 20 stores in Natchez selling wares such as silver, furniture, coins and jewelry. Many antique shops are along Franklin Street.

H. Hal Garner Antiques, 610 to 614 Franklin between Union and Rankin, carries 18th- and 19th-century furniture, silver, estate jewelry, paintings and other fine antiques. **Brown Barnett Dixon's Fine Gifts**, 511 Main, offers upscale gifts and decorative merchandise. **As You Like It Silver Shop** is in the Stanton Hall Carriage Shop and sells fine silver jewelry, sterling flatware and estate jewelry. At 703 Franklin Street is **Sharp Designs and Works of Art**, which sells unique items

including Oriental and English porcelain, silver serving pieces, Victorian jewelry reproductions, framed art and antique china. **T.A.S.S. House Antiques** on 111 N. Pearl Street is across from the Eola and sells estate jewelry, coins, books, glass and porcelain.

Vicksburg has its share of fine antique stores. **Harrison House**, 1433 Harrison Street near McRaven, is in a 115-year-old Victorian home that contains rooms filled with fine gifts. Handily enough, you can come for lunch and tea Monday through Friday. Reservations are preferred for lunch and required for tea. **Douglas-Yeager-Deen Antiques**, 1110 Clay Street, has a large inventory of 18th- and 19th-century furniture as well as cut glass, china, silver, rugs, clocks, books and even artifacts from the Civil War.

Specialty Shops

Cover to Cover sells books and more at 208 Washington Street in Natchez. There are regional and children's books and works by Southern authors. Cover to Cover also hosts book signings. Also in Natchez, the **Canal Street Depot** and **Market** at Canal and State streets is home to the **Pilgrimage Tour Headquarters** as well as several shops that sell gifts, clothes and food. This shopping area has a number of stores and specialty shops. **Kelly's Kids Outlet,** also at Canal and State streets in the depot, has children's playwear (overages and seconds) for sizes 12 months to adult size 16. The **River Boat Gift Shop** can be found at Natchez Under-the-Hill. It sells silver, china, pewter, Civil War items, souvenirs, T-shirts and more. **Daniel's Basketry**, 200 S. Canal Street, Natchez, has collections of angels, bears, Christmas and lots more. The shop also sells T-shirts, silk flowers, Fenton glass, musical water globes, pottery, refrigerator magnets, cards, dolls, books of all kinds and wind chimes.

Downtown Vicksburg has a collection of exclusive boutiques, including some nice clothing stores such as **The Hub** for men's wear at 1312 Washington Street and **Karl's** for women at 1412 Washington Street. **Coury's**, at 1216 Washington, features children's clothes. Unique art can be found at **Alley Cat Artists** at 1415 Washington Street; upstairs the **Attic Gallery** offers folk, regional and primitive pieces. If you're looking for gifts, **Sassafras** at 1406 Washington Street and **The Cinnamon Tree** at 1322 Washington are two good choices. They both have a super selection of gift items. These and many other shops nestled among some interesting attractions can be found lining Washington Street.

The **Book Store**, 2222 S. Frontage Road, specializes in children's literature and Southern authors. This independently owned store carries a good selection of new and used books and also has a small section for comics.

If you're interested in browsing around in an old-fashioned general store, try **Old Country Store** on U.S. 61 in nearby Lorman. Constructed in 1890 with pine floors and 14-foot ceilings, the store began operations in 1875. You'll find history books and cookbooks, mellow hoop cheese cut with a 70-year-old cutter, crafts, dry goods and picnic supplies. Visitors have plastered the walls and ceiling with some 30,000 business cards.

Shopping Malls

Natchez Mall, on John R. Junkin Road, is open Monday through Saturday from 10 AM to 9 PM and 12:30 to 5:30 PM on Sun-

day. The mall contains **McRae's**, **JCPenney**, jewelry stores, a music shop, a bookstore, gift shops plus a video arcade and cinema.

In Vicksburg, **Pemberton Square Mall**, off I-20 at Pemberton Boulevard, has 40 specialty stores anchored by four large retailers: **Wal-Mart**, **McRae's**, **JCPenney** and **Goody's Family Clothing**. Inside are food outlets, a cafeteria and theater. The nearby Pemberton Plaza contains a grocery, sporting goods, hair salon and fast food restaurants.

The Coast

This is a resort area with a large population and a taste for the arts, so finding a good selection in shops is not a problem.

Antiques

There are antique stores in virtually every city along the Coast. Bay St. Louis has a number of antique stores, some of which are in the historic downtown district. One is **Court St. Station Antiques & Gifts**, 200 S. Beach Boulevard, which has fine gifts, linen and jewelry. Lunch is served inside at Tortilla Bay. **The Antiquarian** at 125 Main Street sells a unique collection of photography, tribal art and botanicals. The **Beach Antique Mall and Flea Market**, 108 S. Beach Boulevard, has a dozen or so dealers. **Evergreen Antiques**, 201 Main Street, sells furniture, jewelry, porcelain and paintings.

Countryside Antiques, 151 U.S. 90 in Waveland, is the oldest antique shop in the Bay-Waveland area and is considered the best around. Countryside specializes in estate antiques including English and French 18th- and 19th-century furniture, Old Paris, bronzes, sterling silver, art, porcelain, wicker and jewelry. Also in Waveland is

Atlantic Empire Antiques at 209 U.S. 90. It sells furniture and glassware among other items.

Over in Pass Christian, **Blue Rose Antiques**, 120 W. Scenic Drive, sells fine antiques and accessories in an 1840s-West Indies-style house on the beach that includes an excellent gourmet restaurant. **Community Antique Mall**, 301 E. Second Street, has 95 booths selling Americana, antiques and collectibles. **Wicker N' Wood** at 254 E. Beach Boulevard sells period antiques, wicker and wrought-iron furniture and home accents. **Alston's Antiques and Gifts** offers furniture, primitives and glass at 2208 25th Avenue in Gulfport. In Pascagoula **Bernard Clark's Whitehouse Antiques**, 2128 Ingalls Avenue, shoppers will find furniture, Blue Willow, lamps, cut glass and pottery for sale. **Ward's Antique Brass** at 711 E. Pass Road in Gulfport specializes in antique lighting. He also restores brass lighting.

Specialty Shops

The downtown areas of historic Ocean Springs and Bay St. Louis have wonderful collections of specialty stores and art galleries, plus some appealing restaurants for meals and snacks. Shoppers can easily park and walk from one establishment to the next.

In Ocean Springs, start at the old **L&N Depot**, 1000 Washington Avenue, (the Chamber of Commerce has its office here) and walk down both sides of the shaded Washington Avenue. At the front of the depot is the popular **Gayle Clark Gallery**. Clark has built a reputation as a talented metalsmith and jeweler, and her works are among those available here. Also in the depot is **Realizations**, a great store for new and longtime admirers of the artistry of Walter Anderson. You'll find

clothes, fabrics, silk-screened prints and other items all bearing the artist's distinctive designs. There are also books, reproductions, posters, note cards, Christmas cards and more. Just down the street is **Salmagundi Gifts**, 922 Washington Avenue, which is loaded with original gifts in the form of signed art, figurines, glass, fine jewelry, gourmet food items, prints and much more. Take time to look around. Across the street is **Miner's Doll and Toy Store**, which is filled with games, books, dolls and toys. Keep walking and you'll come to **The Whistle Stop Framing Gallery and Gifts** at 714 Washington Avenue. If you're looking for art, this is a great place for local works and art gifts as well as fine art reproductions. **Bayou Belle**, 622 Washington Avenue, is a nice boutique that carries distinctive women's sportswear and accessories. Take the time to check out the other interesting shops around here. Then drive over to **Shearwater Pottery**, 102 Shearwater Drive, to visit the family compound where the unique works of celebrated artists Walter Anderson and his brothers, Peter and James McConnell Anderson, are featured. Family members carry on traditions begun by the three brothers. Shearwater sells beautiful pottery and prints.

Also check out **Favorites: Books, Art, Etc.** at 1209 Government Street. It's in a Victorian cottage built in 1900 and restored in 1993. The landscaped grounds and beautiful garden are nice touches that add to the enjoyment of visiting here. Inside, you'll find a great selection of mainly new books plus tapes, greeting cards, original local art and small gift items throughout the rooms. There's also a chance you'll find an author signing a new title or a cookbook author giving lessons.

In Bay St. Louis, both sides of Main Street are lined with shops and art galleries that run from the beach for a few blocks and spread out onto adjacent streets, including Beach Boulevard. Start at **One Magnolia Place**, the big building on the corner of Main and Beach Boulevard that contains several stores, including **Riverboat Landing of Mississippi**. Here you'll find a nice collection of delicious food and cookbooks plus gifts such as original design T-shirts. Across the street are **Bay Crafts and Gifts by the Bay** for nice gift items and top-quality crafts. In the first block of Main is **Cat Rock Corner**, the charming working studio of artist Anne Lynch, who turns rocks into cats and other creatures. **Nadic Arts** at 111 Main features original art depicting wildlife and seascapes. **Simply Southern** at 144 Main Street sells contemporary gifts and gourmet coffee. Down the street, stop in at **Creole Kitchen** for food and gift baskets at 207 Main Street. At the end of the block is **Paper Moon**, which features handmade paper and art, vintage clothes and unusual gift items. At 111 U.S. 90 you'll find **Bookends**, a charming independent bookstore that carries an excellent selection of volumes by Southern authors and a good collection of new and used books. **The Kid Company** is an excellent children's clothing store next door to Bookends. It sells clothes and accessories for infants through young juniors. Also on U.S. 90 is **Ellen Kane Gifts**, a great store full of fine gifts, gourmet food items, greeting cards, picture frames and bath items. Across the highway in Bay Plaza Shopping Center is **The Princess Shoppe**, a boutique for women of all ages. Further out on the highway in Waveland is **Lydia's Audubon Shoppe**, 914 U.S. 90, a nature lover's shop filled with Audubon prints, T-shirts, chimes, jewelry, books and other nature-related items.

Also in Waveland, **Your Personal Touch**, 9070 McLaurin, is the only full-line craft and floral wholesaler in Mississippi that offers craft, art, wedding and floral supplies.

There are several interesting shops you shouldn't miss on Scenic Drive in Pass Christian. **Hillyer House**, 207 E. Scenic, has original art, hand-crafted jewelry, hand-sculptured pottery and blown glass by 175 artists. **Parkers Inc.**, 103 E. Scenic Drive, sells fine and fun jewelry that reflects the seasons. **Lynda's Cookery** and **Valentino's** share the same building at 116 West Scenic across from the boat harbor. Lynda's Cookery is the place for cooks, bakers and gourmets or anyone looking to buy gadgets, cookware, cutlery, spices and more. Valentino's has a distinct line of gifts, including candles, room fragrances and interior decorating items.

In Gulfport, **Village Drummer** at E. Beach and Teagarden is an exclusive women's apparel shop that sells jewelry and a nice selection of gifts. Next door, **Warr's** has quality men's clothing, from suits to sportswear.

Great Expectations Ltd., 520 Courthouse Road, is a favorite for maternity and children's wear. **Cornerstone Gifts**, 16th Avenue and Pass Road, is popular with anyone looking for handmade jewelry, Mississippi-made pottery and food items for the gourmet. **SF Alman Ltd.**, 452 Courthouse Road, sells upscale lines of clothing for men and women.

Martin Miazza, 1208 Pass Road at 29th, offers some exclusives for Coast shoppers, including McCarty pottery made in Merigold, Mississippi; Christmas ornaments designed in-house with depictions representing six Southern states; and Original Mississippi Groceries such as fig preserves, barbecue sauce and jams developed especially for this gift shop.

Downtown Biloxi has a good collection of specialty shops, including **The Bay Collection**, 131 Rue Magnolia, for women's casualwear, business apparel and just the right outfit for that special occasion. For the train enthusiast, **The Emporium**, 136 Rue Magnolia, is a Lionel authorized dealer and repair center that sells trains of all sizes and accessories.

Also in Biloxi, **TU J's Treasures Ltd.** has a collection of everything from furniture to tools and collectibles for sale. You'll find the shop at 819 Jackson Street across from Biloxi Regional Medical Center. **Marion's Antique House**, 124 Rue Magnolia, has been serving customers for 28 years. The store sells a little bit of everything according to owner Lola Marion. **Anne Cuevas Gift Shop** is located in Edgewater Village at 2650 Beach Boulevard. The shop is in a converted carriage house and is filled with unusual yet affordable gifts of all kinds. **Magnolia Memories** contains an interesting mix of items, from gourmet food to dolls, jewelry, clothing and works by Gulf Coast artisans. It's located in the courtyard of Mary Mahoney's restaurant on Rue Magnolia.

Stuffed Shirt Factory Outlet, 1830 Beach Boulevard in Biloxi and 100 W. Beach in Pass Christian, is a great place to find denim items such as shorts, jeans, overalls and skirts. T-shirts are also available.

Shopping Malls

There are two enclosed malls on the Coast, Edgewater and Singing River. **Edgewater Mall**, on the beach in Biloxi, celebrated its 30th birthday recently, and after a major renovation a few years ago, the mall is better than ever. Anchor stores are **Gayfers** department store, **JCPenney** and **Sears**. Nearby is **Edgewater Village**, 2650 Beach Boulevard in Biloxi, a great collection of more than 40 stores selling food, shoes, clothes, electronics, houseware, gifts and much more. The shopping center is across from Edgewater Mall.

Singing River Mall, on U.S. 90 in Gautier contains a variety of stores and restaurants and a cinema. **McRae's**, **Sears**, **JCPenney** and **Service Merchandise** are the anchor stores.

Bargain shoppers can look forward to a large factory outlet mall that is under construction in Gulfport. Work is expected to be completed on **Gulfport Factory Stores** in late 1995. The 200,000-square-foot mall, which developers say they will double in size in two subsequent additions, will contain more than 100 shops. No stores had been announced by presstime.

Inside
Attractions

Here in the Magnolia State, we define an attraction as something fun and festive to see and do. And in this state steeped in folklore and tradition, fun and festive generally has a modicum of historical flavor. You'll see it in the many heritage tours and founder's day celebrations, and in others things pertaining to our history or culture.

History lives here — in the plethora of annual Pilgrimages to antebellum homes (notice the capital P for importance, and see the Pilgrimage chapter) — and in so many marvelous small museums. Even the current trend of converting barges into glitzy riverboat gambling casinos reflects a bit of our history.

Some gaming establishments claim to recapture the spirit of the old paddlewheelers that plied the Mississippi River in the 1800s, where the likes of the fictional Rhett Butler enhanced — or lost — their fortunes. Others are redolent of Las Vegas, with little of the rivertown ambiance of long ago.

For those who consider the gaming industry an attraction, there's a whole chapter on it in this book. If you go, good luck. While you're there, take a break and experience a smattering of what really makes this state special: historic architecture, stories handed down from one generation to the next — told and retold for company — and quaint, small towns.

Credit: The Sun Herald

Elvis Presley, the King of Rock'n' Roll, was born in humble surroundings in Tupelo.

The Hill Country

Historic Attractions

ANTEBELLUM HOME TOURS

Columbus Welcome Center
300 Main St., at River Hill
Columbus   329-3533, (800) 327-2686
Selected homes open daily 10 AM-4 PM, 2-4
PM Sun.; admission: $5 adults

Columbus is a town where the antebellum South is never too far back in time. History abounds here, in the customs, architecture and daily activities. Townspeople are proud of their 100 or so historic homes, though "their" isn't quite accurate, for the homes are private residences, and some — at least two each day — are open for tours. The Columbus homes have been impeccably restored and/or lovingly preserved. They're adorned with the finest antiques. A few have been in the same family since they were built in the mid-1800s, so you're assured of a certain authenticity here not always available elsewhere. All the tour homes are listed on the National Register of Historic Places. Information and maps to homes are available in racks all over town. They practice Southern hospitality here, so you'll enjoy a chat with the home owner. The homes are managed by the Columbus Historic Foundation, 329-3533. The CHF has offices in the new Columbus Welcome Center, formerly the first home of playwright Tennessee Williams. It was moved to its present location on Main Street, also Highway 82. The CVB also can answer questions about historic homes, the Welcome Center, or other Columbus attractions; call 329-1191.

WAVERLEY MANSION

Just off Miss. Hwy. 50, West Point 494-1399
Open early morning to sundown, seven days a
week; admission: $7.50 adults

Waverley (1852) is one of north Mississippi's grandest plantation homes, and it is written up in prominent books all over the world. Once the center of thousands of acres of rich cotton-producing land, it is now known more for its architectural excellence. From the foyer/ballroom, twin circular cantilevered stairways wind gracefully around three floors and support balconies on each. The distance from the ground floor to the top of the cupola, or widow's walk, measures 65 feet. Important antiques have been collected by the owners for more than a quarter of a century. Waverley is on the National Register of Historic Places, is a National Historic Landmark and is a National Restoration Award winner. From Miss. 45 N. outside Columbus, take Miss. 50 to West Point; just over the big Tombigbee River bridge, follow the signs to Waverley.

ELVIS PRESLEY BIRTHPLACE

306 Elvis Presley Dr., Tupelo   841-1245
Open 9 AM-5 PM Mon.-Sat.; 1-5 PM on Sun.
Admission to birthplace: $1, museum admission: $4

This house does not actually qualify as a historic home tour by most standards, but it's such a popular house, it must be included. Elvis fans know it well — this two-room shotgun house where the man who changed American music was born. Elvis' father desperately wanted a house for his pregnant wife, so he borrowed $180 and constructed the frame house just in time for the birth of Elvis and a twin, who died shortly thereafter. There's not much to see in the sparse little house, but true Elvis-ites say they "feel the magic." The nearby Elvis Presley Museum has a nice collection of Elvis memorabilia. The Elvis Presley Center and Museum feature the birthplace, a meditation chapel, a gift shop, picnic pavilions and a nearby lake and campground. East Main Street in Tupelo becomes Miss. 6; Elvis Presley Drive turns to the left from downtown. Follow the signs.

ROWAN OAK

Old Taylor Rd., Oxford   234-4651
Open 10 AM-12 noon and 2-4 PM Tues.-Sat.;
2 -4 PM Sun., free admission

This rambling old planter's home was built in the 1840s. William Faulkner bought it in 1930, and it became the home of his heart until his death in 1962. It was here that Faulkner wrote many of his novels, one of which, *The Fable*, is still inscribed on the walls in his study. *The Fable* won the Pulitzer Prize in 1956. Faulkner also won the 1949 Nobel Prize for Literature.

Rowan Oak is now owned and maintained by the University (of Mississippi/ Ole Miss) Museums. Not many changes

have been made, for even Faulkner's old Underwood typewriter rests on his desk as though it's waiting for Mr. Bill to come back and whip out a book or two.

MONTROSE

Salem Ave., Holly Springs   252-2943
Open by appointment only, admission: $5 adults

This 1858 Greek Revival mansion, complete with imposing and impressive towering columns (four across the front) now serves as headquarters for the Holly Springs Garden Club. Montrose is a popular tour home, and it's definitely worth a phone call to see the circular stairway, design elements, ornamentation and period antiques in every room. The landscaped grounds are graced with an arboretum that contains 37 native trees, each labeled with its common and botanical name.

Outdoor Attractions

NATCHEZ TRACE PARKWAY

Inquiries/Information: Rural Rt. 1, NT-143
Tupelo 38801   680-4025

The Natchez Trace Parkway cuts a 400-mile-plus slow-paced and scenic path diagonally across Mississippi and the tip of Alabama and meanders up into central Tennessee. In Mississippi, it begins near Natchez (southwest), and runs up to the uppermost (northeast) corner. On the Trace, as it's called by locals, drive slowly, for the speed limit is 50 mph, and it is strictly enforced by uniformed park rangers. You'll want to mosey along any-

Credit: The Sun Herald

The Lauren Rogers Museum in Laurel holds a fine arts book collection, 19th- and 20th-century American paintings, European and English art and furniture, porcelain, china, silver and other treasures.

way so as not to miss the glorious woodlands, fields, streams and seasonal wildflowers. Don't be surprised to see wild animals darting in and out of view. Deer are common along the Trace, and you may see a wild turkey or two. Getting back to nature is one reason the NTP attracts millions of visitors each year. It's a clean and green escape to earlier times.

The Natchez Trace Parkway appears untouched by time and civilization; there are no billboards, no traffic lights, no commercial vehicles, no litter from fast food chains and not much visible development. Actually, there's only one service station on the entire Parkway, at Jeff Busby Park (milepost 193.1). Plan to gas up there unless you want to venture off the Trace into a nearby town, which requires a slight detour.

Markers along the way tell the Trace's history — some historians say the path is about 8,000 years old — though we know it as a route for frontiersmen heading back to "Kaintuck" and settlers heading west. More than a few bandits roamed the Trace in the 1800s, while soldiers trav-

eled its terrain to fight wars and keep peace in the young United States.

Nature trails are abundant and well-marked. The Natchez Trace Parkway is administered and policed by the National Park Service, U.S. Department of the Interior. En route, stop by the NTP Visitors Center at Tupelo, where you have access to a film about the Trace's development, exhibits, history books and maps.

SUNSHINE FARMS
Rt. 1, Box 92 (Prairie Point Rd.)
Macon 39341   726-2264
Open 9 AM-5 PM Mon.-Sat., admission: $3.50 for everyone

This one's for the kids, for little people appreciate little horses, and there's an entire herd of miniature horses at Sunshine Farms. Children have an opportunity to ride the horses ($1 per child), to see a plethora of birds and a very unusual herd of fainting goats and to go on a hayride, weather permitting. This hands-on introduction to farm life is definitely off the beaten path, but kids consider it well worth the effort.

General Attractions

AMERICAN HERITAGE "BIG RED" FIRE MUSEUM

332 N. Church Ave.
Louisville   773-3421

This museum is private and by appointment only but well worth a phone call. Retired industrialist W. A. Taylor shares his impressive collection of antique fire engines. He has about 20, some of which are in the process of restoration. See an 1888 steam engine and other rare vehicles.

The Delta

Historic Attractions

FLOREWOOD RIVER PLANTATION

U.S. 82 W.
Greenwood   455-3821, 455-3822
Open Tues.-Sat. 9 AM-5 PM; Sun. 1-5 PM
(March -November); short tour Dec.-Feb.;
closed major holidays
Admission: $3.50 adults; $3 senior citizens and groups; $2.50 ages 5-18; younger than 5 no charge

Florewood is a living history re-creation of 1850s plantation life in the Mississippi Delta. It's well-researched and accurate, for Florewood is a state park. At the "big house," also known as the planter's mansion, guests are greeted by costumed docents who conduct tours of the furnished house. On the grounds, visitors view and visit the adjunct buildings, or those outbuildings necessary to plantation life: the school room, the blacksmith shop, the smokehouse, the overseer's house, the carriage house/tutor's home and even a sorghum (cane syrup) mill. A cotton museum and gift shop are at the entrance to the park property; both are open year round.

COTTON ROW

Downtown Greenwood   453-9197

More than one street makes up what is known as Cotton Row, which is now an area listed on the National Register of Historic Places. Front, Howard and Main streets are the location of the offices of cotton factors or those who grade, buy and sell the Delta cotton crops. To date, 24 of the original 57 cotton factors still operate on Cotton Row, which is one of only nine spot cotton markets in the United States. This is a nice stroll down the streets of history and a good look at the Yazoo River that flows near Cotton Row.

GREENVILLE FLOOD MUSEUM

915 Washington Ave.
Greenville   378-3141
Open Monday through Friday, 9 AM- 5 PM; free admission

This cottage museum recalls the catastrophic Mississippi River flood that nearly ruined the Delta back in 1927. It also represents the irrepressible spirit of Deltans, who've rebuilt more than once. Greenville's new Firehouse Museum is also a testament to the people and their survival ability.

OLD FIREHOUSE MUSEUM

230 Main St., Greenville   378-1616
Open weekdays 9 AM-4 PM, Sundays 1-5 PM;
free admission

It's only fitting that Greenville have a firehouse museum, since the town burned three times, once during the Civil War and twice since. Included in the exhibits are two old fire engines and a complete firehouse setting. Children love the fact that they can pretend to be firefighters by donning firefighter garb and climbing aboard the fire engines. Though this is a free museum, donations are accepted and appreciated.

General Attractions

STACKHOUSE/DELTA RECORD MART
232 Sunflower Ave.
Clarksdale   627-2209

This is the best place to go for blues news and music, for the owner, Jim O'Neal, is a blues expert. Expect to find LPs, CDs, 45s, 78s and books and memorabilia. They'll tell you about the Delta Blues Museum, another great stop in Clarksdale (see our Arts and Culture chapter for more information).

AMERICAN COSTUME MUSEUM
104 Ruby St., Ruleville 756-2344, 756-2171
Open by appointment
Admission: $5 adults; $3.50 senior citizens

Costume designer Luster Bayless, a Ruleville native, headed for Hollywood as a young man to seek his fortune in film. Since that time, his designs have appeared on the bodies of the biggest stars in the best films, and many costumes and accessories are now on display at the American Costume Museum. Also on exhibit is a costume collection that goes as far back as the silent film era. Bayless' goal has been to preserve these pieces of film history, for "once it's gone, it's gone," he said. See a beautiful dress worn by Scarlett in *Gone With the Wind* and original designs worn by Marilyn Monroe, Robert Redford, John Wayne, Humphrey Bogart, James Cagney and many more. The costumes are housed in an old but updated brick building, formerly a dry goods store built in 1905, smack in the heart of quaint downtown Ruleville. The store next door has access, but please call in advance. Maybe you can catch Luster there, for he's in and out, between Ruleville and Hollywood, where he has a company that makes costumes for film and TV.

MAMA'S DREAM WORLD
307 Central, Belzoni   247-1433
Open by appointment, $2 admission

The late Ethel Wright Mohamed recreated from memory her beloved Delta traditions and culture in what she called "memory pictures." See more than 100 examples of Mrs. Mohamed's creative stitchery displayed throughout her interesting home. You'll see why her work is on permanent exhibit in the Smithsonian and why the primitive work has earned her comparison with Grandma Moses.

THE CATFISH CAPITOL
111 Magnolia, St. Belzoni   247-4838
Open 9AM-5PM Monday-Friday, free admission

The Catfish Capitol wears many hats, for it serves as the official Catfish Visitors Center for the Delta's catfish industry, as well as a fine example of the way Mississippi artists depict the industry. See handcrafted displays that include paper, metals, wood carvings and ceramics. Outdoor exhibits include hatching tanks, seining nets and a miniature catfish pond. The project was completed in 1994, thanks to funding provided by the local Development Foundation, the City of Belzoni and the County of Humphreys. Located in an old railroad depot, the structure was designed by Mississippi architect John Robbins of Oxford, who also worked on renovations for the Statue of Liberty and the J. Paul Getty Museum.

Outdoor Attractions

WISTER GARDENS
Miss. 7 N., Belzoni   247-3025
Open 9 AM-5 PM daily, free admission

Whatever's blooming down South is what you'll find at the lush and lovely 14-acre Wister Gardens, for there are more than 120 varieties of trees and shrubs. Springtime is the most colorful time, with thousands of azaleas, dogwood, redbud and wisteria competing for attention. Winding paths lead through the manicured grounds and to the lake, where domestic and exotic fowl reside. Of particular interest are black swans and African geese. The gardens are a mile north of Belzoni (pronounced Bell-zon-uh).

CLAIBORNE VINEYARDS AND WINERY
U.S. 49, Indianola   887-2992, 887-2327

This small hybrid grape vineyard offers a tasting tour, free, but by appointment only. If you like the wine you sample, it is for sale. It's a family-owned winery, with local products on display. The location is a mile north of Highway 82 in Indianola.

The Heartland

Historic Attractions

JIM BUCK ROSS MISSISSIPPI AGRICULTURE AND FORESTRY/NATIONAL AGRICULTURAL AVIATION MUSEUM
1150 Lakeland Dr.
Jackson   354-6113, (800) 844-TOUR

Though it is listed in the Arts and Culture chapter, the Ag Museum is such a wonderful asset to the state, we don't mind including it twice. It shows a quaint Mississippi community dating from the 1920s. Not only is the Parkman farm a replica of earlier days, some of the farm buildings were actually moved to the present site from rural in Jeff Davis County. Other replicas open for touring include a general store, a church, and more. Also at the Ag Museum, the Heritage building houses other interesting exhibits depicting Mississippi's history, including little crop duster airplanes used in the business of agriculture. This is a tour appreciated by all ages, and it should be high on a must-see list.

MISSISSIPPI STATE HISTORICAL MUSEUM
100 S. State St., Jackson   359-6920

If you've read about this fine museum in our Arts and Culture chapter, perhaps you won't mind seeing more about it. It is something of which Mississippians are most proud. Called the Old Capitol Museum, it was built in the late 1830s and restored in 1961, and what a grand Greek Revival structure it is. It houses award-winning exhibits spanning the early days of the state's colorful history, through the Civil Rights movement and beyond. Plan to spend a while here, for there's much to see and do, and there's also a bookstore and gift shop. Admission is free.

THE GOVERNOR'S MANSION
300 E. Capitol St., Jackson   359-3175
Open 9:30-11 AM Tues.-Fri.; tours on the half-hour; may be closed to visitors during official state functions, free admission

The people of Mississippi are duly proud of the residence of their governor and its restoration project that represents a $2.5-plus million investment. The Greek Revival structure was built in 1842 and is now one of only two governors' residences to be designated a National Historic Landmark. Museum-quality antiques are displayed throughout the mansion, among them original pieces by Duncan Phyfe. The grand mansion's immaculately manicured lawn is a green and serene respite in the heart of the busy capital city.

THE MANSHIP HOUSE
420 E. Fortification St., Jackson   961-4724
Open 9 AM-4 PM Tues.-Fri.; 1-4 PM Sat.
Free admission

The Gothic Revival house built in 1857 and called a "cottage villa" will be forever known as the home of the Jackson mayor who surrendered the town to Union Army Gen. W. T. Sherman during the Civil War in 1863. Not that the mayor had much choice, since Sherman was wont to ride his fiery trail through the South, wreaking havoc in his wake. Mayor Manship's house-museum uses photos, diaries and letters to interpret family activities and events of the 1800s. The Manship House is administered by the Mississippi Department of Archives and History.

Outdoor Attractions

MYNELLE GARDENS
4736 Clinton Blvd., Jackson   960-1894
Open 9 AM-6 PM, March-Oct., 8 AM-4:15 PM
Nov.-Feb.; admission: $2 adults; 50¢ children younger than 12

Thanks to Mrs. Mynelle Westbrook Hayward, a nationally known aficionado of flower arranging and gardening, Jackson has a seven-acre botanical wonderland near downtown. Mrs. Hayward groomed and nurtured the private gardens for years before the city purchased the colorful showplace in 1973. The grounds feature azaleas, daylilies, camellias, perennials, annuals, naturalized bulbs and evergreens. Mynelle Gardens and the homes on the property are popular wedding sites.

MISSISSIPPI PETRIFIED FOREST
Just off U.S 49, Flora   879-8189
Open 9 AM-5 PM daily
Admission: $4 adults; $3 senior citizens and groups; $3 grades 1-12; preschoolers no charge

The only petrified forest east of the Mississippi, this one boasts giant trees said to be more than 36 million years old. The Mississippi Petrified Forest has been designated a National Natural Landmark, one of the few privately owned Landmarks in the United States. The ancient stone trees are guarded by living trees and bordered by rustic rail fences. A marked-trail guides visitors through the forest. A museum/gift shop is on the premises. From Flora, take U.S. 49 southwest for about 2 miles.

JACKSON ZOOLOGICAL PARK
2918 W. Capitol St.
Jackson   352-2585
Open Memorial Day to Labor Day, Mon.-Sun. 9 AM-6 PM; open the remainder of the year 9 AM-5 PM
Admission: $3.50 adults; $1.75 children 3-12

This old Jackson Zoo (founded in 1919) is the new Jackson Zoological Park, where visitors will be delighted with the animals, the activities and the re-created environments. Enter the rain forest and see chimps and monkeys cavorting around their own islands. Hippos are happy wallowing in their pool, while cheetahs run gracefully on the African Plains. Add elephants and rhinos, and it's Africa revisited. Kids adore the Discovery Zoo, and it's no wonder. There's a barnyard full of exhibits for them to experience, hands-on. More than 100 acres of varied terrain make up the popular Jackson Zoo.

CYPRESS SWAMP NATURE TRAIL
Mile Marker 122, Natchez Trace Pkwy.
North of Jackson near Madison   680-4025

This is perhaps the most intriguing part of the Natchez Trace Parkway and a good look at a true swamp scene. A well-marked trail winds through tall cypress trees and others that form a lush tree-canopy overhead. You'll learn about a cypress swamp, for there are 22 interpretative stops along the way, and as you cross the wooden bridge over the dark swampy waters, it is possible to catch sight of an alligator.

RAINWATER OBSERVATORY
French Camp Academy, Miss. 413
French Camp   547-6113, 547-6865
Open by appointment only, free admission

This is the largest public access observatory in the state. It features 13 telescopes, including five for daytime solar viewing. Since it is open by appointment only, there will be someone there to answer questions. It's located a mile east of the Natchez Trace Parkway.

MERIDIAN NATIONAL FISH HATCHERY AND AQUARIUM

U.S. Hwy. 11 S., Meridian   *483-1362*
Open daily 8 AM-3 PM, free admission

This attraction features spawning ponds used for stocking private and state lakes and an aquarium containing local sport fish plus a few exotic varieties.

Historic Attractions

MERREHOPE

905 Martin Luther King Dr.
Meridian   *483-8439*
Open year round 9 AM - 5 PM Mon.-Sat; 9 AM-4 PM mid-October-March
Admission: $3 adults, $1.50 children

Merrehope is the only antebellum home in Meridian. The original structure, a cottage home, built in 1858, served as headquarters for Confederate Gen. Leonidas Polk. Ten years later the owner added on to the cottage, using the Italianate style of architecture. A 1904 remodeling project was done in the neoclassical style. This stately restored home was spared from destruction by Union Gen. William T. Sherman. Today, visitors can enjoy touring its 20 rooms that feature some unusual woodwork, mantels and columns.

FRANK W. WILLIAMS HOME

905 Martin Luther King Dr.
Meridian   *483-8439*
Open Mon.-Sat. 9 AM-5 PM except Oct. 15-March 15 when the home closes at 4 PM
Admission: $3 adults, $1.50 children

Adjacent to Merrehope, this is the second major restoration project of The Meridian Restorations Foundation. The Queen Anne-style Victorian home was built in 1885 by Frank W. Williams, one of the founding board members of the U.S. Fidelity and Guaranty Insurance Co., as a wedding present for his bride. The structure was actually built on Eighth Street and was moved to its present location behind Merrehope. Many of the home's original features remain on display for visitors to view.

GRAND OPERA HOUSE OF MISSISSIPPI

2206 Fifth St.
Meridian   *693-LADY (5239)*
Open 11 AM-3 PM Tues.-Sat.; Sun. 2 -4 PM
Admission: $3 adults, $1 children

"The Lady," as this downtown landmark is known, was completed in 1890 and is now being restored to its original grandeur. Among the famous performers who appeared on stage were Helen Hayes, Sarah Bernhardt and Otis Skinner. The Victorian-style opera house was closed in 1927, and its sealed contents were not seen again until 1988. Visitors can enjoy a grand collection of memorabilia such as posters and more than 1,000 playbills, an intact stage, box seats and a backdrop. Tours are provided at the hours noted above.

HAMASA SHRINE TEMPLE THEATER

2320 Eighth St., Meridian   *693-1361*
Open 8:30 AM-4:30 PM Mon.-Fri., free admission

Completed in 1928, this Moorish/Revival-style theater began as a movie house and later featured Vaudeville acts. Its stage was one of the largest in the United States, second only to New York's Roxie Theater. The theater houses one of two existing Robert Morton pipe organs, whose sound equals that of a 100-piece orchestra. Today, the Temple is used for live stage shows, plays and concerts. Tours are available upon request during the hours noted above.

HIGHLAND PARK DENTZEL CAROUSEL

39th Ave., Meridian   495-1801
Open Sat.-Sun. 1-6 PM June-Aug., 1-5 PM Sat.-
Sun. Sept.-May; rides: 25¢ per person

Highland Park is home to the world's only two-row stationary Dentzel menagerie. The carousel, made between 1892 and 1899 in Philadelphia by Gustav Dentzel, is a National Historic Landmark. Look for the original museum-quality oil paintings decorating the carousel's crown. From I-20/59, follow the signs to the Jimmie Rodgers Museum.

ROSE HILL CEMETERY

40th Ave., Meridian   483-4225
Open 24 hours daily, free admission

The two founders of Meridian and the king and queen of the gypsies are all buried in this historic cemetery that's opened all year. See the monuments of city fathers John Ball, Lewis Ragsdale and Emil and Kelly Mitchell, Gypsy King and Queen. Gypsies still pay their respects to the royal couple, leaving fruit and juices as gifts. From I-59/20, take the 22nd Avenue Exit to downtown.

CAUSEYVILLE GENERAL STORE

Causeyville Rd., Meridian   644-3102
Open 7 AM-7 PM Mon.-Sat.; Sun. 1-5 PM, free
admission

Approximately seven miles from Meridian, this 1895 general store and gristmill still produces and sells stone-ground meal. Original fixtures and counters are still there, as is a musical museum with the local Grand Opera House's 1920s nickelodeon. Gristmill public demonstrations are held on Saturdays only. Take Miss. 19 south, turn right at Causeyville and go 5 more miles.

LANDRUM'S HOMESTEAD AND VILLAGE

1356 Miss. 15 S., Laurel   649-2546
Open 9 AM-5 PM Mon.-Sat.
Admission $2 adults, $1 for children

This new attraction features a furnished cabin, a waterwheel turning a gristmill, a blacksmith shop, a barn complete with animals, a smokehouse and a chapel, all depicting life in the late 1800s and early 1900s. The setting is a landscaped area behind Landrum's Country, a handmade furniture store located 4.5 miles south of Laurel. This is a popular field trip destination, so large groups should call ahead.

General Attractions

PEAVEY VISITORS CENTER

Marion Russell Rd., Meridian   484-2460
Open Mon.-Fri. 10 AM-4 PM, Sun. 1-4 PM
Free admission

The name Peavey is a familiar one in the music industry and it all started in Meridian. Founder Hartley Peavey started a museum at the Northeast Industrial Park that traces the history of the Peavey Electronics Corp. through guitars, amps and keyboards among its displays. It's situated on more than 40 acres that once was the site of the Department of Agriculture's Experiment Station.

INTERNATIONAL CHECKER HALL OF FAME

220 Lynn Ray Rd., Petal   582-7090
Open weekdays by appointment only; $3 for
adults, $1 for students

Checkers fans will love this celebration of the game at a place that's been featured in Ripley's Believe It or Not. Visitors will marvel at what are billed as the two largest

Insiders' Tips

After a great meal at Weidmann's famous restaurant, take a relaxing walking tour of downtown Meridian.

checker boards in the world. There's also a museum, the world's largest checker library and checkers memorabilia, from the historic to the artistic variety. It's best to call a couple of days before you visit to make arrangements for a tour.

The River Cities

Historic Attractions

History lovers will find plenty to hold their attention in Vicksburg, Natchez and Port Gibson. The remnants of the Civil War and the opulent lifestyle of the antebellum South are the common ingredients of the most popular attractions and events. Good ol' Southern hospitality is also a drawing card, most evident during the Pilgrimages but definitely apparent at other times and places.

VICKSBURG NATIONAL MILITARY PARK AND CEMETERY

3201 Clay St., Vicksburg   636-0583
Open daily from 8 AM-5 PM, USS Cairo Museum open daily from 8:30 AM-5 PM Nov.-March, 9:30 AM-6 PM April-Oct.
Admission: $4 per car or $2 per person in van or bus; for a guide in your car it's $20 a car, $30 a van and $40 a bus; cassette tape rental is $4.50

This 1,858-acre park is called the best-preserved Civil War battlefield in the nation. Visitors travel 16 miles and more than 100 years back in history to the Civil War campaign.

Start out in the visitors center to view the 18-minute film *Vanishing Glory*, life-size exhibits and artifacts telling the story of the Siege of Vicksburg. Then drive through the park's rolling hills, past markers and monuments recounting the military campaign. The driving tour goes through the Vicksburg National Cemetery where nearly 17,000 Union soldiers are buried. Also in the north section of the park are the remains of the Union gunboat USS *Cairo* and its adjacent museum. No credit cards are accepted here.

THE MARTHA VICK HOUSE

1300 Grove St., Vicksburg   638-7036
Open Mon.-Sat., 9 AM-5 PM; Sun. 2-5 PM
Admission: $5 adults

This "mini-mansion," built around 1830, has been authentically restored and furnished with antiques from the 18th and early 19th centuries. There are French impressionist paintings throughout the house, which was built for a daughter of the founder of Vicksburg. A tour takes 30 minutes.

THE DUFF GREEN MANSION

1114 First East St.
Vicksburg   636-6968, (800) 992-0037
Open daily 2-6 PM
Admission $5 adults; children 6-12 $3

A former hospital for Confederate and Union soldiers, this three-story mansion, built c. 1856, offers 30-minute tours daily. Visitors will see what is considered to be one of the finest examples of Paladian architecture in the state. The mansion was built by Duff Green, a wealthy merchant, for his bride, Mary Lake, whose parents donated the property as a wedding gift. In a cave near the mansion, she gave birth to a son during the siege of the city and named him, appropriately, Siege Green. Before the war, the 12,000-square-foot home was the site of many lavish parties. Now it offers bed and breakfast accommodations.

ANCHUCA
1010 First East St.
Vicksburg   631-6800, (800) 469-2597
Open daily 9 AM-5 PM; admission $5 adults, $3 children 6-12

Take a 25-minute tour through this grand mansion filled with magnificent period antiques and gas-burning chandeliers. Built in 1830, Anchuca was one of the city's first mansion-type homes. Additions were made from 1840 to 1845. After his release from serving 2.5 years in prison, Confederate President Jefferson Davis went to Anchuca to visit his oldest brother Joe, who was living in the mansion, and made a speech from Anchuca's balcony. In addition to the two-story main house, Anchuca visitors can see the original slave quarters, also built in 1830, and the turn-of-the-century guest house.

THE CORNERS MANSION
601 Klein St.
Vicksburg   636-7421, (800) 444-7421
Open daily 10 AM-5 PM; admission $5 adults, $2 children younger than 12

This mansion, built in 1872, combines Greek Revival and Victorian architecture. Features include the original parterre gardens, a 68-foot gallery with river and valley views and period antiques. Tours last 30 minutes.

McRAVEN
1445 Harrison St.
Vicksburg   636-1663
Open Mon.-Sat. 9 AM-5 PM, Sun. 10 AM-5 PM, the house is closed Dec.-Feb.; admission: $5 adults, $3 children 12-18, $2.50 children 6-11

No less an authority than *National Geographic* described this home as the South's time capsule. Spend an hour and a half touring this home that was built from 1836 to the 1850s in Frontier, Empire and Greek Revival styles. Watch for the damage done by wartime cannons, and enjoy the antiques and three-acre garden.

CEDAR GROVE MANSION INN
2300 Washington St.
Vicksburg   636-1000, (800) 862-1300
Open 9 AM-4 PM; admission $5 adults, $3 children

This 1840 Greek Revival mansion is furnished with original antiques, gas chandeliers and gold-leaf mirrors. A reminder that it survived the Battle of Vicksburg is a Union cannonball lodged in the wall of the parlor. Tours are conducted daily.

ANNABELLE
501 Speed St.
Vicksburg   638-2000, (800) 791-2000
Open daily 10 AM-4 PM; admission: $5 adults, $2 children younger than 12

This two-story Victorian-Italianate home is in Vicksburg's historic Garden District. It was built c. 1868 by John Klein, who also built Cedar Grove for himself and five other homes for his children in the same square block that was part of the Cedar Grove estate. Annabelle is furnished in period antiques, has 12-foot ceilings and a patio reminiscent of those found in the French Quarter of New Orleans.

BELLE OF THE BENDS
508 Klein St., Vicksburg   634-0737
Open daily 10 AM-5 PM; admission: $5 adults, $2.50 children younger than 12

Italianate architecture and the area's only oval-arched woodwork are the distinctions of this 1876 lovely home. There's also a great river view. Tours last approximately 30 minutes.

TOMIL MANOR

2430 Drummond St.
Vicksburg   638-8893
Open daily 9 AM-5 PM; admission: $4.30 adults,
$2.15 children younger than 12

The entire manor is open to visitors, who take an hour tour of this home, built in the early 1900s. Tomil, named for its current owners, Tom and Mildred Kirkland, is a Spanish-style, two-story structure furnished with antiques. Inside, the beautiful oak, cypress and pine woodwork, 32 stained-glass windows and a spectacular staircase are some of the outstanding features of this home, which was completed in 1910. Every room except the butler's pantry has a fireplace, but only three stacks are seen on the roof. It is believed that the manor's New Orleans architect was a student of Frank Lloyd Wright.

GREY OAKS

4142 Rifle Range Rd., Vicksburg   638-4424
Open Mon.-Sat. 12-5 PM; admission: $5 adults

"Vicksburg's Tara" was built in 1834 and reconstructed on its present six-acre site in 1940. That's when the front facade of Grey Oaks was redone to resemble the *Gone With The Wind* mansion. Landscaped gardens and a nature trail are on the grounds. A tour takes 30 minutes.

BALFOUR HOUSE

Crawford St.
Vicksburg   638-7113, (800) 294-7113
Open Mon.-Sat. 9 AM-4:30 PM, Sun. 1-5 PM
Admission: $5 adults

Built in 1835, Balfour House hosted many prominent military figures during the Civil War and eventually became the headquarters for Union soldiers after the city's fall. Some key features of the Greek Revival house is its elliptical staircase that spirals for three floors. It's named for owner Emma Harrison Balfour, a diarist who recorded events during the city's war years.

STANTON HALL

401 High at Pearl St.
Natchez   442-6282

The Pilgrimage Garden Club restored this 1857 antebellum home that can best be described as palatial, but the words princely and magnificent have also been used. Stanton Hall is one of the largest Greek Revival houses in the South and certainly is one of the most visited (it's featured on our cover). The house, built between 1857 and 1958 by cotton broker Frederick Stanton, has a 72-foot central hallway with high-ceilinged rooms off each side. Elaborately carved and elegant wood moldings and cornices are seen throughout, along with other architectural details that must be seen to be believed.

There's another story to Stanton Hall aside from its impressive Greek Revival facade, crystal chandeliers, white Carrara marble, Victorian parlor sets and Rococo Revival side chairs. Stanton Hall is also the headquarters for the Pilgrimage Garden Club. The club bought the home in 1938 and commenced to furnish it in period style and fashion. Since that time, the

---

The Nanih Waiya Historical Site, near the small town of Noxapater, is believed to be the first home of the Choctaw Indians. At the center of the site is a ceremonial mound referred to by the Choctaw as "mother." Nearby, about 18,000 members of the tribe are buried in another mound. For additional information call 773-7988.

Insiders' Tips

Historic Home is Mississippi's Newest Welcome Center

Columbus is pleased to have a new Mississippi Welcome Center from which to greet guests to this River City and the northeastern part of the state. The Welcome Center is actually a very old home with a new lease on life. It began in 1878 or so as the Victorian-style rectory for St. Paul's Episcopal Church. After more than 100 years of service as the rector's residence and later the parish office, it has a slightly new location, for it was moved about a block, and has a new life as the official information center for the region.

The yellow and gray Victorian structure, now on Main Street, has more historical significance than its age and occupation, for it was also the first home of one of America's most prolific playwrights. Perhaps it's only fitting that the first home of the man who wrote the line, "I've always depended on the kindness of strangers" is now a welcome center. The line was spoken by the character Blanche DuBois, played by both Jessica Tandy and Vivian Leigh, in the Pulitzer Prize-winning play, *A Streetcar Named Desire*. The playwright was Tennessee Williams, who also won a Pulitzer for *Cat on a Hot Tin Roof* and critical acclaim for *The Glass Menagerie*, among others. Tennessee's grandfather was the rector of St. Paul's at the time of the playwright's birth. The young Williams family lived with Mrs. Williams' parents, the Rev. and Mrs. Walter Dakin. The Mississippi Welcome Center-Columbus has a Tennessee Williams Memorabilia Room, as well as brochures and information about the region's attractions. For additional information, contact the Chamber of Commerce, 328-4491, or the Convention & Visitors Bureau, 329-1191, in Columbus.

Credit: Sylvia Higginbotham

Tennessee Williams' first home is Mississippi's newest welcome center.

house has become one of the South's most recognizable tour houses and a major revenue producer for the Garden Club.

As well as Pilgrimage tours in the spring and fall, the house is open for tours each day. Tours are conducted daily from 9 AM to 4:30 PM and last about 30 minutes. Cost is $5 for adults and $2.50 for students. A gift shop and the Carriage House Restaurant, which is internationally known for its delicious Southern specialties and tiny tasty biscuits, is also on the grounds.

LONGWOOD

Lower Woodville Rd.
Natchez   *442-5193*

Longwood is called the largest octagonal house in the country, and its Oriental style gives the structure a distinctive look. Tours of the finished basement, the first floor with the original furnishings and the well-kept grounds are conducted daily from 9 AM to 4:30 PM and take approximately 25 minutes. Cost of the tour is $5 for adults and $2.50 for children. Longwood is off U.S. 84.

THE HOUSE ON ELLICOTT HILL

200 N. Canal St.
Natchez   *442-2011*

The Natchez Garden Club restored this 1798 home of Andrew Ellicott on the hilltop where in 1797 he raised an American flag in an act of defiance against the Spanish. The spot also overlooks the terminus of the Natchez Trace. Tours are given daily every 30 minutes from 9 AM to 5 PM. Cost is $5.

MAGNOLIA HALL

215 S. Pearl St.
Natchez   *442-6672*

Greek Revival architecture is practically defined by Magnolia Hall, one of the last mansions built in 1858 just before the start of the Civil War. In 1862 the house sustained damage by a Union gunboat. Tours are conducted daily from 9 AM to 5 PM and are conducted every 30 minutes. Visitors see six rooms upstairs and six downstairs. Seventy-five percent of the furnishings are original family pieces. There's also a costume museum housed in there. Cost to tour is $5 for adults and $2.50 for children.

GRAND VILLAGE OF THE NATCHEZ INDIANS

400 Jefferson Davis Blvd.
Natchez   *446-6502*
Open Mon.-Sat. 9 AM-5 PM, Sun. 1:30-5 PM
Free admission

Visitors can learn about the Natchez Indian tribe and earlier occupants of this site through reconstructed ceremonial mounds and a dwelling. There is also a museum with a gift shop, nature trails and an area for picnicking.

NATCHEZ TRACE PARKWAY

         842-1572

Starting 5 miles north of Natchez, this scenic highway goes on to Nashville with historic sites and inviting picnic grounds along the way. See the write up under The Hill Country section of this chapter.

Coca-Cola aficionados will be thrilled with the displays of memorabilia in the Coca-Cola Museum in Vicksburg, where the popular soft drink was first bottled.

Insiders' Tips

HISTORIC JEFFERSON COLLEGE

U.S. 61, Washington   *442-2901*
Grounds open daily sunup to sundown, exhibition buildings open daily 9 AM-5 PM, Sun. 1-5 PM; free admission to all buildings

Six miles east of Natchez and named in honor of Thomas Jefferson, the college was incorporated in 1802, making it the first educational institution in the Mississippi Territory. Besides the school's 19th-century buildings, there's a museum with gift shop. This is also the site of the Copper Magnolia Festival and Ghost Tales Around the Campfire, among other annual events. The grounds include two nature trails and picnic areas.

NATCHEZ NATIONAL HISTORICAL PARK

504 S. Canal St., Natchez   *442-7047*
Melrose open daily except Christmas Day; admission: $4 adults, $2 children 6-17

The park contains two historic properties, but lots of plans are in the works for this attraction. Melrose is a Greek Revival mansion completed in 1845. It contains original furnishing and original outbuildings that are open for tours. Nearby, the William Johnson House (1841) is being carefully restored and will eventually open as a museum that will contain artifacts and displays depicting black history in the Natchez area. William Johnson was an African-American barber and former slave in Natchez. His diary details his life as a freed slave. Johnson's 2.5-story brick townhouse is now open only on weekends for tours. Also planned is the acquisition of the site of historic Fort Rosalie, established by the French in 1716.

GRAND GULF MILITARY MONUMENT

Rt. 2, Box 389, Port Gibson   *437-5911*
Open Mon.-Sat. 8 AM-noon and 1-5 PM, Sun. 10 AM-6 PM; admission: $1.50 adults, 75¢ children

Grand Gulf Military Park is dedicated to the former town of Grand Gulf and to the Civil War battle that took place there. The park is 8 miles northwest of Port Gibson, off U.S. 61 and consists of approximately 400 acres that incorporate Fort Cobun, Fort Wade, a cemetery, a museum, campgrounds, picnic sites, hiking trails, an observation tower and a number of restored buildings. The museum contains Civil War memorabilia plus antique machinery and an assortment of horse-drawn vehicles.

OLD COUNTRY STORE

U.S. 61, Lorman   *437-3661*
Open weekdays 8 AM-6 PM; Sun. and holidays noon-6 PM; free admission

This authentic general store has been in operation since 1875 and is one of Mississippi's oldest businesses. The ceilings are 14 feet high, the fixtures are original, and the cheese cutter is about 70 years old and still working. The museum contains relics from the steamboat days. The owners, the E.T. Breithaupt family, close for Easter and Christmas. The store is easy to reach from U.S. 61 and the Natchez Trace via Miss. 552.

Insiders' Tips

Take advantage of the interesting nature and history programs offered by park rangers at the Gulf Islands National Seashore Visitors Center in Ocean Springs.

RUINS OF WINDSOR

Miss. 552, Port Gibson
Free Admission

All that remains today of a gracious mansion 10 miles southwest of Port Gibson is 23 columns. The mansion, completed in 1861, was a Confederate observation post. After the Battle of Port Gibson, it was turned into a hospital to treat Union soldiers. The grounds are generally open year round during daylight hours. If the gate is locked, you can walk the 150 yards from the road to the ruins, but keep an eye out for hunters during deer hunting season (late November through late January). There have been a few isolated instances of illegal hunting near the ruins, and illegal hunters aren't mindful of tourists.

OAK SQUARE

1207 Church St.
Port Gibson   437-4350, (800) 729-0240
Open 9 AM-5 PM Mon.-Sat.; Sun. 1-5 PM
Admission: $5

This fully restored 30-room Greek Revival mansion was built in 1850. Features include nine-foot doors, 12-foot ceilings and a carriage house. Civil War memorabilia is on display

General Attractions

U.S. ARMY CORPS OF ENGINEERS WATERWAYS EXPERIMENT STATION

3909 Halls Ferry Rd.
Vicksburg   634-2502
Guided tours 10 AM-2 PM Mon.-Fri., self-guided tours 7:45 AM-4:15 Mon.-Fri., only stops 1-3 PM open weekends, free admission
Admission free

This is the Army Corps of Engineers' largest research and development facility. On view at the 685-acre facility are scale working models of many of the country's rivers, dams, harbors and tidal waterways. A half-mile nature trail and picnic area are available to visitors.

NATCHEZ UNDER-THE-HILL

Silver St., Natchez
Casino: open 24 hours; shops: 10 AM-5 PM daily, except Sun.; restaurants and bars: midday until closing

Gamblers, highwaymen, river pirates and other such characters brought this landing to life in the early 18th century. It's where the ancient Natchez Trace began and where the first town named Natchez was established in 1716. In the mid-1800s Under The Hill was one of the busiest cotton markets in the world. Nature, plus the end of the steamboating era, brought a decline in the landing. The end came when ferry operations ceased in 1940. But in the last few years Under The Hill has seen a rebirth, thanks to new shops, bars, restaurants and, appropriately enough, a riverboat casino.

OLD SOUTH WINERY

65 S. Concord Ave., Natchez   445-9924
Open 10 AM-6 PM daily, free admission

Muscadine vines have a place in Mississippi history, and the Galbreath family's winery carries on the tradition of wine making. The winery produces table wines with modern techniques and offers tours and tastings daily. There is a $4 per person charge for groups to cover tastings and cheese.

GRAND GULF NUCLEAR STATION

Waterloo Rd., Port Gibson   437-6317
Open Mon.-Fri. 8 AM-4:30 PM
Free admission

Grand Gulf Nuclear Station is the largest boiling water reactor plant in the United States. The visitors center, "Energy Central," features colorful, informa-

The Mississippi Governor's Mansion in Jackson, opened in January 1842 to serve as home to Governor Titghman M. Tucker. Money Magazine *estimates its current value at more thanr $16 million making it the most expensive governor's mansion in the nation.*

tive exhibits. Grand Gulf is west of Port Gibson, off U.S. 61. You can't miss its 520-foot tower.

The Coast

The Mississippi Gulf Coast region, with its mild climate, has been attracting visitors for a century or more when city dwellers in New Orleans and Mobile would pack up and head to the breezy, uncrowded escape the coastal area provided.

The weather is still a drawing card, but now there are many other attractions that bring in visitors from neighboring states and the frozen north.

The centerpiece is the sand beach and the Gulf of Mexico, with a multitude of recreational possibilities. All three coastal counties have white sand beaches, but the granddaddy of them all is Harrison County's 26 continuous miles of beach that run west from Henderson Point to Biloxi along busy U.S. 90. Besides being scenic, with huge live oaks and magnolias growing along the highway, it is the longest man-made beach in the world. And it's all open to the public for sunbathing, strolling, bird watching or whatever. Here's a look at some of the Coast's other popular attractions.

Historic Attractions

GRASS LAWN

720 East Beach, Gulfport   864-5019
Open 10 AM-4 PM Mon., Wed., Fri.
Admission: $2

Built in 1836 as a summer home for a wealthy Port Gibson surgeon, Grass Lawn once sat on 235-beachfront acres surrounded by orchards and gardens. The City of Gulfport bought it from its last owners and opened it to visitors in 1973, a year after the house was placed on the National Register of Historic Places. Constructed of handhewn pine and cypress, the house features 10-foot-wide galleries that are supported by a series of two-story columns, three 20-by-20-foot rooms on each floor and marble mantels. The furniture dates back to the first half of the 19th century.

ANCIENT BURIAL GROUNDS

110 Porter Ave., Biloxi   *435-9615*
Open 10 AM-5 PM Mon.-Fri.; Sat. 10 AM-2 PM
Free admission

While repairs were being made to Moran's Art Studio after Hurricane Camille in 1969, workers discovered this burial site, which contains ancient remains. The skeletons can be viewed from a glass-enclosed deck.

BEAUVOIR

2244 Beach Blvd., Biloxi   *388-1313*
Open daily except Christmas 9 AM-5 PM
Admission: $5 adults; $2.50 ages 6 to 15

The restored last home of the only President of the Confederacy, Beauvoir was the seaside estate of Jefferson Davis. A National Historic Landmark, Beauvoir was built in the mid-1800s, and its 74-acre landscaped grounds and handsome buildings are open to visitors. In addition to the furnished presidential residence, there is a Confederate museum and cemetery where the Tomb of the Unknown Confederate Soldier is located. The beautiful grounds contain large oaks, magnolias, pines, gardens and a lagoon.

OLD BRICK HOUSE

622 Bayview Ave.
Biloxi   *432-5836, 432-5498*
Open by appointment only; donations accepted

Biloxi's oldest documented house was constructed facing Back Bay in the late 1700s. The two-story structure was built with the last bricks made at the brickyard that previously occupied the site. Owners have included two Biloxi mayors, and today the city owns the building, which provides a home-spun look at the Coast's past. Each spring, locals and visitors gather on the lawn for free twilight-time concerts featuring jazz, classical and popular music. Local historians give personalized tours of the house year round by appointment only.

TULLIS-TOLEDANO MANSION

360 E. Beach Blvd., Biloxi   *435-6293*
Open 10 AM-5 PM Mon.-Fri.
Admission: $1.50 adults, $1 senior citizens, 50¢ children 6-16

This antebellum home, built in 1856, features Greek revival architecture with French influences. Look for the two outdoor staircases and twin galleries. The 2.5-acre site contains the Councilor Oak, well more than 600 years old, that is so named because meetings with Indians and Europeans took place in the shade of its massive branches. The manor, owned by the City of Biloxi, is open for public tours starting at 10 AM; the last tour starts at 4:30 PM. Tours take 25-30 minutes.

Outdoor Attractions

THE FRIENDSHIP OAK

U.S. 90, Long Beach   *865-4500*
Open year round, free admission

The Friendship Oak dominates the tranquil beachfront campus of the University of Southern Mississippi-Gulf Coast. This majestic live oak is more than 500 years old and 50 feet high, and its foliage spreads out for more than 150 feet. The oak is so named because, according to legend, those who enter its shadow will remain friends forever. It's a picture-perfect location any time. Souvenirs are available.

Astronaut Fred Haise, a member of the ill-fated Apolllo 13 lunar mission is a native Biloxian who has a street named in his honor in his home town.

BILOXI LIGHTHOUSE

Porter Ave. and U.S. 90, Biloxi   435-6293
Open by appointment only
Admission free; donations accepted

This cast-iron landmark, situated on the median of a busy highway, is a favorite subject for photographers. The lighthouse, built in 1848, stands 65-feet tall and is duly decorated for the winter holidays.

MISSISSIPPI SANDHILL CRANE NATIONAL WILDLIFE REFUGE

I-10 Exit 61, Gautier   497-6322
Open 8 AM-4 PM Mon.-Fri., free admission

Hikers, bird watchers and nature photographers will find lots to hold their attention at this refuge, which is home to approximately 150 sandhill cranes. Twenty of the refuge's 20,000 acres are open to the public. The visitors center contains informative displays and a videotaped slide show about the endangered species. Your best chance of seeing the Sandhill cranes is during January and February when visitors can tag along on feeding tours that leave the visitors center in the morning and afternoon. Call for times. A three-quarter-mile hiking trail winds through two types of terrain along a bayou and past a savanna with different types of birds and wildlife.

CROOKED FEATHER

Davidson Park, U.S. 90
Ocean Springs   875-4424

Visitors approaching Ocean Springs from the west will see this 30-foot-tall cypress structure on their right as they approach downtown. The American Indian figure was carved and donated to the state by Hungarian artist Peter Toth as a gift to commemorate the U.S. Bicentennial in 1976. It took Toth four months to carve the figure from a 2,000-year-old cypress log. The 10-foot feather was carved from a separate log.

General Attractions

JOHN C. STENNIS SPACE CENTER

Miss. 607, near Bay St. Louis   688-2370
Open 9 AM-5 PM daily except Thanksgiving, Christmas and Easter; free admission

Near Bay St. Louis, this 13,500-acre rocket testing facility, one of only nine NASA centers, was constructed back in the days of the race to the moon to "hot fire" rocket stages. Now the center puts the Space Shuttle's main engines through their paces by holding them in concrete test stands and igniting them. Visitors can view this spectacular (and noisy) display from a special area. Stennis is home to more than a dozen other federal agencies. Guided tours and presentations are available throughout the day. Space artifacts and high-tech exhibits are displayed in a museum. There is a snack bar, souvenir shop, picnic area and Teacher Resource Center. The center is easily accessible from I-10 and I-59.

MARINE LIFE OCEANARIUM

U.S. 90, Gulfport   863-0651
Open daily 9 AM-sunset in summer months; 10 AM-3 PM in winter months
Admission: $9.25 adults, $5.95 children 3-11

This family attraction has entertained grown-ups and children since 1956 with its performing Atlantic bottle-nosed dolphins, California sea lions and South American macaws. Visitors peer into windows of the giant reef tanks and watch divers swim with a collection of Gulf sea life, including sharks, sting rays and loggerhead sea turtles. The Touch Pool encourages hands-on introductions to starfish, horseshoe crabs, sand dollars and other inhabitants of the nearby waters.

Rides on the S.S. *Gravity Ship* demonstrate the effects of gravity. The Harbor Tour Train offers a 15-minute narrated trip through the adjacent Port of Gulfport and Small Craft Harbor.

KEESLER AIR FORCE BASE

White Ave., Biloxi   377-3901
Open weekdays 8 AM-4 PM, free admission

Keesler is the home of the 81st Training Wing and is the Air Force's electronics, computer and weather training center. It's one of the largest technical training centers in the Air Force and has a population of 26,000. Keesler also houses the hurricane hunters who track storms for the National Hurricane Center in Miami. The 3,600-acre center marked its 50th anniversary in 1991; at the time, more than 1,780,000 students had graduated from its high-tech training courses. Self-driving tours are available to the public each weekday. Check in at the visitors center at the main gate for instructions.

MARDI GRAS MUSEUM

119 Rue Magnolia, Biloxi   432-8806
Open Mon.-Fri. 10 AM-4 PM
Admission: $1 adults; 50¢ younger than 12

If you're not in town during the Carnival season (and even if you are) you can get a taste of the season by looking at the elaborate costumes and trinkets that dress up the coast krewes and "royalty" for Mardi Gras. The museum is in the Magnolia Hotel, which is the last hotel left on the Coast from the pre-Civil War days.

MISSISSIPPI COAST COLISEUM AND CONVENTION CENTER

2350 Beach Blvd., Biloxi   388-8010

This 100,000-square-foot Coast landmark is the Southeast's largest beachfront complex overlooking the Gulf of Mexico. A favorite facility for conventions and meetings, the Coliseum is also the site of some of the Coast's best entertainment in the form of concerts by top national performers and special events such as the annual Coast Fair & Expo, Coast Blues Festival, Scottish Highlands and Islands Games and Chefs of the Coast.

BILOXI VISITORS CENTER

710 East Beach, Biloxi   374-3105
Open weekdays 8 AM-5 PM; summer weekends 9 AM-5 PM Sat., noon-5 PM Sun.; winter weekends 9 AM-4 PM Sat., noon-4 PM Sun. Free admission

The city's visitors center is in historic Brielmaier House, which is listed on the National Register of Historic Places. The three-room residence, built c. 1895, is distinguished by its Victorian details. The gallery is accented by lattice work and inside are three hand-carved mantels. The city-owned structure was moved to its present site on the Town Green at Main Street and the highway in 1986. Visitors can enjoy the home's features, collect information

Gold in the Hills, an annual melodrama held each spring in Vicksburg, is said to be the world's longest continually running melodrama. It's presented on weekends from mid-March through early April by the Vicksburg Theater Guild.

Insiders' Tips

about coastal attractions and set out on a self-guided walking tour of Biloxi's historic district.

J.L. SCOTT MARINE EDUCATION CENTER & AQUARIUM

115 Beach Blvd., Biloxi   374-5550
Open daily except Sun. 9 AM-4 PM
Admission: $3 adults; $2 senior citizens; $1.50 children 3-17

This is home to Mississippi's largest public aquarium, the 42,000-gallon Gulf of Mexico tank in which sharks, sea turtles, eels and other large inhabitants are on display. The Aquarium Room also houses 40 smaller aquariums containing native creatures found in large and small bodies of water. You'll see snakes, turtles and alligators, a seashell collection, a partial whale skeleton, videos in the auditorium and art exhibits. Watch staff researchers at work in the research center's laboratories, and try your hand at the Touch Tank and Discovery Island exhibits. The gift shop sells educational material and standard souvenirs. The center is at the western end of the Biloxi Bay Bridge.

SHEARWATER POTTERY

102 Shearwater Dr., Ocean Springs 875-7320
Showroom open 9 AM-5:30 PM Mon.-Sat.; Sun. 1-5:30 PM; workshop open 9 AM-noon and 1-4 PM Mon.-Fri.; free admission

Potter James Anderson carries on his family's artistic tradition at the pottery established in 1928 by his father, Peter Anderson. Works by brothers Peter, Walter and James Anderson are displayed at this family compound situated on 28 wooded acres. Visitors are welcomed in the showroom, where artwork is displayed and sold, and in the workshop, where the pieces are made.

GULF ISLANDS NATIONAL SEASHORE

3500 Park Rd., Ocean Springs   875-9057
Seasonal hours of operation, generally 8 AM-5 PM
Free admission

The visitors center here is where you can view short films about the barrier islands and their historic forts, enjoy displays of art and nature and take in interesting programs on weekends at the nearby campgrounds. Ask about special tours conducted by park rangers.

GULF COAST WINERY

1306 29th Ave., Gulfport   863-0790
Open 10 AM-6PM daily; free admission

The Coast's only winery offers free tours at its location in the historic downtown district, just off the beach. Along with the tour, the winery offers free tastings of the dozen or so wines made here. Wine-related gift items are also sold.

CROSBY ARBORETUM

1986 Ridge Rd., Picayune   799-2311
Open 10 AM-5 PM Wed.-Sun.
Admission is $2 adults, $1 for children 12 and under, $5 per family

Take a nature walk through the pines and magnolias at this 67-acre native plant study center, and enjoy educational programs in the Pinecote Pavilion, designed by noted Arkansas architect Fay Jones. The facility, just north of the Coast, has a total of 1,000 acres dedicated to ecological restorations. Take Exit 4 off I-59 and look for the signs.

PALESTINE GARDENS

201 Palestine Gardens Rd.
Lucedale   947-8422
Open 8 AM-6 PM Mon.-Sat., 1-6 PM Sun.
Admission: $2 adults, $1 children.

Take an hour to enjoy a quarter-mile walking tour through this replica of the Holy Land, including such features as the Sea of Galilee, the Mediterranean and Dead seas and 22 cities and villages. There's also a life-size replica of Calvary and the Garden Tomb. The facility is available for self-contained RV hook-ups with reservations. A sheltered picnic area and cold drinks are available. Lucedale is just north of the Coast.

Inside
Gaming

After a frantic race to get dockside casinos up and running along the Mississippi River and the Coast, the booming new industry is settling down. Already, stiff competition has forced a few casinos to file for bankruptcy and close; others have adjusted their operations with an eye on the bottom line and the competition.

Still, gambling continues to make a tremendous impact on the state's economy in terms of revenue generated and jobs created. *U.S. News & World Report* noted in late 1993 that gambling had become a $500 million industry and that unemployment in the state has been cut from nearly 11 percent to 5.4 percent. Spin-off benefits are evident at local air-

ports, where charter flights bring in gamblers from other states. New hotels adjacent to some casinos will soon be a permanent part of the landscape. Local governments are spending gaming revenues on new equipment and infrastructure improvements. Casinos provide major support to local charitable organizations.

On the downside, communities are seeing a proliferation of pawn shops, increased crime statistics in some areas and the formation of support groups for those addicted to gambling. Traffic problems are now a full-blown nightmare in some casino-congested areas, however, some roads have been ex-

Credit: Treasure Bay Casino

Treasure Bay Casino in Biloxi closely resembles a giant pirate ship like this one.

panded to accommodate the influx of cars.

Basically, every casino has the same type of flashing, noisy slots and standard table games where players try to beat the house at poker, craps, blackjack and roulette. Because of this inherent similarity, each casino tries to cast itself in a unique light by using different themes that include the turn-of-the-century Mississippi riverboats, costumes, tournaments, entertainment, cheap or free food, valet parking, giveaways and whatever the marketing department can dream up to lure customers. What follows is a brief look at the casinos that were up and running at press time.

Tunica Area

HOLLYWOOD CASINO
Commerce Landing
Tunica County   (800) 871-0711

Hollywood Casino boasts a hotel and RV Park, all located on Robinsonville Road. The casino has 54,000 square feet of gaming space that is decorated with a Hollywood theme, complete with art deco decor. It's got 1,353 slots, a 12-table poker room and 53 tables. For dining there's a buffet, deli, steak house, lounge and bar. The hotel has 154 rooms and suites, and the RV park has spaces for 50 vehicles.

HORSESHOE CASINO AND HOTEL
7 Casino Center
Robinsonville   (800) 303-SHOE

Horseshoe opened in February 1995 with a three-story facility including a 200-room hotel. The 30,000-square-feet of gaming, all on one level, has 49 table games, more than 1,000 slots, video poker and keno games. The hotel has an 1890s Victorian style and is located

on the second and third floors, directly above the gaming action on the first floor. There are three restaurants: a buffet, steak house and snack bar.

CIRCUS CIRCUS CASINO
11 Casino Center Dr.
Robinsonville   357-111

Circus Circus opened in August 1994 with 66 tables and 1,451 slots in 60,000 square feet of gaming area. The facility covers a total of 83,000 square feet and cost $82 million. The Big Top Buffet covers 11,000 square feet; the Amazing Linguini Brothers serves Italian dishes; JoJo's Sideshow Deli is open 24 hours with traditional sandwiches.

HARRAH'S CASINO TUNICA
711 Harrah's Dr.
Robinsonville   363-7200

Harrah's opened its Tunica-area casino November 29, 1993. Since then gamblers have been playing the slots and table games spread out over three floors of this Southern-style casino at Commerce Landing, 24 miles south of Memphis. The three-level casino has 24,000 square feet of gaming on two floors and a conference center on the third floor. There are 929 slots, 44 tables, two video poker bars and an entertainment lounge. The land-based Magnolia Gardens Restaurant has seating for 255 and is open 24 hours a day for breakfast, lunch and dinner buffet meals.

FITZGERALD'S CASINO
Off Rt. 304
Tunica County   (800) 766-5825

Fitzgeralds opened in June 1994 with an Irish theme set in a bi-level castle on two barges. To get there, you drive through an enchanted forest. Inside the castle diners can enjoy an Irish menu in Molly's Country Kitchen, a full-service restaurant, or The Shamrock Express for quick service. For refreshments, there's The Blarney Stone Pub and The Lucky Lounge. Players pick from more than 1,000 slot machines and 55 table games spread out in 36,000 square feet. There's also Progressive slots, jackpot prizes and the Friendly Craps table for new players. Fitzgeralds Casino plans a hotel on its 121 river front acres.

SAM'S TOWN
HOTEL & GAMBLING HALL
Robinsonville Rd. at Commerce Landing
Robinsonville (800) 456-0711

North of Tunica and 20 minutes south of Memphis, Sam's Town calls itself Mississippi's largest casino and entertainment complex with 500,000 square feet in a Old Western town setting. It also touts itself as more than a casino and has devoted three-fourths of this "town" to non-gaming activities. They include Tunica's first casino hotel (with 508 rooms), four restaurants, nine bars and lounges, a 1,400-seat River Palace Entertainment Arena and Cotton Eye'd Joe's dance hall. Visitors can also play 1,900 slot machines, 75 table games, poker in a separate room and live keno.

SHERATON CASINO
1 Casino Center Dr.
Robinsonville 363-4531, (800) 391-3777

Sheraton opened at its site 12 miles from the Tennessee state line near Memphis in August 1994. It's Tudor style, three-story manor has hand-painted murals on the exterior and turn-of-the-century European touches throughout the interior. A sweeping staircase leads to the Grand Salon, a 12,000-square-foot event center for concerts and parties. The Hemmings River Club provides elegant dining, and the Landing Buffet and Rotisserie serves casual meals. There's also a snack bar and deli lounge. The River Stage offers local talent and wide screen viewing for sporting events. The 31,000 square feet of gaming space houses 1,000 slot machines and 57 table games.

LADY LUCK
RHYTHM & BLUES CASINO-HOTEL
777 Lady Luck Pkwy.
Lula (800) 789-5825

This Lady Luck is in Coahoma County on the Mississippi side of the Helena Bridge connecting Mississippi and Arkansas. It's exterior sports two 112-foot guitars and 62-foot saxophones. Inside, the casino has 60,000 square feet including 25,000 square feet for gaming. There are 740 slots, 33 table games, three restaurants, a lounge and gift shop. Food is served in a 250-seat buffet, a 24-hour cafe and sandwich shop. Lady Luck's hotel has 173 rooms and suites and offers special casino packages.

Greenville

Vicksburg

COTTON CLUB CASINO

333 Washington Ave.   355-1111
Greenville   (800) WIN-MORE

This downtown waterfront casino, Greenville's first, is a replica of a 1920s ocean liner that's 250 feet long and 60 feet wide. The entire facility, including the casino and adjacent restaurant and bar area, is 49,000 square feet. On the main casino deck, players will find the 205 gaming machines, 29 tables and two bars. Forty more gaming machines are on the mezzanine deck. On one deck there are 315 machines and a bar; the poker room on the second deck has 10 tables and a bar.

LAS VEGAS CASINO

242 S. Walnut   335-5800
Greenville   (800) VEGAS-21

The second casino to open in Greenville, the Las Vegas Casino on the river front has 529 slots, 27 tables for blackjack and other games and a mezzanine with six poker tables — all in more than 18,000 square feet of gaming space. State-of-the-art lighting illuminates the casino, and 19-foot ceilings with an air-filter system cuts down on smoke.

Natchez

LADY LUCK

21 Silver St.
Natchez   (800) 722-5825

Lady Luck Natchez has more than 500 slot machines and 12 black jack tables in its riverboat on the Mississippi at the city's famous and historic Under the Hill area. Other features of the casino are Bayou Lane for dining, the Burgundy Room for live entertainment, a gift shop and three bars. The Comedy Zone offers weekly entertainment by top comedians. The casino opened February 27, 1993.

AMERISTAR CASINO

4144 Washington St.
Vicksburg   638-1000

This three-deck, 84,000-square-foot riverboat features approximately 1,000 slots, 52 table games and the three-tiered, 350-seat Delta Grand Showroom. Other entertainment is available in the Cabaret Lounge. Guests can dine onshore at the Delta Point Restaurant, a Vicksburg favorite, in the 300-seat Veranda Buffet for breakfast, lunch and dinner and at the 200-seat Pilot House that's open 24 hours. All have river views. Plans call for a 250- or 300-room hotel to be constructed on 18 adjacent acres.

HARRAH'S VICKSBURG CASINO

Clay and Mulberry Sts.
Vicksburg   634-0711, (800) 427-7247

This downtown casino opened in late 1993, in a 297-foot, 36,000-square-foot riverboat in the tradition of the 1800s vessels that traveled the Mississippi. There's gaming on all three decks (516 slots and 43 table games). The casino is docked next to a shoreside entertainment complex featuring the Vicksburg Station food court, Winning Streak sports bar and Faulkner's Gifts retail outlet. For a small fee, there's a child-care facility available. Harrah's luxury hotel has 117 rooms, including 16 suites.

ISLE OF CAPRI CASINO

3990 Washington St.
Vicksburg   636-5700, (800) WIN-ISLE

This tropical paradise casino opened August 9, 1993, and is the sibling of the Biloxi Isle of Capri. This was the first in town to open to players. On board two levels are 745 slots and 40 table games, plus a poker player's paradise. It has 24,000 square feet of gaming space. On the land-based portion, there's live entertainment in the Tropical Atrium, the 200-seat, 24-hour Calypso Buffet Restaurant. You'll also find Banana Cabana Gift Shop and the 50-seat Tradewinds Deli.

RAINBOW CASINO
1380 Warrenton Rd. off I-10
Vicksburg　　　　　　　　　*631-0233*

Rainbow Casino opened July 12, 1994, and is just the first phase of what will eventually be an entertainment park, complete with an 88-room hotel and an entertainment complex to be built by Six Flags. The hotel is nearly completed; reservations are being accepted. The inside of the entertainment complex is complete; work on the exterior is under way. Rainbow Casino is the only gaming facility in town that's all on one level. Inside players will find 24,000 square feet with a vaulted ceiling, chandeliers and mirrored walls. Rainbow has 20 blackjack tables, four dice tables, two roulette wheels and two Caribbean Stud poker games, in addition to 574 gaming devices. The casino is off I-20 along the Mississippi River. Take Washington Street Exit 1A and drive 1.5 miles south on Warrenton.

Philadelphia

SILVER STAR HOTEL & CASINO
Hwy. 16 W.
Philadelphia　　　　　　*(800) 557-0711*

The Mississippi Band of Choctaw Indians and Boyd Gaming Corp. of Las Vegas have teamed up to open Mississippi's only land-based casino. Their joint venture, a $37

million hotel and casino package, is 3 miles west of Philadelphia. Silver Star opened its doors for business July 1, 1994, and less than six months later the casino opened its first expansion. The 165,000-square-foot complex includes a 100-room hotel, an RV park, four restaurants, three bars, a 125-seat entertainment lounge and a gift shop. The 65,000-square-foot casino has more than 1,550 slots, 10 poker tables, 71 tables and live keno. In June 1995, the Silver Star opened a state-of-the-art conference center with 55,000 square feet of available space. Take advantage of a grand ballroom, five break out rooms and a full-service catering staff.

Bay St. Louis

CASINO MAGIC
BAY ST. LOUIS RESORT
711 Casino Magic Dr.
Bay St. Louis　　　　*(800) 5MAGIC5*

This casino, the first to open in Hancock County, likes to say it's "a cut above!" It includes more than 150,000 square feet of total space with 40,000 square feet of gaming space featuring 1,100 slot machines, 65 table games and 35-seat live keno. Food and beverages are served in Torgy's Restaurant, the Veranda Buffet and Cafe Magic Food Court. Special events such as concerts, boxing matches and dog shows are held in the Magic Dome. There's also a 200-room Casino Magic Inn, an RV park with full hookups and 50 lighted marina slips. Plans call for a golf course and Arnold Palmer Golf Academy.

Insiders' Tips

Several casinos have child-care facilities and entertainment especially for teens.

Clermont Harbor/Lakeshore

BAYOU CADDY'S JUBILEE CASINO
5005 S. Beach Blvd.
Clermont Harbor/Lakeshore (800) 552-0707

This is Hancock County's second casino, and it points out that it's the one closest to New Orleans and "the jazziest casino on the Coast." Visitors could get the feeling they're in the Crescent City when they see the Jubilee's New Orleans-style architecture, hear live jazz and taste the spicy Cajun-Creole fare. There's even a Lucky Dog vendor on the French Quarter Pier at the casino's entrance. Inside, players will find more than 860 slots and 60 tables. Three restaurants give a choice of casual buffet or fine dining, and top entertainers perform in the 400-seat show room. The casino's mascot is Jubilee Joe, a hospitable alligator in top hat. The neon depiction of Joe at the casino's Highway 90 welcome center near Waveland is the world's tallest neon gator. The sign is 10 stories high and is illuminated by 4,633 feet of neon.

Biloxi

ISLE OF CAPRI CASINO
151 Beach Blvd.
Biloxi *(800) THE-ISLE*

The first to open in the South back on August 1, 1992, the Isle spreads Caribbean style over a 50,000 square foot, multilevel gaming complex and land-based facility. Slot players will find more than 1,230 machines plus 49 table games and seven tables in the Poker Paradise Room. The Isle offers regularly scheduled slot, black jack, craps and poker tournaments. The land-based Calypso's restaurant has outstanding local cuisine and house specialties plus tropical beverages and live entertainment in the lounge. There's live entertainment daily. Banana Cabana gift shop is also a winner. In April 1994, the Isle broke ground on a new phase of development — a 370-room Crowne Plaza hotel scheduled for completion in summer 1995. The hotel will also include a fitness center, indoor and outdoor pools, a child-care facility, a high-tech theater and space for meetings and conventions.

GRAND CASINO BILOXI
265 E. Beach Blvd.
Biloxi *(800) 946-2946*

This casino has a total of 250,000 square feet, including 100,000 square feet of gaming space where guests can play one or more of the 1,800 slot machines, 84 table games and 18 poker tables. Hungry visitors can choose from menus in the Market Place buffet, Roxy's diner, LB's Grill-Steak and Stuff and Sister's casual dining. Like its Gulfport counterpart, the Grand here has a Kids Quest children's activity center for little guests and the Grand Arcade with video games for teens. Next door is the new Grand Hotel, a 12-story, 500-room property that also includes a seafood restaurant, meeting facilities, a spa and other amenities.

Revenues derived from casinos have been a tremendous boom to the state's various departmental budgets.

Insiders' Tips

Casino Magic Biloxi

195 E. Beach Blvd.
Biloxi *(800) 5MAGIC5*

The dimensions of the casino's permanent structures (115,000 square feet with twin 139-foot towers) make it the tallest building on the Mississippi Gulf Coast. Gaming is done in 60,000 square feet, where players can try their luck on 1,100 slots, 50 table games and a 35-seat live keno parlor. The 300-seat Odyssey buffet, Southern Traditions fine dining restaurant, McDonald's fast-food restaurant and three cocktail lounges are inside.

The President Casino

2110 Beach Blvd.
Biloxi *388-PRES, (800) THE-PRES*

In early 1995, President Casinos Inc. announced its plans to lease the former Gold Shore Casino facility and move it to the President's site at the Broadwater Beach Resource Hotel Marina. The new President is larger (from 20,500 to 38,000 square feet) and has more slots (more than a 1,000) and more tables (50). Enjoy a world-class buffet facility and expanded entertainment facilities.

The President is affiliated with the Broadwater Beach Resort, which has more than 800 rooms, two 18-hole golf courses, eight tennis courts, pools and other amenities. The restaurants include the Marina Restaurant, featuring fresh seafood. The Royal Terrace offers fine dining. Mariner's Restaurant and Pier 90 are also located on the property.

Lady Luck Biloxi

316 Beach Blvd.
Biloxi *435-7639, (800) 539-5825*

Lady Luck introduced its unique Asian theme in Biloxi when the casino opened its doors in December 1993. The dramatic setting inside and outside, officials say, reflects "the growing ethnic population along the coast regional of Mississippi." It's hard to miss the prominent theme, what with a robotic fire-breathing dragon at the entrance and a Chinese buffet where dishes are prepared in woks. Patrons can also dine in the adjacent Fisherman's Wharf, a longtime Coast favorite now run by the casino. There's also a gift shop and lounge in the 38,000-square-foot facility. Games include more than 600 slots and approximately 40 tables.

The Palace Casino

158 Howard Ave.
Biloxi *436-4200, (800) PALACE9*

The Palace is said to be the largest floating glass palace in the world. It's three stories high, contains 85,000 square feet and offers more than 50 table games, 750 slots and other electronic games. You can't miss this one. The amethyst glass dome houses a laser-light system that flashes colors across the sky, and the exterior neon lighting paints the glass-plated casino in changing colors and designs. Inside, the Palace's three restaurants are the Crown Room for gourmet dining, the Emerald Courtyard for buffet service, and Pearl Diver's for seafood, pasta and sandwiches. The Royal Palladium Showroom seats 450 and presents American Superstars, a popular show featuring celebrity tributes, dancing and music.

Treasure Bay Resort Hotel and Casino

1980 Beach Blvd.
Biloxi *(800) PIRATE-9*

As the name implies, there's a pirate theme here. The casino is an authentic replica of an 18th-century pirate ship, nearly 400 feet long. Inside the 65,000 square feet of gaming space are 1,023 slot machines and 47 table games.

Scalawag's Show Bar has entertainment in a 200-seat lounge. Rogue's Gallery offers brick oven pizzas and fast food. Next door is a 48,000-square-foot fort that houses Laffite's Feast, a 350-seat buffet serving "Around the World in 80 Dishes." Across the street is Treasure Bay Resort Hotel with 254 rooms and suites, convention space, pool and a restaurant. Plans include child-care facilities, more restaurants and an outside lounge.

BOOMTOWN CASINO

460 Caillavet St.
Biloxi   *(800) 627-0777*

Boomtown brought the Old West to the Coast when it opened the first casino on Biloxi's Back Bay in July 1994. The casino has 43 table games and 963 slots. The Western theme is carried out in the 400-seat Longhorn Buffet Restaurant, the 50-seat Stagecoach Deli and Boots Cabaret. One unique feature is the Fun Center, which contains the Dynamic Motion Theater with 11 movies, the Family Entertainment Center with 90 redemption games and a 24-hour video arcade. Boomtown has announced plans for a 300-room hotel.

Gulfport

COPA CASINO

East Pier, Gulfport   *(800) WIN-COPA*

While the other Coast casinos have barges as their foundations, the Copa Casino is a real ship, with 30,000 square feet of gaming, restaurants and entertainment. Docked at the State Port of Gulfport, this 503-foot former world-class cruise ship has a 26,000-square-foot gaming floor, where guests will find 670 slots and 32 tables. There is a 30,000-square-foot entertainment complex in addition to the full casino. The Copa also has the deli-style Cabana Cafe and a lounge open 24 hours daily, and the Atrium Buffet open for lunch and dinner. The elegant design of the Copa was created by the same individual who worked on Caesar's Forum in Las Vegas.

GRAND CASINO GULFPORT

3125 W. Beach Blvd.
Gulfport   *(800) WIN-7777*

This gigantic structure isn't called grand for nothing. Both the Gulfport and Biloxi versions are billed as "the world's largest floating casinos." Total space in the Gulfport Grand's three floors is 225,000 square feet, and that houses more than 1,900 slots and 90 table games in a colorful Mardi Gras-style decor of lights and colors. Kid's Quest is a fully supervised children's activity center for ages 6 weeks to 12 years. For older kids there's the Grand Arcade with more than 40 video games and games of skill to hold their attention. The Grand is at the State Port of Gulfport. You'll find Banana's, a large buffet; Nifty Fifties, a snack bar; and Magnolia's, a fine dining restaurant. The Grand's 17-story, 400-room hotel will be completed in October 1995. Adjacent to the casino is a new 45,000-square-foot entertainment complex. The $12 million complex features four entertainment venues and two restaurants.

Inside
Pilgrimages and Historic Preservation

Southern belles and columned mansions have symbolized and romanticized parts of the Deep South since Scarlett O'Hara swept down the stairs at Twelve Oaks in the 1939 film *Gone with the Wind*. Before and since, good Southern girls, with Scarlett as a role model, imagined themselves fairly floating down a spiral staircase, with hoop skirts swaying and all eyes watching, as they made their grand entrances to the glamorous Old South of films and novels. The opulent lifestyle is gone, but the grand old homes still stand, and throughout Mississippi, many towns capitalize on increased interest in antebellum architecture by hosting annual pilgrimages to the Old South.

Webster defines 'pilgrimage' as "A journey made by a pilgrim to a shrine or holy place." That's an apt definition of the way some Mississippians view Pilgrimages, the first of which began in Natchez in 1932.

The nation was in the Great Depression when Natchez hosted its first Pilgrimage, and it was quite by accident, for the flower gardens were to have been featured. Perhaps it's a Southern thing, but no matter how hard the times, damsels of Dixie work in their gardens. Even with some of the magnificent homes peeling and reeling, the gardens of Natchez were truly grand. As it happened, a state garden club convention was to be held in Natchez for the explicit purpose of tour-

Longwood in Natchez stands unfinished as it was at the start of the Civil War.

Credit: Sylvia Higginbotham

ing the lovely gardens. The blooms were out; the flowers would surely be full and colorful by convention time. Mother Nature had other plans, however, for just days before the arrival of the garden clubbers, a hard freeze killed the buds. Natchez was not to blossom that spring. The ladies of Natchez were distraught — but as true sisters of the South are wont to be — they were also resilient and resourceful.

Katherine Grafton Miller (Mrs. J. Balfour) of Hope Farm (c. 1780) was said to have been the first to suggest opening the homes for tours since the gardens were dead. Some of the Natchez dowagers disagreed, but Mrs. Miller waged a campaign, and the homes of history were spiffed up to greet the distinguished guests. The event was a tremendous success; the garden club members were enthralled with the grand and gracious homes that Natchezians took for granted.

So thanks to the late Katherine Miller and friends, Pilgrimage was born. The garden clubs, two big ones, in fact, still ultimately manage and oversee the Natchez Pilgrimage. The Pilgrimage Garden Club and the Natchez Garden Club are the driving force behind Pilgrimage in Natchez. They've each purchased property, including the beautiful Stanton Hall, Longwood and Magnolia Hall, and are in the daily tours business. The focal point, however, is Pilgrimage, and in Mississippi, Pilgrimage warrants a capital P. It's a rite of spring; the time when towns across the state put their best foot forward and roll out the red carpet for visitors from far and near. Visitors come time and again for this colorful foray into the past, and apparently, they are not disappointed. The heritage tour homes in such towns as Natchez, Columbus, Vicksburg and Holly Springs are listed on the Na-

tional Register of Historic Places. These grand vestiges of the past are impeccably maintained and furnished with period European and American antiques.

During Mississippi Pilgrimages, local folks dress up in period costume, which includes elegant gowns over full hoop skirts. Look closely, and more than likely a Confederate uniform or two can be seen in most towns. Expect lots of old lace and crinoline, and notice the delicate Southern accents as hostesses or docents tell of each house's history. Some accents are a bit more pronounced than usual, for Pilgrimage is a theatrical, festive time. In some towns, New Orleans-style krewes (groups of people who band together to build floats or help celebrate Mardi Gras) were formed to be the fun arm of a somewhat formal event. Other towns have big Pilgrimage balls, where "royalty" reigns. Kings and queens of some Pilgrimage courts are highly guarded secrets until pageant night.

Deep down in Dixie, the Old South lives each spring, and behind every Pilgrimage tour home lies a deep and abiding interest in historic preservation. Preservation is big business down South, and what a shame it didn't catch on much earlier. Buildings of the past contribute to the present and the future, and to date, too many historic structures in Mississippi have been torn down to make room for parking lots or fast-food establishments. Towns that recognize that heritage tourism is a viable revenue source — actually economic development in its purest form — are to be commended for their efforts, and the first is Natchez, the one that called national attention to historic preservation through hosting the nation's first Pilgrimage.

As befitting the first, Natchez is the supreme queen of Pilgrimages. Their event is the biggest and the best, the one to which others aspire. And it's a title well-deserved, for Natchezians are serious about Pilgrimage. After all, it has saved the town's economic standing more than once. The most current saving grace was during the oil-related money slump of the early 1980s. Natchez is tied to Louisiana's oil industry, and when the industry all but collapsed, Natchez felt the crunch. Once again, tourism saved the day, for New Orleans tour operators stepped up their packaging of bus tours into Natchez, and as those in the business of tourism know, when tourists come, they bring money.

With the advent of more tourists, the Natchez Pilgrimage Tours and the Natchez Convention & Visitors Bureau, two separate entities, offered more activities in hopes that visitors would linger longer. The outstanding Spring Pilgrimage ran a month, from early March to early April, so they decided to feature the homes in a Fall Pilgrimage too. Natchez also offers activities other than home tours; see information below.

NATCHEZ PILGRIMAGE

(The River Cities)
Canal at State St.,P.O. Box 347   446-6631
Natchez 39121   (800) 647-6742

During the spring and fall events, 30 antebellum mansions are open to the public for organized tours. Tickets, maps and general Natchez information are available at Pilgrimage headquarters at the corner of Canal and State streets; it's open daily. Pilgrimage-time tickets are $20 per five-home tour; $18 per four-house tour, and $15 per three-house tour. Year-round tour tickets to individual homes (12 are open year round) are $4.50 for one home; $12 for three homes; $15 for four homes, and $20 for five homes.

Evening entertainment includes the *Confederate Pageant*, a popular depiction of the Old South at party time. Local performers don elaborate costumes for four performances each week of Pilgrimage. Tickets are $10 per person; performances begin promptly at 8:30 PM on selected evenings.

Southern Exposure is a satirical look at Pilgrimage behind the scenes. It is presented five times a week at the Natchez Little Theatre Playhouse during spring Pilgrimage; tickets are $10 per person.

Southern Road to Freedom is a stirring musical tribute to the trials and tribulations of black Americans, from Colonial times to the present. It's performed three days each week during spring Pilgrimage; tickets are $10 per person. Fall Pilgrimage features the *Mississippi Medicine Show*; tickets are $10 per person.

Other things to do and see in Natchez during Pilgrimage, or anytime, include antique shopping in a plethora of shops, horse-drawn carriage rides through the historic streets, double-decker bus rides, riverboat gaming at The Lady Luck Casino, the infamous "Natchez Under the Hill"; the Grand Village of the Natchez Indians and wonderful sunsets over the Mississippi River as seen from the bluff.

Natchez, settled by the French in 1716 two years before the founding of New Orleans, once boasted, after New York City, more millionaires than any other city.

Insiders' Tips

COLUMBUS PILGRIMAGE

(The Hill Country)

P.O. Box 46   329-3533
Columbus 39703   (800) 327-2686

This Pilgrimage began in 1940 and ranks right up there with Natchez in its reputation for quality homes and furnishings. Columbus features 12 to 16 antebellum homes, most of them Greek Revival in style, but Italianate influences are seen too. A few homes have a combination of design elements in a style called "Columbus eclectic." Some of these homes are ornate and grand; others are comfortable and livable, but they all meet the requirements of quality, inside and out, and they're all private residences of local people.

Two of the Columbus homes, Liberty Hall and Amzi Love, are still inhabited by descendants of the original builder. It is indeed refreshing to see authentic family treasures that have been lovingly preserved by generations of fmily members.

During Pilgrimage only, tickets, maps and pertinent information are available at Pilgrimage headquarters, the new Mis-sissippi Welcome Center/Tennessee Williams Home at Main and Third streets. Tickets are $15 per two-home tour ($8 for students through high school). The price includes an optional church tour, but this may change for future Pilgrimages. Some of the homes present re-enactments of things done in the period of their construction, such as quilting, lacemaking, doll restoration, weaving or tatting. Five homes are open year round on a rotating basis, so at least two homes are open each day, at $5 per person per home. Daily tour tickets (not Pilgrimage tickets) are available at the new Mississippi Welcome Center on Main Street, downtown Columbus.

Entertainment during Pilgrimage focuses on history, as in Tales from the Crypt, a nighttime graveyard tour of Friendship Cemetery. Students from a high school portray characters who have had significant roles in local history. A musical revue is on the agenda, and it's sure to be high-spirited. Dates and rates change yearly; call in advance.

Credit: Mississippi Department of Economic Development

French Camp Museum in French Camp on the Natchez Parkway is open all year.

Columbus also offers the Blewett-Harrison-Lee Museum, a driving-tour map, a walking-tour map, riverboat rides and historical displays at the library. And, about 10 miles from Columbus stands an outstanding example of historic preservation — Waverley Mansion, one of the most photographed houses in the country (see our attractions chapter for more information). It is open for daily tours from early morning to dusk; there's a $7.50 admission fee. For additional information about activities and offerings in and around Columbus, contact the Convention & Visitors Bureau, P.O. Box 789, Columbus 39703, 329-1191 or (800) 327-2686.

VICKSBURG PILGRIMAGE

(The River Cities)
P.O. Box 110   636-9421
Vicksburg 39181   (800) 221-3536

This old river city is lively throughout the year, but during Pilgrimage in mid-March for two weeks, it's at its best. They celebrate the past, and justly so, for Vicksburg has withstood onslaughts of war and flood and has survived all with spirit intact. Along with tours of 12 historic houses, expect to hear legends from the mythical antebellum days, heroic episodes from the 47-day Siege of Vicksburg, hard times during Reconstruction and the 13 years following Reconstruction when the city was under military rule. Tickets for this Pilgrimage, which began in 1974, are $12 per three-house tour; half-price for students younger than 12. Tickets are available at the Vicksburg Convention & Visitors Bureau; exit at 4-B off U.S. I-20.

Highlights of the Vicksburg Pilgrimage include the nationally known melodrama, *Gold in the Hills*, which is now in its 60th year. It is available on Friday and Saturday evenings during Pilgrimage. A must-see are tours of the town's other interesting sites: the impressive Vicksburg National Military Park and the ironclad *Cairo*; Toys and Soldiers Museum, the Old Court House Museum, Biedenharn Coca-Cola Museum, Gray and Blue Naval Museum, U.S. Army Corps of Engineers Waterway Experiment Station and riverboat casinos for those who wish to try their luck.

Vicksburg offers a wealth of historic homes and churches — including the impressive Christ Episcopal Church (1839), itself a treasured piece of history — wonderful views of the mighty Mississippi River and many good restaurants.

HOLLY SPRINGS
PILGRIMAGE HEADQUARTERS

(The Hill Country)
Marshall County Library
109 E. Gholson Ave.
Holly Springs 38635   252-2943

Holly Springs features eight of its antebellum homes for this annual weekend tour in mid- to late April, and it includes Pilgrimage royalty presentations. The queen is crowned; she and her escort begin the festivities and lead the way to the tour homes. The Garden Club of Holly Springs sponsors the Pilgrimage, and these innovative members offer activities in each tour home, from a harpist to a potter to a wildlife artist. The popular Rust College Acappella Choir will perform on the Courthouse lawn, and carriage rides will be available. Three historic churches offer organ recitals during Pilgrimage; the Kate Freeman Clark Art Gallery and the Marshall County Historical Museum open for special tours. Adding authenticity to the Holly Springs Pilgrimage, a Civil War camp is set up at nearby Wall Doxey State Park. This Pilgrimage is a top-20 tourism event for April.

Tickets are $20 for adults, $18 for senior adults, $8 students ages 12 to 17. Tickets for morning tour only or evening tour only are $12 each.

GULF COAST PILGRIMAGE

(The Coast)	452-9287
Mississippi Beach CVB	(800) 237-9493

The Coast Pilgrimage is a function of the Gulf Coast Council of Garden Clubs. There's a chairman of the event who may change periodically, so rather than list an address and phone number that could be temporary, the CVB will be pleased to forward inquiries. This is an eclectic tour that includes private homes, the Mississippi Welcome Center, the Stennis Space Center and such historic sites as Beauvoir, last home of CSA President Jefferson Davis, the Tullis-Toledano home and the Old Spanish Fort. Expect to see the Walter Anderson Museum and other private endeavors too.

With so many garden clubs and so many locations and sites involved, tour times vary according to the tour. Dates are mid- to late March, and the admission is free. Call to verify dates. Other Coast attractions include the J.L. Scott Marine Education Center, Mardi Gras Museum in the old Magnolia Hotel, Marine Life, Old Town in Bay St. Louis, Gulf Islands National Seashore, Shearwater Pottery, numerous Las Vegas-style casinos and so much more. See our Gaming, Attractions and other chapters for more information.

ABERDEEN PILGRIMAGE

(The Hill Country)
Aberdeen-South Monroe
Chamber of Commerce
P.O. Box 727, Aberdeen 39730   369-6488

The clean, green town of Aberdeen features 10 historic homes on its Pilgrimage tour. The styles are both antebellum and Victorian, and they run the gamut from lacy-look cottages to grand mansions. Usually held the first full weekend in

Insiders' Tips

Longwood, on Lower Woodville Road in Natchez, is the largest octagonal house in the country. It remains unfinished, as it was at the outbreak of the Civil War. The house, begun in 1858, was to be the residence of Haller Nutt and family. It's a superb example of Oriental-inspired architecture and is crowned by a large dome. The basement is finished and furnished with family heirlooms, though the most interesting aspect of this tour is seeing the complicated architecture in its original form, including three floors of rough brick and exposed beams.

April, the townspeople entice visitors with a full slate of activities, including the "Our Town" historical pageant. The First Presbyterian Church Tea Room is the perfect place for lunch during Pilgrimage, and an antiques show and sale caps off the weekend (individual admission prices apply). Pilgrimage tickets are $10 per three-home tour, $12 per four-home tour, $15 per five-home tour and they are available at the Elkin Theatre on Commerce Street in downtown Aberdeen.

PORT GIBSON PILGRIMAGE
(The River Cities)
Chamber of Commerce
P.O. Box 491, Port Gibson 39150   437-4351

The town that Union Gen. Ulysses S. Grant said was "too beautiful to burn" back in the 1860s has gotten better with age. Those who attend the Pilgrimage and accompanying 1800s Spring Festival at the stellar home, Oak Square, will get a sample of what Gen. Grant meant, for about 200 costumed participants at the festivities present living history at its best. Period activities including music, dancing, fencing, duels, lawn games, and a genuine Maypole dance take place on the lawn of the antebellum Oak Square. Locals and guests join in to enjoy other events too, such as an 1800s fashion show, arts and crafts, and a Civil War re-enactment. Also in late March, a quilting exhibition and other outstanding African-American exhibits at the Mississippi Cultural Crossroads, 508 Market Street, 437-8905.

Usually held the last weekend in March, the Port Gibson Pilgrimage tour of seven antebellum homes sells tickets for $3 per home; tickets are available at the Chamber of Commerce, on Church Street.

Other Pilgrimages

Other towns in Mississippi have Pilgrimages, though they are smaller in scale than the ones listed above. Not all the tour homes are historic, but they are billed as "architecturally interesting" or as the town's "finest homes." The following towns in the state have Pilgrimages that usually coincide with the blossoming of spring flowers: Brookhaven, 833-1411; Carrollton, 237-4380; Laurel, 649-3031; Pontotoc, 489-5042; and Yazoo City, 746-2088 or (800) 381-0662; which they call a Spring Spectacular. The towns of Oxford and Monticello sometimes have Pilgrimages as well. Their chambers of commerce can answer questions.

To confirm which towns have Pilgrimages and the exact dates, contact the Mississippi Department of Economic and Community Development, Division of Tourism, P.O. Box 1705, Ocean Springs 39566, (800) WARMEST . . . "warmest" meaning "The South's Warmest Welcome."

Inside
The Civil War

No event in the state's history, to date, has defined Mississippi's historical consciousness as much as the Civil War. You're apt to hear as many opinions about it as there are names by which it is known. The Civil War has been referred to by Southerners as The War of Northern Aggression, The War of Southern Independence, Mr. Lincoln's Folly and, more universally, the War Between the States. Whatever its name, it was a tragic four-year life-and-death struggle that devastated the South and forever changed a way of life for Mississippians. The Civil War was a fire relatively slow to ignite, but once it began to burn, the flame swallowed everything in its path.

Beginnings of War

Throughout the 1850s, the best parlors in the state held groups of men who talked of states' rights and slavery. There was an odd thing about the War Between the States: The central issue was slavery via states' rights, though the vast majority of those who fought for Mississippi owned no slaves. Those who did own slaves had a culture of their own.

The cotton-based culture in Mississippi abruptly ended at the onset of the war. It had been a lifestyle of opulent architecture and furnishings, literary pursuits, fine art and serious socializing. Before the war, people came to the grand homes from surrounding towns and

Source: John Fitzhugh, The Sun Herald

A "wounded" Confederate soldier is wheeled to surgery during a battle as part of Fall Muster. This event is held annually at Beauvoir, home of Confederate President Jefferson Davis in Biloxi.

counties to attend parties. They came with trunks of clothing including hoop skirts and corsets, for the young ladies of the family. Some of them had their "mammies" along for support. Those who lived the farthest away stayed for days.

There was a creed, devised and adopted by planters, and it was based on luxury. The creed, summed up by prominent lawyer of the day Rueben Davis, was simple: "A man ought to fear God, and mind his business. He should be respectful and courteous to all women; he should love his friends and hate his enemies. He should eat when hungry, drink when thirsty, dance when merry, vote for the candidate he likes best, and knock down any man who questions his right to these privileges."

Indeed, Mississippians felt these privileges were questioned by the federal government, and on January 9, 1861, the state followed South Carolina in seceding from the Union. At first, patriotic volunteers clamored to sign up to defend their new republic. Many Mississippians thought it would be a short-lived defense of their way of life; they considered it a "glorious revolution."

The Confederacy was formed in February of 1861, with the esteemed Jefferson Davis as its president. In March, Mississippi ratified the constitution of the Confederate States of America (CSA). The first shot of the War Between the North and South was fired on Fort Sumter, just across the way from Charleston, South Carolina, in April — with Mississippi officer, Col. Stephen D. Lee, giving the order to attack. U.S. President Abraham Lincoln called for volunteers to stop "the rebellion" — Mississippi sent troops to Florida, Virginia and Tennessee. Much to the dismay of Gov. John J. Pettus, Mis-

sissippi was left virtually undefended and unnoticed, for the CSA was in the process of moving its capital from Montgomery, Alabama, to Richmond, Virginia. It was essential that Richmond be defended, and, in so doing, the Mississippi Valley suffered lack of attention and the beginning of very hard times.

Battle Scars

As the war gained momentum, the once-prosperous state of Mississippi was on the brink of economic ruin. After all, this state's money was in its land, its cotton and the slaves who tended it. With more than 78,000 Mississippi men off defending the sovereignty of the Confederacy, the tilling of local soil was left to loyal slaves and often the women of the plantation. Even after Lincoln's Emancipation Proclamation ordered the freeing of slaves, many in Mississippi remained on the plantations, continuing to work as before.

Cotton still grew during the war, but enemy blockades prohibited its sale. Often, entire crops were burned to prevent valuable cotton from falling into enemy hands. At one time, as the war was raging, Mississippi was land poor, cotton poor and slave poor. None of these assets brought much-needed cash or the return of loved ones from the battle fields. Throughout the South, death was feared but almost expected.

When we think of the war, we think of the suffering and hardship of the men who fought it. Consider the suffering of women. They were left to tend the land, grow the food, feed the livestock, chop the wood for stoves and fireplaces, nurse the sick, clean and clothe the family, do their best to protect their belongings from looters and all the while wonder if their husbands, fathers or brothers would ever return. One man who chronicled the events of the day said this: "What shall I say of the Confederate women? They were the greatest patriots of the War. They endured, in silent struggle, at home." Perhaps they endured silently, but they wrote vociferously. Some of the best and most accurate accounts of the day came from diaries kept by women. One is quoted below.

When we read of battles in India, in Italy, in the Crimea, what did we care? It was only an interesting topic, like any other, to look for in the paper. Now you hear of a battle with a thrill and a shudder. It has come home to us. Half the people that we know in the world are under the enemy's guns. A telegram comes to you and you leave it on your lap. You are pale with fright. You handle it, or dread to touch it, as you would a rattlesnake, or worse; for a snake could only strike you. How many, many of your friends or loved ones this scrap of paper may tell you have gone to their death.

When you meet people, sad and sorrowful is the greeting. They press your hand, and tears stand in their eyes or roll down their cheeks as they happen to have more or less self control. They have brothers, fathers, or sons as the case may be in the battle; and this thing now seems never to stop. We have no breathing time given us. It cannot be so at the North, for the papers say gentlemen do not go in the ranks there (the North). They are officers, or clerks of departments. That is why we see so many foreign regiments represented among our prisoners;

Germans, Irish, Scots. But with us (Southerners), every company in the field is filled with our nearest and dearest as rank and file, common soldiers.

— June 1862. Mary Boykin Chestnut: A Diary from Dixie

Though evidence of war was everywhere, not all Mississippians agreed with the prevailing politics and willingness to fight. A few fiercely independent Piney Woodsmen from around Jones County, namely areas now known as Cracker's Neck and Sullivan's Hollow, decided they wanted no part of "a rich man's war and a poor man's fight." The Piney Woods region spawned no actual plantations and no slave holders of note, but many articles and a few books were written then — and long afterward — about Newt Knight and the Free State of Jones.

Legend has it that throughout the swamps and hills of the county, the band of "Free Staters" assembled to the sound of a black horn. The echo of the black horn became the stuff of legend and lore, and even a film, *Tap Roots*, was based on a book about this era by Laurel native James Street. One of Newt Knight's descendants also wrote a book called *The Echo of the Black Horn*.

Let it be said that not all Jones Countians sympathized with Newt Knight, for several rifle companies were organized and deployed. They fought with honor and distinction throughout

The "Billy Yanks" of the North called the Civil War, "The War of the Rebellion," much to the dismay of the Johnny Rebs, who fought heartily to ensure states' rights.

Insiders' Tips

Credit: Division of Tourism, Mississippi Department of Economic and Community Development

The Mississippi State Historical Museum is inside the Old Capitol Building in Jackson and contains important Civil War documents and exhibits.

the war then returned home to hard times and veiled hostility.

War Strikes Mississippi Soil

Though skirmishes had occurred along the Mississippi Gulf Coast earlier in the war, the Battle of Shiloh, part of the Campaign of Corinth, was the first actual military invasion of the state's soil. The bloody battle was fought just across the state line in Tennessee in April 1862. The Confederates were greatly outnumbered and retreated into the new railroad town of Corinth, which was touted as a prize for both armies. After Shiloh, more than 128,000 Federal forces began their march to invade Corinth, which was guarded by CSA Gen. P.G.T. Beauregard. Again, the Confederates were vastly outnumbered, so Gen. Beauregard used a bit of subterfuge to stymie the Yankees. He decided to retreat to Tupelo, but left enough troops to fool the Yanks camped nearby. Dummy cannons guarded the rail lines, and when an empty train came in, buglers serenaded and loud cheering was heard so that the Federals thought the Rebels had reinforcements. When Union Gen. Halleck's men stealthily entered Corinth at daybreak on May

30, they found a deserted town. They occupied Corinth for months, then in October of that year, the Confederates attempted to retake the town but failed after a bloody battle of hand-to-hand combat.

The first invasion of Mississippi by federal troops brought widescale destruction and downright thievery, according to reports of the day. Yankee soldiers pillaged and burned many grand mansions; furnishings, including everything from expensive pianos to imported furniture, were stolen or burned. Entire towns, such as Prentiss in the south-central part of the state, were torched. Yankees later boasted of having burned the courthouse in Prentiss, the jail, a tavern and about 25 homes. Damage was done throughout the countryside, in scattered communities and lone houses. We must say that not all Yankees were murdering marauders, for stories abound about the kind and gentle men who stopped to help a family in some way or the soldiers who did not pillage and destroy. Supposedly, Union Gen. U.S. Grant refused to torch the town of Port Gibson because the little town on the Natchez Trace was "too pretty to burn." It maintains its beauty today, and it lies between two other wonderful old Mississippi treasures, the river towns of Natchez and Vicksburg.

USA Gen. William T. Sherman, though he was responsible for burning a wide swath across Dixie, also commandeered choice items of household goods, according to historic documents. In Warren County, Sherman took for himself wagonloads of fine furniture from one home and supposedly told the woman from whom he took it, "You have so much, you deserve to lose it." Accounts of Sherman's confiscation of property he didn't burn were almost as rampant as his fires.

Another highly respected Union general, who later became president of the United States, was reported to have helped himself to fine furnishings from some Southern homes. Perhaps Gen. Ulysses S. Grant considered it "spoils of war," but those from whom he allegedly took things considered it looting. This account was found in an old Corinth, Mississippi, newspaper:

According to a letter written after the incident, the famed Union warlord apparently spent a great deal of time methodically looting a fine Southern mansion near Corinth and crating its luxurious furnishings for shipment to his own home in Springfield, Illinois. When Grant commandeered the plantation home of Col. F.E. Whitfield, Sr., it was reputedly one of the most beautiful and prosperous plantations in northeast Mississippi . . . when he left for Holly Springs, little remained other than the original 900 acres of land, a few trees and a section of fence.

Here's how Col. Whitfield described the pillage in a letter written in 1885:

The entire timber on 30 acres of my woodland was cut down by the Federal troops to obstruct the approach to a fortification which the Federals had erected near my dwelling. All my corn fences were torn down and rails partly burned.

About 1,000 horses and mules were turned inside my fields, pastures and woodlands, thus destroying my entire granary, crops of 200 acres, also the nursery, vineyard, orchards, gardens, etc. Now what became of all this property?

When I returned to Corinth it had all disappeared except the land, a part of the original trees, one gate post, and two or three fence posts that stood where the fish pond had been. All the house, furniture, fences, granary crops, stock, farming implements, vineyards, orchards, tree nursery, provisions and carriages had disappeared. Even my cistern was torn up and every brick carried off. But I held, and still hold a note from Gen. U.S. Grant admitting that he had taken my entire property.

According to the article in the Corinth paper, Col. Whitfield later learned that his furnishings had not been destroyed. Fourteen wagonloads of Whitfield's luxurious furniture were traced to the Corinth depot. From there they had been shipped to Illinois, where Grant's wife lived.

Surely such things as looting and stealing happen in war zones, but during the Civil War, it happened all over the South. Family homes and treasures were willfully destroyed, and the sad thing is that it was Americans stealing from Americans; the war zone was personal property.

During the fighting in north Mississippi, the Union army outnumbered the Confederates nearly two to one, and the Union had northern industrial money that purchased artillery and uniforms. The Union Army under Grant invaded Corinth, captured Holly Springs and occupied Oxford and Water Valley.

New Orleans was captured by the Union Army; Memphis was taken later, so the next Confederate power base on the Mississippi River was Vicksburg. Military strategists in both armies were hard at work; Vicksburg was to be the prize plum. In December 1862, Union Gen. Sherman was left in charge of the Vicksburg conflict, with 120 boats and 33,000 men. By the end of December, Sherman was repulsed by CSA Gen. Stephen D. Lee and about 2,500 of the 5,000 Confederate troops in Vicksburg. Sherman lost 1,776 men; Lee lost only 120. Sherman withdrew, and Vicksburg appeared to be temporarily out of danger, though President Lincoln continued to say that Vicksburg was the key. "The war can never be brought to a close until that key is in our pocket."

After the first of the year, 1863, about 50,000 Union soldiers arrived and camped in Louisiana, just across the Mississippi River from Vicksburg. Grant's forces tried to reach Vicksburg but were turned back by industrious Confederates. Followed by several months of maneuverings and major battles at Champion Hill and Jackson, Grant succeeded in reaching Vicksburg. The 47-day Siege of Vicksburg was the beginning of the end of the war, and the 32,000 Confederates who withstood the siege of 75,000 Federals were approaching starvation. Many of the citizens of Vicksburg left their homes and moved to caves in the bluff for a better chance of surviving the steady bombardment.

One Vicksburg woman, Emma Balfour, kept a journal in which she described the siege of her city. She told of hearing conversations and jokes exchanged between the soldiers of the two warring armies. Sometimes the blue and the grey were nearly face to face, and she heard the cannon balls whiz by her house. More than one hit; a cannon ball is still lodged in the wall of the Balfour House, which today stands tall and proud.

Insiders' Tips

When the Union Army occupied Oxford in 1864, according to legend, spiteful Union troops rode their horses through the cherished halls of Ole Miss.

As I sat at my window, I saw mortars from the west passing entirely over the house and the parrot shells from the east passing by — crossing each other and this terrible fire raging in the center. One or two persons who had passes to leave the city if they could returned last night, Grant saying that no one should leave the city until it surrendered. I have almost made up my mind not to think of retiring at all at night. I see we are to have no rest. They are evidently trying to harass our army into submission. All night they fired so that our poor soldiers have no rest and as we have few reserves, it is very hard on them.

— The Diary of Emma Balfour

Many historians consider the Campaign of Vicksburg the country's best example of military action, though it was devastating for those Mississippians and others involved.

Surrender

On July 4, 1863, CSA Gen. John Pemberton, with starving troops, surrendered to Gen. Grant, whose troops finally occupied Vicksburg. Vicksburg was the most significant military effort in Mississippi and one of the most significant of the Civil War.

Fighting continued in parts of Mississippi, with Confederate Gen. Nathan Bedford Forrest by then the major defender of the state. A Union general tried to subdue Forrest's army in June 1864, and the Battle of Brice's Crossroads ensued. Forrest, outnumbered by more than two to one, was not defeated; rather, the Federals are said to have been in a state of "panic."

The bedraggled Army of the South made a valiant effort to no avail. The war ended in the spring of 1865. More than 3 million men fought in the Civil War; 600,000 died. Mississippi sent 80,000 soldiers to fight; 20,000 were accounted for at the end of the war. Hundreds of thousands of slaves were freed, and the Union was finally restored.

As the War Between the States came to an end, Gen. Robert E. Lee, with less than 8,000 men, stood surrounded by about 80,000 Union forces. Surrender was inevitable. When word reached Lee that support was not forthcoming, he said: "Then there is nothing left me but to go to Gen. Grant and I had rather die a thousand deaths than to do it." But indeed he did. The proud Confederate general and the victorious Union general met at Appomattox Court House. Gen. Grant's terms were almost generous. The two leaders of men faced each other with great dignity and solemnity.

When Gen. Lee returned to his headquarters, he was met by his men, many of them in tears because the cause they so loved, and would have died for, had itself died. Their general issued this statement on April 10, 1865:

After four years of arduous service, marked by unsurpassed courage and fortitude, the Army of Northern Virginia has been compelled to yield to overwhelming numbers and resources. I need not tell the brave survivors of so many hard fought battles, who have remained steadfast to the last, that I have consented to this result from no distrust in them; but feeling that valor and devotion could accomplish nothing that could compensate for the loss that would have attended the continuation of the contest, I have determined to avoid the useless sacrifice of those whose past services have endeared them to their countrymen. By the terms of the agreement, officers and men can return to their homes and remain there until exchanged. You will take with you the satisfaction that proceeds from the con-

sciousness of duty faithfully performed; and I earnestly pray that a Merciful God will extend to you His blessing and protection. With an unceasing admiration of your constancy and devotion to your Country, and a grateful remembrance of your kind and generous consideration for myself, I bid you an affectionate farewell.

Rebuilding

So the war had ended, but more struggles were met by those who returned to their homes, if indeed they had homes left. They mustered their strength and began to rebuild, though progress was hampered by carpetbaggers and outlaws. Near-starvation and abject poverty prevailed for a while, but irrepressible Mississippians bounced back, stronger for the effort and determined to overcome.

Civil War historian and native Mississippian Shelby Foote has said, "Any understanding of this nation has to be based, and I mean really based, on an understanding of the Civil War."

Civil War Sites and Cemeteries

After the Battle at Brice's Crossroads north of Tupelo in June of 1864, CSA Gen. Nathan Bedford Forrest said this to his men: "Soldiers! Do not forget the gallant dead upon these fields of glory. Many a noble comrade has fallen, a costly sacrifice to his country . . . the most you can do is cherish their memory."

Indeed we do here in Mississippi. Since 500 battles and skirmishes took place on Mississippi soil, the state has a plethora of sites and museums. The most significant battle, according to historians, was in Vicksburg. The war in Mississippi, however, began in the northern part of the state, with the bloody Battle of Shiloh,

so that's where we'll begin to list cemeteries and sites.

The Hill Country

CORINTH BATTLEFIELD AND NATIONAL CEMETERY
Horton St.
Corinth   386-8311

More than 7,000 graves are here; most are marked "Unknown Soldier." This cemetery includes the graves of many Union soldiers as well as Confederates.

NORTHEAST MISSISSIPPI MUSEUM
Corner of Fourth and Washington
Corinth   287-3120

This museum contains artifacts from the Battle of Corinth. It is open Friday through Wednesday 1 to 4 PM or by appointment. Admission is $1.50 for adults.

HILLCREST CEMETERY
Elder Ave. at Center St.
Holly Springs   252-3757

Confederate soldiers, known and unknown, rest beside the graves of 13 Confederate generals.

BRICE'S CROSSROADS BATTLEFIELD
Hwy. 370
Baldwyn   842-1572

Six miles west of Baldwyn, find a park, a monument and graves of soldiers from both armies in nearby Bethany Cemetery.

BRICE'S CROSSROADS MUSEUM
Hwy. 45 N.
West of Baldwyn   356-5281

This museum contains replicas and artwork representing the Battle of Brice's Crossroads. It is open by appointment.

TUPELO NATIONAL BATTLEFIELD
West Main St., Tupelo   842-1572

This one-acre site features a memorial that honors both armies that fought here. You'll find cannon, an interpretive marker and a map.

TUPELO MUSEUM

Hwy. 6 W., Tupelo   *841-6438*

See artifacts recovered from the Battle of Tupelo. This museum is open daily except Monday. Admission is $1 for adults.

FRIENDSHIP CEMETERY

Fourth St. S., Columbus   *329-1191*

After the war, the nation's first Me-morial Day was held here. CSA graves form somber lines among the magnolias in Friendship Cemetery.

BLEWETT-HARRISON-LEE HOUSE

316 Seventh St. N.
Columbus   *327-8888*

Once the home of CSA Gen. Stephen D. Lee, this small museum houses Civil War artifacts and Lee's personal effects; it also displays antebellum toys and bridal gowns. It is open Tuesday and Thursday afternoons and at other times by appoint-ment.

Source: The Herald Sun

A statue of Gen. Ulysses S. Grant stands among the trees in the area of Grant's Headquarters at Vicksburg's Battlefield Park.

The Delta

COTTONLANDIA MUSEUM
Hwy. 49/82 Bypass
Greenwood   453-0925

Exhibits of Fort Pemberton and an ironclad are housed at Cottonlandia. It is open daily.

CONFEDERATE CEMETERY
Strong Ave.
Greenwood   (800) 844-7141

Graves of known and unknown soldiers line rows here.

The Heartland

LAUDERDALE SPRINGS
CONFEDERATE CEMETERY
Hwy. 45 N.
Lauderdale   693-1306, (800)748-9970

This haunting reminder of a sad war is alone in the countryside.

MARION CONFEDERATE CEMETERY
Hwy. 45 N.
Meridian   693-1306, (800) 748-9970

Known and unknown Confederate soldiers rest peacefully here.

DOOLITTLE CSA CEMETERY
½ mile east of Newton on Hwy. 80
Newton   683-2201

Memories linger of the valiant soldiers who died for their cause.

MISSISSIPPI STATE HISTORICAL
MUSEUM/OLD CAPITOL
100 S. State St.
Jackson   359-6920

This magnificent building survived the torching of Jackson and now includes important Civil War documents and maps and outstanding exhibits. It was here that the Ordinance of Secession was passed in 1861. And it was here, at the end of the war, where the governor was arrested. Jefferson Davis spoke here periodically. The museum is open daily.

The River Cities

Vicksburg, on the Mississippi River, was called the "Gibraltar of the Confederacy" and was the site of a most important Civil War campaign. The city was literally surrounded and townspeople nearly starved by Gen. Grant's troops in 1863 during the 47-day siege. Good accounts of this campaign are available at the Vicksburg National Military Park, at various other locations in the city and in the film *The Vanishing Glory*.

VICKSBURG
NATIONAL MILITARY PARK
3201 Clay St., Vicksburg   636-0583

About 1,800 acres of rolling hills harbor fortifications and earthworks, with Union and Confederate lines marked.

Insiders' Tips

One military historian said that the Confederate loss of the Battle of Champion's Hill, near Edwards, did irreparable damage to the Confederate cause. He said, "The drums of Champion's Hill sounded the doom of Richmond." The battle occurred on a 70-foot ridge near the plantation of the Champion family.

Friendship Cemetery

Columbus, Mississippi, is a town where history lives and memories linger. CSA Gen. Stephen D. Lee, who made his home in Columbus, quoted the historian McCauley while reminding participants at a Memorial Day service of this true and timeless fact: "A people who take no pride in the noble achievements of remote ancestry will never achieve anything worthy to be remembered with pride by remote descendants."

Indeed, Columbians remember with pride a gracious gesture by a small band of women back in 1866 — a gesture that helped to heal the wounds of the War Between the States.

Credit: Columbus Convention and Visitors Bureau

Friendship Cemetery

During the war, following the bloody Battle of Shiloh, Columbus served as a hospital zone for armies of Mississippi and Tennessee. Amazingly, since 500 battles and skirmishes were fought on Mississippi soil, Columbus was never officially invaded by Federal troops. After the chaos of Shiloh, it was hard to distinguish blue from gray, so uniformed soldiers of both colors apparently joined the march. About 3,000 wounded soldiers made their way to Columbus, where they were tended day and night by the noble women, black and white, of the town. Many brave young soldiers died from battle wounds and were quietly laid to rest at a local cemetery.

Columbus survived the Civil War physically intact but economically and spiritually devastated. In 1866, a year after the war ended, the group of women met at the home Twelve Gables to plan a way to honor the war dead at the local cemetery. Their intention was to decorate Confederate graves, but the sight of Union soldiers' graves caused them to change their course of action. After all, the war was over. Those formerly distinguished as Confederate and Union soldiers were Americans, one and all. The women began to place flowers on every grave, regardless of the army represented, until all graves were laden with flowers.

In the mid-1860's, newspapers were delivered by slow mail and horseback and were quite influential, especially Horace Greely's New York paper. Reports indicate that this one small paragraph appeared in Greely's publication in 1866: "The women of Columbus, Mississippi have shown themselves impartial in their offerings made to the memory of the dead, They strewed flowers alike on the graves of the Confederate and the National soldiers."

To a nation still in mourning, this simple gesture became significant to the healing process and caught the attention of young New York attorney Francis Miles Finch, who wrote a poem depicting the deed of the ladies of Columbus. His poem, "The Blue and the Gray," first appeared in the September 1967 issue of the *Atlantic Monthly*.

Afterward, Finch's poem was recited by school children throughout America. Here's an excerpt:

By the flow of the inland river,
Whence the fleets of iron have fled,
Where the blades of the grave-grass quiver,
Asleep are the ranks of the dead;
Under the sod and the dew,
Waiting the judgement day;
Under the one, the Blue,
Under the other, the Gray

This poem became so popular and Friendship Cemetery in Columbus so well known, Congress, in 1868, designated May 30 as Decoration Day. This tradition of honoring the war dead has evolved into Memorial Day, and Columbus is still known as the town where flowers healed a nation.

No more shall the war cry sever,
Or the winding rivers be red;
They banish our anger forever
When they laurel the graves of our dead.
Under the sod and the dew,
Waiting the judgement day;
Love and tears for the Blue,
Tears and love for the Gray.

Monuments tell the story of the 28 states that sent soldiers to Vicksburg. Also on the site is the USS *Cairo*, a Union ironclad. The park is open daily. Admission is $3 per car.

SOLDIERS REST CSA CEMETERY
Sky Farm Ave., Vicksburg   636-9421

Soldiers Rest is the Confederate Cemetery, which is part of the City Cemetery.

Most of those buried here were killed during the Seige of Vicksburg. For more information contact the historian at the Vicksburg National Military Park.

OLD COURTHOUSE MUSEUM
1008 Cherry St., Vicksburg   636-0741

This historic building suffered the onslaught of Union shells during the siege until the wily Confederates housed

Union prisoners there. This maneuver saved the building, which today offers an extensive collection of Civil War letters and diaries.

ROSEMONT PLANTATION
Hwy. 24 E.
Woodville   *888-6809*

Original family furnishings are still within the walls of Jefferson Davis' boyhood home, and windowsills feature the names of the Davis children. The house is open periodically, therefore it is best to call ahead for times and admission information. We hear that once a year Davis descendants gather there for a family reunion. Woodville is near Natchez, so if you go, don't miss the opportunity to see the many antebellum mansions of lovely Natchez, the country's best representation of the Old South.

The Coast

BEAUVOIR
2244 Beach Blvd., Biloxi   *388-1313*

It was at this spacious house facing the Gulf of Mexico that Confederate President Jefferson Davis, after his release from a federal prison, wrote *The Rise and Fall of the Confederate Government*. Here's an interesting anecdote about Jefferson Davis: According to local legend, Davis was visited at Beauvoir by the Union soldier who had captured him. After the visit, the man had no money, so

Davis loaned him enough to get back home and gave him this suggestion: "If you ever meet any of our boys in want, relieve them if it be possible." The Davis family showed their appreciation for Confederate veterans even after Davis died in 1889, for his widow refused to sell Beauvoir and the surrounding property to a hotel developer for $100,000; instead, she sold it to the Sons of Confederate Veterans for $10,000. Beauvoir is now a museum and a major tourist destination for the Gulf Coast. It is open daily. Admission is $4 for adults, $3.50 senior adults and $2 children.

FORT MASSACHUSETTS
Ship Island, Gulf of Mexico   *875-9057*

After its capture by Union forces, Ship Island became a prison for Confederates. It's now a part of the Gulf Islands National Seashore and sits about 12 miles out in the Gulf; the visitor center is at Ocean Springs. Call for departure schedule and fare information.

Civil War Re-enactments

Civil War buffs who want to witness a re-enactment or two have a plethora of choices. Skirmishes and battles have been thoroughly researched by the soldier/actors who in turn portray the actual event. Here's some information, though it's best to contact the Mississippi Division of Tourism for updates; call (800) WARM-

---

Insiders' Tips

After CSA Gen. Nathan Bedford Forrest soundly defeated Union forces at Brice's Crossroads, Union Gen. W.T. Sherman told Gen. A. J. Smith to ". . . follow Forrest to the death, if it costs 10,000 lives and breaks the U.S. Treasury."

EST. Locations sometimes change, and a fee is charged; verify prior to trip.

February

BATTLE OF WEST POINT
West Point
(The Hill Country) 329-1191, (800)327-2686

BATTLE OF OKOLONA
Okolona
(The Hill Country) 447-5913, 327-9704

March

CONFEDERATE ENCAMPMENT
Ag Museum, Jackson
(The Heartland) 354-6113

April

CONFEDERATE DAY CELEBRATION
Beauvoir, Biloxi
(The Coast) 388-1313
Clinton Civil War Re-enactment and various related activities Clinton
(The Heartland) 924-5912
Hillman Berry Campus, Leake St.

May

BATTLE OF CHAMPION HILL
Near Edwards, off I-20
(The River Cities) 852-2705

FEDERAL MEMORIAL DAY
Old Courthouse
Vicksburg
(The River Cities) 636-0741

June

BATTLE OF BRICE'S CROSSROADS
Baldwyn
(The Hill Country) (800) 748-8687

July

THE SIEGE AND FALL OF VICKSBURG
Vicksburg
(The River Cities) 636-0741

October

FALL MUSTER
Beauvoir, Biloxi
(The Coast) 388-1313

BATTLE OF CORINTH
Corinth
(The Hill Country) 287-5269

November

MECHANISBURG CORRIDOR CIVIL WAR RE-ENACTMENT
Near Yazoo City
(The Delta) 746-1815, (800)381-0662

RE-ENACTMENT AND LIVING HISTORY DEMONSTRATION
Florewood River Plantation
Greenwood
(The Delta) 455-3821

Inside
Arts and Culture

Mississippi is no stranger to arts and culture, for the Magnolia State is home to outstanding writers, artists, musicians, entertainers, amazing architecture, and more museums than anyone north of the Mason/Dixon line would imagine. One of the country's finest small museums is the Lauren Rogers Museum of Art in Laurel; it's truly a treasure.

Many towns in Mississippi have similar offerings, such as Oxford, where an active literary community is gaining international attention. Among the many noted writers from this small town are William Faulkner and John Grisham.

It may be a circuitous route from Biloxi to Broadway, but that doesn't mean theater lovers won't find very good talent on local stages. Community theater flourishes throughout the state, and so do civic arts organizations that bring in national touring companies and internationally known performers.

The capital city of Jackson has a high-profile arts community, with two major groups in residence: the Mississippi Arts Commission and the Jackson Arts Alliance. Jackson has the distinction of hosting the USA's International Ballet Competition, along with other host cities of Moscow; Helsinki, Finland; and Varna, Bulgaria. Jackson is the new kid on the block for the IBC, a prestigious organization that sponsored such dancers as Mikhail Baryshnikov, a gold medal winner in Moscow in 1969, and Alexander Gudunov, another gold medal winner in Moscow in 1973. The IBC began in 1964; Jackson became a part of the Olympic-style dance competition in 1979.

The International Ballet comes to Jackson every four years (the next appearance is June 1998) and, in the process, casts an international cultural spotlight on Jackson. Jacksonians who support the arts serve as host families for junior dancers, world-renowned artistic directors, teachers and choreographers who are affiliated with the IBC as jurors and teachers in the International Dance School.

New Stage Theatre in Jackson is Mississippi's first professional theater, and with several thousand loyal subscribers, New Stage attracts regional and national actors and playwrights. It lends credence to Jackson's vibrant arts environment.

Lovers of Southern literature know that writer Eudora Welty is from Jackson. In fact, Miss Welty is a lady older than 80 who continues to live in her family home. Fans of Welty's books may not realize that she painted before she wrote and is also a remarkable photographer. Joining Welty in Jackson's literary spotlight are Margaret Walker Alexander, Willie Morris, John Stone and others.

On campus stages throughout the state, colleges and universities offer student productions of Broadway's best. And university art galleries provide opportunities to discover new talent. Some Mississippi artists have permanent exhibits in galleries dedicated to their work, among them the late Walter Anderson of Ocean Springs and George Ohr, known as the Mad Potter of Biloxi. Anderson was a talented but eccentric painter who spent much of his time on Horn Island. He rowed 12 miles out in a small skiff, then explored, painted, wrote in his journals and communed with the island's wildlife. As well as the Walter Anderson Museum and museums dedicated to the seafood and maritime industries, the Coast is also home to thriving art colonies in historic, picturesque Bay St. Louis and Ocean Springs.

Mississippi's museums are nothing short of impressive. From exhibiting very good art to showing examples of lifestyles no longer existent, there's something for every taste. Some museums have admission fees of $1 to $4 for adults; if this is a factor, call before you arrive. In this chapter, we will feature a proud cultural heritage and hope that visitors and locals

Credit: Division of Tourism, Mississippi Department of Economic and Community Development

A Choctaw Indian woman practices the art of basket weaving on the Choctaw Indian Reservation in Philadelphia.

take the time to visit some of Mississippi's museums and participate in some of its many other cultural opportunities.

The Hill Country

Museums

HISTORICAL SOCIETY MUSEUM
318 Seventh St. N., Columbus   327-8888

This museum is also called the Blewett-Harrison-Lee Home and locally, the Lee Home, for it was once the graceful Italianate residence of CSA Gen. Stephen D. Lee, from all accounts the officer who gave the first command to fire at Fort Sumter at the outbreak of the Civil War. The Museum, upstairs at the Lee Home, contains a varied collection of Civil War artifacts and memorabilia. Bridal gowns of the period are displayed, too, in all their old lace and timeworn glory. The Lee Home is open Tuesday and Thursday from 1 to 4 PM; other times by appointment. It is also the headquarters for the Columbus Spring Pilgrimage.

COBB INSTITUTE OF ARCHAEOLOGY
Mississippi State University, Starkville   325-3826

The Cobb Institute houses an impressive collection of artifacts from excavations of Indian mounds in the Southeastern United States. Also presented are replications of Middle Eastern and Biblical artifacts. The Institute is a closed June through August.

C.C. CLARK MEMORIAL COCA-COLA MUSEUM
Miss. 12 W., Starkville 323-4150, 323-4317

Fans of Coca-Cola memorabilia will love this museum, for it boasts more than 2,300 items dating back to the early days of the soft drink. It's closed weekends.

TEMPLETON MUSIC MUSEUM AND ARCHIVES
46 Black Jack Rd., Starkville   325-8301

If ragtime music pulls at your heart strings, this museum is for you. It helps that it's in a 1910 structure, and that it houses an extensive collection of antique phonograph music boxes, recordings, sheet music and Nipper dogs. It is affiliated with the Department of Music Education, MSU; it's open by appointment only.

EVANS MEMORIAL LIBRARY
105 N. Long St., Aberdeen   369-4601

There's more than a library here. Inside, a museum awaits those who are interested in historical materials and documentation. This is said to be one of the best sources in the state for genealogical research. It is closed Sundays.

AMORY REGIONAL MUSEUM
715 S. Third St., Amory   256-2761

This museum honors Amory's railroad heritage, for the railroad developed this town. An old passenger coach on the grounds now holds railroad memorabilia. Since the museum is housed in the old Gilmore Hospital, it is only fitting that

The Old Jail Museum in Canton was built in 1870 and is available for tours, by appointment. The Canton CVB has details, 859-1307.

Insiders' Tips

early medical instruments and photographs are displayed. Very early Native American artifacts blend amicably with contemporary art. Hours are 9 AM to 5 PM Monday through Friday.

TUPELO MUSEUM OF ART

211 W. Main, Tupelo   *844-ARTS*

Housed in an old store, this museum is a branch of the Mississippi Museum of Art in Jackson. The exhibits are provided by the parent museum; they sometimes feature Mississippi artists.

THE TUPELO MUSEUM

Miss. 6 W. at Ballard Park
Tupelo   *841-6438, (800) 841-6438*

No matter what you're interested in, the Tupelo Museum has something for you, with exhibits featuring Native Americans, astronauts, Elvis Presley and much more. An old train caboose shares billing with a space hangar that includes a lunar lander and a simulated rocket launch. This museum is indeed eclectic. Hours are 8 AM to 4 PM Tuesday through Friday; 1 to 5 PM Saturday and Sunday; it's closed Monday.

ELVIS PRESLEY MUSEUM:
TIMES AND THINGS REMEMBERED

306 Elvis Presley Dr., Tupelo   *841-1245*

This tribute to Elvis Presley contains treasures fans will love, such as a jumpsuit from his Las Vegas act. Candid, never published Elvis and friends photographs are a bonus. It's open 9 AM to 5 PM Monday through Saturday, 1 to 5 PM Sunday. Admission is $4 for adults and $2 for children.

NATCHEZ TRACE
PARKWAY VISITORS CENTER

On the Trace
6 miles north of Tupelo   *680-4025*

The museum houses artifacts concerning the early days of the Natchez Trace, and it offers a 12-minute audiovisual presentation of the Trace's history. A bookstore on the premises sells educational material about this National Park and others. It is open daily.

NORTHEAST MISSISSIPPI MUSEUM

Fourth St. at Washington
Corinth   *287-3120*

Since Civil War battles occurred here, expect documents, replicas and artifacts of the war as well as Native American exhibits. Open limited hours; it's best to call before arriving.

UNIVERSITY MUSEUMS

University Ave. and Fifth St.
Oxford   *232-7073*

Plan to spend a while at this museum near the Ole Miss campus, for there's much to see, beginning with a fine collection of Greek and Roman antiquities, scientific apparatus from the 18th and 19th centuries, a doll collection and more than 6,000 objects of Southern folk art. It's open Tuesday through Saturday 10 AM to 4 PM, Sundays 1 to 4 PM; it's closed Mondays.

MARSHALL COUNTY HISTORICAL MUSEUM

220 E. College Ave., Holly Springs   252-3669

Trace the development of the area here, where old farm tools and wonderful quilts show ingenuity and creativity. A doctor's office equipment, textiles, toys of yesteryear and war relics make this an interesting stop. The museum is open 10 AM to 5 PM Monday through Friday; it's closed Sundays.

The Performing Arts

Most cities and towns in northeast Mississippi have active community theater groups that usually play to packed houses. Money is often a factor in community theater in small towns, so the plays are sometimes limited in cast and set decoration. One musical a year is the goal, and if it's not a local production, arts councils or other presenter groups manage to bring in touring shows of Broadway classics.

The University of Mississippi (Ole Miss) in Oxford, Mississippi State University in Starkville and Mississippi University for Women in Columbus all have good theater departments that offer performances throughout the year. Ole Miss' annual Festival of Summer Theatre attracts a huge audience from across the region.

Tupelo has a symphony and a city ballet, as well as an active theater group, but Oxford is the performing arts leader in the Hill Country. The annual Ole Miss Jazz Reunion is a big alumni event each spring, and it usually includes a nationally known guest artist or two. The Artist Series includes theater, dance and music. Oxford Tourism Council has details, 234-4651 or (800) 880-6967.

Theater

COLUMBUS ARTS COUNCIL

P.O. Box 1248
Columbus 39703   *328-ARTS*

This multipurpose arts group is among the state's best, for they are presenters of touring company shows and sponsors of local functions, among them the highly acclaimed Young People's Artist Series. The season for YPAS consists of four major productions each school year. The CAC's goal is to present four concerts per year for adult audiences, and in between the CAC often picks up block-booking opportunities. Tickets are available in advance or at the door and range from $5 to $15, depending on the production. Most performances are held on the MUW campus at Whitfield Auditorium.

COLUMBUS COMMUNITY THEATRE

P.O. Box 83
Columbus 39703
Call the Arts Council for Information
                                   328-ARTS

A small but active group, CCT tackles major Broadway plays and dinner theater, about two or three performances a year. Non-dinner plays are held at the historic Princess Theater. Purchase tickets at advance locations or at the door; it's usually $5 for non-dinner plays.

STARKVILLE COMMUNITY THEATRE

P.O. Box 1254, Starkville 39759
Call the Visitors and Convention Council for information   *323-3322*

Starkville Community Theatre presents three or four plays each year, and they have an enviable pool of talent from which to cast: Mississippi State University staff and students. The season starts in September. Season tickets may be purchased in advance or at the door; all performances are held on campus.

MISSISSIPPI STATE
UNIVERSITY LYCEUM SERIES
Box HY, MSU 39762   325-3228

The university's Lyceum Series of performances usually runs January through April, one per month. Performances are varied — from brass ensembles to dance

— and always professional or professional quality. An admission fee is charged; campus locations vary.

TUPELO COMMUNITY THEATRE
P.O. Box 1094, Tupelo 38801   844-1935

Not only does this well-organized group perform quality plays, they also worked toward the restoration of the old Lyric Theatre, now the performance site

Credit: Division of Tourism, Mississippi Department of Economic and Community Development

The International Ballet Competition is held in Jackson every four years. It's next appearance is 1998.

for their quarterly productions. Season tickets are available, or single tickets may be purchased at the performance.

CORINTH THEATRE-ARTS
P.O. Box 127, Corinth 38834   287-2995

Unlike most theater groups in small Southern towns, this one has a professional resident director — and it shows. CT-A presents eight hit shows each season, plus a summer day camp for area children, an after-school program and more. Better still, CT-A has won numerous awards for dramatic and technical quality. Season tickets are $40 for adults, $25 students.

THE UNIVERSITY THEATRE (OLE MISS)
Central Ticket Office, Oxford   232-7411

The theater season at Ole Miss offers eight shows, with a major musical over Homecoming weekend. Here you'll see contemporary American plays and a smattering of European drama. Season ticket packages are available at the Central Ticket Office.

FESTIVAL OF SOUTHERN THEATRE
Central Ticket Office, Oxford   232-7411

Each summer, selected Southern playwrights converge upon Ole Miss to see their work premiered. The festival attracts a national audience of theater critics and lovers of Southern literature. Tickets are available at Central Tickets.

ARTISTS' SERIES
Central Ticket Office, Oxford   232-7411

This series of four annual performances includes theater, dance and music of international status; events are held at Fulton Chapel, Ole Miss. Series tickets are available; the cost is slightly more if tickets are purchased individually.

Visual Arts

There are organized groups of artists in the Hill Country who pool resources and talents to rent or buy old houses or buildings to use as studios. From these studios, or galleries, the artists sell their work. It's fun to discover artists here, and it's not uncommon to find good art at low prices. Local chambers of commerce or convention and visitors bureaus have information on art studios and associations and their location and hours of operation, which often vary.

In Columbus, for example, the local art association rented a rambling old house and named it Studio 206. It's a good bet for good art. Stonegate Gallery on Main Street is another place that showcases local artists. The ladies of Stonegate, as they're called, and one lone male who frames the works of art, are proud to show their paintings.

E. TALBOTT GALLERY
116 Fifth St. N.
Columbus   328-7181, 328-5534

This is a new gallery and working studio for local artist Eugenia Talbott, who paints on canvas, wood and furniture. She also paints exotic scenes on room divider screens and a series of painted pets. An

> Coast community theater groups are not only crowd-pleasers, many have won awards and honors in national competitions.

obvious animal-lover, Talbott makes yearly treks to the Canadian Northwest in pursuit of animals to portray and Inuit art. This versatile artist's work is frequently exhibited in museums, and it has been featured on Australian national television and in films about the Arctic region.

THE KATE FREEMAN CLARK ART GALLERY

292 E. College Ave.
Holly Springs   *252-4211, 252-2511*

The Kate Freeman Clark Art Gallery houses more than 1,200 paintings by a young woman of the 1890s who, with her mother, went to New York City to study art with William M. Chase. She returned to Holly Springs and never showed her prolific paintings. At her death, Clark's paintings were willed to the city. The museum is open by appointment.

UNIVERSITY MUSEUMS

University Ave. and Fifth St.
Oxford   *232-7073*

Along with Greco-Roman antiquities, the museum exhibits a fine collection of Mississippi artist Theora Hamblett's paintings. It's been called primitive and naive; perhaps interesting will work.

MISSISSIPPI STATE UNIVERSITY ART GALLERIES

McComas Hall, MSU
Starkville   *325-2970*

The galleries here exhibit works of students, so if you're lucky, perhaps you'll spot and sponsor a talented new artist. Faculty and visiting artists exhibit too. Call for information on current exhibits, for they change often.

MISSISSIPPI UNIVERSITY FOR WOMEN FINE ARTS GALLERY

1100 Fifth Ave., Columbus   *329-7341*

Printmaking, fine art, pottery and other art forms are exhibited at this gallery, and it is the work of students, faculty and visiting teachers. Permanent and changing exhibits are featured.

Other Cultural Attractions

CENTER FOR THE STUDY OF SOUTHERN CULTURE

Barnard Observatory, University of Mississippi
Oxford   *232-5993*

Those who cherish Southernese — and fans are apparently legion in number — are probably familiar with the Center for the Study of Southern Culture. The Center has been telling about the South since 1977, through publications, media productions, lectures, performances and exhibitions. And they've sponsored the popular program that draws national recognition and international participation each August, the Faulkner and Yoknapatawpha Conference. Each year, participants study different themes appearing in William Faulkner's novels.

Among the center's publications: the *Encyclopedia of Southern Culture*, a 1,634-

---

page reference work supported by the National Endowment for the Humanities and the Ford Foundation; *Cultural Perspectives on the American South*; and a new literary magazine called *Reckon*. The center offers bachelor's and master's degrees in Southern Studies. It is a research center for Southern literature, folklore and blues music. The center is housed in the 135-year-old Barnard Observatory on the University of Mississippi campus. Hours are 8:15 AM to 4:15 PM Monday through Friday; it's closed weekends.

UNIVERSITY OF MISSISSIPPI BLUES ARCHIVES
Farley Hall, Room 340, UM Campus
Oxford   232-7753
Bluesman B.B. King's personal collection is housed here, and it includes more than 10,000 records, promo materials, posters and photographs. The archives is a library collection for blues music. Make an appointment in advance if you wish to listen to music. Hours are 8:30 AM to 5 PM Monday through Friday; it's closed weekends.

The Delta

Museums

COTTONLANDIA MUSEUM
U.S. Hwy. 82 W., Greenwood   453-0925
This is a perfect museum for the Delta, for it lauds King Cotton and the soil-rich cotton growing region. See exhibits of early citizens, including the Delta's own Greenwood LeFlore, the Frenchman/Indian who was a Choctaw chieftain and local politico. Also shown are early farm implements, furniture and much more. It's open 8 AM to 5 PM Monday through Friday, Saturday and Sunday, 2 to 5 PM. Admission is $2.50 adults, 50¢ for children younger than 12.

THE GREENVILLE WRITER'S EXHIBIT
Memorial Library, 341 Main St.
Greenville   378-3141
The Delta is a breeding ground for writers, and this exhibit showcases the talents of Shelby Foote, Hodding Carter II and III, Ellen Douglas, David L. Cohn, Walker Percy, Bern Keating and more. It's open from 9 AM to 5 PM weekdays, 9 AM til noon Saturday, closed Sundays.

DELTA BLUES MUSEUM
Carnegie Public Library, 114 Delta Ave.
Clarksdale   624-4461
Before there was jazz, current country or rock 'n' roll, there was the blues, the pure music of the Delta. Indeed, it is still around, stronger than ever, and this museum heralds its importance to the world of music. Ongoing blues-related events are held throughout the year, and maps are provided for those who want to see the roots of the blues or homesites of former blues greats and other popular sites. You'll learn at the museum that Issaquena Avenue is a top choice to see, and so is Stackhouse/Rooster Blues Records on Sunflower Avenue. The museum and gift shop are open from 9 AM to 5 PM Monday through Friday, 10 AM to 5 PM Saturday.

JIM HENSON MUSEUM
U.S. Hwy. 82, Leland   686-2687
Most of the world knows Kermit the Frog and his creator, the late Jim Henson. Now, learn more about Henson, a Delta native, and see some of his Muppets on loan from Henson Productions in New York City. The museum overlooks Deer Creek, where Henson played as a child. It's open 10 AM to 4 PM Monday through Friday, Memorial Day through Labor Day, Saturday and Sunday 1 to 5 PM.

AMERICAN COSTUME MUSEUM

104 Ruby St.
Ruleville   756-2344, 756-2171

This museum contains what one would least expect in a tiny Delta town: original costumes from classic Hollywood films, including a dress worn by Vivian Leigh as Scarlett in *Gone With the Wind*. The costume collection is varied — from items worn by Cagney and Bogart to John Wayne. Luster Bayless is the collector. Call first to be sure the museum is open. It's a treat to see.

YAZOO HISTORICAL MUSEUM

332 N. Main St.
Yazoo City   746-2273, (800) 381-0662

This town and its museum are on the fringes of the Delta and the Heartland, though it bills itself as the "Gateway to the Delta." The museum is in the old Main Street School building, and it houses other civic offices, such as the Triangle Cultural Center. Changing exhibits run the gamut of old photographs to quilts and permanent exhibits of artifacts from the Civil War to the present. Hours are 10 AM to 4 PM Monday through Friday.

The Performing Arts

The Delta Symphony Association is a merger of two of the Delta's oldest arts organizations, the Greenville Symphony and Delta Music Association. The combined forces and funds assure Deltans the best in musical presentations, about six per year. It's based in Greenville, but Deltans from far and wide attend performances.

Greenwood Arts Foundation sponsors symphonies, choirs and concerts throughout the year; the Greenwood Little Theatre offers three or four productions each year. Arts for Success is a program specifically for young people.

Theater

GREENWOOD LITTLE THEATRE

P.O. Box 246, Greenwood 38930
Call the CVB for information   453-9197

These presenters offer three or four Broadway plays each year and usually play to big audiences. Season tickets are available, and the cost per ticket is slightly more if purchased individually.

GREATER GREENWOOD ARTS FOUNDATION

P.O. Box 1491
Greenwood 38930
Call the CVB for information   453-9197

This umbrella organization presents some performances, usually by national touring companies, and sponsors others. A fee is charged for performances by touring companies. The foundation also sponsors fine art exhibits.

DELTA CENTER STAGE

P.O. Box 14, Greenville 38701
Call the Arts Council for information   378-3141

It's Greenville's local group of nonprofessional actors who love the theater. They present four plays each year, with a big summer musical that features the talents of area children. Season tickets or tickets to individual performances are available at the E.E. Bass Cultural Center.

DELTA CHILDREN'S THEATRE

P.O. Box 1194, Greenville 38701
Call the Arts Council for information   378-3141

Touring productions of children's classics make regular appearances in the Delta. An admission fee is charged. Events are held at the E.E. Bass Cultural Center.

Credit: Jack Mitchel, Columbia Artists Management

In 1955 Leontyne Price became the first African American to sing the title role in an opera on television. Price was born in Laurel Mississippi.

DELTA STATE UNIVERSITY
Cleveland 846-3000

The Theatre Arts department of this university presents various productions during the academic year. Reviews are usually excellent, especially when the professors perform. A small admission fee applies; performances are held on campus.

Music

DELTA SYMPHONY ASSOCIATION
723 S. Main, Greenville 334-4168

A merger generally means more and better; this surely occurred when Delta Music joined forces with the Greenville Symphony to become Delta Symphony. Locals perform, as well as touring talent, several times a year. Season tickets are available, or tickets may be purchased at the door. Events are held at the E.E. Bass Cultural Center.

DELTA STATE UNIVERSITY
Cleveland 846-4615

Delta residents can name their preference, for the DSU Music Department's productions include opera theater, wind ensemble, jazz band, chorale, clarinet choir, brass ensemble and the resident faculty Brass Quintet. Expect musical performances throughout the school year. Some are free; others require a small fee. Performances are held on campus.

Visual Arts

Throughout the Delta towns, local artists exhibit at museums, banks, shops, festivals and elsewhere. Those interested in certain areas should contact the chambers of commerce or visitors and convention bureaus to inquire about upcoming exhibit dates.

THE FIELDING L. WRIGHT ART CENTER
Delta State University
Cleveland 846-4720

The Fielding L. Wright Art Center at Delta State has performed a coup: It has a Salvador Dali original. The Art Center houses a permanent exhibit of the work of Kate Kolwitz. Changing exhibits and good contemporary art show a variety of art forms. Hours are 7:30 AM to 4:30 PM Monday through Friday.

The Heartland

Museums

MISSISSIPPI STATE HISTORICAL MUSEUM
100 S. State St., Jackson 359-6920

Since this outstanding museum is a division of the Mississippi Department of Archives and History, one expects it to be better than most, and it is. The museum's collection of artifacts began in 1902 when the Department was established. Today, more than 30,000 cataloged items are housed in this restored former capitol building, which in itself is a showplace. Permanent exhibits and texts depict Hernando DeSoto's explorations, the Civil War, Reconstruction, the Great Depression, civil rights and more. Completed in 1840, the Old Capitol is one of America's finest examples of Greek Re-

vival architecture. To better understand and appreciate this complex state, visit the State Historical Museum and its bookstore and gift shop. Hours are 8 AM to 5 PM Monday through Friday; 9:30 AM to 4:30 PM Saturday and 12:30 to 4:30 PM Sunday.

MISSISSIPPI MUSEUM OF NATURAL SCIENCE
111 N. Jefferson St.
Jackson 354-7303

Today more than a quarter million specimens of the state's flora and fauna are exhibited in this museum of living heritage. Also see exciting dioramas, a massive aquarium system, a lush garden and hands-on displays. Hours are 8 AM to 5 PM Tuesday through Friday; 9:30 AM to 4:30 PM Saturday; closed Sunday and Monday.

JIM BUCK ROSS MISSISSIPPI AGRICULTURE AND FORESTRY/NATIONAL AGRICULTURAL AVIATION MUSEUM
1150 Lakeland Dr.
Jackson 354-6113 , (800) 844-TOUR

If you're interested in the real Mississippi and have limited time on a trip to Jackson, you won't want to miss the Jim Buck Ross Mississippi Agriculture and Forestry/National Agricultural Aviation Museum. Once visitors get past the long name and discover that this museum is a living history treasure, most people are very glad they came. Locals call it the "Ag Museum," but it involves much more than agriculture, for it's a chance to see a small Mississippi town of the 1920s. Visit a working farm and all its daily activities, a general store and an Episcopal church. Gift items and refreshments are available in the general store. In the nearby 40,000-square-foot exhibit center, agriculture and forestry — complete with aviation relative to farming, which is crop-dusting —

are well documented and exhibited. This museum, and the State Historical Museum, make one proud to be a Mississippian, native or temporary. Hours are 9 AM to 5 PM Monday through Saturday; Sunday 1 to 5 PM. Admission is $3 adults, $1 children older than 6.

SMITH ROBERTSON MUSEUM AND CULTURAL CENTER

528 Bloom St., Jackson   *960-1457*

Follow the development of a culture — from working in the fields to contributions to history, art and music — at this museum dedicated to African-American Mississippians. The museum is housed in the old Smith Robertson Elementary School, which was Jackson's first public school for blacks. It was built in 1894 and named for City Alderman Smith Robertson. Included with historical exhibits are folk art demonstrations, workshops and a museum gift shop that offers hand-crafted items. Hours are 9 AM to 5 PM Monday through Friday, 9 AM to 12 PM Saturday and 2 to 5 PM Sunday. Admission is $1 adults, 50¢ children.

DIZZY DEAN MUSEUM

1202 Lakeland Dr., Jackson   *960-2404*

See personal effects and baseball memorabilia of Mississippian Dizzy Dean, former St. Louis Cardinal pitcher and sportscaster. The museum is seasonal, open April 1 to September 1, noon to 6 PM Tuesday through Saturday; 1 to 5 PM Sunday. Admission is $1. This museum may, in the future, be a part of the

eagerly anticipated Mississippi Sports Hall of Fame and Museum, a project in the works, spearheaded by the Mississippi Sports Foundation, Inc. For information, telephone (800) 280-FAME or 981-1515.

CHOCTAW MUSEUM OF THE SOUTHERN INDIAN

Choctaw Indian Reservation, Miss. 16 W.
Philadelphia   *656-5251*

Choctaws have long valued living in harmony with nature. They appear to have a deep and different spirituality that few of us understand. Perhaps the museum, a good tribute to a grand culture, will help to fill in the gaps. See highly prized Choctaw baskets plus other exhibits and archives, and see why Chahta Hapia Hoke (we are Choctaw) evokes such pride. Hours vary; call first.

KOSCIUSKO MUSEUM

Natchez Trace Pkwy.
Kosciusko   *289-2981*

The town is named for Tadeusz Kosciusko, a Revolutionary War hero, and the museum is dedicated to the town's namesake. Changing exhibits show the early history and development of this town where television talk show hostess/actress Oprah Winfrey was born. Hours are 9 AM to 5 PM Monday through Saturday, limited hours on Sunday.

MERIDIAN MUSEUM OF ART

628 25th Ave., Meridian   *693-1501*

The museum, which opened in 1970, presents more than 30 exhibitions of traditional and contemporary works each year, as well as lectures, symposia and special events. It also hosts the region's most prestigious art competition, the annual Bi-State Art Competition for Mississippi and Alabama artists. Admission is free. The museum is open Tuesday through Sunday 1 to 5 PM.

JIMMIE RODGERS MUSEUM
1720 Jimmie Rodgers
Meridian 485-1808

The "Father of Country Music" called Meridian his hometown, and the town pays homage to this music pioneer with a collection of memorabilia honoring his contributions to the music world. The items on display include family photographs, musical instruments and other personal items. Hours are 10 AM to 4 PM Monday through Saturday and 1 to 5 PM on Sunday. Admission is $2.

KEY BROTHERS AVIATION PICTORIAL EXHIBIT
Key Field, U.S. Hwy. 11 S.
Meridian 482-0364

The Key brothers made history by setting the world's endurance flight record back in 1935. This museum reviews their accomplishment and the history of aviation in the terminal of the Meridian Airport. This museum is open from 7 AM to 9 PM when the terminal is open to passengers.

PEAVEY VISITORS CENTER
Marion-Russell Rd., Northeast Industrial Park
Meridian 484-2460

The Hartley Peavey Museum, inside a 1931 building, showcases the hugely successful Peavey Electronics Corp. and its founder. Visitors will see artifacts, displays and a demonstration room containing the latest Peavey guitars, amplifiers and keyboards. Also located on the 42 acres of a former U.S. Department of Agriculture Experiment Station is the original caretaker's lodge and greenhouse. Tours are available on request, and admission is free. The center is open weekdays from 10 AM to 4 PM and weekends 1 to 4 PM.

LAUREN ROGERS MUSEUM OF ART
Fifth Ave. at Seventh St.
Laurel 649-6374

This museum housed in Georgian splendor was the first art museum in Mississippi. It contains an outstanding collection of 19th- and 20th-century American landscapes and European salon paintings. Also on display are 18th-century English silver and decorative arts, a large collection of baskets and rotating exhibits. Gallery hours are 10 AM to 5 PM Tuesday through Saturday and 1 to 4 PM Sunday. Admission is free.

Insiders' Tips

For a trip back in time, we recommend a stop at Sciple's Mill, north of DeKalb, off Miss. 39. The mill, built in 1790, is run by a water-turbine wheel and has the capacity to grind 32 bushels of corn or wheat per hour. It's open and operational daily, but if you need to call for exact directions, dial 734-2295 or 743-2754.

CAMP SHELBY
ARMED FORCES MUSEUM
South Gate, U.S. 49, Hattiesburg   558-2757

This military museum contains more than 5,000 items from the Civil War, Mexican War, both world wars, Korea, Vietnam and the Persian Gulf War. A special exhibit is a rare sky crane helicopter used in Vietnam. The museum is 12 miles south of Hattiesburg and is open Monday through Friday 9 AM to 4 PM and Saturday and Sunday 1 to 4 PM. Tours must be prearranged. Admission is free.

Elsewhere in the Heartland, community theater and local music groups perform several times each year.

Performing Arts

Jackson has an array of remarkably diverse performing arts groups. Here's a quick rundown of a few of the best-known organizations: Ballet Mississippi, International Ballet Competition (every four years), Black Arts Music Society, Mississippi Symphony Orchestra, New Stage Theatre, Ballet Magnificat, The Modern Dance Collective, Mississippi Opera, Capital City Concert Band Society, The Mississippi Chorus, Metropolitan Chamber Orchestra Society, Mississippi Academy of Ancient Music and the Repertory Theatre. Add the performing arts groups from Millsaps College, Belhaven College, Mississippi College and Jackson State University, all in or near Jackson, and see that choices are indeed plentiful.

Another suggestion to best enjoy dance and music: Attend the many annual festivals, such as Jubilee!JAM, a big arts and music festival held each May. Even the Jackson Zoo gets in on the performing arts with a Zoo Blues concert in the spring. Free noon concerts each spring in downtown Jackson are compliments of the Arts Alliance of Jackson and Hinds County.

Ballet Mississippi performs concerts in Mississippi and elsewhere, including the full-length ballets *Coppelia* and *The Nutcracker*. The Mississippi Opera tackles top productions and executes them beautifully, including *Carmen* and the Puccini masterpiece *La Boheme*.

Elsewhere in the Heartland, community theater and local music groups perform several times each year.

Theater

NEW STAGE THEATRE
1100 Carlisle St., Jackson   948-3531

Founded in 1965, New Stage is Mississippi's only professional theater. It presents a full professional season, including current Broadway and off-Broadway productions. Season tickets are available and suggested.

The Palaces of St. Petersburg Come to Mississippi

March 1 through August 31 of 1996 will be a memorable time for Mississippians and visitors, for those dates are when they'll have an opportunity to see The Palaces of St. Petersburg: Russian Imperial Style. The major exhibition, held at the Mississippi Arts Pavilion in Jackson, will feature authentic recreations of grand and opulent rooms from five imperial palaces, complete with original furnishings and priceless works of art. Also included are about 500 objects that belonged to the Russian imperial families, including Peter the Great through the last czar, Nicholas II.

THE PALACES OF ST. PETERSBURG
RUSSIAN IMPERIAL STYLE

Among the objects in the exhibition are a coronation throne, 24-settings of the spectacular Guriev Imperial Porcelain Service, lapis lazuli furniture from the Lyon Room, Alexander II's golden coronation carriage and much more.

This is indeed a rare opportunity, for the exhibition is the first major showing presented outside Russia in which the palace museums of St. Petersburg have jointly collaborated. The exhibition represents a collaboration of Mississippians as well. The principal sponsors are the Mississippi Department of Economic and Community Development, Division of Tourism Development; Metro Jackson CVB and the City of Jackson. Major sponsors include Deposit Guaranty National Bank; Trustmark National Bank; The Clarion-Ledger; Chevron; South Central Bell, and Bank of Mississippi. Also involved is the Mississippi Commission for International Cultural Exchange, Inc., a nonprofit educational and cultural organization.

The Mississippi Arts Pavilion is in downtown Jackson. The exhibition will be open seven days a week from 9 AM until 10 PM. All tickets are for specific dates and times with entries for 150 visitors every 15 minutes. Tickets prices are $10 for adults, $9 for seniors older than 60 and $5 for youth 5 to 16. For additional information, write P.O. Box 2447, Jackson 39225, or call 960-9950.

REPERTORY THEATRE OF MISSISSIPPI
P.O. Box 17927, Jackson 39236   354-0976

The Rep Theatre provides local artists the opportunity for broad-based experience in dance, drama, music and the technical end of theater. A small fee is charged for performances.

PUPPET ARTS THEATRE
1927 Springdale Dr.
Jackson   956-3414

Since 1967, this touring puppet theater group has been combining arts, education and entertainment. A fee is charged, and locations for performances vary.

COMMUNITY CHILDREN'S THEATRE
1000 Monroe St.
Jackson 354-1191

Each year, this volunteer group produces one play for area children, and it's a collective effort in set design, costumes, props and more. About 10,000 children see the annual play.

MERIDIAN LITTLE THEATRE
State Hwy. 39 N., Meridian 482-6371

This community theater group claims the largest membership of any in the state and is one of the most active groups. Each season features dramatic and musical presentations.

CAREY DINNER THEATER
William Carey College
Hattiesburg 582-6221

The Carey Dinner Theater presents musicals from mid-June to late July and other major productions in April, October and November. A Madrigal Dinner, with music and all the pageantry from medieval times, is presented in December. There is an admission charge for most shows.

USM COLLEGE OF THE ARTS
USM Campus, U.S. 49 and Hardy St.
Hattiesburg 266-ARTS

Each year the college puts on more than concerts, recitals, plays, dance programs, art exhibits and multimedia events for the public. Among the events are performances by USM's Symphony Orchestra, Dancers, Hartwig Theatre, Choral, Southern Chamber Winds, School of Music, Jazz Lab Bands, Opera Theatre, Wind Ensemble and String Chamber Music quartets and trios. Many of the performances are free and open to the public.

Musical Theater

THE MISSISSIPPI OPERA ASSOCIATION
201 E. Pascagoula St.
Jackson 960-1528

A season of grand opera is available through this group as well as recitals and special events. The performance of Verdi's tragic *Rigoletto* received rave reviews, as have other operas performed by the Mississippi Opera. Two productions are staged each year at Municipal Auditorium; an admission fee is charged.

OPERA SOUTH
P.O. Box 18016
Jackson 39236 968-2700

Opera South is one of the three black professional opera companies in the United States. This group performs operas in English and has performed world premieres of various operas, one of which, *A Bayou Legend*, aired on PBS and received the International Film and Television Festival of New York Bronze Award and an Emmy Award nomination. Admission fee applies; most performances are held at Jackson State University.

Music

STARKVILLE-MISSISSIPPI STATE UNIVERSITY SYMPHONY ASSOCIATION
P.O. Box 1271
Starkville 39759   325-3070

This symphony association has been in operation for more than 25 years, which gives Starkville the distinction of being the smallest community in the United States to support a symphony orchestra consecutively for 25 years. All performances, six per year, are free to the public and are held on campus.

TUPELO COMMUNITY CONCERT
Civic Auditorium, Tupelo
Call the CVB for information   841-6521

Local talent performs with Tupelo Community Concert in about four performances per year held at the Civic Auditorium. You may purchase season tickets or get them at the door.

MISSISSIPPI SYMPHONY ORCHESTRA
201 E. Pascagoula St., Jackson   960-1565

The symphony performs for more than 400,000 Mississippians each year, and it's the largest performing arts organization in the state. It functions as a full orchestra, a chamber orchestra or a touring orchestra. The Masterworks Series brings in top concert pianists and violinists who share billing with outstanding local talent. In conjunction with the Arts Alliance, outdoor concerts are held on certain spring days, in downtown Jackson at noon. There's no admission charged for outdoor concerts. Other concerts are held at the Municipal Auditorium and a fee is charged.

METROPOLITAN CHAMBER ORCHESTRA SOCIETY
3615 Hawthorne Dr.
Jackson   992-9880

Hear quality classical music, and encourage local performers to solo with an orchestra. More than 40 musicians play in this volunteer group, which performs several times a year. A small admission fee is charged, and performance locations vary.

TUPELO SYMPHONY
Civic Auditorium
Tupelo   842-8433

The classics come alive, and locals perform several times per year at the Civic Auditorium. Season tickets are available, or tickets may be purchased at the door.

OLE MISS JAZZ REUNION
Office of Alumni Activities
Oxford   232-7377

Alumni of the Ole Miss jazz and music programs return each spring to perform. The reunion also includes nationally renowned guest artists who conduct workshops during the week-long event that begins with a Jazz Interlude. The reunion is held annually late April-early

Insiders' Tips

The Marie Hull Gallery in the Denton Art Building on the campus of Hinds Community College in Raymond offers permanent exhibits by Mississippi artists. Call 857-3275 before you go; hours are limited and the gallery is closed May through August.

May. All performances and workshops are open to the public and are held at various locations in town. Call for details and performers.

MERIDIAN SYMPHONY ORCHESTRA
Meridian Community College
Meridian   *693-2224*

Seventy musicians perform five subscription concerts and one pops concert each season at the Meridian Community College auditorium, 910 Highway 19 North. Tickets to single performances are in the $6 to $12.50 range.

MERIDIAN SYMPHONY POPS CONCERT
Highland Park,
1720 Jimmie Rodgers Memorial Dr.
Meridian   *693-2224*

This free outdoor concert follows the American Cancer Society's Pig in the Park benefit in early July. Highland Park is located at 1720 Jimmie Rodgers Memorial Drive.

ST. PAUL'S CHAMBER SERIES
St. Paul's Episcopal Church, 1116 23rd Ave.
Meridian   *693-2502*

This is a series of free musical programs presented at noon. Recent concerts have featured classical guitarists, a piano trio, a symphony string quartet and jazz vocalists.

CHUNKY BLUES FESTIVAL
Chunky Amphitheater, Chunky   *693-6260*

Top recording artists bring their rhythm and blues to this annual festival held in July at the natural amphitheater on a farm 12 miles west of Meridian.

MAIN STREET SALUTES THE BLUES
Downtown Meridian   *485-1996*

This festival and talent contest held in July showcases up-and-coming blues performers.

SANDY RIDGE SPRING BLUEGRASS FESTIVAL
Sandy Ridge Blue Grass Park, Hwy. 45 S.
Meridian   *693-2996*

Regional bands play bluegrass each May at Sandy Ridge Blue Grass Park behind Clarkdale School between Meridian and Quitman. Campers can stay for $6 per day. Otherwise, admission is $6 to $8. The event starts at 6 PM Wednesday and continues through Saturday.

JIMMIE RODGERS MEMORIAL COUNTRY MUSIC FESTIVAL
Meridian   *483-5763*

The Father of Country Music is honored each May with nightly concerts, talent contests, a celebrity golf tournament, a fishing rodeo and conference on country music. Activities take place downtown, at Highland Park, 1720 Jimmie Rodgers Memorial Drive, and at the Temple Theater, 2320 Eighth Street.

Dance

TUPELO BALLET
775 Poplarville
Tupelo   *844-4352, 844-1928*

The Tupelo Ballet boasts a well-respected dance school, which is the Academy of Dance Arts. Expect at least three productions per year at the Civic Auditorium, including the annual presentation of *The Nutcracker* each December. Local dancers train diligently for each performance. Admission is charged.

MISSISSIPPI UNIVERSITY FOR WOMEN
College St., Columbus   *329-7437*

Though no dance major is offered at the university, an active dance department performs major ballets each year. The resident dance professional works with students and local children who participate in the Children's Dance Division. The annual *Nutcracker* performance in December features locals and guest artists from national companies, including the Joffrey. A nominal admission fee is charged; tickets are available in advance or at the door.

MISSISSIPPI BALLET INTERNATIONAL, INC.

200 S. Lamar St., Jackson   355-9853

Jackson is the United States host city for the International Ballet Competition held once each year in each of four world cities. Along with Jackson, IBC is held in Varna, Bulgaria; Helsinki, Finland; and Moscow. Jackson is the only IBC city to hold an International Dance School for competing and non-competing dancers. The school is held during the competitions. The next IBC in Jackson will be held in 1998. Advance tickets are certainly suggested for this event, and rates vary depending on times and location of seating. Most performances are held at the Municipal Auditorium.

BALLET MISSISSIPPI

201 E. Pascagoula St.
Jackson   960-1560

This is a professional ballet company. It boasts an artistic director who once toured with the London Festival Ballet. The company is best known for its outstanding productions of *Coppelia* and *The Nutcracker*. Season tickets are available; tickets also are on sale at the Municipal Auditorium before performances.

BALLET MAGNIFICAT

4459 N. State St.
Jackson   982-1920

Jackson is proud to be the home of Ballet Magnificat, the world's only known professional Christian ballet company. Since its founding in 1986, the ballet has

performed throughout the United States and Canada. Ballet Magnificat offers a summer workshop at Belhaven College that attracts international dancers. A nominal fee is charged.

Visual Arts

MISSISSIPPI MUSEUM OF ART

201 E. Pascagoula St.
Jackson   960-1515

This museum is pleased to offer an extensive collection of masterworks by American and European artists. MMA, as it's called by locals, is a good place to go to contemplate the essential importance of art, for here the spirit is refreshed and the soul restored. MMA boasts seven galleries and about 40 exhibits per year, with more than 5,000 works of art in a permanent collection that includes 18th-century British paintings and furniture. MMA admirably fulfills its goal of "bringing the visual arts to the people of Mississippi." Hours are 10 AM to 5 PM Monday through Friday, 12 to 5 PM Saturday and Sunday. Admission is $3 adults, $2 children.

JACKSON MUNICIPAL ART GALLERY

839 N. State St., Jackson   960-1582

This champion of Mississippi artists rotates exhibits each month, and art works are nicely displayed in a Victorian structure. The Municipal Art Gallery has been promoting artists for more than 40 years. It's a good place to buy good, original art. Hours are 9 AM to 5 PM Tuesday through Saturday, 2 to 5 PM Sunday.

CHIMNEYVILLE CRAFTS GALLERY

1150 Lakeland Dr.
Jackson   981-2499

This gallery near the Ag Museum is where some of Mississippi's finest arti-

The Robert Johnson Memorial at Mt. Zion M. B. Church near Itta Bena marks the grave of the "King of the Delta Blues Singers."

sans — those in the Craftsmen's Guild — exhibit, demonstrate and sell their work. Guild members include printmakers, woodcarvers, jewelrymakers, painters and more. Hours are 9 AM to 5 PM Monday through Saturday; it's closed Sunday.

MISSISSIPPI CRAFTS CENTER
Natchez Trace Pkwy., Exit 105A
Ridgeland 856-7546

The Crafts Center is operated by the Craftsmen's Guild of Mississippi. They are among the state's best artists, and they provide a grand opportunity to see and buy traditional and contemporary folk arts and crafts. This dogtrot-style house is a good setting from which to exhibit handmade quilts and Choctaw baskets. Hours are 9 AM to 5 PM daily.

USM DEPARTMENT OF ART
Fine Arts Building
Hattiesburg 266-4972

The University of Southern Mississippi's Department of Art maintains a permanent display of artwork and hosts rotating exhibits available for free viewing each weekday. The Woods Art Gallery features changing exhibits and works by graduate students. Of interest is an exhibit of works by Richmond Barthe, an African-American sculptor and Bay St. Louis native whose works are also on display at the Whitney Museum and Metropolitan Museum of Art in New York. Admission is free.

ARTS IN THE PARK FESTIVAL
Meridian 693-2787

Come to this annual event held in the spring in Highland Park and presented by the Meridian Council for the Arts. Enjoy live entertainment and browse as artists and craftspeople display their work.

MERIDIAN COUNCIL FOR THE ARTS
601 24th Ave. 693-2787
Inside City Hall (800) 748-9970

The Meridian Council for the Arts is the umbrella agency for local arts. That includes the local art museum, little theater, symphony orchestra and Grand Opera House.

Other Cultural Attractions

ALLISON'S WELLS SCHOOL OF ARTS & CRAFTS, INC.
158 West Center
Canton 859-5826, (800) 489-2787

This teaching center for the arts and crafts replaces the original Allison's Wells Art Colony that burned in the 1960s. It now occupies the renovated Trolio Hotel and offers intensive workshops and classes in everything from fine arts to blacksmithing. It is the nation's first known arts and crafts school with a formal incubator center. Master seminars are offered in basketry, quilting, painting and more. The Colony Gallery features paintings and crafts by faculty, students and locals. Call for upcoming classes and registration and tuition information.

The River Cities

Museums

OLD COURT HOUSE MUSEUM
1008 Cherry St.
Vicksburg 636-0741

More than 10,000 artifacts from Mississippi's Native American cultures, the Civil War and the steamboat era are on display in this 1858 building constructed on the highest hill in Vicksburg. The courthouse was converted to a museum in 1948. Exhibits include furniture, clothing, paintings, china and silver. The museum is open Monday through Saturday from 8:30 AM to 4:30 PM and on Sunday from 1:30 to 4:30 PM. Hours are extended until 5 PM during daylight-saving time. Admission is $2 for adults, $1.50 for senior citizens and $1 for students.

GRAY & BLUE NAVAL MUSEUM
1211 Washington St.
Vicksburg   *638-6500*

The museum houses the world's largest collection of Civil War gunboat models, plus paintings of naval battles, artifacts and reference files on naval history from the war. Rates are $1.50 for adults and $1 for children younger than 12. The museum sells books, videotapes and model kits. It's open Monday through Saturday 9 AM to 5 PM.

BIEDENHARN MUSEUM OF COCA-COLA MEMORABILIA
1107 Washington St.
Vicksburg   *638-6514*

The Biedenharn Candy Company was the site in 1894 where Coca-Cola was first bottled. The faithfully restored 1890 building contains every kind of Coke advertisement and memorabilia, a reproduction of the original bottling equipment, a turn-of-the-century soda fountain and a restored candy store from 1890. Cokes, candy, ice cream and more than 100 soft drink items are sold in the gift shop. The museum is open all year except New Year's Day, Easter, Thanksgiving and Christmas. Hours are 9 AM to 5 PM Monday through Saturday and 1:30 to 4:30 PM on Sunday. Admission is $1.75 for adults, $1.25 for children younger than 12.

TOYS AND SOLDIERS MUSEUM
1100 Cherry St.
Vicksburg   *638-1986*

This privately owned and operated museum and gift shop houses the largest, most diversified collection on display in North America — more than 30,000 old and new toy soldiers of every kind, plus a miniature circus, a Mickey Mouse collection, pewter statuettes, soldier figurines and Civil War artifacts. Adults pay $2 admission, students $1. It's open March through September only Tuesday through Saturday from 9 AM to 5 PM.

USS CAIRO MUSEUM
National Military Park
Vicksburg   *636-2199*

The museum, adjacent to the restored Union gunboat, contains artifacts from the vessel. During winter months the museum is open Monday through Sunday from 8:30 AM to 5 PM; spring and summer hours are 9:30 AM to 6 PM.

MUSEUM OF AFRO-AMERICAN HISTORY AND CULTURE
307 Market St.
Natchez   *445-0728*

More than 600 original items from the 1890s to the 1950s are on display, along with special visiting exhibits. Call for hours. Donations are accepted.

Greenville boasts more published writers, per capita, than any other town in the USA, among them William Alexander Percy, Ellen Douglas, Walker Percy, Shelby Foote and many more. See the Percy Library Writers Exhibit for complete details.

Insiders' Tips

GRAND GULF MILITARY MONUMENT PARK

Rt. 2, Box 389
Port Gibson 39150   437-5911

Grand Gulf Military Park is dedicated to the former town of Grand Gulf and to the Civil War battle that took place there in 1863. The park is 10 miles northwest of Port Gibson, off Highway 61, and consists of 400 acres that incorporate Fort Cobun, Fort Wade, a cemetery, a museum, campgrounds, picnic sites, hiking trails, an observation tower and a number of restored buildings. The museum is open Monday through Saturday, 8 AM to noon and 1 to 5 PM, 9 AM to 6 PM on Sunday.

Theater

GOLD IN THE HILLS

3101 Confederate Ave.
Vicksburg   636-0471

The Parkside Playhouse presents this old-time melodrama where the audience takes an active role in booing the villain and cheering the hero. This production, a sentimental favorite, is almost 60 years old. Call for show dates during Pilgrimage and summer months. Admission is $7 for adults, $5 for children 12 and younger.

Music

THE NATCHEZ OPERA FESTIVAL

Natchez   (800) 862-3259

Get set for opera and much more during a month of music from late April through May. Audiences are treated to everything from Broadway musicals to plantation recitals, a cabaret and full-length operas. Ticket prices vary ($5 to $45) and so do the sites.

Literature

NATCHEZ LITERARY CELEBRATION

Natchez   (800) 862-3259

The focal point of this annual event, begun in 1989 and held in early June, is literature and the area's multicultural history. The theme changes each year. There are lectures, tours to literary landmarks and parties. Most presentations are held in the municipal auditorium, and the fees range from $10 each for one day's lectures and a gala reception at Stanton Hall to $20 each for three days' worth of lectures and the all-day writers' conference at the Natchez Eola Hotel. Free events include tours of the Melrose mansion, a book sale, book signings and movies. Sponsors are Copiah-Lincoln Community College, Mississippi Department of Archives and History and the National Park Service.

Visual Arts

PICTURING OUR PAST: PHOTOGRAPHS FROM THE ALLEN COLLECTION

City Hall, 1005 College St.
Port Gibson   437-4234

Leigh Briscoe Allen began photographing life in the rural South in 1906, capturing such scenes as river baptisms, county fairs, molasses cooking, train platforms and other images of the early 20th century. Fifty of his pictures are on display. The collection can be viewed Monday through Friday from 8 AM to 4 PM.

THE ATTIC GALLERY

1406 Washington St.
Vicksburg   638-9221

Upstairs in Sassafras Gift Shop, this gallery is crammed full of original regional art and fine crafts, including hand-blown glass, Walter Anderson prints, stained glass, lamps, jewelry, folk art and Native American crafts. It's open Monday through Saturday 10 AM to 5 PM.

The Coast

Museums

WALTER ANDERSON MUSEUM OF ART
510 Washington Ave.
Ocean Springs   872-3164

Walter Anderson was a prolific artist and naturalist known for his creations and eccentricities, such as rowing out to Horn Island and tying himself to a tree during a hurricane. He died in 1965, and only recently has he begun to receive recognition for his artistry. This new museum showcases more than 150 pieces of Anderson's work. Private docent tours are available and there is a nicely stocked museum shop. It's open 10 AM to 5 PM Monday through Saturday, 1 to 5 PM on Sundays. Admission is $3 for adults, $1 for children 6 to 12.

BEAUVOIR-
THE JEFFERSON DAVIS SHRINE
2244 Beach Blvd.
Biloxi   388-1313

The last home of the Confederate President features the Davis Family Museum, which highlights the life of the South's "First Family." This National Historic Landmark is open daily except Christmas from 9 AM to 5 PM. Admission is $5 for adults, $4.50 for seniors and active military, $2.50 for kids 6 through 15.

MARDI GRAS MUSEUM
Rue Magnolia and Croesus St.
Biloxi   432-8806

Inside the historic Magnolia Hotel is a collection of colorful costumes and memorabilia from the Coast's own carnival celebration. The museum is open Monday through Friday, 11 AM to 3 PM. Admission is $1 for adults and children 12 and older, younger than 12, 50¢.

GEORGE E. OHR ARTS
AND CULTURAL CENTER
136 G.E. Ohr St., Biloxi   374-5547

Adjacent to the Biloxi Library, the center features a permanent Ohr gallery that exhibits more than 120 exquisite pieces of pottery created by the "Mad Potter of Biloxi." The Lila Wallace Gallery showcases regional art that rotates quarterly. Guided tours by docents are available on request. Ohriginals, the Center's gift shop, features pottery, artwork and gift items. It's open 9 AM to 8 PM Monday through Wednesday, 9 AM to 5 PM Thursday through Saturday. A $2 suggested admission is appreciated.

OLD SPANISH FORT AND MUSEUM
4602 Fort Ave., Pascagoula   769-1505

Built in 1718, the fort is said to be the oldest building in the Mississippi Valley. Its 18-inch-thick walls are made from oyster shells, mud and moss. The museum contains 18th-century artifacts for the local area and a special hands-on exhibit for kids. It is open 9:30 AM to 4:30 PM Monday through Saturday and noon to 4:30 PM on Sunday. Admission is $2 adults, senior citizens $1.50, children 6 to 16 $1.

SCRANTON FLOATING MUSEUM
River Park, Pascagoula   762-6017

This unusual museum is an authentic, 70-foot shrimp boat that contains natural history and environmental displays. It is open 10 AM to 5 PM, Tuesday through Saturday and 1 to 5 PM on Sunday. Admission is free, but donations are accepted.

FORT MASSACHUSETTS

West Ship Island   875-9057

You'll have to travel 12 miles out into the Gulf to reach this historic fort, which is one of the last masonry coastal fortifications ever built. Constructed from 1859 to 1866, the fort was occupied by Confederate soldiers during the Civil War. National Park Service personnel conduct guided tours every day in summer. There is no charge for admission to the fort.

MARITIME AND SEAFOOD INDUSTRY MUSEUM

Point Cadet, Biloxi   435-6320

Biloxi was once known as the Seafood Capital of the World, and this local museum presents a number of exhibits that trace the city's once thriving industry. Learn about Native American tribes, boat building, marine blacksmithing and hurricanes through a collection of photographs and artifacts. The museum also sponsors the annual Race of the White Wing schooners and the Gulf States Model Boat Exhibit in November and Christmas Open House in December. The replica Biloxi Schooners *Glenn L. Swetman* and *Mike Sekul* were built under the museum's Biloxi Schooner Project. The museum is open Monday through Saturday 9 AM to 4:30 PM. Admission is $2.50 for adults and $1.50 for senior citizens and kids 6 to 16.

STENNIS SPACE CENTER

State Hwy. 607
Near Bay St. Louis   688-2370

The visitors center at this NASA propulsion system test facility contains everything from a Navy sub to a Space Shuttle external tank. The space-oceans-earth theme reflects the work of all of the agencies located at this scientific community. It's open daily, except Christmas Eve and Christmas Day, Thanksgiving and Easter, from 9 AM to 5 PM. Guided bus tours leave from the center on a regular schedule. The NASA Center is on State Highway 607, with easy access from I-10 and I-59. Just follow the signs to the guard gate for directions to the visitors center. Admission is free.

Theater

Coast theater audiences enjoy local and touring company productions throughout the year. The professional road companies perform at the Coast Coliseum and the Saenger Theatre, both in Biloxi. The community colleges in Biloxi and nearby Perkinston also stage productions. And there's a theater group for practically every community.

But whether the production is small or big in scale, the participants put everything they've got into the shows. The high quality will be a pleasant surprise to new audience members. There are many groups, each producing several shows a season. You will find musicals, classics, Broadway hits and even some original works offered on a regular basis. Check *The Sun Herald's* entertainment guide on Fridays for the latest, or call the following community theater groups directly.

BAY ST. LOUIS LITTLE THEATER

301 Boardman Ave.
Bay St. Louis   467-2587

The Bay St. Louis Little Theater presents productions in a quaint old playhouse in a quiet residential neighborhood. The group has been putting on shows for many seasons, including comedies, musicals and children's productions.

BILOXI LITTLE THEATER

220 Lee St., Biloxi   432-8543

Biloxi Little Theater's productions are always crowd pleasers, including its recent production of the popular *Under the Yum Yum Tree*.

CENTER STAGE

240 Eisenhower Dr., Biloxi   388-6258

Center Stage has its own modern building where some very talented actors perform. This group is known not only for its consistently fine productions but also for some outstanding set designs.

GULFPORT LITTLE THEATER

2600 13th Ave., Gulfport   864-7983

Gulfport Little Theater is an award-winning company that entertains audiences with various productions in its Lee Street theater. It features performances such as *The Taffetas* and *Barefoot in the Park* as well as an annual night of one-acts. This theater group has an active children's theater and theater camp and will proudly celebrate its 50th anniversary in the 1995-'96 season.

KINETIC NEO
SKENE THEATER

Biloxi   435-0450

Kinetic Neo Skene Theater is unique among Coast groups in that it puts on only musical productions, and it does so very well. KNS started its eighth season in the summer of 1995 with *Damn Yankees* at the Biloxi Saenger Theatre.

Music

MISSISSIPPI GULF COAST
BLUES FESTIVAL

Biloxi   388-8010

Blues, soul and gospel music are available all day long from several stages set up inside and outside the Coast Coliseum. The festival takes place in September and presents local, regional and national talent. An added attraction is lots of good food.

MAGNOLIA STATE
BLUEGRASS FESTIVAL

Wiggins   (800) 228-8779

Lovers of bluegrass music have two opportunities a year to enjoy those sounds if they take a short drive from the Coast north to Wiggins. The local radio stations sponsor festivals in June and in October. Camping on the grounds is available. A three-day pass to three days of concerts costs $25. Individual tickets run from $8 for one show to $9 and $10 for both evening and night concerts.

MISSISSIPPI COAST JAZZ SOCIETY

Biloxi   864-4000

The Society presents an annual festival and monthly parties celebrating the sounds of Dixieland.

GULF COAST OPERA THEATRE

Biloxi   388-6547

Members put on two or three productions per season, from full-blown costumed operas to the concert version,

---

The Delta Blues Museum in Clarksdale houses blues music memorabilia second to none. It also features a life-size replica of McKinley Morganfield, known by blues fans worldwide as the inimitable Muddy Waters.

Insiders' Tips

sometimes with guest artists. Every production is performed at the Saenger Theatre in Biloxi.

MISSISSIPPI COAST CHORUS
255-9975, 863-5335

This a cappella group stages shows at the Biloxi Saenger, Gulfport Little Theater, festivals and special events year round throughout the Coast.

GULF COAST COMMUNITY BAND
832-1256, 388-0142

Musicians perform for civic functions and festivals as well as at concerts in Edgewater Mall in Biloxi and West Side Community Center in Gulfport. Among the 30 or so members playing marches, overtures and show tunes are a few "snowbirds" who return each summer from the Midwest and New England.

SEACHORDS BARBERSHOP MEN'S CHORUS
832-1270

This barbershop group began as a quartet and grew to about 15 members who gladly perform at special events and other gatherings all year long.

BAY AREA CHORALE
8454 Kimo Ct.   452-3537
Diamondhead   255-5827

Members present several concerts throughout the year at various locations. The chorale also presents other choral groups, including some from neighboring Louisiana, in concert.

Dance

There are several dance schools and companies listed by the Gulf Coast Arts Council, including the following.

BALLET THEATER SOUTH
102 J Shearwater Dr. Gulfport   896-1724

Dancers present two ballet performances a year — in the spring and fall — at the Saenger Theatre in Biloxi. In addition to full-length productions, the group stages original choreography.

THE AIRTH CENTER
102 J Shearwater Dr.
Ocean Springs   875-6028

Interpretive dancer Leif Anderson, daughter of artist Walter Anderson, performs at the Walter Anderson Museum of Art and at workshops for children and adults. She also holds open houses at her Ocean Springs dance studio.

COAST BALLET CO. AND SCHOOL
Gulfport   864-4503

This nonprofit group presents repertory performances throughout the year. Its two big performances, at Christmas at the Biloxi Saenger and in the spring at the New Orleans Saenger, are presented jointly with Ballet Hysell of New Orleans.

STAR TWIRLERS SQUARE DANCE FESTIVAL
832-1392

This annual event, sponsored by the Star Twirlers Square Dancers, attracts dancers from all over the country. Attendance has been anywhere between 500 and 1,200. It's held the first full weekend of August. Visitors are welcome to watch the dancers free of charge. The event had been held at the Convention Center in Biloxi for years, but organizers are looking for a new permanent location.

MAGNOLIA SWINGERS SQUARE DANCE CLUB
D'Iberville   388-8320

Dancers get together every Friday night at the local community center.

Visual Arts

The Coast more than 30 art galleries and frequent events showcasing local talent as well as regional and national artists. There are two thriving art colonies on both sides of the Coast in the historic towns of Bay St. Louis and Ocean Springs as well as a great deal in between. Check *The Sun Herald's* "Marquee" entertainment guide published each Friday for a complete listing of galleries and details on special events such as art festivals.

GREATER GULF COAST ARTS COUNCIL
2511 13th St.
Gulfport   864-4000

A permanent collection of works by Coast artists and changing cultural exhibits are available for viewing free of charge. The council office is open weekdays from 10 AM to 5 PM.

GILLESPIE ART GALLERY
1856 Beach Dr. , Gulfport   865-1500

On the campus of William Carey College on the Coast is a collection of Mississippi art on permanent display. The gallery also presents changing exhibits. Admission is free.

ART WAVE
Ocean Springs   374-5547

This alliance of professional artists from Mississippi, Alabama and Louisiana sponsors two popular events each year. The annual juried show, held during the summer at the George E. Ohr Arts and Cultural Center in Biloxi, presents works by artists from the three member states. The members' show is held for a month during the spring at different gallery locations on the Coast.

ART WALK
Ocean Springs   872-5000

The many fine local art galleries sponsor special events, an outdoor sculpture exhibit in Marshall Park, demonstrations by artists and performing arts in the city's downtown historic district each year on a Saturday in early September.

OCEAN SPRINGS ANNUAL FALL SHOW
Ocean Springs   875-4424

The 300 members of the Ocean Springs Art Association sponsor this popular art show in the community center during the first two weeks of November. The event is nearly 30 years old, and it coincides with the Peter Anderson Festival.

A PLACE OF ART
Bay St. Louis   467-9092

The historic Main Street area, with its galleries and shops, takes center stage with indoor and outdoor exhibits by Bay area artists. The annual show is held on a Saturday in early October.

"Soldiers" clash sabers during a Calvary demonstration at Fall Muster, an annual event at Beauvoir, home of Confederate President Jefferson Davis in Biloxi.

Inside
Annual Events and Festivals

Here in Mississippi, annual events run a close second to big, raucous family reunions, where distant cousins come from far and near to pay homage to ties that bind. At annual events and reunions, vaguely familiar folks can become fast friends before home beckons. Some festivals, such as Jackson's Jubilee!JAM, are so big it's not easy to circulate and socialize. Others, such as the Calico Fair-type, are perfect places to meander among the wares and meet new people. Whatever your preference in weekend gatherings, you'll find some appealing events and celebrations here in the festival-filled Magnolia State.

After years of observing Southern festivals, we've come to this conclusion: The most successful ones have three key ingredients — barbecue, bands and beer. The latter can be replaced with "co-cola" if it's a church or family affair, but barbecue and bands are *de rigueur*. We'll feature a few festivals in this overview, then list the specifics of each region's biggest and best. For a listing of the state's festivals, contact the Mississippi Division of Tourism at (800) WARMEST. They print a nice calendar of events in six-month increments (January through April and May through December) for the upcoming year that covers all the festivals they know about. Area chambers of commerce usually have events calendars as do local Convention and Visitors Bureaus.

The Magnolia State is known for its stately antebellum mansions, and springtime is when most are open for annual "pilgrimages" to historic homes. The biggest pilgrimages are held in Natchez, Vicksburg, Columbus and Holly Springs. The Coast hosts a nice one too, though their houses are not all pre-Civil War, as in the other towns mentioned. For descriptions and details, see our Pilgrimages chapter.

Seafood of all varieties is celebrated in a collection of festivals in cities and towns along the Mississippi Gulf Coast. Crawfish, crabs, shrimp, oysters, catfish and even the mullet has its day (or weekend) to shine during appropriate seasons. The featured food becomes the menu's star attraction, which is accompanied by live entertainment and good times.

Monthly events of note include First Monday Trade Day in Ripley, said to be one of the 10 largest flea markets in the United States. It sometimes draws up to 50,000 people each month, and it covers about 27 acres. Meridian's East Mississippi-West Alabama Collector's Fair is a popular event each month, too, and the two major Canton Flea Markets — on the second Thursdays of May and October — are much anticipated and well-attended events at Court House Square in downtown Canton. About 800 crafters exhibit and sell here.

In the following pages we've organized our favorite annual events according to when and where they take place. Treat yourself to some good ole Mississippi fun and stop by as many as you can.

January

The Hill Country

TUPELO GIGANTIC FLEA MARKET
Tupelo Furniture Market, 1301 Coley Rd.
Tupelo (800) 533-0611

This is one of the Southeast's largest flea markets, with offerings of furniture, clothes, antiques and collectibles. Expect vendors/dealers from several states.

MID-SOUTH FAIR TALENT SHOW CONTEST
Civic Auditorium, Tupelo (800) 533-0611

Held in the hometown of Elvis Presley, participants hope that more exceptional talent will be noticed here. This is a search for entries for the Fair talent show. Admission is charged.

The Heartland

DIXIE NATIONAL
LIVESTOCK SHOW AND RODEO
The Coliseum, 1207 Mississippi St.
Jackson 961-4000, 354-7050

The capital city of Jackson is known for its many festivals, though few are better known than the Dixie National Rodeo and Western Festival. It's the second-largest

livestock show and the largest rodeo east of the Mississippi — and a crowd-pleaser to boot. This event is sponsored by the Mississippi Department of Agriculture and Commerce. It runs late January through late February.

COLLECTORS' FAIR
41st Ave. and 19th St., Meridian 483-5575

This monthly fair at the Frank Cochran Center at Highland Park is where vendors sell crafts, antiques, baseball cards and other collectibles. Admission is 75¢.

The River Cities

ELEVENTH MOON
STORYTELLING FESTIVAL
400 Jeff Davis Blvd., Natchez 446-6502

Regional storytellers present tales with Native-American subjects in this free event held in late January at the Grand Village of the Natchez Indians. Admission is free. Organizers recommend young visitors be at least 8 years old.

February

The Hill Country

BLACK HISTORY MONTH
Contact Welcome Centers 359-3297

Special events recognizing the contributions of black Americans are held statewide. Events including museum exhibits and school programs are well-publicized and well-attended. Choose one near you.

CIVIL WAR RE-ENACTMENT
Off Miss. 50   329-1191
Outside Columbus   (800) 327-2686

Local battles are thoroughly re-searched and re-fought 130 or so years after the fact. Re-enactors wear uniforms of both armies; cannon are fired, bugles are blown, and "suttlers' stores" sell souvenirs to onlookers. This usually takes place the second weekend in February, but call to be sure.

The Heartland

DIXIE NATIONAL LIVESTOCK SHOW, RODEO, AND WESTERN FESTIVAL
The Coliseum, 1207 Mississippi St.
Jackson   961-4000, 354-7050

The Mississippi Coliseum is the site of this month-long livestock show and rodeo. It's also a western festival extraordinaire, complete with food, crafts and lots of family entertainment.

ANNUAL GEM, MINERAL, JEWELRY & FOSSIL SHOW
Jackson   859-1240

Call for exact location, and then expect to find gems, minerals, fossils and working demonstrations of how to cut and polish gemstones.

The River Cities

MARDI GRAS
Natchez   (800) 647-6724

Natchez celebrates the carnival season with colorful day and night parades, parties and balls. The festivities are held at various locations throughout the city. Dates vary from year to year, so call for details.

RIVER CITY CLASSIC
Broadway and Franklin Sts.
Natchez   (800) 647-6724

Runners and walkers take to the streets for this classic 10K run, 5K walk and 1-mile fun run/walk. The 10K is a Mississippi Track Club-sanctioned Grand Prix event. Of course there's a celebration on the bluff after the race.

The Coast

MARDI GRAS
(800) 237-9493

If you've never been to Mardi Gras, or even if you have, don't miss the lively celebrations in just about every community along the Coast. The parades, with costumed riders on floats and accompanying marching bands, start as early as January. Riders reward the crowd's shouts of "Throw me something, mister" with colorful beads, doubloons and other prized trinkets. The culmination of all this carnival revelry is on Mardi Gras, the day before Ash Wednesday, when the final parades roll through the streets.

MISSISSIPPI COAST HISTORY WEEK
360 Beach Blvd., Biloxi   435-6320

A week of living history centered on the re-creation of an 18th-century French encampment is presented on the grounds of the historic Tullis-Toledano Manor in early February.

March

The Hill Country

TUPELO GIGANTIC FLEA MARKET
Tupelo Furniture Market
1301 Coley Rd., Tupelo   (800) 533-0611

This is one of the largest flea markets in the northern part of the state, where a wide variety of items are for sale. Big and small items are plentiful.

The Delta

DELTA SPRINGFEST
Convention Center, Raceway Rd.
Greenville   334-2711, (800) 467-3582

Homemade crafts, a carnival, food and ongoing entertainment are on the agenda for this family affair in mid-March. Rumor has it that a celebrity and more are scheduled.

BIG SPRING ROUND-UP, TRAIL RIDE, AND RODEO
Convention Center, Raceway Rd.
Greenville   334-2711, (800) 467-3582

This is said to be the biggest cowboy party in the state, with about 2,000 horses and riders in attendance in late March. Cowboy vendors are there to sell saddles, hats, tack and more. There's a western dance on Friday and Saturday nights, which promises outstanding entertainment. Proceeds benefit the burn center at the local hospital.

SPRING SPECTACULAR
Downtown Yazoo, Yazoo City   (800) 381-0622

Tour the outstanding homes and buildings of the early days of Yazoo City. You'll enjoy historic house tours and other special activities in the best festival form on the fourth weekend in March.

The Heartland

MAL'S ST. PADDY'S PARADE AND FESTIVAL
100 E. Captial, Jackson   984-1100

This event spans a couple of weeks in early and mid-March and includes a golf tournament, spring dance, regatta, children's parade and festival and adult parade. Festivities end with a big street dance.

MISSISSIPPI FORESTRY AND WOOD PRODUCTIONS EXPOSITION
Laurel Fairgrounds, Laurel   649-3031

The expo is fun for everyone, with log rolling, informational seminars and demonstrations about forestry, games and contests for all ages plus good food. The expo takes place on the last Friday and Saturday of March.

LIGHTED AZALEA FESTIVAL
McComb   684-2291

McComb and other communities throughout Pike County light up when the azaleas are in full bloom. For a two-week period, residents illuminate their azaleas and dogwoods, and visitors can enjoy the sights on driving tours by following directional signs and arrows. Also during this time, the Pike Alive celebration of spring features live entertainment and food at various locations in McComb.

WALKING AND RACKING HORSE SHOW
Collins City Park, Collins   765-6012

Winners in more than two dozen classes take home prize money and ribbons in this chamber-sponsored event. There's also live entertainment, rides and games to enjoy.

The River Cities

RUN THROUGH HISTORY
3201 Clay St., Vicksburg   (800) 221-3536

The Vicksburg National Military Park is the setting on the first Saturday in March for this annual 10K road race, 5K walk and 1-mile fun run.

SPRING PILGRIMAGE
Natchez   (800) 647-6742

The city opens its doors to visitors as 30 or more of its antebellum homes open their doors for inspection. There's also a Confederate Pageant depicting the city's colorful history, the comical play *Southern Exposure!*

and *Southern Road to Freedom*, a tribute set to music to entertain visitors with lively performances by actors and musicians.

SPRING PILGRIMAGE

Vicksburg   (800) 221-3536

A dozen antebellum and Victorian homes are opened to visitors during this annual tour in March and April. *Gold in the Hills*, a 60-year-old melodrama with a national reputation, is presented during Pilgrimage at the Vicksburg Theatre Guild. Audiences are encouraged to boo the villain and cheer the hero at the weekend performances.

SPRING PILGRIMAGE

Oak Sq. and Main St., Port Gibson   437-4351

This annual event is a weekend filled with tours of nine historic homes. There's also the 1800s Spring Festival, a living history fest at Oak Square Mansion where costumed participants show how life was in earlier times — from dances to fencing duels. The accompanying Main Street Heritage Festival features live music, arts and crafts vendors, a 5K walk/run, music, a food fair, guided tours of historical sites, a venison cook-off, an antique car show and more.

ST. PATRICK'S DAY PARADE

Natchez   442-1422

Wear green and join the Krewe of Killarney to watch St. Patrick drive the snakes into the Mississippi. The parade starts at Memorial Park and ends on Broadway. The fun lasts all day, and it's free.

POW-WOW AT THE GRAND VILLAGE OF THE NATCHEZ INDIANS

400 Jeff Davis Blvd.
Natchez   446-5117

Native Americans display their dancing, music, costumes and crafts at this popular annual event held in late March. Admission is $1.

PIECES AND STRINGS

507 Market St., Port Gibson   437-8905

Quilting artists display their talents and compete in contests at Mississippi Cultural Crossroads. Some of the African and European-American style quilts are for sale.

The Coast

SPRING PILGRIMAGE

The Coast   (800) 237-9493

This Coast-wide pilgrimage of homes, gardens and historical buildings is nearly 50 years old and is sponsored by the Mississippi Gulf Coast Council of Garden Clubs. The Coast Pilgrimage features private homes as well as historic homes such as Tullis-Toledano in Biloxi and Jefferson Davis' Beauvoir. Also welcoming visitors during this time are such diverse facilities as the John C. Stennis Space Center in Hancock County and the Old Spanish Fort in Jackson County.

City dwellers who want to see the South at work will enjoy an agricultural tour of catfish farms, cotton gins and animal farms. Self-guided tours via a new Mississippi map offer a chance to enjoy the scenic back roads off the beaten path, though a more organized tour is available. To receive a free, updated map, contact the Mississippi Division of Tourism Development, (800) WARMEST.

Insiders' Tips

ST. PATRICK'S DAY

Biloxi   896-6363

Biloxi's celebration includes the annual parade and the Irish Greens golf tournament and derby. Events are held at various locations.

ST. PATRICK'S DAY PARADE

Waveland   467-7400

Waveland welcomes everyone who is Irish for the day at this fun parade held in the downtown area.

OYSTER FESTIVAL

Point Cadet, Hwy. 90, Biloxi   374-2330

Fresh seafood, live entertainment, arts and crafts and family fun are featured at the annual benefit for the Biloxi Boys and Girls Club.

April

The Hill Country

April is Pilgrimage time in Mississippi; historic homes display fine antiques and period furnishings to guests who pay a call. Festive gowns worn over hoop skirts add even more authenticity to a visit to the Old South. Antiques are polished; old chandeliers sparkle; lovely gardens are in full bloom. Dates vary each year, though many Pilgrimages coincide with the blossoming of spring flowers, usually in early April. It's best to call for specifics before planning a trip. More detailed information on Mississippi Pilgrimages will be found in the Pilgrimages chapter of this book.

COLUMBUS PILGRIMAGE

316 Seventh Ave. N.
Headquarters, The Lee Home
Columbus   329-3533, (800) 327-2686

The Columbus Pilgrimage kicks off annually in very late March or early April.

Usually 14 to 16 antebellum homes are open for tours on a rotating basis. This heritage tour event is one of the state's best and named a Top 20 Event by the Southeast Tourism Society; all the homes are antebellum and listed on the National Register of Historic Places. Candlelight tours are available some evenings.

TALES FROM THE CRYPT

Fourth Ave. S.   329-1191
Columbus   (800) 327-2686

History is brought to life by candlelight and lanterns as students from the Mississippi School for Mathematics and Science don period costumes and portray the historically significant persons laid to rest at Friendship Cemetery. It's a most impressive history lesson in early April, as it coincides with Pilgrimage.

ABERDEEN PILGRIMAGE

The Magnolias, Commerce St., U.S. 45
Aberdeen   369-6488

Tour historic homes and churches, and expect lots of extras, such as a stroll along "Silk Stocking Avenue," the historical pageant *Our Town*, and lots more, all weekend.

OXFORD CONFERENCE FOR THE BOOK

Ole Miss Campus   232-5993
Oxford   (800) 880-6967

Gather among readers, writers, agents, publishers and scholars. This big event includes workshops for aspiring writers, lecturers, panel discussions and readings. Call for specifics on this April weekend-long event.

BLUE MARBLE CELEBRATION

Mumphrey Coliseum
MSU Campus, Starkville   323-3322

This festival features the performing arts, with a wide variety of performers from the state and far beyond.

TUPELO GIGANTIC FLEA MARKET
Tupelo Furniture Market
1301 Coley Rd., Tupelo 842-4442

You can snatch up some good bargains in glassware, furniture, clothing, lamps and more. Many vendors attend.

CARROLLTON SPRING PILGRIMAGE
Carrollton 237-6943

Tour historic homes and other structures, and enjoy a flea market, food, music and more. It all happens in mid-April. Call for specifics and to see if it's on this year.

TRASH TO TREASURES
Columbus Fairgrounds
Miss. 69 S., Columbus (800) 327-2686

Great finds and great fun are at this big annual event. And it is, literally, trash to treasures! Vendors and visitors from Mississippi and Alabama gather for arts and crafts and more.

HOLLY SPRINGS PILGRIMAGE
Holy Springs 252-2943

Seven pre-Civil War heritage homes are open for scheduled tours along with the museum, the Kate Freeman Clark Art Gallery and more.

SPRINGTIME IN THE ROCKERS
Columbus 329-1191, (800) 327-2686

This special treat is a trip back in time, when folks visited on front porches and heard the latest news. Springtime in the Rockers is a front porch tour of Columbus' historic Southside, complete with friendly visits along the way. It be-

gins at the front porch of the first home of playwright Tennessee Williams, now the Columbus Welcome Center, then proceeds to other porches and interesting stories. It's a guided tour, with staggered tours beginning throughout the weekend. Call sponsor Columbus Convention & Visitors Bureau for exact dates and times for this mid-April event.

REDLANDS FESTIVAL
Downtown Fulton, Fulton 862-4929

Family fun is on the agenda for this one, including arts and crafts, a 10K run, children's rides, antique cars and more.

AMORY RAILROAD FESTIVAL
Amory 256-7194

This big festival held the third week in April celebrates Amory's early days as a railroad town with arts and crafts, entertainment, train exhibits and a 10K run. It is also one of the Southeast Tourism Society's Top 20 Events for April.

PICNIC AT THE POPS
MUW Campus, Poindexter Hall 329-1191
Columbus (800) 327-2686

The Mississippi Symphony Orchestra offers a concert once each year on the lovely grounds of the spectacular Mississippi University for Women. This is a top priority for lovers of history and music in late April.

SUPER BULLDOG WEEKEND
MSU campus, Starkville 323-3322

This big event is the university's springtime homecoming, and it offers a chance to

Mardi Gras parade crowds can be large, so get to your viewing spot early, and stick to legal parking spaces.

Insiders' Tips

cheer at football scrimmages and base-ball games. It's also the place to be for the popular pork barbecue cookoff. There are lots of activities all weekend for all ages. The Starkville Visitors & Convention Council has details.

SPRINGFEST
Hwy. 51 and Stateline Rd.
Southaven   393-7738

Southaven is next door to Memphis, so it stands to reason that a Memphis-in-May sanctioned barbecue cooking contest is on the agenda. You'll also enjoy arts and crafts, entertainment and a lovely sunset symphony performance.

The Delta

WORLD CATFISH FESTIVAL
Belzoni   247-4838

Help locals and guests celebrate the importance of King Catfish at this festive day that offers more than 200 arts and crafts booths, races, catfish lunches, music, children's activities, a 10K run and so much more. It's held downtown around Court House Square in early April. While there, don't miss the new and exciting Belzoni Catfish Capital Museum; it's a museum of which to be proud and a good sample of Mississippi artists' work. This is billed as an international festival.

RIVERGATE FESTIVAL
Downtown Tunica   (800) 541-3823

Barbecue cooks and fans converge on Rivergate Park in downtown Tunica. This festival comes complete with bands, arts and crafts, children's activities and the big Memphis-in-May-sanctioned bar-becue cooking contest. More than 6,000 came last year, and future years are ex-pected to bring larger crowds. This is an early-April weekend event.

LELAND CRAWFISH FESTIVAL
Downtown Leland   (800) 467-3582

This festival not only boasts red hot Cajun crawfish, but also entertainment, arts and crafts and more. And while there, don't miss a stroll along the beautiful Deer Creek in early April.

LEVEE BREAK CELEBRATION!
Schelben Park, City Waterfront
Greenville   (800) 467-3582

This event celebrates the prevailing spirit of Greenville and the town's ability to bounce back from disaster, such as the Great Mississippi River Flood of 1927. It's two weeks of entertainment, commu-nity profiles and more in mid-April.

CROSSTIE ARTS FESTIVAL
Courthouse Lawn, 200 Court St.
Cleveland   846-4087

A juried arts festival makes this a well-attended event. You'll enjoy concessions, en-tertainment and a day of fun in mid-April.

ARTZAPOPPIN' IN YAZOO
Downtown Yazoo, Yazoo City (800) 381-0662

Celebrate the arts, history, drama and music surrounding this interesting town. Also available as part of Artzapoppin' are alternate performances —meaning they alternate each year — of *Chronicles of Yazoo* and a stage play by New Stage the-ater group out of Jackson. *Chronicles of Yazoo* tells the town's history and hap-penstance in the form of a dramatic per-formance. Organizers expect it will be on again in 1996.

The Heartland

OLDE TOWNE CLINTON
CIVIL WAR REENACTMENT
Hillman-Berry Campus
Leake St., Clinton   924-5912

Clinton was caught in a path of destruc-

Credit: Mississippi Department of Economic and Community Development

Fox hunting is a featured event at the Neshoba County Fair in Philadelphia.

tion as Union forces marched from Vicksburg to Jackson. See it re-enacted 1860s-style in early April. You'll enjoy living history displays and more.

BRICK STREETS FESTIVAL

Jefferson St., downtown Clinton   924-5912

Artisans and exhibitors from the Southeast line the old brick streets of historic downtown Clinton. It's part of the "Arts in April" observance, an early-April Arts Council event.

ZOO BLUES

Jackson Zoological Park, Jackson 352-2582

Listen to this great blues concert served up as a fund-raiser for the Jackson Zoo, and enjoy good food and cold drinks all the while. Big-name blues bands attract about 8,000 fans in early April. Many choose to come early (before 1 PM) to visit zoo animals, then venture next door to the afternoon's outdoor concert. Call the Zoo for specific bands and latest developments.

CANTON PILGRIMAGE AND ANTIQUE CAR SHOW

Canton   859-1307, (800) 844-3369

Tour Canton's historic homes and the downtown Court House Square around the first of April. Also, admire the antique cars that line the streets along Court House Square.

FIDDLERS' JAMBOREE

Attala County Coliseum
Kosciusko   289-2986

Musicians of all skill levels compete in fiddle, mandolin, banjo contests and more at the Attala County Coliseum in late April.

NATCHEZ TRACE FESTIVAL

Courthouse Square
Kosciusko   289-2986

For more than 25 years, this popular festival has celebrated the area's heritage. You'll enjoy food, entertainment, a 10K run and kids' activities at Courthouse Square in late April.

MISSISSIPPI MULE FESTIVAL

The Ag Museum, 1150 Lakeland Dr.
Jackson   354-6113

This old-fashioned festival is sure to please all age groups. It takes place in late April or early May at the Agricultural and Forestry Museum, which is one of Mississippi's untouted treasures. Mules helped clear the land and till the soil during the settlement of Mississippi, and that's cause for a celebration.

PINE FEST

Laurel   428-0574

This chamber event began as a salute to the timber industry and its impact on the area. A special feature is a tour of private homes in the historic district, which are not usually open to the public. Admission is $3. A free event is an original musical production depicting the history of Jones County. Pine Fest is held in late April.

RAILFEST

Hazlehurst   894-3752

Hazlehurst celebrates springtime and the railroad's place in its history with a walking tour of historic homes, live music, delicious food, a 5K walk/ run and lots of other fun on the third Saturday of March. Activities are held in the downtown area.

MISSISSIPPI SHAKESPEARE IN THE PARK

110 Beaver Dam Rd.
Lucedale   947-2123

Lucedale City Park is the stage for this free celebration of Shakespeare's works and the Elizabethan period, complete with costumes and period food (plus present-day favorites).

The celebration marks the beginning of National Library Week.

The River Cities

RIVERFEST

Vicksburg   (800) 221-3536

Enjoy three days of food, music and entertainment in Vicksburg's downtown area and City Park in mid-April. The Spring Arts and Crafts Show in Old Courthouse Square is held in conjunction with the fest.

The Coast

COASTCON

2350 Beach Blvd., Biloxi   435-5217

For almost 20 years, the Coast Con-

Insiders' Tips

Madison, a Jackson neighbor growing in leaps and bounds, was first settled in the 1800s and called Madisonville. The advent of the railroad in the 1850s brought the name Madison Station, and today, the town is enjoying a population boom as the City of Madison. It's also a place where churches are involved in community activities. Three historic churches in the area host big festivals, among them the Germanfest at St. Joseph's in Gluckstadt in September; the Cajun Fest at St. Francis of Assisi in October; and Day in the Country hosted by the Episcopal Chapel of the Cross. The Chamber of Commerce, 856-7060, has information.

Source: The Sun Herald

Sincerely yours Mary Ann Mobley Miss America 1959

Mary Ann Mobley from Brandon was crowned Miss America in 1959. Mississippi has had three other Miss Americas since then – Lynda Lee Mead, Natchez, 1960; Cheryl Prewitt, Ackerman, 1980; and Susan Akin, Meridian, 1986.

vention Center has been the setting for this science fiction and fantasy convention. Activities include special guests, costumes, movies, games and panel discussions.

LANDING OF D'IBERVILLE
Front Beach Dr., Ocean Springs   872-2766
French explorer Pierre LeMoyne D'Iberville first set foot in the area now known as Ocean Springs in 1699. The city celebrates the exploration for a week

in late April. Festivities include a costumed re-enactment of his arrival.

CONFEDERATE MEMORIAL DAY
2244 Beach Blvd., Biloxi   388-1313
Soldiers of the Confederacy are honored in late April with tributes and music at Beauvoir, the last home of Confederate President Jefferson Davis. A wreath is placed at the Tomb of the Unknown Soldier.

May

The Hill Country

GUMTREE FESTIVAL
Courthouse Lawn, 200 W. Jefferson
Tupelo   841-6521, (800) 533-0611

Gumtree features a juried arts and crafts show with more than $12,000 in prizes, a songwriter's competition, theatrical performances, a 10K run and lots of food and fun. It's usually held the second weekend in May.

A FAIR IN THE SQUARE
Courthouse Square
Hernando   429-9055

Tours of homes are a big feature here in early May as well as arts and crafts, a barbecue cook-off, music and performing arts.

GOLDEN TRIANGLE POWER BOAT REGATTA
Columbus   329-1191, (800) 327-2686

Enjoy special events, entertainment and concessions at this two-day Southeastern Championship held on the Tennessee-Tombigbee Waterway. The event is sponsored by the Columbus Jaycees and is called "Thunder on the Water."

The Delta

MAINSTREAM FESTIVAL
Greenville   334-2711, (800) 467-3582

This big festival is three-in-one, and it's held on the Courthouse lawn. An arts and crafts festival and children's activities make for a lot of family fun, while a world-championship barbecue, catfish cook-off and hot tamales are the fare for the bluegrass picnic. The *Delta Democrat Times* sponsors the popular Grande Prix Catfish Races. All takes place on the Saturday before Mother's Day.

WITCH WAY TO YAZOO
Main St., Downtown
Yazoo City   746-1815, (800) 381-0662

Graveyard stories, a block party, food, a scavenger hunt and games will assure that this day in late May will be memorable.

MISSISSIPPI CROSSROADS BLUES FESTIVAL
Greenwood   453-9197, (800) 748-9064

It's a day in the park, complete with performances by well-known Delta Blues musicians. The festival is held at Whittington Park near the U.S. 82 Bypass in late May.

The Heartland

PEPSI POPS AT THE RESERVOIR
Jackson   960-1565

In early May you'll hear great music provided by the Mississippi Symphony at the Old Trace Park on the Ross Barnett Reservoir. This is a popular event, so plan to come early and claim a prime spot to see the hot-air balloons and hear the outstanding music.

JUBILEE!JAM
Downtown
Jackson   960-1891, (800) 354-7695

This is Jackson's big arts and music

festival in the heart of the city. It includes theater, dance, art, bands on several stages, activities and huge crowds in mid-May. The downtown area is the place to be for this big event, and it's well worth the trip!

CANTON FLEA MARKET

Courthouse Square 859-1307
Downtown Canton (800) 844-3369

The big twice-yearly Canton Flea Market Arts and Crafts Show has an excellent reputation. More than 800 superior artists from 29 states display and sell here, and they are by invitation only. This is truly one of the South's finest arts and crafts offerings, and a Top 20 event, according to the Southeast Tourism Society. It's held the second Thursday in May and October.

ARTS IN THE PARK

41st Ave. and 19th St.
Meridian 693-ARTS

Enjoy art, food, music and kid entertainment at this regional arts festival held at Highland Park for three days in early May. This popular annual event is almost 25 years old.

SANDY RIDGE SPRING BLUEGRASS FESTIVAL

U.S. 45 S., Meridian 693-2996

Bluegrass music is provided by top bands from around the country in mid-May. Admission is $6 to $8. The fall version of this event is held in late August.

JIMMIE RODGERS MEMORIAL COUNTRY MUSIC FESTIVAL

41st. Ave. and 19th St.
Meridian 483-5763

This is a versatile salute in late May to the legendary Mississippian known as the father of country music, with everything from a fishing rodeo to a talent show for kids and a beauty pageant. Events are held at Highland Park and Temple Theater, 2320 Eighth Street.

DAY IN THE PARK

Clarkco State Park
U.S. 45 776-6651

This Memorial Weekend event is nearly 20 years old and still going strong. The day's activities include crafts, food booths, live entertainment, a 5K and 1-mile fun run. The site is 18 miles south of Meridian. Admission is $2 per car for four people and 50¢ for each additional person.

OLD TIME FESTIVAL

Downtown, Hattiesburg 545-4595

Enjoy a showcase of the area's heritage through entertainment, arts and crafts and something special for the kids. More than 50,000 people come out to enjoy the music and food, making it one of Hattiesburg's top events. Things get kicked off with the annual Crawfish Festival, held on Friday night before the Old Time Festival. There's music and mudbugs for everyone. The Crawfish Festival is held at Elks Lake Music Park, about 3 miles south of Hattiesburg.

OKATOMA FESTIVAL

Courthouse Lawn, Collins 765-6012

Covington County celebrates in early May with an award-winning, week-long festival featuring carnival rides, arts and crafts, a horse show, canoe racing, live entertainment, food and street a dance. Actor Gerald McRaney, a native son who starred in the television series "Major Dad," and entertainer Jerry Clower have been past grand marshals in the festival's parade.

The River Cities

NATCHEZ OPERA FESTIVAL
Natchez   (800) 862-3259

See opera plus Broadway, cabaret and other music in a month-long series of recitals held at various locations. Ticket prices range from $5 to $45, depending on the event.

The Coast

BLESSING OF THE FLEET
Small Craft Harbor, Biloxi   435-5578

For more than 60 years, fishermen have maintained this Old-World tradition of receiving spiritual blessings for a safe season and bountiful catch. The colorfully decorated boats form a water parade as part of the ceremony. Blessings are also held in Pascagoula, 762-4423, and Pass Christian, 452-2252.

RIVER JAMBOREE
Moss Point   475-6492

A day of fun in early May for the family features entertainment, games, rides and crafts. It is held at various locations in town.

ANNUAL MISSISSIPPI
GULF COAST FAIR & EXPO
2350 Beach Blvd., Biloxi   388-8010

The fair features more than 40 amusement rides plus musical entertainment, a petting zoo, fireworks and lots of fun on the grounds of the Coast Coliseum in late May.

June

The Hill Country

OLEPUT FESTIVAL
Courthouse area, downtown Tupelo   841-6521
                              (800) 533-0611

Observant festival-goers will notice that Oleput is Tupelo spelled backward, and it is a Mardi Gras-style festival that's gotten bigger and better since it began in 1990. Celebrate at the Oleput Festival the first weekend in June.

JUNETEENTH DAY CELEBRATION
Downtown Aberdeen   369-6488

Join with those who celebrate the African-American heritage and culture and enjoy the festivities in this special Mississippi treasure of a town.

The Delta

DELTA JUBILEE
U.S. 49 S.
Clarksdale   627-1313, (800) 626-3764

This event features a championship barbecue cooking contest, arts and crafts, sports tournaments, concessions and more. You'll also enjoy great entertainment performed by popular local and national groups each night of the event. Join more than 30,000 people in Clarksdale on the first weekend in June.

INDIAN BAYOU ARTS
AND CRAFTS FESTIVAL
Downtown Indianola   887-4454

This one boasts native Indianolan B.B. King in the "B.B. King Homecoming" outdoor concert on Friday night. The weekend features lots of goods to see and buy as well music and entertainment on the first weekend in June.

GRENADA LAKE FESTIVAL
At the lake, Grenada   226-2851

There's something here for the entire family: music, a 10K run, tennis and softball tournaments, a car show, arts and crafts, a children's fishing rodeo and more in early June. This amazing new festival focusing on water safety attracted more than 75,000 people in 1994.

MISSISSIPPI INTERNATIONAL BALLOON CLASSIC

Whittington Park, Sycamore St. 453-9197
Greenwood (800) 748-9064

Here's a full four days of fun for balloonists and spectators who gather to see the 75 or so hot-air balloons soar above the Delta fields. Partake of all the festival food, entertainment, children's rides and more in late June and early July.

The Heartland

GREAT CHUNKY RIVER RAFT RACE

U.S. 80, Chunky 482-6161

Rafters race the Chunky River for prizes and cash aboard flat bottoms, canoes, homemade rafts and inflatable vessels in early June. Boyette's Fish Camp is the site.

LONESOME PINE BLUEGRASS FESTIVAL

Lonesome Pine Park, Miss. Hwy. 28
Laurel 729-2691

This 15-year-old festival is considered one of the oldest and largest in three states. It's even gotten national exposure for its combination of bluegrass music by big-time musicians, good food and arts and crafts. The festival is held the second weekend in June and in October. Admission is $8 a day for the music only. Camping spaces for 250 RVs are also available, but reservations aren't. Come early.

The River Cities

NATCHEZ LITERARY CELEBRATION

Natchez (800) 862-3259

Scholars and literature lovers take in lectures, entertainment and other activities at this award-winning literary conference. Events are held at various locations in early June. The focus changes each year, but Southern writers always take center stage. Some events have limited seating, so call for information about reservations. The celebration is sponsored by the Copiah-Lincoln Community College, the Mississippi Department of Archives and History and the National Park Service.

STEAMBOAT JUBILEE AND FLOOZIE CONTEST

Natchez (800) 647-6724

The *Mississippi Queen* and *Delta Queen* steamboats pause in Natchez in late June during their yearly race to St. Louis. The passengers and crews compete as floozies, and a panel of local dignitaries judge who's best in this raucous contest. The audience gets into the act by cheering for their favorites.

The Coast

ST. CLARE SEAFOOD FESTIVAL

234 S. Beach Blvd., Waveland 467-7071

Good food, kid's games, live entertain-

Credit: The Sun Herald

On Biloxi's beach in front of Edgewater Mall, teams compete in the world's largest sand sculpture contest of its kind. This September event is sponsored by The Sun Herald.

ment and more are on tap at this local fest held at St. Clare School.

BLUEBERRY JUBILEE
STORYTELLING FESTIVAL

Poplarville   795-8378

The storytelling part of the already popular Blueberry Jubilee is getting more popular each year. Storytellers share their magical talents with audiences of all ages, and they come from all over the country to do just that. Organizers are members of the Poplarville Storytellers Guild, whose members include artists from other states as well as Mississippi. The event takes place in early June, a day before the emphasis turns to blueberries, crafts and arts.

JUNETEENTH CELEBRATION

Division St.
John Beck Park, Biloxi   388-4038

This annual event in mid-June cel-

ebrates black heritage and culture with entertainment, arts and crafts and food.

MAGNOLIA STATE
BLUEGRASS FESTIVAL

Magnolia Dr., Wiggins   (800) 228-8779

Bluegrass music takes center stage the first weekend in June and again in October. Both festivals are held in a pecan grove just a short drive from the Coast into Stone County.

July

Most cities and towns in Mississippi have some kind of Independence Day celebration, including arts and crafts shows, fireworks exhibits and barbecue cook-offs. Check local papers, Division of Tourism information, or the brochures available at local CVBs and chambers of commerce for July 4th celebration opportunities in specific areas.

The Hill Country

SLUGBURGER FESTIVAL

The Depot, Filmore St.   287-1550
Corinth   (800) 748-9048

Those who remember the Great Depression will know that a "slugburger" is a nickel's worth of a soybean-type hamburger, and Corinth celebrates those days. You'll find good food, great fun, games, a magician, entertainment, arts and crafts, a tour train and more on the first of July.

GOLDEN TRIANGLE RODEO

Beart Arena on Plymouth Rd.
Columbus   327-3822

Professional contestants compete in calf roping, steer wrestling, barrel racing, team roping, bareback riding and more. There are activities for kids too. The event is sponsored by the Golden Triangle Cowboy Association.

KUDZU FESTIVAL

Downtown Holly Springs   252-2943

This celebration of the great green vine includes a barbecue cook-off, a carnival, arts and crafts and live entertainment, sometimes by such groups as the Coasters. Don't miss the pig races and more on the first full weekend in July.

The Delta

GREENVILLE CELEBRATES AMERICA

Greenville   334-2711, (800) 467-3582

This big fireworks expo is compliments of Greenville's casinos, and they truly light up the sky. Entertainers of the caliber of Percy Sledge appear at the amphitheater at the downtown waterfront park on July 4th.

The Heartland

MISSISSIPPI CHAMPION HOT-AIR BALLOON FESTIVAL

Canton   859-1307, (800) 844-3369

Races and top prize money all add to the excitement at this big balloon event. At night enjoy the balloon glows, exhibitions that light up the sky. You'll enjoy a talent show, parade, music and more on July 4th weekend.

HOG WILD IN JULY

Mississippi Ag and Forestry Museum
Jackson   354-6113, (800) 844-TOUR

Early July is the time for fun at the Ag Museum, where a big barbecue-cooking contest gets top billing with musical entertainment and children's activities.

CHOCTAW INDIAN FAIR

Choctaw Reservation, Miss. 16 W.
Philadelphia   656-1742

See American Indian culture at its best, including native arts, social dancing, stickball, native food and other competitions. This annual event, held in mid-July, garners much media attention and it is one of the state's best-known events.

CHUNKY BLUES FESTIVAL

Chunky-Duffee Rd.
Chunky   693-6260

Nationally known recording artists display their talents at this popular annual music fest in mid-July. The site is a natural amphitheater on Richardson's Farm 12 miles west of Meridian on I-20; go north on Exit 121. Tickets are $15 in advance and $20 at the gate.

ZOOFARI FESTIVAL

Park Ave. at Hardy St.
Hattiesburg   545-4576

The Hattiesburg Zoo is the place to be for live music and other entertainment at this annual event sponsored by the local Zoological Society and the city. Enjoy arts and crafts, train rides and artists demonstrations.

SUMMERFEST
110 Beaver Dam Rd.
Lucedale   947-2755

Lucedale City Park is the site of dozens of crafts booths, live music, a petting zoo, rides and various other fun attractions in early July.

The River Cities

NATCHEZ BICYCLE CLASSIC
Natchez   (800) 647-6724

Pro and amateur cyclists compete in this exciting race. The weekend also features live music and other entertainment.

The Coast

DEEP SEA FISHING RODEO
Rice Pavilion, U.S. 90
Gulfport   388-2271

The mother of all fishing rodeos, this one is billed as the world's biggest. It's almost 50 years old and is still drawing crowds. It takes place during the July 4th weekend.

4TH OF JULY CRAB FESTIVAL
228 S. Beach Blvd.
Bay St. Louis   467-6509

A crustacean weekend celebration that the whole family can enjoy features namesake crab dishes and other great food, live entertainment, games and fireworks.

ST. PAUL'S
ANNUAL SEAFOOD FESTIVAL
151 E. Beach, Pass Christian   452-4686

Gumbo and fresh seafood are two of the menu items offered at this mid-July festival. There's also live entertainment and activities for kids.

August

The Hill Country

FAULKNER AND
YOKNAPATAWPHA CONFERENCE
Ole Miss Campus, Oxford   232-5993

This is an informative round of lectures and workshops concerning the life and works of Oxford's Pulitzer Prize-winning author. Each year's conference has a different topic; in 1994, it was Faulkner and Gender. The conference is a project of the Center for the Study of Southern Culture. It is held the last week in July or the first week in August. Early registration is best for this popular conference.

WATERMELON FESTIVAL
Old City Park, Water Valley   473-1122

This fun festival offers a music fest, talent show, arts and crafts, a downtown flea market and much more. A street dance kicks it off on the Friday evening before the big day, which is the first Saturday in August. More than 5,000 attend and enjoy the Watermelon Festival and its reunion ambiance.

ELVIS PRESLEY
COMMEMORATION DAY
306 Elvis Presley Dr., Tupelo   841-1245

This is a part of Elvis Presley Week, an annual event that garners much media attention. It's held on the grounds of his birthplace, and it showcases the Elvis museum, Times and Things Remembered. The commemoration is usually held the first week in August.

First Monday Trade Day

Start off your month by traveling the back roads to Ripley, where highways 5 and 15 intersect. You won't be disappointed when you arrive at First Monday Trade Day. This event has been going on since the late 1890s, and locals say it's getting better all the time.

Over the years, the First Monday site has moved from the courthouse square to an abandoned drive-in theater that amounts to acres and acres of chaotic fun. It's the setting for a giant treasure hunt, where you can buy or sell anything legal within reason.

About 600 traders set up booths; some spread their wares on the ground. Vendors often arrive early, say on a Thursday, to set up for the weekend-long sale that ends on the first Monday of the month.

The Delta

CROP DAY

Cotton Row, Greenwood   (800) 748-9064

CROP is an acronym for Cotton Row on Parade, and Cotton Row is Greenwood's answer to Wall Street . . . almost. It's the financial district for cotton brokers. The day celebrates cotton with juried arts and crafts, children's rides, canoe races, music, food and more in early August.

SUNFLOWER RIVER BLUES FESTIVAL

Old Train Depot, Clarksdale   627-1313
(800) 626-3764

This major Delta festival is dedicated to "preserving, promoting, and perpetuating the living blues musicians of the Delta." Indeed it does, and it offers lectures, educational programs, films, fun and food and more; it's held annually the second weekend in August.

KUDZU IN YAZOO

Fairgrounds   746-1273
Yazoo City   (800) 748-8875

Entertainment begins Friday evening and lasts all day Saturday, complete with arts, a barbecue-cooking contest and more on "Hawg Day Afternoon" in late August.

The Heartland

NESHOBA COUNTY FAIR

Fairgrounds, Philadelphia   656-1742

This popular fair is an annual event that's been around for more than a hundred years, and it keeps getting better. It's an old-fashioned "camptown" where camphouses are passed down from one generation to the next. The event features camptown races, national politicians, well-known entertainers and exhibits. It's truly a one-of-a-kind experience held in late July or early August. *National Geographic* called the Neshoba County Fair "America's Giant Houseparty."

SANDY RIDGE
FALL BLUEGRASS FESTIVAL

U.S. 45 S.
Meridian   693-2996

For almost 10 years audiences have been enjoying bluegrass at this site between Meridian and Quitman, behind Clarkdale School. The spring version of this event is held in May. Admission is $6 to $8. Concessions are available.

Zoo Blues

Historic Downtown Hattiesburg   545-4507

This blues festival takes place in the city's historic downtown district. Local cuisine is served up along with good music.

The Coast

Square Dance Festival

2350 Beach Blvd., Biloxi   863-1856

This annual event started back in 1963 and features workshops as well as square and round dancing in early August.

September

The Hill Country

Prairie Arts Festival

Downtown West Point   494-5121

One of the region's major arts festivals, Prairie Arts has a juried show and features hundreds of artisans from across the South. Booths and shoppers fill Sallie Kate Winters Park in downtown West Point on the Saturday before Labor Day each year. Thousands attend!

Hog Wild in Corinth

Corinth Train Depot
Downtown Corinth   287-5269

This is a day for barbecue and bands, for both are plentiful at Hog Wild. Showmanship is a big part of this barbecue cooking contest, and good times are on the agenda.

Northeast Mississippi Blues and Gospel Festival

Rust College, Holly Springs   252-8000

This festival in early September is sure to be enjoyed by blues and gospel fans. Performers come from throughout Mississippi and the mid-South.

Boardtown Jubilee

McKee Park
Starkville   323-3322

Browse as more than 120 exhibitors from throughout the South display a variety of goods. Expect to find antiques, paintings and a flea market in mid-September.

Pelahatchie Muscadine Jubilee

Downtown Pelahatchie   854-5224

Ever stomped a grape? Well, you can try it out at this early September festival that also features arts, crafts, food, entertainment and children's activities.

Possum Town Pigfest

Fairgrounds, Miss. 69 S.   328-4532
Columbus   (800) 327-2686

This gigantic barbecue cook-off in late September usually has about 80 teams vying for the big championship. You'll find lots of theme booths and Cajun and country music. Pigfest means party-time for cookers and a multitude of their guests, though it is open to the public and is a popular event.

Tallahatchie River Festival

The Park Along the River, New Albany 534-4354

Native crafts and tribal dancers offer a look at Chickasaw Indian culture in late September. History is a part of this festival that also features bands and a street dance.

The Delta

Delta Blues Festival

Miss. 1 and Rt. 454   334-2711
Greenville   (800) 467-3582

The Blues Festival has gotten consistently bigger and better since it began in 1977, and now it attracts more than 25,000 blues fans from across the country and Europe. Down-home Delta blues reverber-

Neshoba County Fair

This major event has been called "Mississippi's Grand Reunion" by *National Geographic*, though Mississippians call it the Neshoba County Fair. Politicians say it's a way to be elected, for it is indeed an important stop on the campaign trail for state and national politicians. The grand reunion, or giant houseparty, as it's also been called, is an institution in the Magnolia State. It's the last remaining camptown fair, where more than 600 colorful and coveted camphouses line the festive midway of this 100-plus-year-old event. For one week each summer, adults and their friends play in the rough and tumble camphouses that are cherished legacies. Often handed from one

Credit: Philadelphia/Neshoba Chamber of Commerce

The Camptown races in Philadelphia.

generation to another, the folks who converge on the fair each August don't seem to mind the heat, for they come to rest and relax and visit with old friends.

The community of camphouse dwellers increases by thousands when the day visitors arrive, and the good times always roll in this down-home, one-of-a-kind environment. Fair-goers stroll the midway, visiting and partaking of traditional fair festivities that include rides, games of chance, exhibits and food. They see painted ponies and real ones too, the latter of which strut their stuff at the camptown harness races held each afternoon. Crowds cheer for their favorite horse and driver as they streak like lightning around the track, though the cheers compete with the thunder of the horses' hooves and the rattle of the carriage wheels. Excitement is in the air!

In the center of the fairground is Founder's Square, where benches are positioned around fat old trees and the politicians podium is in plain view. Young and old, rich and poor find friends and camaraderie at the Neshoba County Fair. This is one of the state's favorite annual events, and one eagerly anticipated. For more information about the Neshoba County Fair, contact the Philadelphia-Neshoba County Chamber of Commerce, P.O. Box 51, Philadelphia, Mississippi, 39350; 656-1742.

ate throughout the weekend in mid-September, with well-known blues greats on the scene. Sometimes B.B. King, Coco Taylor, Dr. John and Bobby Rush appear. Follow the signs, and the crowd, to Highway 1 S., and Route 454. Expect to stay from noon til dark or after.

DEER CREEK ARTS & CRAFTS SHOW
Downtown, on Deer Creek   334-2711
Leland   (800) 467-3582

You'll find handmade arts and crafts, great food, music and a 5K run on the banks of beautiful Deer Creek in mid-September. About 100 exhibitors sell handmade items. Paddleboat rentals are available too.

The Heartland

SKY PARADE
Jackson International Airport
Off I-20 E., Jackson   982-8088

This is the largest aerial show in Mississippi. See 200 hot-air balloons, amusements, rides, nightly fireworks displays and a major crowd in early September. There's usually a special crowd-pleaser, such as a fly-by by the USAF Thunderbirds. Traffic is congested, so plan to leave early.

GERMANFEST
St. Joseph's Catholic Church, Gluckstadt
Madison   856-4977

Enjoy German foods and festivities served up by local descendants of German farmers in late September. This is one of the region's most diverse festivals, and a fun one to attend. It's also called the Gluckstadt German Festival.

OUTDOOR FEST
Blue Bluff Harbor on the Tenn-Tom Waterway
Aberdeen   369-6488

Enjoy this outdoor mid-September event that includes a fishing rodeo, arts and crafts, a 5K run, a boat regatta, concessions, entertainment and more. You'll usually find hot air-balloon rides too.

STAMPIN' STOMPIN' BLUES FESTIVAL
Lake Hazle City Park, Lake Hazle Dr.
Hazlehurst   894-3752

Hazlehurst is where blues man Robert Johnson was born in 1911, and the

Bishop Joseph Howze on the Glen Swetman *blesses shrimp boats as they pass at the Biloxi channel behind the small craft harbor by Deer Island.*

city honors the legendary musician with a festival featuring live entertainment and much more. The day-long event is held the last Saturday of September. Tickets are $10 in advance, $15 at the gate.

LABOR DAY ARTS AND CRAFTS FESTIVAL
Chautauqua Park, U.S. 51
Crystal Springs 892-2711

Exhibitors by the hundreds present their arts, crafts and food at this well-attended event sponsored by the chamber of commerce.

The River Cities

OVER-THE-RIVER RUN
4210 Washington St.
Vicksburg (800) 221-3536

Runners start on the Vicksburg side of the Mississippi, race across the bridge to Delta, Louisiana, and back in this annual 5-mile event in early September.

COPPER MAGNOLIA FESTIVAL
U.S. 61
Washington 442-2901

Beautiful Historic Jefferson College hosts this crafts fair that also has food and entertainment for the kids in late September.

The Coast

MISSISSIPPI
GULF COAST BLUES FESTIVAL
2350 Beach Blvd., Biloxi 388-8010

Music is performed by regional and national performers of blues, soul and gospel on various indoor and outdoor stages at the Coast Coliseum in mid-September.

GREAT OAKS STORYTELLING FESTIVAL
Downtown Ocean Springs 875-4424

This new weekend event takes place in historic downtown Ocean Springs and brings in storytellers from the Southeast and across the globe. Tickets are sold for the day or by event.

BILOXI SEAFOOD FESTIVAL
Point Cadet Plaza
Biloxi 374-2717

Taste seafood of all kinds is prepared and sold by individuals and restaurants at this mid-September festival. There is a small admission fee.

ANYTHING THAT FLOATS
CARDBOARD BOAT REGATTA
Chicot Rd., Pascagoula 762-4423

People-powered cardboard boats compete on Whitehead Lake at I.G. Levy Park. "Sailors" get the cardboard and the rules from the city's parks and recreation department and construct their own vessels. Some make "instant boats" while the more competitive take months to fashion what they hope will be a winner. Dozens compete, and many sink.

SAND SCULPTURE CONTEST
Beach Blvd., Biloxi 896-2434

It's the world's largest sand sculpture contest of its kind and as many as 100 teams have dug-in to compete for cash prizes. Sponsored by *The Sun Herald*, the event has been featured on the Disney Channel. It's held on the beach in front of Edgewater Mall.

October

The Hill Country

STARS OVER AMORY
High School Stadium, Amory 256-7194

"Stars" meaning film and TV stars from Hollywood. Indeed, they do come out for education the first weekend of October every other year, thanks to Amory native Sam Haskell, now a senior vice-president with the William Morris Agency in Los Angeles. His clients and friends fly into Amory to participate in the fund-raiser for an education scholarship in the name of Haskell's mother. Those who buy tickets buy outstanding entertainment as well. In 1994 (the next event is in 1996), showstoppers were Sela Ward, Nell Carter, Debbie Allen, Sinbad, Susan Anton, Collin Raye, Mary Donnelly Haskell (Sam's wife, an actress and singer and a former Miss Mississippi) and Malcolm-Jamal Warner. MCs were Mary Ann Mobley and hubby Gary Collins. Haskell, who initiated the scholarship, said that this is not an Amory event but a Mississippi event. It's held the first weekend in October. Call early for tickets to this high-quality show.

BLACK HILLS FESTIVAL

West Side Park, off U.S. 82
Starkville 323-3322

This event focuses on Mississippi's cultural heritage by including music from rhythm 'n' blues to gospel as well as arts and crafts. It's held near the first of October.

BATESVILLE FALL FESTIVAL PECAN GROVE

Behind the elementary school, Pecan Grove
Batesville 563-3126

This annual outdoor arts festival has been gaining popularity for about 30 years. It features hand-crafted items and an upscale flea market with antiques for sale in early October.

COLUMBUS ARTS FESTIVAL

Probst Hill
Columbus (800) 327-2686

Formerly the popular "Calico Fair," a name you never forgot, the less-inspirationally named festival still draws lots of booths and attendees on the first week-

end in October. It's a nice place to pick up original art for Christmas, and it's not too pricey.

GALA FALL WEEKEND AND
EUDORA WELTY WRITER'S SYMPOSIUM

MUW campus
Columbus 329-4750 , (800) 247-6724

This three-day celebration of Southern literature in mid-October attracts celebrity journalists from TV and magazines from across the country. A Book and Author Dinner is a black-tie affair that helps fund the Eudora Welty Chair. The dinner, held at the Trotter Convention Center, honors Welty, a Pulitzer Prize-winning writer from Mississippi. She attended Mississippi University for Women, host of the weekend symposium.

COLUMBUS DECORATIVE ARTS FORUM
AND ANTIQUE SHOW AND SALE

Convention Center, downtown Columbus
329-3533, (800) 327-2686

This show attracts lecturers and about 30 or so select dealers from the South and beyond in late October. It's a gala weekend-long event known for quality merchandise, including silver, porcelain, jewelry, linen and furniture.

DANCING RABBIT FESTIVAL

Downtown Macon 726-4456
(800) 487-0165

A big, fun-filled day is on the agenda in Macon at the Dancing Rabbit Festival. A talent contest, flea market, arts and crafts, live entertainment, food and more are available in this historic northeast Mississippi prairie town.

The Delta

CLEVELAND OCTOBERFEST AIRSHOW

Cleveland Airport, Cleveland 843-27122

See vintage World War II airplanes,

crop duster demonstrations, static displays and concessions at the Cleveland Airport in early October.

THE TENNESSEE WILLIAMS FESTIVAL
U.S. 49 and U.S. 61
Clarksdale   624-4461

Fans of playwright Tennessee Williams are here for the three-day mid-October event that includes panel discussions, a juried art show, a literary conference, music and walking tours of Tennessee's old neighborhood. This is becoming an important literary event in the state, thanks to astute organizers, most of whom are volunteers.

The Heartland

MISSISSIPPI STATE FAIR
The Coliseum, Mississippi St.
Jackson   961-4000

It's just what you expect a big state fair to be: midways, games, shows, livestock and exhibits in early October. You'll enjoy exciting rides as well!

DAY IN THE COUNTRY
CHAPEL OF THE CROSS
Miss. 463
Madison   362-0669, 856-2593

The popular festival features more than 100 artists and craftspeople, plus a country store, live entertainment, a run and lots of good food, including the famous 63-Egg Cake. This family festival is held around the first of October.

FRENCH CAMP HARVEST FESTIVAL
French Camp Academy
French Camp   547-6482

This is a lovely place to be in the fall because it is adjacent to the pristine Natchez Trace. Folks come in early October for the handmade quilt auction and sale of many other homemade items.

PIONEER AND
INDIAN HERITAGE FESTIVAL
Natchez Trace Pkwy.
Ridgeland   856-7546

Members of the Mississippi Craftsmen's Guild demonstrate period crafts from the pioneer era, including breadmaking and traditional dance in mid-October. There's also musical entertainment at the Crafts Center on the Natchez Trace Parkway.

CANTON FLEA MARKET
Downtown Canton 859-1307, (800) 844-3369

Known far and wide as a special event, this gigantic flea market boasts about 800 dealers from across the country. It's held the first Thursday (of each October and May).

UNION STATION RAILFEST
Front St. under 18th Ave. overpass
Meridian   485-1802

Rail buffs will want to head for Meridian Railroad Museum in late October. On display are artifacts from the old-time railroading days as well as a collection of photos, paintings and prints depicting rail travel. A popular new feature is a syrup mill that turns sugar cane into delicious syrup that is sold during the fest. Admission is free.

HUBFEST
Downtown Hattiesburg   (800) 63TOURS

Hundreds of booths offer food and arts and crafts throughout the downtown area. Other festivities include tennis and golf tournaments and 5K and 1K runs. This highly popular event is cosponsored by the city, the Area Development Partnership and the Columbus CVB.

CLARKE COUNTY FORESTRY
AND WILDLIFE FESTIVAL
Archusa Creek Water Park, Rt. 4
Quitman   776-5701

This water park is 28 miles south of

Credit: Tim Isbell, The Sun Herald

A ground crew prepares their balloon for takeoff at a hot air balloon festival in Canton.

Meridian. Festivities include arts and crafts, fun for kids, canoe racing and more. Good food is also available at this Clarke County Chamber of Commerce event held on the first Saturday in October.

The River Cities

FALL PILGRIMAGE
Natchez   (800) 647-6742

Hoop skirts are back in fashion with the fall version of the classic open house at 24 antebellum homes around town. The Natchez Fall Pilgrimage is held for three weeks starting in early October. Tickets to view the lovely homes are available at Natchez Pilgrimage Tours, Canal at State streets.

FALL PILGRIMAGE
Vicksburg   (800) 221-3536

Morning and afternoon tours of 12 beautiful antebellum and Victorian homes are offered to visitors. The Vicksburg Pilgrimage is a week-long event during which visitors can tour the elegant antebellum homes. Styles include Greek Revival, Italianate, Gothic Revival and Creole cottages. You can purchase tickets at the individual homes or the CVB.

GREAT MISSISSIPPI RIVER BALLOON RACE
Rosalie Gardens, Natchez   (800) 647-6724

Hot-air balloons race overhead in mid-October while music, food and games are available at Rosalie Gardens on the Bluff.

GHOST TALES AROUND THE CAMPFIRE
Hwy. 61
Washington   442-2901

Area storytellers tell Halloween tales in late October by the light of a bonfire at Historic Jefferson College, 6 miles east of Natchez.

OLD COURT HOUSE FLEA MARKET
1008 Cherry St., Vicksburg (800) 221-3536

Vendors offer food, arts and crafts, antiques and collectibles at the Old Court

House Museum on the first Saturday of October.

The Coast

INTERNATIONAL FOOD FESTIVAL
228 S. Beach Blvd.
Bay St. Louis   467-7048

All sorts of delicious ethnic foods are offered at this annual event held in early October on the grounds in front of Our Lady Academy.

MULLET FESTIVAL
Hwy. 90 W., Gautier   497-1878

Held in early October at the Jackson County Campus of the Mississippi Gulf Coast Community College, this city fest has food, music and family fun.

COLUMBUS DAY FALL FESTIVAL
366 Cowan Rd., Gulfport   896-3147

Enjoy games, arts and crafts, food and live entertainment at this fund-raiser sponsored by the St. James Catholic Church.

JACKSON COUNTY FAIR
Shortcut Rd., Pascagoula   762-6043

This traditional county fair in late October has carnival rides, food, contests and more, all at the Jackson County Fairgrounds.

BEAUVOIR FALL MUSTER
2244 Beach Blvd., Biloxi   388-1313

Beauvoir, Jefferson Davis' last home, is the site for the re-creation of an 1861 Confederate boot camp. Participants "skirmish" and play period music in late October.

SCOTTISH HIGHLANDS
AND ISLANDS GAMES
2350 Beach Blvd., Biloxi   388-3791

Scottish games, highland dances, entertainers, food and fun pay tribute to this ethnic group.

TOAST TO THE COAST
Pass Christian   452-9442

Thirty restaurants and caterers prepare dishes for this fund-raiser that benefits Coast Episcopal schools. The entertainment is top-notch too. The location varies, but this event is always held at a beautiful home on the beach in mid-October.

GEORGE E. OHR EXTRAVAGANZA
136 George Ohr St.
Biloxi   374-5547

The city celebrates the work of native son and renowned "mad potter" George Ohr at the Ohr Arts and Cultural Center the fourth weekend in October. The extravaganza starts with the Mad Potter's Ball on Friday night. On Saturday it's the arts and crafts festival with regional artists displaying and selling their work, juried art exhibits, pottery-making exhibitions and kids' activities. Food and music complete the festivities.

November

The Hill Country

FOUNDERS' DAY CELEBRATION
Rust College
Holly Springs   252-8000, ext. 4077

You'll enjoy a parade, entertainment, drama and a band concert at Rust College campus.

UNION CRAFTS FAIR
Mississippi State University
Starkville   325-2930

More than 50 artisans display and sell handmade goods . . . just in time for Christmas. It is also called MSU Christmas Bazaar, and it's held at Colvard Union in late November.

The Delta

DELTA WILDLIFE EXPO
Washington Co. Convention Center
Greenville   686-4062, (800) 467-3582

This weekend-long event is a boon for Delta hunters and others who appreciate wildlife. It's sponsored in part by Delta Wildlife Foundation, the Delta's only conservation organization. The Expo features about 125 exhibitors selling hunting and fishing gear, wildlife art and books, outdoor apparel, trucks, conservation exhibits, guided trips and an exhibit of special interest to anglers: a "hawg trough" aquarium, which is a portable 42-foot fish tank that holds about 5,000 gallons of water. The Mississippi Department of Wildlife, Fisheries and Parks stock it with largemouth bass, crappie, bream, catfish and other native species. Expect these events and so much more at this Expo in early November.

The Heartland

MISTLETOE MARKETPLACE
Trade Mart, 1207 E. Mississippi St.
Jackson   948-2357

The Mississippi Trade Mart is the site for this pre-Christmas (early November) shopping spree where 100 specialty stores and dealers sell their merchandise. Proceeds benefit the Junior League charities. This is Mississippi's largest charity fund-raiser.

VICTORIAN WINTER FESTIVAL
Town Square
Canton   859-1307, (800) 844-3369

This historic town square and its Christmas decorations make us nostalgic for seasons past. Enjoy a merchants open house, entertainment and more in late November through December.

The River Cities

PILGRIMAGE
GARDEN CLUB ANTIQUES FORUM
110 N. Pearl St.
Natchez   (800) 647-6742

An educational gathering to discuss antiques is held in early November at the Natchez Eola Hotel. In addition to lectures, there are tours, entertainment and delicious meals served in some of the city's historic settings.

The Coast

PETER ANDERSON
ARTS AND CRAFTS FESTIVAL
Downtown Ocean Springs   875-4424

In and around the historic railroad depot, fest-goers will find arts and crafts, musical entertainment and a food show with an international flavor in early November. This is one of the Southeast Tourism Society's Top 20 Events.

RACE OF THE WHITE WINGS
Biloxi   435-6320

The *Glenn L. Swetman*, a replica Biloxi schooner, and other vessels race for the historic Heidenheim Cup in late November. Spectators from the shore will enjoy seeing these beautiful ships compete.

CHEFS OF THE COAST
2350 Beach Blvd., Biloxi   388-5162

Coast restaurants serve their specialties at this food extravaganza, complete with live entertainment, at the Coliseum.

December

The Hill Country

CHRISTMAS IN COLUMBUS
Columbus   329-1191, (800) 327-2686

This month-long city-wide event includes antebellum home tours, Christmas trees at the library, many outstanding church seasonal specials and theatrical performances, such as *The Nutcracker* at MUW. It also includes a Downtown Historic Christmas Weekend of open houses, tours of downtown apartments and businesses and a Christmas Parade on the Water. Call for a brochure listing all the Columbus offerings.

HOLIDAY TOUR OF HOMES
Aberdeen   369-6488

Tour private residences in Aberdeen's historic district; all are tastefully decorated in seasonal splendor the second weekend of December. The Chamber of Commerce has specific information on the tour, which includes Christmas Trees Around the World, with authentic ornaments imported from 10 countries.

TOUR OF HOMES
Holly Springs   252-3369

Rare and unusual historic homes are open for special tours the first weekend in December. Expect beautiful, seasonal decorations.

The Delta

CHRISTMAS CANDLELIGHT TOUR
Greenwood   455-3821

Revisit an 1850s Christmas at Florewood River Plantation, complete with tour and refreshments in early December. This is nostalgia at its very best.

CHRISTMAS ON DEER CREEK
Leland   334-2711, (800) 467-3582

Christmas on Deer Creek in Leland features Santa's arrival by water-propelled sleigh and other Christmas merriment on the first Friday in December. Floats on the creek remain lighted the entire month of December. In Greenville, the Christmas parade, a huge bonfire, the singing of carols and hot wassail evoke the Christmas spirit; call for exact dates and other activities for Christmas in Washington County.

The Heartland

HOLIDAY JUBILEE
Downtown Jackson   960-1084

This is a collective one-day effort that combines the annual Christmas Parade, merchants open houses, choral groups and entertainment. It ends with the lighting of the Christmas Tree at City Hall and a fireworks display. Call for the exact early December date.

FESTIVAL OF CHRISTMAS TREES
Smith Robertson Museum
Jackson   960-1457

Visit this collection of trees decorated by different clubs and church groups throughout Jackson in early December.

HOLIDAY STUDIO TOURS
Jackson   960-1550

This annual event pays tribute to about 50 Mississippi artists including printmakers, painters and potters. Tour the decorated studios and meet the artists in early December.

CHIMNEYVILLE CRAFTS FESTIVAL
Trade Mart, 1207 E. Mississippi St.
Jackson   981-0019

The Mississippi Craftsmen's Guild demonstrates traditional and contemporary crafts, plus Mississippi foods, music and more. An early December three-day event, this offers a grand opportunity to peruse and purchase original art for Christmas and support Mississippi artists in the process.

CHRISTMAS AT THE OLD CAPITOL
Jackson   *359-6920*

This history lesson with seasonal finery is a favorite Christmas activity for Mississippians. See antebellum decorations, a giant cedar tree and antique toys. Festivities are carried on most of the month of December, and this event is a Top 20 in the area, according to the Southeast Tourism Society.

VISIONS OF CHRISTMAS PAST
The Manship House, 420 E. Fortification St.
Jackson   *961-4724*

This property is administered by the Mississippi Department of Archives and History, which means that authenticity is always emphasized. The Victorian decorations bring the house to life, as it must have been when it was built in 1857. It remains decorated throughout December.

CHRISTMAS IN JACKSON

Most all of Jackson's many churches have wonderful Christmas programs in December, and so do many of the schools. Watch the *Clarion-Ledger* for event dates closer to Christmas, but in the meantime, here are a few of the most spectacular seasonal offerings:

Handel's Messiah is performed by the Mississippi Chorus and Mississippi Symphony Orchestra in early December, 960-1565.

Belhaven Singing Christmas Tree is an outdoor Christmas choral extravaganza presented by the Belhaven College

choir on the college green in early December, 968-8707.

The **Tougaloo Choir Christmas Concert** is in the Coleman Library on the Tougaloo campus in early December, 977-7834.

Carols by Candlelight are presented by First Baptist Church in early December, 949-1918.

Christmas Music and Midnight Mass is celebrated at St. Andrews Episcopal Cathedral on Christmas Eve, 354-3897.

TREES OF CHRISTMAS
905 M.L. King Dr.
Meridian   *483-8439*

Two historic homes, Merrehope and the Frank W. Williams House, are decorated for the season. Merrehope is a 20-room Victorian mansion, and the adjacent Williams house is a Queen Ann style of the same period. Both homes have been restored to their original beauty.

VICTORIAN CANDLELIT CHRISTMAS
Historic District, Hattiesburg   (800) 638-6877

This nighttime display shows off the holiday season in more than two dozen historic city blocks. Adding to the festivities are carriage rides and tours of homes decked out for Christmas.

The River Cities

CHRISTMAS IN NATCHEZ
Natchez   *(800) 647-6724*

This is a month-long celebration of the season featuring music, food and tours of beautifully decorated antebellum and Victorian homes. Churches present seasonal programs, pageants and candlelight services, and children's choirs sing in the downtown district. Shoppers will find plenty to choose from, and so will restaurant guests who are looking for tasty specialties of the area. Other holiday events include a presentation of *The Nutcracker* and a display of Christmas trees.

The Coast

TULLIS TREES OF CHRISTMAS
360 Beach Blvd., Biloxi   435-6293

The coast population is a mix of many ethnic groups, and this holiday display reflects that. Ethnic Christmas trees are on view at the historic Tullis-Toledano Manor during December. Each tree bears the authentic decorations of a specific country, reflecting the ways that the holiday is celebrated there.

ANNUAL CHRISTMAS ON THE WATER
U.S. 90, Biloxi   435-6250

A parade of beautifully decorated boats, holiday lights and other activities take place in early December around the downtown area and along the beach in Biloxi.

BEAUVOIR CANDLELIGHT CHRISTMAS
2244 Beach Blvd., Biloxi   388-1313

This is a Christmas celebration with a historical flavor, complete with Victorian-era decorations and refreshments made from the recipes of Mrs. Jefferson Davis. Visitors tour the buildings and grounds of this beautiful and popular attraction.

Credit: The Sun Herald

Insiders know the best spots on the Coast to catch delicious blue crabs. This catch came from the Biloxi Lighthouse pier.

Inside
Sports and Recreation

Outdoor sports come to mind when thinking about Mississippi's unspoiled environment and moderate climate. Indeed, the state is perfect for hunting, fishing, golf, tennis, ballooning, skydiving, biking, hiking and more. Enjoy freshwater fishing in the plethora of lakes, streams, rivers and reservoirs, actually more than 294,600 acres of public fishing waters where more than 150 species tempt anglers. And there's deep-sea fishing and boating on the Gulf of Mexico along the Mississippi Gulf Coast, where captains and charter boats work for hire.

College and other spectator sports deserve their own category on Mississippi's sports agenda. After all, this is serious Southeastern Conference (SEC) country, where loyal football fans wear school colors with pride. Most fall Saturdays are taken up with football, in some form, and each play is replayed in workplaces throughout the state. Football fever in the Magnolia State is almost universal.

Hunting seems to be another category that transcends occupations and income levels. Physicians, mechanics, lawyers, truckers and others seem to have a religious-like affinity for the sport. Here's a word of caution: Steer clear of hunters on the first day of a season. They are intent upon getting to the woods first in order to bag the biggest. Innocent onlookers would do well to step aside, then watch the dust that emanates from the wheels of hunters' trucks or ATVs. Since the state boasts more than 2 million acres of outdoor wonderland and other perks that might mean a memorable hunt, expect a flurry of activity during certain seasons.

Mississippians and their Department of Wildlife, Fisheries and Parks are indeed conscientious about their sports and sporting events, so remember to follow all the rules and honor all appropriate licenses and limits.

Hunting

Here's an overview of the hunting basics: All persons, except those exempt under state law, are required to purchase a hunting license and have it on their person while hunting. Exemptions apply to residents younger than 16, older than 65 and those who are legally disabled. All persons born after January 1, 1972, must complete a hunter-education course before obtaining a license. See our "Responsible Hunters" sidebar in this section for more information on hunter education.

Hunters have a choice of Mississippi environments: marshy swamps, pine or hardwood forests and open fields. There are more than a million acres of prime game land in 36 Wildlife Management Areas, WMAs, and nine National Wildlife Refuges, NWRs. Hunting on the state's national forest land is permitted in all areas except developed, administrative or recreation sites or unless prohibited as posted. Also, public waterfowl hunting is allowed on some reservoirs that were constructed for flood control in the 1940s and '50s by the U.S. Army Corps of Engineers. They are Arkabutla, near Coldwater; Okatibbee, near Meridian; Sardis, near Sardis; Enid, near Batesville; Grenada, near Grenada; and Ross Barnett, near Jackson. The latter reservoir is owned by the Pearl River Valley Water Supply District; the others are owned by the Corps of Engineers. For current, accurate information concerning hunting and fishing, call (800) ASK FISH, or contact the Mississippi Department of Wildlife, Fisheries and Parks, P.O. Box 451, Jackson 39205; 362-9212 or (800) 467-2757.

Resident Hunting Fees

These license fees were current at press time. The license year begins July 1 and ends June 30 of the next year. A sportsperson's license costs $32 and entitles the holder to hunt and fish for all legal game, including deer and turkey, with all weapons. All-game hunting and fishing licenses cost $17 and are required for use with modern weapons only. Small-game hunting and fishing licenses cost $13 for all legal game except deer and turkey. Fourteen dollars entitles the holder of an archery and primitive weapon license to hunt all legal game by archery and with primitive weapons (this is included in the sportsperson's license but must be purchased with an all-game license). A state waterfowl stamp costs $5 plus a $1 agent fee. For additional information on licenses, residency requirements or regulations, call (800) ASK FISH or pick up a Mississippi *Hunting*

& Fishing Digest at sporting goods stores across the state.

Nonresident Hunting Fees

Nonresident hunting fees are as follows: All-game hunting, $225; five-day all-game hunting, $105; small-game hunting, $75; five-day small-game hunting, $30; state waterfowl stamp, $5; archery and primitive weapons, $30 (must accompany all-game or five-day permit). You'll also need to factor in a $3 agent fee.

The Hunting Season

Season dates vary, though the general rules are:

Squirrel season begins in October for certain zones and continues through the month of January.

Rabbit season runs October through February.

Deer season begins in October for archers and continues through November. Gun season for deer is November and December, though dates vary depending on the sex of deer and whether or not dogs are used.

Turkey season runs from November into December and then from March to May.

Quail season is in November and December.

Dove season includes one date in September and one in October.

Duck season runs early December through early January.

Fox, crow and blackbird may be hunted in any season.

Again, public hunting and fishing in Mississippi is so varied and plentiful, the best sources for exact information on sites and locations are the State Department of Wildlife, Fisheries and Parks or the Mississippi *Hunting & Fishing Digest.*

Wildlife Management Areas

Scattered over the entire state are wildlife management areas that offer managed environments for small and big game. Hunters may choose from any of the WMAs listed in this chapter or contact Wildlife, Fisheries and Parks, (800) 467-2757, for a complete listing.

The Hill Country

In the upper northeast part of the Hill Country, along the Tennessee-Tombigbee Waterway, lies a bountiful region enjoyed by hunters and fishermen. Deer and waterfowl hunting is allowed with proper permits. Maps of hunting zones are available from the U.S. Army Corps of Engineers, Resource Manager, Box 2800, Fairlane Station, Columbus 39704.

Chickasaw Wildlife Management Area near New Albany is composed of 27,259 acres in Chickasaw and Pontotoc counties. Expect deer, dove, quail, turkey and waterfowl. Contact the area managers, 568-7400 or 534-9235. The **Divide Section WMA** near Iuka is also near the Tenn-Tom Waterway. Here 12,000 acres of land and water offer deer, dove, quail and duck. The area supervisor can answer questions, 423-1455.

John Bell Williams WMA in the upper northeast section of the state, north of Fulton, offers 9,930 acres on which to hunt deer, dove, duck, quail, rabbit, turkey, woodcock and furbearers. You may contact the area manager at 728-5057.

Upper Sardis WMA near Oxford is a big 47,274 acres of prime hunting land; hunt for deer, dove, duck, rabbit, squirrel, turkey, woodcock and furbearers. Call the area manager, 236-2360. **Choctaw WMA** near Ackerman and Louisville consists of 24,314 acres. Expect to find deer, dove, quail, rabbit, squirrel, turkey, duck woodcock and furbearers. The biologist can be reached at 726-5573. Also in the Hill Country, the big **Noxubee Wildlife Refuge** near Starkville is a 42,000-acre wonderland where deer, squirrel, turkey and duck roam and can be hunted periodically. For specifics, call the Refuge office, 323-5548.

The Delta

Anderson-Tully WMA is near the Mississippi River and the town of Mayersville. The 4,385 acres here offer deer, duck, rabbit, squirrel, turkey, woodcock and furbearers. Contact the area manager, 873-6968. **Twin Oaks WMA** near Rolling Fork has 5,800 acres where deer, turkey, rabbit, squirrel, raccoon and waterfowl can be hunted. The area manager's number is 873-4141.

Malmaison Wildlife Management Area borders the Delta, not far from Grenada, and consists of 9,483 acres of deer, dove, duck, quail, rabbit, squirrel and turkey. For more information call the area managers, 453-5196 or 453-5409.

The Leroy Percy Wildlife Management Area near Hollandale is about 2,300 acres where deer, dove, rabbit, squirrel,

Insiders' Tips

turkey and duck live. You can reach the area manager at 827-5436.

Sunflower Wildlife Management Area near Rolling Fork offers 58,480 acres of prime hunting land and boasts deer, dove, quail, rabbit, squirrel, turkey and furbearers. Call the area manager, 247-2213.

The Delta also has several National Wildlife Refuges, though the biggest is **Panther Swamp NWR** near Holly Bluff and Yazoo City. On these 22,000 acres, deer, dove, turkey, duck, squirrel, raccoon opossum and beaver can be hunted during specific seasons. For information, call the Refuge office, 839-2638.

The Heartland

Pearl River WMA near Canton provides 6,000 acres for deer, dove, quail, rabbit, squirrel, duck, woodcock and furbearers. Contact the area manager, 856-5140.

Choctaw Wildlife Management Area between Louisville and Ackerman is proud to provide 24,314 acres for hunting deer, dove, quail, rabbit, squirrel, turkey, waterfowl and furbearers. Reach the area manager at 726-5573.

Bucatunna Wildlife Management Area, 12 miles south of Meridian, offers turkey, deer, dove, rabbit, quail, squirrel and woodcock hunting on 19,000 acres. Contact the area manager, 693-3977, for details.

Chickasawhay Wildlife Management Area near Laurel has more than 150,000 acres for hunting squirrel, quail, rabbit, dove, woodcock, deer and turkey. The area managers' numbers are 428-5860 and 344-7443.

Copiah County Wildlife Management Area covers 6,500 acres near Hazlehurst. Hunters can find deer, quail,

rabbit, turkey, dove, squirrel and woodcock. The area manager can be reached by phoning 277-3508.

Mahannah Wildlife Management Area is 13,000 acres where hunters go after turkey, squirrel, dove, waterfowl, deer, rabbit and raccoon. Call the area manager, 636-2045.

Marion County Wildlife Management Area, 736-0066, near Columbia, consists of 7,200 acres. Game includes dove, deer, quail, rabbit and turkey.

Leaf River Wildlife Management Area is almost 42,000 acres near Lucedale. Expect deer, dove, quail, squirrel and turkey. Contact the area manager, 598-2367.

Tallahala Wildlife Management Area has deer, quail, dove, squirrel, rabbit, woodcock, turkey and furbearers on its 28,000 acres. The area manager can be reached at 536-2203.

Bogue Chitto National Wildlife Refuge, near Picayune in Pearl River County, is where hunters find deer, turkey, rabbit, duck and squirrel. To find out more, call (504) 646-7550.

The River Cities

Sandy Creek Wildlife Management Area near Natchez has more than 16,400 acres for hunting deer, quail, rabbit, squirrel, turkey, woodcock and furbearers. Call 384-2658 for rules and regulations. Also near Natchez, **St. Catherine's Creek National Wildlife Refuge**, 442-6696, has deer (archery), rabbit and squirrel hunting.

Homochitto Wildlife Management Area offers rabbit, dove, quail, deer, turkey, squirrel and woodcock on 25,000 acres near Meadville. For more information call 384-5154.

The Coast

The **Little Biloxi Wildlife Management Area**, 795-4686, is in Harrison and Stone counties. You'll find 14,540 acres for hunting rabbit, deer, turkey, quail, squirrel and woodcock.

Pascagoula River Wildlife Management Area, 947-8631 and 588-3878, is in Jackson and George counties near Vancleave and Lucedale. It offers 37,000 acres for hunting duck, quail, rabbit, turkey, deer, squirrel, woodcock and furbearers.

Ward Bayou Wildlife Management Area, 392-5138, in Jackson County consists of 12,000 acres. Rabbit, waterfowl, deer, squirrel, turkey and furbearers are the game here.

Red Creek Wildlife Management Area, 872-1459, in Harrison, Jackson, George and Stone counties, offers hunters 89,400 acres for bagging deer, rabbit, quail, squirrel and turkey.

Fishing

The Mississippi Gulf Coast attracts sport fishermen from across America. They come to fish the blue waters offshore from Biloxi, Gulfport and all the coastal cities, and they often take home a trophy. Knowledgeable charter boat captains ply the waters of deep-water spots near islands and oil rigs in search of grouper, bonitos, lemon fish, red snapper and king mackerel. Farther out in the Gulf, harbor marlin and sailfish offer challenges and excitement.

Inland, the many lakes, rivers, streams and reservoirs in Mississippi have loyal followers, and some of those anglers include tournament fishermen who have earned pro status. According to those "in the know," some of the state's best fishing is along the lakes and inlets created by the construction of the 234-mile long Tennessee-Tombigbee Waterway. Tournaments are abundant here, and big-money events are major attractions. Sports magazines have named the waterway's Columbus Lake "one of America's top-20 hot spots" for bass.

Mississippi's six reservoirs are said to offer about the best fishing in the South. The reservoirs are engineering masterpieces and great favorites of serious fishermen. Crappie is good at Enid, near Batesville, where the world-record white crappie (5 pounds, 3 ounces) was caught back in 1957. Mississippi's record black crappie (4.33 pounds) was caught at Coldwater's Arkabutla Reservoir in 1991. The state's record hybrid striped bass (17.77 pounds) was caught at Sardis Lake in 1991.

The big Ross Barnett Reservoir (33,000 acres) near Jackson offers outstanding bass fishing. It's not bad for paddlefish, either, since the state's record (66 pounds) was caught at the spillway here in 1974. The Reservoir features a full-service marina and ample boat launching.

The Mississippi Department of Wildlife, Fisheries and Parks owns or leases prime fishing lakes throughout the state. About 21 lakes in all are situated on a combined total of more than 5,100 acres of scenic inland waters. Some fees are charged for maintenance, and as with all Mississippi fishing, licenses are required. They can be obtained from full-time lake managers. Indeed, Mississippi's endless and ever-changing hot spots on rivers, lakes, creeks, reservoirs, brackish waters and salt water in Mississippi Sound and the Gulf of Mexico offer variety and challenges to the most astute fishermen.

Persons not exempt under state law (see the regulations under our Hunting section) must have a valid fishing license in their possession. Residents may fish if they hold all-game sportsperson's licenses and an annual fishing license, which may be purchased for $8 freshwater and $4 saltwater, plus a $1 agent fee. Nonresidents can purchase a three-day freshwater fishing permit for $6; also $6 for saltwater, or an annual nonresident license for $25. Add a $3 agent fee.

For recorded information on fishing and licenses, call (800) ASK-FISH, the Mississippi Sport Fishing Information Line. To talk with a person about the state fishing laws, call the Department of Marine Resources in Biloxi, 385-5860.

The Hill Country

All state parks (see listing later in this chapter) offer fishing, though the Mississippi Department of Wildlife Conservation Lakes are prime spots. We'll list a few of these along with a few others that we're told are the true hot spots in this part of the state; some say the hottest for big bass is Columbus Lake on the Tennessee-Tombigbee Waterway.

Chewella Lake, off Highway 78, County Road 634, southeast of Holly Springs in the Holly Springs National Forest, is a favorite of serious local fishermen. In the same general part of the state awaits **Lakeview**, also known as Horn Lake, in Desoto County near the Tennessee state line. Lakeview is a major oxbow of the Mississippi River, and it is known to yield massive bream, especially in June, weather and river permitting. Big bass bite here as well.

Lake Lamar Bruce is about 1.5 miles northeast of Saltillo, near Tupelo. Anglers say it's one of the best bream lakes of all those maintained by the Mississippi Department of Wildlife and Fisheries. You'll find good year-round fishing too, and hefty sizes are a plus. **Lake Monroe**, between Aberdeen and Amory, off U.S. 45, offers good fishing for bass, bluegill, redear and catfish.

Tippah County Lake, 2.5 miles north of Ripley on Miss. 15 W., then 2.5 miles on a paved road, boasts the largest bream ever recorded in Mississippi, a redear weighing in at 3.33 pounds.

The Delta

Bordering the Delta is **Grenada Lake**, an all-time favorite of dedicated anglers. Near Grenada, it's easy to find. In the Delta proper, all lakes along the Mississippi River offer superb fishing. Try **Eagle Lake**, **Lake Lee** and **Lake Ferguson**. A variety of fish bite in these lakes. Locals like **Lake Chotard** and **Lake Albemarle**, about 20 miles north of Vicksburg. Bluegill love these oxbow lakes once the Mississippi River is down. Fifteen miles west

of Cleveland, **Lake Boliver County** is a good place for bream, crappie and bass.

The Heartland

It's hard to compete with the Ross Barnett Reservoir if you want to fish around Jackson, but little **Lake Dockery**, 10 miles south of Jackson, off U.S. 51, has plenty of bass, bluegill, redear and channel catfish.

Tom Bailey is a state lake covering 234 acres 8 miles east of Meridian on U.S. 11. This is where a 45.8-pound channel catfish — a state record fish — was caught. Anglers can try their luck bringing in bass, redear, bluegill and channel cats. Seventy-one-acre **Lake Claude Bennett** in Jasper County is east of Bay Springs off Miss. 18. It contains channel catfish, bass and bluegill.

Lake Ross Barnett in Smith County, southwest of Mize, also has bass and bluegill plus channel catfish and redear. This lake, off Mississippi 35, covers 87 acres. Just north of Magee on U.S. 49 is **Simpson County Legion Lake**. On U.S. Highway 84 in Jones County, east of Laurel, is

1,200-acre **Lake Bogue Homa**. The catch of the day here can be crappie, striped bass, bluegill or channel catfish. Eight miles west of Collins in Covington County is **Lake Mike Conner**, an 88-acre state lake that contains bass, channel catfish, bluegill and coppernose. It's off U.S. Highway 84.

In Jefferson Davis County is **Lake Jeff Davis**, a 164-acre lake with crappie, redear, bass, channel catfish and bluegill. The lake is on Miss. Highway 42, 3 miles south of Prentiss. **Lake Mary Crawford** contains bass as well as channel catfish, redear and bluegill. This lake is in Lawrence County on Highway 84, 5 miles west of Monticello. Eight miles southeast of Tylertown is **Lake Walthall**. It's got a water area of 62 acres. Fishermen there can catch bass, bluegill, channel catfish and redear. **Lake Columbia** has crappie plus bass, bluegill and channel cats in 90 acres of water area. Columbia is on the Marion County Wildlife Management Area 12 miles southeast of Columbia. Two-hundred-acre **Lake Bill Waller** is in the same location. Perry County is the site of **Lake Perry**, with a water area of

125 acres for catching bass, crappie, channel catfish and bluegill. The smaller **Lakeland Park** (12 acres) in Waynesboro is off U.S. Highway 84.

The River Cities

There aren't any state fishing lakes in the River Cities but, anglers will still find plenty of action, and maybe get into the record books. **Natchez State Park Lake**, off U.S. 61 at Stanton, is the former home of an 18.15-pound largemouth bass, brought in 1992. That's a state record catch. Fishing is available in **St. Catherine Creek Wildlife Refuge**, along the Mississippi from Butler Lake to Cloverdale Road, and area oxbow lakes. **Clear Springs** and **Pipe's** lakes, off Miss. 33, both in the Homochitto National Forest near Natchez, offer fishing opportunities. So does **Eagle Lake Recreation Area**, U.S. 61, northwest of Vicksburg, where there's a fishing pier and a place to launch a boat.

The Coast

No matter what kind of fishing you like, or what your skill level is, the coast is the place to try your luck and enjoy the fishing in numerous rivers, bays, lakes, bayous and, of course, the Gulf of Mexico. And don't forget the state parks and public recreation areas found throughout the area. Information about these spots is included later on in this chapter.

According to the Sea Grant Advisory Service, fishing in the fresh and brackish waters is good all year long, and with luck you'll pull in largemouth bass, bluegill and shellcrackers, also known as redear sunfish. Speckled trout await fishermen in salt and brackish waters, as do black drum, redfish, flounder, sheepshead and other catches for fun and for feasting. For best results, try your luck during the spring and fall, when the weather is great and the fishing can't be beat. There are a number of public piers along the coast and these make great places for fishing. For example, in **Bay St. Louis**, the public piers at Ulman Avenue and at Washington Street (also a boat launch) are good spots for specs and redfish. Nearby, the **Jourdan River**, off I-10 and Miss. 43, provides some great fishing opportunities for boaters. Also try **Heron Bay** near the mouth of the Pearl River when you're after redfish and gafftop. North of Pass Christian, near U.S. 90, are two other popular spots, **Bayou Portage** and **Mallini Bayou**. There's great Gulf fishing off the seawall right in front of **Buccaneer State Park** on South Beach Boulevard in Waveland. Wadefishing is popular all along the coast, and specs are a prized catch for this effort.

The advisory service publishes a se-

Parasailing over the beautiful Mississippi Sound is a watersport that is popular with locals and visitors to Mississippi's Gulf Coast.

ries of fishing waters guides for the entire Mississippi coastal area from Hancock to Jackson counties. These maps show where public boat ramps are located and where fishing licenses are required inland.

CHARTER BOATS

Fishing for Spanish and king mackerel, Jack Crevalle, pompano, grouper, lemon fish, shark, Atlantic bluefin tuna and other sport fish is an exciting experience, and the coast has dozens of deep-sea charter boats available for half-day, full-day and overnight trips. These boats are available in all three counties, with the majority docked at various cities in Harrison County. Some fish at rigs, near the islands; some troll and bottom fish; others let you surf fish and spear fish. Most of the boats furnish tackle, bait and ice, so all you do is step aboard and get ready to fish. For short trips, however, you probably will have to bring your own food and beverages. On full-day trips, you may be asked to provide food and beverages for the captain and crew.

The crews are experienced in finding good fishing spots and are patient in assisting less-than-expert anglers. You probably won't need a fishing license if you're covered by the boat's license. Ask to make sure, since a saltwater license is required by law. The mate will clean your catch for a reasonable fee. You'll probably need an ice chest to take your catch with you at trip's end.

When you go, it's best to wear comfortable clothing and footwear appropriate for moving about on a boat, such as deck shoes. Be prepared for lots of sun. Pack a hat, sunglasses and enough sunscreen to protect yourself for the whole trip. Except during the hot summer months, it might be a good idea to bring extra clothing to protect against chilly winds. And don't forget any medication that might be necessary to avoid seasickness.

Cost of a full-day trip for a party of four to six is about $400, but prices vary. Reservations are required, especially during busy holidays and weekends. It's

Hunters enjoy pursuing quail and other game in the state's fields and forests.

slower during the week, but it's still a good idea to book ahead.

Many of the charter boats are listed in the *Sun Herald's* "Marquee" entertainment guide that's published every Friday. Lists of charter boats are available from local chambers of commerce. Call the Mississippi Beach Convention and Visitors Bureau at (800) 237-9493 for charter boats listings, then contact the boat directly to make arrangements for an unforgettable trip.

In Gulfport, *Fishy Business*, 865-9801, is available for charter from Pier 1, Slip 1. Capt. Lenny Desrouche can lead you to big catches, especially shark. Capt. Mike McRaney's *Outrageous*, 875-9462, awaits crews in Biloxi's Point Cadet. Capt. Hugh Bodden's *Gulf Dancer*, 875-9491, in Ocean Springs will take you for a tour of Horn Island off Jackson County.

Camping

Overnight accommodations are available in Mississippi's State Parks, however, if you prefer the comforts of indoors,

please make cabin reservations well in advance. Some of the popular parks are booked for cabins months in advance. However, primitive camping is always available. Tent campers may set up in developed areas or hike into the wild for real outdoor adventure. RV pads are available in most parks. Some areas have private campgrounds, and most of them are advertised along the routes.

The Tennessee-Tombigbee Waterway also provides public use facilities, and some include campsites. Approximately $40 to $50 million in public recreation facilities are completed or planned for the waterway, so it's a good bet that outdoor recreation is a priority along the Tenn-Tom in northeast Mississippi. We'll highlight a few of the campsites below, though the TTW Development Authority in Columbus, 328-3286, can provide information on campsites and recreational opportunities along the entire waterway.

The state parks are built around water, with the exception of the historic parks, so water sports are the focus. Expect fishing, canoeing, swimming, boating and skiing. You'll find nature trails, scenic vistas, wildflowers and some organized playground sports, such as tennis and basketball, on the premises.

For more information on camping, contact any of the parks listed in this section or the Department of Wildlife, Fisheries and Parks, (800) 467-2757.

The Hill Country

The next four campgrounds are along the Tennessee-Tombigbee Waterway. They are impeccably maintained by the U.S. Army Corps of Engineers, and the surrounding scenery is nothing short of spectacular.

Town Creek Campground, 494-4885, just off Miss. 50 near Columbus, west of the Tenn-Tom Bridge, is scenic and serene. It offers campsites, a bathhouse, a playground and a boat ramp.

Try **Blue Bluff Campground**, 369-2832, off U.S. 45 near Aberdeen. Blue Bluff offers campsites, a bathhouse, a picnic shelter, fishing, an activity area, a boat ramp, swimming and a nature trail.

Piney Grove Campground, 728-1134, is just off Miss. 30 in the upper northeast, about 15 miles from Dennis, near the Tenn-Tom Waterway and the Natchez Trace Parkway. Here you'll find campsites, a bathhouse, a picnic shelter, an activity area, a boat ramp, swimming and a nature trail. Also in the vicinity, **Mill Creek Boat Dock**, 423-6129, 4 miles east of Iuka on County Road 242, offers camping amenities and water sports.

The Delta

Near Yazoo City off Miss. 16, **Barge Lake** and **Blue Lake**, 873-6256, offer primitive campsites, while **Leroy Percy State Park**, 827-5436, near Hollandale offers campsites and a bathhouse.

The **Great River Road State Park**, 759-6762, in Rosedale, about 35 miles north of Greenville, is a big favorite because of its location on the Mississippi River. A four-level observation tower offers an outstanding view of the River and surrounding land. Developed and primitive camping is available.

The Heartland

A favorite Heartland place for camping and other outdoor activities is the **Ross Barnett Reservoir**, 354-3448, near Jackson. Certain areas are set aside for primitive camping, though developed sites are available too. **Timberlake Campground**, 992-9100, has 66 RV pads, 16 pop-ups and 16 tent sites. It's on the Rankin County side, off Spillway Road. There are also campsites at Goshen Springs, 829-2751; Coal Bluff, 654-7726; and Leake County Water Park, 654-9359.

Meridian/Toomsuba East KOA, 3953 KOA Kampground, (800) 553-7740, in Toomsuba, is 12 miles east of Meridian, 2 miles off I-20. Eight of the 45 sites are full service, the remainder have water and electricity. Also available are showers, laundry facilities, a grocery store, a swimming pool, a water slide, a kid's playground and a game room.

Pat Harrison Waterway Campgrounds, (800) 748-9403, in Meridian has log sites and **Okatibbee Water Park**, 737-2370, northwest of Meridian just off Miss. 19 N., has developed camping spurs on 3,800 acres. **Dunn's Falls Water Park**, 655-8550, 15 miles south of Meridian on the Chunky River, has primitive camping only on 69 forested acres. Both are open year round.

Pep's Point, U.S. 49 N., 582-8461, is 3 miles north of Hattiesburg. Pep's Point offers camping with waterfront sites. The centerpiece of this location is a spring-fed lake.

Lake Lincoln, 833-8910, in northeast Lincoln County near Brookhaven and Wesson has a nature trail, a large picnic area, formal and primitive camping and a 550-acre lake for fishing, swimming and skiing. Access is available from I-55, U.S. 51 and Miss. 27.

The River Cities

Natchez State Park, 363 State Park Road, 442-2658, is on Highway 61 N. 10 miles from Natchez. This campground has no limit on the size of units. There are no restrooms here.

Campers who travel 8 miles from Natchez will find full hookups available plus showers and restrooms at **Traceway Campgrounds**, 101 Log Cabin Lane, 445-9894. **Battlefield Campground**, 4407 I-20 Frontage Road, 636-2025, is adjacent to the Vicksburg National Military Park and is convenient to other local historical attractions. The shaded campsites have all hookups, and campers will also find a swimming pool, a playground, a grocery store, laundry facilities, showers, cable and tent sites.

New in Vicksburg is **River City RV Park**, 211 Miller Street, 631-0388, with 66 campsites, all with pull-throughs and full hookups, plus picnic tables at each pad and laundry facilities. Campers here will also find a swimming pool and playground. River City is open year round from 6 AM to 9 PM. It's near Pemberton Mall, the historic downtown and local casinos. Take Exit 1-B 1 mile to Miller Street.

The Coast

The coast has a number of private campgrounds near Biloxi, Gautier, Gulfport, Bay St. Louis and Ocean Springs. These campgrounds and RV parks, many of which are on the beachfront, offer a range of services, including utility hookups, laundry facilities and boat launches. **Casino Magic** in Bay St. Louis, 467-9257, has a new RV Park with 100 camping sites. Here is just a sampling of other camping options.

McLeod Water Park, 8100 Texas Flat Road, 467-1894, is near Bay St. Louis north of I-10 on Miss. 603. Campers can enjoy the activities in the park and along the Jordan River in addition to 91 camp sites.

Insiders' Tips

For pristine floating and fishing, head for the Okatoma, in the upper headwaters of the Pascagoula River watershed in lower east central Mississippi.

Credit: Mississippi Department of Economic Development

The Chunky River with its imposing Dunn's Falls is a popular float trip for canoeists. Located in east central Mississippi near Meridian, the waterfall is more than 50 feet high.

Ocean Springs KOA, 7501 Miss. 57, 875-2100, has 105 sites plus hookups with water, electricity, sewer, phone and cable, a swimming pool and laundry.

Bay St. Louis KOA, 822 U.S. 90, 467-2080, offers complete pull-through hookups, cable TV, a store and souvenir shop, playground, showers and laundry. It's close to the beach and casinos.

Boating

Boaters in the Magnolia State may drift lazily downriver or race the rapids on one of the many rivers or reservoirs, the latter of which also offer full-service marinas, campgrounds, picnic areas and water sports. The slack current of the Tenn-Tom Waterway makes it ideal for pleasure boaters and skiers. The most popular freshwater spot in the state is the Ross Barnett Reservoir near Jackson. It offers 33,000 acres for skiing, sailing and fishing.

Other reservoirs, six in all, accommodate all water sports and provide coastline and inlets to explore. The reservoirs were constructed by the U.S. Army Corps of Engineers. The lakes of Arkabutla, Sardis, Enid, Grenada and Okatibbee each have 40 to 50 miles of water surface. All the reservoirs have plenty of boat launching ramps.

The Hill Country

TENNESSEE-TOMBIGBEE WATERWAY
Columbus   328-3286

This waterway, called "America's newest river," is a 234-mile-long, safe and scenic waterway that connects the inland south with the Gulf of Mexico — it's a boater's paradise. The Tenn-Tom is ideal for pleasure boaters, some of whom come from points farther north en route to Southern destinations. It's a project of the U.S. Army Corps of Engineers, which monitors and maintains it. The U.S.

Coast Guard's Inland Navigation Rules govern the waterway. Excessive speeds in narrow sections of the waterway are prohibited, and boaters in small craft must never come within 1,200 feet of tows nor should they anchor in the channel.

Boaters can put in the Tenn-Tom at West Lowndes Landing on the West Bank, in Aberdeen at Morgan Landing and near Amory at Miss. 278. For detailed information, contact the Tenn-Tom Development Authority, 328-3286.

ARKABUTLA LAKE
Coldwater   562-6261

This quarter-moon-shaped lake is just off I-55 N., south of Memphis. You'll find about 45-square miles of water surface, shaded coves and great boating opportunities. Boaters can put in at Coldwater Point, near Coldwater, on County Road 304.

SARDIS LAKE
Sardis   563-4531

This big lake of approximately 32,000 acres on the Sardis Reservoir offers most things an outdoors lover could want, and boating is nothing short of spectacular. Boat ramps are readily available.

ENID LAKE
Batesville   563-4571

This lake is bordered by lush foliage and is home to native wildlife species. It offers excellent boating, including water skiing and sailing. Plentiful boat ramps are here.

The Delta

GRENADA LAKE
Grenada   226-5911

A favorite lake for Southerners, this reservoir and lake borders the Delta and offers more than 40 miles of water surface and great scenery. It's ideal for boating and offers easy access.

The Heartland

ROSS BARNETT RESERVOIR
Jackson   354-3448

This big reservoir is 33,000 acres of surface water, hidden coves and inlets and outstanding scenery. Organized water sports and major annual events are held at the Reservoir; nightlife is close by too. Boaters and skiers love this lake. Boat ramps are plentiful along the reservoir.

OKATIBBEE LAKE
Near Meridian   626-8431

This is a large public lake 8 miles west of Meridian via Miss. 19. Features include a full-service marina, restaurant and a motel. Fishing tournaments and other special events are held here.

BONITA LAKES
Meridian   485-1802

This public park on Miss. 19 S. near I-20/59 has 3,300 acres for hiking, horseback riding, boating and fishing. It's only open during daylight hours.

Insiders' Tips

The rich Delta fields and their adjacent rolling hills offer some of the South's finest habitat for quail. Delta Outfitters, (800) 270-DELTA, can make all the arrangements for a spectacular hunt.

Responsible Hunters

Hunters in Mississippi do more than enjoy the state's outdoor bounty. Most of them utilize it safely and responsibly, thanks to the Hunter Education Course offered by the Department of Wildlife, Fisheries and Parks. In fact, all persons born after January 1, 1972, are required to complete the course before purchasing a Mississippi hunting license. The courses, held in counties throughout the state {call (800) 354-5033 for specific details}, are a minimum of 10 hours and include a live firing exercise. Volunteer instructors teach the courses. The Hunter Education program is designed to reduce hunting accidents, teach hunter ethics and responsibility, promote wildlife conservation and teach firearm safety.

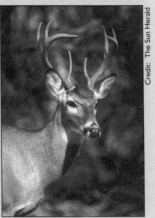

Credit: The Sun Herald

Another area in which hunter's show responsibility is through "Mississippi Sportsmen Against Hunger." To date, in two years, Mississippi's needy have received more than 50,000 pounds of ground venison from this enterprising group of hunters who share their deer meat, after it has been professionally dressed, ground

The Hunter Education Course, sponsored by the Department of Wildlife, Fisheries and Parks, promotes wildlife conservation.

and frozen, with participants in the Mississippi Food Network. Hunter-sponsored collection centers operate throughout the state. Indeed, this is a most worthwhile project. For additional information about the collection centers and helping fight hunger, call (800) 777-5001.

LAKE LINCOLN

Wesson   833-8910

This is a 550-acre lake near Brookhaven that boaters as well as fishermen and swimmers enjoy. There are three boat ramps and a floating dock for use by the public.

BIG CREEK WATER PARK

Near Laurel   763-8555

Big Creek, part of the Pat Harrison Waterway District, is on U.S. 84 between Laurel and Collins. It's open all year for camping, boating, fishing, swimming, picnics and hiking.

DRY CREEK WATER PARK

Mount Olive   797-4619

Dry Creek offers boating on a 150-acre lake filled with fish. The lake is also popular for swimming, and camping is available here too. It's off U.S. 49 south of Magee. This is another park in the Pat Harrison Waterway District.

LITTLE BLACK CREEK WATER PARK

Near Purvis   794-2957

Off I-59 between Lumberton and Purvis, Little Black Creek is open year round for boaters and campers. This Pat

Harrison Waterway District park has a lodge and marina.

The River Cities

The oxbow lakes along the Mississippi River provide lots of leisure boating and fishing action in the River Cities area. These include Lake Centennial across from Vicksburg, Lake Bruin near Port Gibson and Lake St. John and Lake Concordia just north of Natchez.

The Coast

Along the Coast, boaters have plenty of opportunity to enjoy outings in the numerous rivers and bays as well as in the Gulf.

Boaters may want to try the calm waters of the Mississippi Sound, the Gulf beyond the barrier islands, the Bay of St. Louis or Biloxi Bay.

McLeod Water Park

Near Bay St. Louis   467-1894

McLeod is north of I-10 on Miss. 603 near Bay St. Louis in Hancock County. Visitors can boat in the Jourdan River, which runs through the park. Besides a boat launch, there are picnic spots with pavilions and grills.

Crossroads Water Park

Crossroad Community   772-9042

This Pearl River Boatway Park is located on the Pearl River north of Hancock

County off Miss. 26. Besides a boat launch, the park has two open-air pavilions, a nature trail, a comfort station and sites for primitive camping.

Water Excursions

There are a plethora of private vessels in the Hill Country and the Heartland but none operating for the public at this time.

The Delta

Mississippi River Cruise Vacations

The Delta Queen Steamboat Company
     (800)458-6789, (800) 543-1949

The *Delta Queen* and the *Mississippi Queen* run scheduled paddlewheel cruises up and down the Mississippi River. They dock at Natchez, Vicksburg and Greenville. Prices vary depending on such factors as length of cruise and location of stateroom, etc. Call for specifics.

River Cities

Mississippi River
Adventure Hydro-Jet Boat Cruise

City Waterfront
Vicksburg   638-5443

From March 1 through November 15, take in the history and scenery of the Mississippi and Yazoo rivers on a 40-mile jet-boat tour. Cost is $25 for adults and $7.50 for children 12 and younger.

The Coast

SHIP ISLAND EXCURSION FERRY
Gulfport   864-1014

Offshore adventure is readily available via a leisurely 70-or-so-minute cruise from Gulfport to Ship Island, one of the picturesque barrier islands a dozen miles out in the Gulf of Mexico. Passengers are sometimes accompanied by playful dolphins racing alongside the boat and by pelicans and gulls flying overhead.

This family-owned and operated ferry service has been a popular attraction on the coast for three generations.

Ship Island, part of the Gulf Islands National Seashore, was cut in two by Hurricane Camille in 1969. West Ship, with its white-sand beach facing clear Gulf waters, is the site of Fort Massachusetts, a Civil War fortress open daily for guided tours in summer and by special arrangement in spring and fall.

There is also a picnic pavilion, shower and restroom facilities and a snack bar. A boardwalk stretches a third of a mile from the pier to the beach. You can surf and pier fish, explore, swim and sun. Watch for numerous species of birds, tidal-pool creatures and even alligators in the inland pools. Just don't forget the sun screen, hats and other protection.

From Gulfport there are three seasonal schedules:

Spring (first Saturday in March to second Saturday in May) — Weekends: two trips daily departing 9 AM and noon; return trips arrive at 3:15 PM and 6:15 PM. Weekdays: one trip daily, departing noon, returning 6:15 PM.

Summer (second Saturday in May through Labor Day): Two trips daily, departing 9 AM and noon, returning 3:45 PM and 6:45 PM.

Fall (day after Labor Day through last Sunday in October): Same as spring schedule.

Round-trip tickets are $14 for adults and $7 for children 3 to 10. Group, senior-citizen and military discounts are available. No reservations are accepted, so get there early on weekends.

GLENN L. SWETMAN
Point Cadet Marina
Biloxi   435-6320

The *Swetman* is a replica of the famous Biloxi schooners that plied the waters a century ago. It and the *Mike Sekul* were built as a project of the Maritime and Seafood Industry Museum's Biloxi Schooner Project to preserve that part of Biloxi's heritage.

The schooner operates from Point Cadet Marina and is available for day-long, half-day and two-hour day sailing along the Biloxi waterfront and for special charters to the barrier islands. If weather permits, moonlight cruises are also offered. Day sailing costs $15 for adults, $10 for kids 3 to 12. Call for reservations.

BILOXI SHRIMPING TOUR
Small Craft Harbor
Biloxi   385-1182

Climb aboard the *Sailfish* and see how shrimp (and other sea life) are caught on this fun, educational 70-minute trip. You'll sail the calm strip of water between the shore and nearby Deer Island. There is a $9 admission charge for adults and a $5 charge for kids 4 through 12.

CAPTAIN ED'S
Small Craft Harbor
Gulfport   864-8736

Rent tackle or bring your own when you try your luck pulling in the fish from aboard the 35-foot *Sea Surrey*. The boat is docked at the Gulfport Harbor (Pier 1, Slip A). It costs $20 for the trip and $2.50 to rent tackle.

GULF ISLANDER
CHARTERED EVENING CRUISES

Small Craft Harbor
Gulfport   864-3797

From those folks who provide ferry-passenger service out to Ship Island comes this 110-foot vessel available for special events worthy of a charter cruise that includes meals, music and dancing.

COOKIE'S BAYOU TOURS

Miss. 603
Bay St. Louis   466-4824

Explore the bayous, Jourdan River and Bay of St. Louis during a one-hour and 45-minute ride in a pontoon boat. Tours depart at 9 AM, 11 AM, 1 PM, 3 PM and, during daylight saving time, 5 PM. Cost is $15 for adults and $7 for passengers 12 and younger. The office is on Miss. 603 between U.S. 90 and I-10.

WILD CHILD SAILING CHARTERS

Point Cadet Marina
Biloxi   374-1936, 861-75252

Sail from Point Cadet to the barrier islands or anywhere you wish. The 37-foot sailboat accommodates one to six passengers on one-hour excursions anywhere the groups wants to go. Passengers bring their own food, drinks and whatever else to make their day in the sun memorable. Rates are $375 (off-season rates are available) and include life jackets, ice and snacks. Call for reservations.

THE GULF SCREAMER

Point Cadet Marina
Biloxi   875-9901

See the shoreline from this 53-foot speed boat that starts out at a slow pace and then picks up speed. The boat accommodates 56 passengers and departs from Point Cadet. Call for schedules, which change in winter. Reservations aren't required. Cost is $10 for adults and $6 for children younger than 13. The *Screamer* is available for charters and night cruises.

Canoeing

The Hill Country

BEAR CREEK FLOAT TRIP

Tishomingo State Park
Tishomingo   438-6914

This is an exciting and scenic 8-mile float trip down rocky-bottomed Bear Creek that runs through the upper east Mississippi high hills. Between mid-April and mid-October the float trips leave from the swinging bridge at 9 AM and 1 PM daily. Participants must register at the park office 30 minutes prior to departure. The trip lasts from two to three hours and costs $15 for the canoe rental. Park staff will meet participants at the end of the trip and return them to the park. For additional information, please call the park office.

The Heartland

BLACK CREEK NATIONAL WILD & SCENIC RIVER

Brooklyn   582-8817

There are six schedules for canoeing, camping, fishing and hiking in the beautiful National Forest every day except Monday from March through October. You can make arrangements for canoes any time of year.

OKATOMA OUTDOOR POST FLOAT TRIPS

Sanford   722-4297

Okatoma Creek near Hattiesburg promises some of the state's best stream canoeing. The Upper Run covers 13 miles and three waterfalls. The Lower Run is 6 miles and has two small waterfalls. Rental includes a canoe, paddles, life vests, cushions and transportation for $18 (one day).

LONNIE'S CANOE RENTAL

U.S. 49 N. at Miss. 590
Seminary   722-4301

Year-round float trips are available at this facility 20 miles north of Hattiesburg. Trips last from three to eight hours. Cost for renting a canoe is $18 for two adults.

The River Cities

For those with their own canoes, the nearby **Homochitto River** in the Homochitto National Forest is the site for do-it-yourself trips. The river has white sand beaches.

Also, enthusiasts can make a daytrip to the McComb area for canoeing and tubing in the **Pearl River Basin** water parks. Pearl River Basin Boatway covers an area from Neshoba County in the northern part of the state to the Coast in the south. There are 17 water parks in the Pearl River Basin Development District, all offering outdoor fun along the river. Visitors can launch their boats and enjoy good fishing, or stay on dry land for a picnic and playground activities. Whitewater canoes are rented at three water parks: Lake Lincoln, Bogue Chitto and D'Lo, all part of the boatway system. When you rent a canoe, the fee includes life jackets, paddles and put-in service.

LAKE LINCOLN BAHALA CREEK

Lincoln County near Brookhaven   643-5216

There's plenty of water activity at this 550-acre lake 6 miles east of Wesson and 15 north of Brookhaven.

BOGUE CHITTO WATER PARK

U.S. 98, McComb   684-9568

In Pike County on the Bogue Chitto River, this water park is a favorite spot for those who enjoy the outdoors. Canoe rentals are just part of the attraction here. There's picnicking, a nature trail and mapped float trips.

D'LO WATER PARK

U.S. 49, Mendenhall   847-4310

This popular water park is on the Strong River at a spot called "The Rocks," where canoe and float trips are available.

The Coast

WOLF RIVER CANOES

Long Beach   452-7666

Canoeists travel at their own pace down scenic Wolf River in Harrison County. Full trips include canoe and paddles, life jackets, parking and transportation up the river. Rentals are $25 per canoe. A group rate of $22 per canoe is available for seven canoes or more. Wolf

River Canoes is at the end of Tucker Road, north of Long Beach and south of the interstate. Take the Long Beach Exit off I-10.

Water Parks

The Hill Country

RIVERPARK
WATER PARK & GOLF RANGE

Columbus   327-4700

Off Miss. 45 on Wilkins-Wise Road en route to the waterway lock and dam, the big slide at this park is a favorite of all ages; some appreciate the go-carts and minigolf too. Summer hours are 8 AM to 10 PM; you can swim til 6 PM.

LAKE TIAK-O'KHATA

Off Miss. 25
Louisville   773-7853

This private, family-owned resort offers a lake with swimming, a slide, a playground, a restaurant, rustic cabins, A-frame efficiencies and a motel. Paddleboats and fishing boats are available for rent, and the scenery on the lake and adjacent land is quite outstanding. Families use Lake Tiak-O'Khata (some say Lake of the Pines) for summer reunions. It's good for business meetings too. The restaurant is open and popular year round. This place is known for down-home cooking and a huge luncheon buffet. Since it is lake swimming, it's available in the summer only. Small sandy beaches and piers add a little diversity, while lifeguards watch the water. Adults swim for $5, children $2.75. Swim from 10 AM to 6 PM.

The Heartland

RAPIDS ON THE RESERVOIR

1808 Spillway Rd.
Brandon   992-0500

This is a water park for the family, complete with wave pool, kiddie water playground, five water slides and an amusement park. It's open during the spring and summer from 10 AM to 6 PM. Daily rates for adults are $10.95 plus tax; children's rates are $9.95.

WATERLAND USA

727 Ridgewood Rd.
Jackson   957-1322

Families can enjoy the 15 acres of water attractions, including a covered pavilion, arcade, snack stands, miniature golf and a kiddie city. It's open weekends spring and summer; hours are 10 AM to 6 PM daily in summer Monday through Saturday; 12 to 6 PM Sundays. Daily adult rates are $11.95 plus tax, $9.95 children. Children 2 and younger get in free. Family season rates are available.

Insiders' Tips

Civil War historian and novelist Shelby Foote has a tie to Mount Holly, the 1850 Italianate mansion in the Delta that on occasion hosts sportspeople. It was owned by Foote's great-grandfather and then by his grandfather. Mount Holly is on lovely Lake Washington, just off Miss. 1, about 20 miles south of Greenville.

OKATIBBEE WATER PARK

Near Meridian   737-2370, (800) 748-9403

Enjoy Splashdown Country's four water slides, including an inner-tube river ride and small slide in the children's pool. The 350-acre water park also has several picnic areas and lodging facilities. The park is open from June through Labor Day. Call for the schedule. Admission is $6 to $8. Lake Okatibbee is 15 miles northwest of Meridian. Take Miss. 19 N., and turn right at the Okatibbee Lake sign.

DUNN'S FALLS WATER PARK

Off I-59 S., Enterprise   655-8550
(800) 748-9403

Power from this 65-foot waterfall near Meridian once ran a gristmill, which is open for tours. The recreation area includes a natural wildlife refuge, hiking, swimming and picnic areas with grills. It's open all year, and admission is $1. From October through April, hours of operation are 9 AM to 5 PM, Wednesday through Sunday. From May through September 30, hours are 11 AM to 7 PM. Take I-59 S. to the Savoy Exit and follow the signs.

MAYNOR CREEK WATER PARK

U.S. 84
Waynesboro   735-4365

Maynor Creek, a mile west of Waynesboro, contains Swampy Hollow with three giant water slides. It's open weekends during May and all day from June through August.

FLINT CREEK WATER PARK

Miss. 29 N.
Wiggins   928-3051

The park contains a 600-acre lake filled with bass, bream, crappie and catfish. There's a separate beach for swimmers, a ski area and boat launches. Other features include tent and developed camping, fishing, swimming, picnicking, skiing, hiking and boating. Hikers can take the nature trail that follows the lake. Flint Creek also has Water Town, which sports four giant water slides and a kid's water slide. Water Town is open May through Labor Day, Wednesday to Sunday.

The River Cities

Although there aren't any water parks in the River Cities, you have plenty to choose from and enjoy in other parts of the state.

The Coast

BUCCANEER BAY WATER PARK

1150 S. Beach Boulevard
Waveland   467-2580, 467-3822

This new water park at Buccaneer State Park consists of Pirate's Lagoon with a large wave pool for body surfing and such; Pirate's Plunge with two 300-foot-long water slides; Kid's Kove, a small pool for young swimmers; The Galley snack bar; and The Surf Shop for souvenirs and other items.

Buccaneer Bay is open from mid-April through Labor Day, daily during summer. Hours are 11 AM to 6:45 PM. Admission is $9 for adults and $7.50 for children. Seniors get in free. Group rates and season passes are available.

FUN TIME USA

1300 Beach Blvd.
Gulfport   896-7315

Watery fun for the family includes bumper boats, rides for adults and kids, go-carts, batting cages, miniature golf, skee ball and an arcade with 70 games, including the video and pinball varieties. There's also a snack bar.

Admission to the grounds and parking are free. Bumper boats, golf and go-carts cost $3 each. Amusement ride prices vary; 10 tickets cost $6. Group rates are available.

WET WILLIE'S WATER SLIDE
1200 E. Beach Blvd.
Gulfport   896-6592

This place is adjacent to Fun Time USA. Here, there's even more family fun on the triple water slide and in the kiddie pool. Concessions are available. There is a $5 per hour charge, or you can pay $10 to ride all day. Latecomers can slide from 7 to 10 PM for $5. Wet Willie's is open May through Labor Day from 9 AM to 10 PM daily.

SLIPPERY SAM'S
3080 Beach Blvd., Biloxi   435-3140

Across from Magic Golf, this water park offers a triple water slide, a speed slide, bumper boats, a pool and rides especially for small kids. It's open 10 AM to 10 PM daily during warm weather. Admission is $1 for an all-day outing or $6 an hour.

BLUFF CREEK WATER PARK
Vancleave   826-9963

Bluff Creek is a day-use park with seasonal primitive camping only. Bass, catfish and bluegill are the resident catches here. There's also a swimming hole, a beach, picnic areas with barbecue grills and tables and giant water slides that are open weekdays May through Labor Day. A Pat Harrison Waterway District park, Bluff Creek is off Miss. 57.

McLEOD WATER PARK
Bay St. Louis   467-1894

This park on the Jourdan River near Bay St. Louis. It has a bathhouse, a boat ramp, developed and primitive camping, canoeing, fishing, a nature trail, picnic shelters and swimming.

Watersports

ALOHA PARASAIL AND WATERSPORTS
U.S. 90
Gulfport   452-0299, 341-DO-IT

This new Coast attraction is on the beach in front of the Holiday Inn in Gulfport. Here you can choose from several exciting options such as parasailing, Waverunners, Hobie Cats and Windsurfers. Sailing and windsurfing lessons are available. The owners have more than 20 years' experience to help you enjoy a few hours or a whole day on the beach. Aloha offers free transportation from hotels within 10 miles of its location.

SKI SKI
On the beach
In front of the Biloxi Lighthouse   374-9720

If you want to take to the water at high speeds, check out Ski Ski. Choose from six Jet Skis in the summer from 10 AM to around 7 PM. Cost is $20 for 15 minutes.

Swimming

The Hill Country

Public swimming is available at most of the state parks that are listed in the State Parks section of this chapter. Normally the fee is $2 per vehicle for park use. Swimmers may swim in lakes at designated sites at their own risk. Though there are many swimming pools throughout the state, most are private pools for members only, except those included with water parks. Certain private establishments such as Lake Tiak-O'Khata are open to the public with an admission charge. Colleges, universities, YMCAs and YWCAs have pools too, but enrollment fees in a swim or recreational program are usually necessary.

The Heartland

Anyone looking for a place to swim can try the state parks in the Heartland region. Be aware that not all parks offer swimming.

MERIDIAN

In Meridian, public swimming is offered at **Highland Park**, 41st Avenue and 19th Street, 485-1801, which is open daily except Wednesday during the summer months from 2 PM to 5 PM. Admission is $1. There is also a swimming beach at **Lake Okatibbee**, Okatibbee Dam Road, 626-8431.

HATTIESBURG

In Hattiesburg, the **Jaycees Pool** is open from mid-June through mid-August. Admission is $1. At the E. Fifth Street Community Center admission is 50¢, and the hours are 1 PM to 5 PM daily. Swimming is also available in USM's Lake Sehoy.

The River Cities

NATCHEZ

Duncan Park in Natchez has a swimming pool among its other attractions, all set in the heart of the city on 200 beautiful acres. The pool ranges from 3 to 10 feet deep. From June to mid-August, it's open daily except Monday from 1 PM to 6 PM. Admission is $1.50 per person per session; sessions are 1 to 3 PM and 3:30 to 6 PM.

The Coast

Swimmers don't have a problem finding places to go in the Gulf, although locals look carefully before entering the water at the beach. Water at the islands is clearer.

There are several swimming pools open to the public.

BILOXI

The **Biloxi Natatorium**, 1384 Father Ryan Avenue, 435-6205, is an Olympic-size pool open daily all year long with two low diving boards and one high board, dressing rooms and showers. Adult lap swim hours are 6 AM to 8 PM Monday through Friday, when a section is roped off for laps. Recreation swimming is 1 PM to 8 PM weekdays, noon to 5 PM on Saturday and 1 PM to 4 PM on Sunday. Cost is $1 per person.

LONG BEACH

The **Long Beach YMCA**, 20134 Pineville Road, 864-1223, has a four-lane, 25-yard outdoor pool that's open all year and every day. Hours for nonmembers are 4 PM to 6 PM on weekdays and noon to 5 PM on weekends.

GULFPORT

The **Mississippi Gulf Coast Community College's** Jefferson Davis campus in Gulfport, 2226 Switzer Road, 896-3355, has an Olympic-size outdoor pool that's open to the public. Swimmers are welcome weekdays from 1 PM to 6 PM and Saturday from 1 PM to 5 PM.

OCEAN SPRINGS

In Ocean Springs the **YMCA** pool, 1810 Government Street, 875-2966, is a heated, Olympic-size indoor pool that has a $2 fee for swimmers. It's open daily. Adult lap swim times are 6 AM to 7 PM weekdays, 9 AM to 5 PM Saturday and 1 to 5 PM on Sunday. Swimmers younger than 18 are allowed to swim weekdays from 5:30 to 7 PM and 1 to 5 PM on weekends.

Bicycling

Bicycling appears to be an up-and-coming sport in the Magnolia State, perhaps because of the vast outdoors and moderate climate. This sport is a popular activity, especially along the Natchez Trace, and it attracts individual bikers and biking clubs from across the country. Bicycling along the Trace is governed by Title 36, Code of Federal Regulations, which states that riders must comply with traffic regulations; riders must keep well to the side of the road, and bicycles should not be ridden abreast of one another. It further states that each bicycle must exhibit a white light on the front and a red light or red reflector on the rear.

If you're biking on the Trace, be careful of heavy traffic around cities, and expect to depart the Trace in Jackson. The Natchez Trace Parkway consists of two completed, but disconnected, sections: 79 miles south of Jackson and 335 miles be-

tween Jackson and Leipers Fork, Tennessee. The width of the parkway varies from 400 to 1,000 feet. Lands outside this boundary are private property except for two state parks in northeast Mississippi. Natchez Trace Parkway literature for bikers advises cyclists to be off the parkway by sundown for safety reasons.

The Heartland

Though there are bike shops and bikers throughout the Hill Country and the Heartland, the biggest races and most avid bikers appear to be in and around Jackson. Races begin there and run up or down the nearby Natchez Trace. Bike rentals are scarce along the Trace, so BYOB (bring your own bike). **Indian Cycle** in Jackson offers assistance to bikers as well as lots of supplies and equipment. They also know about local biking events. Call them at 956-8383 or (800) 898-0019.

Another bike shop in Jackson, **The Bike Rack**, organizes four mountain bike races each year in the capital city. Mountain racing occurs also in Tupelo and Meridian. Each April, there's a two-day road race in Jackson organized by Bo Bourne, with pro-bikers in attendance and big sponsor money. The Bike Rack's two locations can answer questions, 956-6891 or 372-6722, about local races and the Tour de Trace, a major charity race sponsored by the local chapters of MS Society.

Credit: Tim Isbell, The Sun Herald

Mississippi heat and humidity can be brutal so locals and visitors use any means available to keep their cool.

The River Cities

The **Natchez Bicycling Center**, 446-7794, has bikes for rent. Costs are $14 for the day, $10 for three to five hours and $7.50 for one to three hours. Cyclists can tour the city's historic homes and other attractions such as the scenic Natchez Trace and quiet country roads outside town. The center is open Tuesday through Friday from 10 AM to 5:30 PM and Saturday from 10 AM to 3 PM, otherwise by special arrangements.

The Coast

Scenic Ocean Springs has a new 15-mile bike trail, the **Live Oaks Bicycle Route**, which takes riders past nine points of interest. The trail begins at the old L&N Depot, 1000 Washington Avenue. From there riders follow signs on the right-hand-side of city streets and pedal through downtown, past the Walter Anderson Museum of Art, through the city's historic district, along Front and East beaches, past Fort Maurepas, Shearwater Pottery, Gulf Coast Research Laboratory and Gulf Islands National Seashore Mississippi District. Maps of the route are available at the Chamber of Commerce, 1000 Washington Avenue.

Ballooning

This high-adventure sport is catching on in certain areas, especially along the Mississippi River in Natchez and in the Delta. These folks are most enthusiastic, and their enthusiasm is contagious.

The Hill Country

ROSCOE TURNER BALLOON RACE
Corinth Airport
Corinth   *(800) 748-9048*

Corinth sponsors this event that appeals to history buffs as well as balloonists. Roscoe Turner was an early aviator and native son. About 55 balloons are on the scene in the mid-August sky. This event awards thousands of dollars in prize money.

The Delta

MISSISSIPPI INTERNATIONAL BALLOON CLASSIC
Whittington Park, Sycamore St.
Greenwood   *(800) 748-9064*

This event is said to be one of the biggest and the best. More than 150,000 visitors converge upon this Delta town to see the 80 or so balloons and learn who wins

the most money in cash prizes. This major event is held the last of June; the Greenwood CVB has details.

The Heartland

MISSISSIPPI CHAMPIONSHIP HOT AIR BALLOON FEST
Canton Balloon Field
Canton   *(800) 844-3369*

This July 1 to 4 annual event features about 50 balloons and attracts in excess of 60,000 onlookers. The Canton CVB will provide specific information.

MISSISSIPPI SKY PARADE
Jackson International Airport, off I-20 E.
Jackson   *982-8088*

This stellar event in ballooning is held around the first of September, and it attracts big prize money, said to be in excess of $100,000. About 300,000 spectators gather at Jackson International Airport to see 200 balloons take to the sky. An air show is on the agenda, plus entertainment, fireworks and amusement-park rides.

The River Cities

GREAT MISSISSIPPI RIVER BALLOON RACE
On the bluff
Natchez   *(800) 647-6724*

Natchez is the place to be in mid-October for a chance to see colorful balloons crossing the mighty Mississippi and flying over

Insiders' Tips

The locks and dams along the Tennessee-Tombigbee Waterway in northeast Mississippi offer outstanding bass and crappie fishing. Large channel catfish are known to prosper here too. The highly prized walleye swims in many of the streams and tributaries of this waterway.

he flat Delta. This is spectacular. Natchez xpects about 80 balloons and 50,000 folks. The CVB has more information.

The Coast

At this time the coast doesn't have any allooning events, so visitors and residents ake advantage of the nearby River Baloon Race in Natchez as well as other state events.

Golf

Ask those who come to play golf in Mississippi from all points north, and they'll say the golf is great in the Magnolia State. Indeed it is, and some of the public courses are excellent. We'll list only public courses here or those that welcome the public. Most private clubs have reciprocity with other private clubs, though play must be OK'd through the club pro. Generally, Mississippi's public courses can be played for around $30 including cart rental. Many hotels on the Gulf Coast offer golf packages, and these include play at some top private clubs.

The Hill Country

HOLIDAY GOLF
E. Goodman Rd., Olive Branch   895-3500

This challenging (but not so challenging you won't enjoy it) course has water on two holes and multiple-dogleg fairways. It's an 18-hole, par 72 course with a

pro shop and available pros. It's just outside Memphis, on the Mississippi side, so the course can get pretty crowded on weekends. A tee time is essential on weekends and helpful at all times.

UNIVERSITY GOLF COURSE
College Hill Rd., Oxford   234-4816

This 25-year-old club hosts Ole Miss players and others who like the very old trees, hills and doglegs. This interesting layout has a course rating of 69.8 and a slope rating of 124, middle tees. It's best to call for a tee time here.

BEL AIR PARK
Country Club Rd.
Tupelo   841-6446

Expect an easy play on these nine holes, with a par 36. Find three lakes and a pro shop too.

MISSISSIPPI STATE UNIVERSITY GOLF COURSE
U.S. 82 E., Starkville   325-3028

Area golfers say this course has the best layout in the state. It has also garnered some national recognition of late. The course rating is 71.0, and the slope rating is 124, middle tee. It's a busy, 18-hole, par 72 course.

The Delta

DELTA STATE GOLF COURSE
Sunflower Rd., Cleveland   846-4585

This college course offers a challenge

Turkey hunting is one of the most dangerous sports because of the amount of camouflage worn. Avoid wearing white, red or blue clothing, for these colors are found on a male gobbler when he is ready to breed. Other hunters may mistake the colors for a turkey.

Insiders' Tips

for the most skilled golfer on holes 5 and 9. It's a nine-hole, par 36 course.

GREENVILLE MUNICIPAL GOLF COURSE
Municipal Rd., Greenville   332-4079

This is a good example of a town that utilized a former military air base; the old base is now an 18-hole, par 72 public golf course. The course rating is 70.8 on the back tee, and the slope rating is 116, back.

The Heartland

LEFLEUR'S BLUFF STATE PARK
2140 Riverside Dr.
Jackson   987-3998

In a state park near downtown Jackson, this course is popular and busy. It's a nine-hole, par 35 course that is not as easy as it looks. There's a pro shop on the premises.

SONNY GUY MUNICIPAL GOLF COURSE
3200 Woodrow Wilson Dr.
Jackson   960-1905

This 18-hole, par 72 course offers a challenge, according to local golfers. You'll need a dash of luck as well as skill on some of these holes.

EAGLE RIDGE GOLF COURSE
Hwy. 18 S., Raymond   857-5993

Hinds Community College owns and manages this 18-hole par 72. It has a pro shop and not as many college players as non-college.

GROVE PARK
1800 Ave. J, Jackson   960-2074

This nine-hole, 36 par club is not rated, but it's said to be fun to play.

LAKEVIEW MUNICIPAL GOLF COURSE
Causeyville Rd., Meridian   693-3301

This par 70, 18-hole course is open to the public seven days a week. There's a driving range, three putting greens and a snack bar. Carts are available. Lakeview is near Long Creek Reservoir.

OKATIBBEE GOLF RANGE
Meridian   483-4653

This range on Highway 19 N. has nine holes and is par 3 and 4. This is a flat course, but the greens are somewhat elevated. A couple of water holes help make this a fun course (that is, if you clear them!).

COPIAH-LINCOLN COMMUNITY COLLEGE
Lester Furr Dr.
Wesson   833-5801

This public course near Brookhaven is open seven days a week. Hours are 8 AM until dark on Monday through Saturday and noon to dark on Sunday. The course has nine holes and is par 72.

TIMBERTON GOLF CLUB
3900 U.S. 11 S.
Hattiesburg   584-4653

Golf Digest calls Timberton one of the top-three in Mississippi. It's an 18-hole, par 72 championship course that's open daily to the public. There's a pro shop

Insiders' Tips

Mississippi's top spots for crappie fishing are Enid Lake, Pickwick Lake, Tunica Cutoff, Eagle Lake, all north of I-20. The choice bait of most crappie anglers is the minnow.

and a restaurant. Golfers are required to call for a tee time.

VAN HOOK GOLF COURSE
1 Golf Course Rd.
Hattiesburg   264-1872

This is the University of Southern Mississippi's championship 18-hole, par 72 course, open daily from sunup to sundown. There's a pro shop, rental clubs and snack bar.

The River Cities

DUNCAN PARK
Auburn Ave. at Duncan Ave.
Natchez   442-5955

City-owned Duncan Park's 200 acres in the middle of town include an 18-hole golf course with a driving range. The beautiful course is a par 71, with a USGA rating of 68.9. The course is open daily except Christmas. Carts are available.

WINDING CREEK GOLF COURSE
U.S. 84, Natchez   442-6995

Winding Creek is an 18-hole par 72 championship course that's open daily. Golfers will also find a driving range, putting greens and a pro shop. Take the Cranfield Exit.

CLEAR CREEK GOLF COURSE
1566 Tiffentown Rd.
Vicksburg   638-9395

This 18-hole, par 72 public course is a wide, forgiving course that's open seven days week. It has a driving range.

The Coast

"Snowbirds" from up north travel to the coast every winter to leave behind the dreary cold and hit the golf courses. They've been doing it for years, taking advantage of the weather, the relatively low fees, and the uncrowded and challenging courses. For complete information on golf on the Gulf, contact the Mississippi Beach CVB, 869-6699 or (800) 237-9493. Remember, many hotels offer golf packages.

Here is a rundown of the courses that are open to the public:

BILOXI PAR THREE & FOUR
1734 Popps Ferry Rd., Biloxi   388-3631

This 18-hole course is open daily from 8 AM to dark, and there's a onetime green fee. A putting green is also available. Sixteen holes are par 3; two are par 4. There's one water hole and a pro shop.

BROADWATER BEACH RESORT
2110 Beach Blvd., Biloxi   388-2211

This resort has two courses, the Sea Course and Sun Course. The Sea Course is a par 71 and has the most photographed hole on the coast, with the Gulf as a picture-perfect backdrop. It claims the title of Mississippi's oldest golf course. The Sun Course is a par 72. It's a tough course with lots of water hazards and nice scenery. Extras include a pro shop, carts, snack bar and a lounge.

DIAMONDHEAD COMMUNITY
7600 Country Club Cir.
Diamondhead   255-3910

There are two courses in this resort community in Hancock County. Both the Cardinal Course and the Pine Course are wooded and roll gently, and both are par 72. Diamondhead has a country club and pro shop. It's just off I-10 near Bay St. Louis.

DOGWOOD HILLS GOLF COURSE
Miss. 67, Woolmarket   392-9805

Dogwood Hills, the Coast's newest course, has 18 holes and a driving range. The greens on the front nine are in excellent shape; the newer back nine holes are coming along. A new clubhouse is set to be completed in 1995. Take Exit 41 off I-10 and travel north 7 miles.

EDGEWATER BAY

2674 Pass Rd., Biloxi　　　*388-9670*

Edgewater Bay is a gently rolling par 71 course with lots of woods and water. There's a snack bar and pro shop. Carts are available.

GULFPORT PAR THREE

700 34th St., Gulfport　　　*868-3809*

This 18-hole par 3 course is lighted year round. There's a lighted driving range here too. Carts, a pro shop, a 19th hole and lessons are also available.

MISSISSIPPI NATIONAL GOLF CLUB

900 Hickory Hill Dr., Gautier　　*497-2372*

Formerly named Hickory Hill, this is an 18-hole, 7,000-yard championship course with water on 12 of the holes. It's ranked as the 10th best course in the state. There's a complete pro shop. Take the I-10 Exit 61 in Jackson County.

PASCAGOULA COUNTRY CLUB

2703 Washington Ave.
Pascagoula　　　　*762-1466*

This club welcomes visitors. The nine-hole course is a par 72. Extras include a lounge and pro shop.

PASS CHRISTIAN ISLES GOLF CLUB

150 Country Club Dr.
Pass Christian　　　*452-4851*

This course, one of the coast's oldest, presents a good challenge as it winds through pines and water. Pass Christian Isles is a par 72 course. There's a pro shop, and golf equipment is available.

PINE ISLAND GOLF COURSE

Marsh Island Dr., Gulf Park Estates
Ocean Springs　　　*875-1674*

Pine Island was designed by Pete Dye and is built on three islands. It's a par 71. In addition to a pro shop and driving range, there's a restaurant, lounge and snack bar.

TRAMARK GOLF CLUB

13831 Washington Ave.
Gulfport　　　*863-7808*

Tramark is a well-kept 18-hole golfing facility that's a par 72 and 6,045 yards. Tramark officials describe this course as "the best golfing value on the Coast" and welcome all players to judge this value for themselves.

TREASURE BAY'S GULF HILLS

13701 Paso Rd.
Ocean Springs　　　*875-4211*

This is an 18-hole championship course in a resort setting. The 17th hole here is called one of the more challenging in the country according to *Golf Digest*. Par is 71.

WINDANCE COUNTRY CLUB

19385 Champion Cir., Gulfport   832-4871

Golf Digest ranked this par 72 course in Gulfport as the second best in Mississippi. Windance was home to the annual Nike Mississippi Gulf Coast Classic tournament Mark McCumber designed this fine course.

ST. ANDREWS COUNTRY CLUB

2 Golfing Green Dr.
Ocean Springs   875-7730

This 18-hole course is well known for its beautiful setting on the Gulf and its fairways. It's a par 72. The clubhouse is newly remodeled.

SOUTHWIND COUNTRY CLUB

15312 Dismuke Ave., Biloxi   392-0400

Southwind is a par 72, 18-hole course with a pro shop and driving range. It opened in 1991 and has some of the largest greens of any coast course.

SUNKIST COUNTRY CLUB

2381 Sunkist Country Club Rd.
Biloxi   388-3961

This 18-hole, par 72 course has nice wooded fairways plus 17 bunkers and dangerous water hazards. Sunkist has a pro shop and driving range, in addition to a lounge and a restaurant.

Tennis

The Hill Country

COLUMBUS

Tennis is an active and popular sport in northeast Mississippi. Several major tennis clubs prosper in this area, such as **Magnolia Tennis Club** in Columbus, where near-professional quality players are often on the courts, and big tournaments are held annually. Many clubs are private, and guests play by invitation only. Whether or not a private club game is on the agenda, players never have to go too long without a game, for the region is rife with public courts. In Columbus, **Propst Park**, off U.S. 82 W., has lighted courts, while several schools have public courts. Call the city's recreation department, 327-4935, to see if a court should be reserved on a given day.

HOLLY SPRINGS

The Holly Springs Recreation Department manages the **City Parks** public courts at 160 S. Memphis Street, where lights are available for evening play. Call City Parks at 252-2019 for information about court reservations.

TUPELO

Tupelo boasts two parks where courts are usually available: **Lee Acres** at Lawndale and **City Park** on Joyner Avenue; both areas are lighted. The City Park Tennis Complex has 11 courts. Call 841-6440 for reservation information. Tupelo also has multiuse facilities at the new **Tupelo Coliseum** and the **Sportsplex** at Ballard Park.

OXFORD

In Oxford, it's easy to find a game at the **John Leslie Tennis Complex Activity Center**, 321 S. 15th Street, or at the University courts; all are lighted. Call 232-2380 to reserve courts.

The Delta

GREENVILLE

At Greenville's **Carrie Stern Park** expect to pay a fee for night play, also at the **Elwyn Wards Park**, **Frisby Park** and **Sam Balogna Park**, all of which are part of the Recreation Department, 400 Robert Shaw. The **Cypress Hills Tennis Club** on

Oakwood Drive hosts the NTRP Delta Doubles Tennis Tournament each Spring. For additional information, call the pro shop, 335-8790.

GREENWOOD

In Greenwood, both the **Veterans Memorial City Park** and **Whittington City Park** are part of the Park Commission; fees apply. Call 378-1670 for reservation information.

The Heartland

JACKSON

Jackson has a plethora of public tennis courts, which means players have a nice selection. The city's Parks Maintenance keeps up the courts at **Battlefield Park**, **Grove Park**, **Legion Complex**, **Presidential Hills I**, **Sykes Park** and **WestSide**. For reservations or more specific information on these city courts, call Parks Maintenance, 960-1630.

Other public courts in Jackson are **LeFleur's Bluff**, in the state park, off Riverside Drive. To reserve a court at LeFleur's Bluff call 987-3923. **Parham Bridges**, 5055 Old Canton Road, hosts the Mississippi Adult Open and Closed championships and U.S. Tennis Association/Mississippi junior qualifying. To reserve a court at Parham Bridges, call 956-1105. **The Tennis Center**, 2827 Oak Forest Drive, offers the state's only public indoor courts. To reserve courts, call 960-1712. Expect to find good players at many of these public courts.

The **H.B. Wolcott Park** is near Jackson, but it has a Ridgeland address. This athletic complex boasts 12 tennis courts with a pro shop. Call 853-1115 for information.

MERIDIAN

The public can hit the courts at **Meridian High School**, **Highland Park** and the **Sammie Davidson Complex**. Parks and Recreation, 485-1801, can provide further details. Also, the courts at **Meridian Community College** are open to the public from 8:15 AM to 8:15 PM during summer and on weekends. When school is in session, the courts open Monday through Friday at 4 PM and close at 8:15 PM and on weekends when the MCC tennis team isn't using them. Sammie Davidson Sports Complex, 485-1803, also has four softball diamonds, tennis courts and a track.

BROOKHAVEN

In Brookhaven, public courts are on **Adams Street**, where players compete in singles and doubles matches. The city recreation department, 833-3791, also offers lessons there.

HATTIESBURG

In Hattiesburg six public tennis courts are available at **Kamper Park**, 545-4578, and three are at **Hattiesburg High School**, 582-4366. The **University of Southern Mississippi**, 266-5405, has 14 courts open all year long on a free, first-come, first-served offering. And **William Carey College**, 266-5051, has courts open to the public at no fee.

The River Cities

NATCHEZ

In Natchez, tennis players will find eight lighted courts available at **Duncan Park**, 442-1589. They're available daily all year from 9 AM to 8:30 PM. Cost is $2 per person per hour.

The Coast

Tennis players won't have any trouble nding courts on the Coast. Here are just a w suggestions. In Bay St. Louis, there's **City ark**, 467-9092, on Second Street where ou'll find two courts available daily.

In Waveland, the **Elwood Bourgeois ark** on Central Avenue, 467-4134, has a ublic court. Biloxi has a dozen tennis ourts throughout the city. Call the parks nd recreation department for details, 35-6294. There are seven courts in)cean Springs that the recreation depart- nent offers to the public. Call 875-8665 or details.

Horseback Riding

The Hill Country

Horseback riding is permissible in all national forests but not in camping ar- eas; there are no developed trails unless indicated. There are trails available at **Trace State Park**, 489-2958, near Belden and **Witchdance Horse Trail**, 285-3264, near Ackerman.

Columbus has a plus for horseback riders. It is the 700-acre **Rock Hill Stables**, 5975 Old West Point Road, 327-7820, where a selection of horses may be rented for $10 an hour. Guided trail rides give riders the extra treat of seeing the Tenn- Tom Waterway and outstanding native foliage; reservations are necessary. Rock Hill also teaches riding and hosts various horse shows.

Starkville's **Ninebarks Stables Riding Center**, 2212 Oktoc Road, 323-1800, gives lessons for beginners and advanced riders. They offer a covered riding arena, horses for sale and boarding.

The Heartland

Jackson's **Red Brick Farm**, 1629 Hilda Drive, 362-9069, offers 900 riding acres, and they specialize in hunters and jump- ers. Call this full-service facility for avail- able rentals and lessons. The Jackson area has tack and equipment shops as well. Try **Tackfully Yours**, 969-3136, **Running Horse Saddlery**, 939-0644, or **Dutchman's Tack Shop**, 856-7373. For horse transportation, if locals can't pro- vide it, try **All-State Horse Express**, (800) 451-7696, or **Horsein' Around**, (800) 234- 4675.

In Hattiesburg, the **University of Southern Mississippi's Equestrian Cen- ter** has horses for rent for guided trail rides in a 200-acre area. Call Coach Mickey Herrington, 266-5405, for hours and rates. Ask about the USM horsemanship day camps for kids in the spring and sum- mer.

The River Cities

It's not exactly horseback riding, but visitors to Natchez can take a horse drawn carriage ride and tour of the his- toric district. Call **Natchez Pilgrimage Tours**, (800) 647-6742 or 466-6631, for day and evening schedules.

The Coast

Lonesome Duck Stables near Pass Christian, 255-5043, has one- and two- hour guided rides, full-moon trail rides and pony rides for the kids. The price is $10 an hour, $15 for two hours. The full- moon trips cost $25 per person. Reser- vations are required. Lonesome Duck also has wagons for rent for groups. Just north of the coast, between Picayune and Kiln, is **Circle G Riding Stables**. The owners have 25 years of experience. Rent horses for trail rides to a picnic area and the beach along a nearby creek. Reservations are necessary. Cost is $30 a day per person.

Spectator Sports

Baseball

JACKSON GENERALS
Lakeland Dr., off I-55
Jackson 981-4664

Mississippi's baseball fans have seen some of their favorite players show their stuff at the 5,200-seat capacity Smith-Wills Stadium in Jackson, home of the professional baseball team, the **Jackson Generals**, a Double-A farm club in the Houston Astros' minor-league system. Jackson has been home to the Generals for about 20 years, and before that, to the Mets of the New York farm system. The team has won three Texas League championships, much to the delight of local fans. You can get tickets to see Generals' home games during the season, April through August, at the stadium office. The office is open from 9 AM to 5 PM daily. Reserved tickets cost $5; bleacher seats are $4. Call 981-4664 for more information.

The stadium is located near the A Museum.

DIZZY DEAN MUSEUM
1204 Lakeland Dr.
Jackson 982-826

Near the Smith-Wills Stadium, you' find the Dizzy Dean Museum, name for the Wiggins, Mississippi, native wh became pitcher for the St. Louis Cardi nals and later a broadcaster. The museun houses artifacts and personal effects span ning this baseball great's long career. Thi museum will soon house the Mississipp Sports Hall of Fame.

NEW ORLEANS ZEPHYRS
139 Robert E. Lee Blvd.
New Orleans, La. (504) 282-677

Coastal fans of baseball follow "home team" **New Orleans Zephyrs**, the city' AAA minor league team. The Zephyr home games are played at Privateer Par next to the University of New Orleans Lakefront Arena. Games are played from April through September. Tickets are available at the Zephyrs office, at the ballpark on the night of a game o through Ticketmaster. Reserved seats are $7; general admission is $5; kids younge than 12 pay $2 for general admission The $2 general admission is also available for seniors and active military with ID. Call the Zephyrs for directions and in formation.

Boxing

Not long after the dockside establishments floated into town, some of the casinos began to sponsor pro boxing bouts that are often broadcast nationally from local rings in Biloxi and Bay St. Louis. In addition to the main events featuring such familiar names as Larry Holmes and Roberto Duran, the casino boxing cards often feature up-and-coming local talent. Check the Marquee entertainment guide in Friday's *The Sun Herald* or in the paper's daily sports section for information on the upcoming boxing matches and ticket information.

Football

NEW ORLEANS SAINTS
The Superdome, Central Business District
New Orleans, La. (504) 522-2600

Many Mississippians, and particularly those in the southern part of the state, have been loyal supporters of the New Orleans Saints since the pro football team was established more than 25 years ago. The loyalty deepened when Ole Miss standout Archie Manning, a genuine sports hero, took over the Saints quarterback position in the early 1970s.

Despite some heartbreaking losses and dismal seasons, Mississippi fans have remained true to the team. They travel to the Superdome to cheer in person or pack local sports bars to watch on big screens. If the Saints ever advance to the Super Bowl, they can count on loads of Mississippians to be in that number, enthusiastically cheering them on. The preseason games start in August, and the regular season is from early September to late December. Home games are played in the Louisiana Superdome in the central business district. Single-game tickets range from $30 to $37 and are sold at the Saints ticket office, (504) 522-2600, and through Ticketmaster, (504) 522-5555.

Rodeo

The Mississippi Coliseum, 961-4000, at the Fairgrounds near downtown Jackson hosts major events, beginning with the big **Dixie National Rodeo and Livestock Show** held at this complex each February. It's one of the city's most popular events.

Basketball

The Mississippi Coliseum hosts the Mississippi high school basketball championships each March, and most of the 10,000 seats are in use. For ticket information call 353-0603.

College Sports

Jackson's Veterans Memorial Stadium is indeed a popular and well-known place. It is home to **Jackson State University's Tiger football team** and the famous Tiger marching band, and it's where the Southeastern Conference (SEC) games are played in Jackson. Veterans Memorial Stadium hosts another big event, when most

The wild turkey population in the state is the result of a cooperative effort between hunters, agencies, and the National Wild Turkey Federation. In 1942, only 253 turkeys were harvested here; in 1988, 58,000 birds were harvested.

Insiders' Tips

all of the 60,000-plus seats are filled. Folks from across the state attend the **Mississippi High School All-Star Football Game** each summer.

Football loyalties run deep here. Ask any loyal fan of the University of Mississippi (Ole Miss) or **Mississippi State University**, both SEC schools in football, basketball and baseball. The major annual rivalry game for football is the infamous **Egg Bowl**, played either in Oxford or Starkville. This major football match keeps rivalries revved up and fans in a frenzy. For current dates and schedules for football, baseball, or basketball at these two SEC colleges, call Ole Miss, 232-7512, and MSU, 325-2703.

The **University of Southern Mississippi** in Hattiesburg fields football, baseball and basketball teams (among other sports) with a strong following, especially in the southern part of the state. For information about the USM teams' schedules, call 266-4503; for ticket information call 266-5418 or (800) 844-8425.

Hall of Fame

MISSISSIPPI SPORTS HALL OF FAME & MUSEUM

Sports Foundation
P.O. Box 16021   *982-8264*
Jackson 39236   *(800) 280-FAME*

The Mississippi Sports Hall of Fame and Museum is working hard to become what its founders intended: a hall of fame and museum in which Mississippi's great athletes are recognized and honored. The Mississippi Sports Foundation, Inc. was established in 1992 as a nonprofit corporation to support the construction and operation of the hall of fame and museum. The idea was born in 1960 when Jimmie McDowell, then sports editor of the now defunct *State-Times* recognized Mississippi's proud sporting heritage and wanted to figure out a way to show it off. He proposed his idea to honor sports heroes while speaking to a Jackson civic club, and in 1961, four members were inducted into the new Mississippi Sports Hall of Fame. Unfortunately, no permanent home was available to hang the plaques, so they were displayed on the ground floor of the Mississippi Coliseum, where the Hall of Fame is still temporarily located.

A few years back, sports fans became even more serious about wanting a home for their heroes, and some met to discuss the feasibility of a permanent site. From this meeting, the Mississippi Sports Foundation, Inc. was formed to establish a museum, and since that time much progress has been made. The museum is the recipient of various bonds and grants and is to be located on Lakeland Drive in Jackson, adjacent to the Ag Museum and the Smith-Wills Stadium. If all goes as planned, the existing Dizzy Dean Museum is scheduled

Insiders' Tips

Old Waverly, near West Point and Columbus in northeast Mississippi, is included among *Golf Digest's* prestigious "America's 100 Greatest Golf Courses" for the 1995-1996 ranking.

to be incorporated into the new facility at its completion.

Among the 154 inductees in the Mississippi Sports Hall of Fame and Museum are star quarterback Archie Manning, Felix "Doc" Blanchard, Bruiser Kinard, Baily Howell, Dizzy Dean, Ray Guy and Walter Payton.

Credit: The Sun Herald

A sign at Gulf Islands National Seashore in Ocean Springs reminds guests that wildlife is always very close by.

Inside
Parks

If you've never taken advantage of Mississippi's beautiful parks, you're missing a great treat. Our parks are clean, green and not too crowded. They're nearly perfect places to get back to the basics and experience firsthand the solace of nature. With that in mind, we suggest that you not try to see the best of nature's bounty by car. Do yourself a favor and walk, hike or bike. Keep alert though, for as wonderful as the parks are, there can be inherent dangers. Snakes are seen on occasion, and Lyme disease can be a serious threat, so consider using tick repellent. It's always a good idea to take a first-aid kit when nature trips are planned.

The national parks are maintained by the U.S. Department of the Interior. They are: Natchez Trace Parkway, Vicksburg National Military Park, Natchez National Historical Park and Gulf Islands National Seashore. Each park has a visitors center where information is available on all aspects of the park.

Mississippi State Parks boast camping, swimming, hiking, fishing, cabins, boat launches and some of the most beautiful scenery in the South. There are 22 recreational parks throughout the state and five historic parks. Historic parks are living-history exhibits, among them Florewood Plantation near Greenwood, which is an actual working plantation from the 1850s.

National forests in Mississippi comprise the largest holding of public land in the state, and they offer a full agenda of outdoor recreation, even for the serious hunter and outdoor enthusiast. Lace up your hiking boots and read on to find out more about Mississippi's parks. We hope that you'll visit and enjoy many and as Walt Whitman said, "Live each season as it passes; breathe the air, drink the drink, taste the fruit, and resign yourself to the influences of each."

State Parks

Mississippi boasts 22 recreational state parks and five historic parks, the difference being that the recreational parks offer a variety of outdoor activities while the historic parks feature living history only. For example, Florewood State Park near Greenwood is a re-created river plantation of the 1850s, complete with a Greek Revival-style planter's home and the outbuildings necessary to run the plantation. For information about Mississippi State Parks, call (800) 467-2757.

The Hill Country

TRACE STATE PARK
Belden   489-2958

Ten miles east of Pontotoc off Miss. 6, this 2,500-acre park offers tent camping, 25 camping pads with electricity and water and four cabin units. Fishing, water skiing, rental boats and a launch ramp are also available.

HUGH WHITE STATE PARK

Grenada   226-4934

Five miles east of Grenada off Miss. 8, this popular park on pretty Grenada Lake offers outstanding outdoor amenities. The 64,000-acre lake invites all water sports. It boasts exceptional fishing, rental boats and a broad sand beach with a concession stand. There's a bait shop, tennis courts, a pool for cabin guests, an 8-mile nature trail and a restaurant.

WALL DOXEY STATE PARK

Holly Springs   252-4231

This park is 7 miles from Holly Springs on a clear, clean, spring-fed lake. Guests enjoy the beach, a three-level diving pier, good fishing and a nature trail. There are nine cabins, a group camp and 64 camping pads.

J.P. COLEMAN STATE PARK

Iuka   423-6515

This is one of the state's prettiest parks, nestled in the mini-mountains of Pickwick Lake on the Tennessee River 13 miles north of Iuka. Wonderful water sports and fishing are available as well as a full-service marina. Here on Pickwick Lake, Mississippi's record smallmouth bass (7 pounds, 15 ounces) was caught in 1987. Twenty cabins, a three-unit motel

and 57 camping pads accommodate all who enjoy the great outdoors. A restaurant is open during peak summer season.

GEORGE P. COSSAR STATE PARK

Oakland   623-7356

On a peninsula-like arm jutting onto the 42-square-mile Lake Enid, Cossar is 8 miles east of Oakland, off Miss. 32. On the premises is a pool, beach, lodge, nature trail and miniature golf course. A restaurant specializes in catfish and all the trimmings. The park has 12 cabins and 156 camping pads.

JOHN W. KYLE STATE PARK

Sardis   487-1345

Nine miles east of Sardis, this park includes the big Sardis Lake and offers all water sports, a seasonal pool, tennis courts, a playing field and an indoor sports hall for basketball and skating. (The sports hall is open weekends only during the off-season.) The park has 20 cabins, a group camp and 200 camping pads.

TISHOMINGO STATE PARK

Tishomingo   483-6914

Tishomingo is a favorite because of its sheer beauty. It's in high hills and thick forests and offers a float trip down the Bear Creek from April to mid-October. The 13-mile nature trail includes a swinging bridge over a river. The seasonal pool, six cabins, a multiuse playing field, group camp, tent camping and 62 camping pads make this a popular destination. It's located 3 miles north of Dennis off Miss. 25, just off the Natchez Trace Parkway or mile marker 304 off the Trace.

TOMBIGBEE STATE PARK
Tupelo   842-7669

Only 6 miles from Tupelo off Miss. 6, this park is diverse and close to city amenities. It has a game room, a lodge with fast food service, a lake for swimming and fishing, a group camp, a nature trail, seven cabins and 20 camping pads.

LAKE LOWNDES STATE PARK
Columbus   328-2110

This is a good, quiet lake for fishing, and there's a nice swimming and picnic area. The indoor multi-sports complex offers basketball, volleyball, badminton, Ping-Pong and six tennis courts. Four guest cabins are booked far in advance, though there are 50 camping pads.

LEGION STATE PARK
Louisville   773-8323

An old Civilian Conservation Corps-built lodge dates back to the 1930s, and it's for rent when available. There are two lakes, picnic grounds, tent camping, nature trails and three cabins. This park is 2 miles north of Louisville on N. Columbus Avenue.

The Delta

GREAT RIVER ROAD STATE PARK
Rosedale   759-6762

The mighty Mississippi River rolls by this park, and it can be photographed endlessly from a four-level observation tower in the park. There's also plentiful fishing, boating, a lodge with a game room, fast-food service and 67 camping pads. The park is about 35 miles north of Greenville, off Miss. 1, which runs through the heart of the Delta.

LEROY PERCY STATE PARK
Hollandale   827-5436

Located 5 miles west of Hollandale, off Miss. 12, this is a favorite of hunters because it includes a wildlife refuge. Other features include a Delta wildlife interpretive center, a lodge, a pool, wildlife compounds, eight cabins and 16 camping pads.

The Heartland

LEFLEUR'S BLUFF STATE PARK
Jackson   987-3923

It's not often that you find a state park in the state's capital city — Lefleur's Bluff is one of those rarities. This park is just off I-55 at the Lakeland Exit in Jackson. The Bluff offers a campground bathhouse, 30 camping pads with water and electricity, comfort stations, a camp store and a deck overlooking Mayes Lake, a boat ramp, a large playground, a nature trail, a pool, three picnic pavilions and sites, a lighted tennis court, a nine-hole golf course and a pro shop.

HOLMES COUNTY STATE PARK
Durant   653-3351

This park is almost in the center of the state, 4 miles south of Durant, off I-55, Exit 150. It boasts two fishing lakes, a nature trail, an amphitheater, a skating rink, a group camp with meeting room, tent camping, 28 camping pads and 12 cabins.

GOLDEN MEMORIAL STATE PARK
Walnut Grove   253-2237

The memorial here is a post-Civil War one-room schoolhouse once located on the site. It offers picnic tables and pavilions, grills and seven camping pads. Find it off Miss. 35 on Miss. 492, 5 miles east of Walnut Grove.

Visitors enjoy nature along a swamp trail at Percy Quinn State Park near McComb.

ROOSEVELT STATE PARK

Morton   732-6316

Lighted tennis courts and a softball field attract the health conscious, and a stocked lake attracts anglers. This park has two campgrounds, 16 cabins and a group camp and a mini-convention center that seats up to 200. Catering is available in the lodge.

CLARKCO STATE PARK

Quitman   776-6651

The park features a 65-acre lake, natural trails, picnic pavilions, lighted tennis courts, a visitors center and a camp store. Also available are 43 camping pads and 15 cabins with individual lake piers. Clarkco is off U.S. 45, 20 miles south of Meridian.

PAUL B. JOHNSON STATE PARK

Hattiesburg   582-7721

This park, 10 miles south of Hattiesburg, has just about everything — boat ramps, cabins, camping sites, canoe-

ing, fishing, self-guided nature trail, picnic shelters, rentals, sailing, skiing and swimming.

PERCY QUIN STATE PARK

McComb   684-3938

This state park on Lake Tangipahoa is 6 miles south of McComb off I-55's Exit 13. Percy Quin makes the most of its lake location by offering lots of water sports, plus 22 cabins, 161 camping pads, a tent camping area and facilities for groups of up to 200. Visitors can also enjoy the picnic area, visitors center, game room and camp store.

The River Cities

NATCHEZ STATE PARK

Natchez   442-2658

This is a 3,000-acre park with trails for hiking and biking, two rental cabins, campgrounds and a large lake containing record-book bass. It offers a bathhouse, a boat ramp, a nature trail, picnic shelters and rentals. The park, 10 miles north of Natchez off U.S. 61, is open year round.

The Coast

BUCCANEER STATE PARK
1150 S. Beach Blvd.
Waveland   *467-3822*

This popular beachfront park occupies a beautiful wooded site once favored by pirates. Today the park is home to 50 primitive camp sites and enough developed camping to accommodate up to 500 units.

Buccaneer offers fishing from the seawall, 50 picnic sites, nature trails and tennis. Also, there's Buccaneer Bay, an attraction in itself, consisting of a wave pool for body surfing, two giant water slides, a kid's pool, concessions and souvenirs. Admission to Buccaneer Bay is separate, and hours are seasonal. Call 467-2580 for details.

SHEPARD STATE PARK
Gautier   *497-2244*

Shepard's 400 acres feature secluded primitive camping in the Cherokee and Mohawk campgrounds off Graveline Road. Campers and visitors can enjoy fishing and other water sports in Bayou Pierre and the Mississippi Sound. You'll also find a nature trail and picnic facilities here.

Historic State Parks

Mississippi's five Historic State Parks showcase the state's cultural heritage and history, from the time of early Native Americans to the antebellum period. The historic parks do not offer camping, but you can enjoy nature walks, picnicking and living history sites.

The Hill Country

NANIH WAIYA HISTORIC SITE
Rt. 3, Louisville   *773-7988*

This site actually borders the Hill Country and the Heartland. It is 12 miles northeast of Noxapater off Miss. 490. The park is at the legendary birthplace of the Choctaw Nation and included is the site of the Choctaw Indian sacred mound, Nanih Waiya. It includes an activity building, picnic area and nature trail. It is also near the Choctaw Reservation out from Philadelphia, and this is considered sacred ground by these Native Americans. It is closed Monday and Tuesday. Call for hours before arriving.

The Delta

FLOREWOOD RIVER PLANTATION
Off U.S. 82, Greenwood   *455-3821*

Located 2 miles west of Greenwood just off U.S. 82, this outstanding historic park recreates a Delta plantation of the 1850s. It includes "the big house," a plantation store, school, blacksmith shop and other buildings that depict this era in Delta history. It is a living history park, which means that demonstrations are in progress at certain times of the year. There is an admission charge for the plantation tours and tram ride to the site, but the Cotton Museum, at the park entrance, may be toured free of charge. A gift shop is on the premises. This is a popular tour site for school and church groups as well as individual tourists who want a glimpse of a real working plantation. It is closed Monday.

WINTERVILLE MOUNDS
Rt. 3, Greenville   *334-4684*

There's an aura about this park. You can imagine the presence of early Indian spirits, and you notice the natural inclination to speak in a subdued voice. Three miles north of Greenville, on Miss. 1, this is the site of one of the largest Indian mound groups in the Mississippi Valley. It is believed by experts to be the ceremonial site of predecessors of the Choctaw and Chickasaw tribes. Park employees are available to answer questions, and there is a gift shop and museum at the entrance to the site. It is closed Monday and Tuesday. Call for hours of operation before making the trip.

The Heartland

CASEY JONES MUSEUM
Vaughan   *673-9864*

Off I-55 north of Jackson, Exit 133, near Vaughan, the Casey Jones Railroad Museum is the state's historic park that honors folklore hero and railroad engineer Casey Jones. There is a 1923 oil-burning steam engine on display and an interpretation of railroading in Mississippi.

SAM DALE HISTORIC SITE
Daleville   *364-2120*

This site is 15 miles north of Meridian, off Miss. 39 in Daleville. It is a memorial to Gen. Sam Dale, a 19th-century frontiersman and patriot. A statue of Dale, by a Mississippi artist, is on the site. There are picnic shelters here, but there aren't any restrooms.

The River Cities

You'll find a state park (see previous section) among other beautiful parks in the River Cities, but no historic state parks.

The Coast

Among its many recreational features, the coastal area has two state parks but no historic state parks.

National Forests

National forests in Mississippi compose the largest holding of public land, more than 1,139,000 acres. Forest land offers some of the best outdoor recreation opportunities in the entire South. Included are 276 miles of hiking trails; 230 campsites; 140 picnic sites; eight swimming beaches; boating; plus excellent hunting and fishing. Don't let the addresses listed below fool you. Some of the forest land borders several towns in the region. For more information, contact the U.S. Forest Service, 100 W. Capitol, Suite 1141, Jackson 39269, 965-4391.

The Hill Country

HOLLY SPRINGS NATIONAL FOREST
Holly Springs   *252-2633*

Just a short drive from the city of Memphis, Tennessee, this northwest Mississippi forest offers 147,000 acres of prime

Insiders' Tips

The Tennessee-Tombigbee Waterway offers outstanding outdoor recreational opportunities along its 234-mile route. Campsites, playgrounds and supreme fishing and boating are just a few of the reasons for the waterway's popularity.

lakes and lush land for fishing, hunting and camping.

TOMBIGBEE NATIONAL FOREST

Houston   285-3264

In northeast Mississippi, this 66,000-acre forest is near the Natchez Trace. At Davis Lake you'll find campsites, fishing lakes, a horse trail and other park amenities. The southern end borders the big Noxubee Wildlife Refuge, near Starkville, one of the state's prettiest sites.

The Delta

DELTA NATIONAL FOREST

Near Rolling Fork   873-6256

This 59,000-acre forest near the town of Rolling Fork offers several lakes for excellent fishing, including Barge and Blue Lakes, near Yazoo City. Its greentree reservoirs attract migratory waterfowl, and it is proud to be the nation's only bottomland hardwood national forest.

The Heartland

BIENVILLE NATIONAL FOREST

Forest   469-3811

In the geographic center of the state, this 178,000-acre forest is a multi-sports area. It includes swimming and a nature trail. Its namesake, Jean Baptiste Bienville, was important to the settlement of Natchez and New Orleans.

DESOTO NATIONAL FOREST

Wiggins   928-4422

By far the state's largest national forest, this 500,000-acre wonderland runs throughout the Piney Woods section of the state. It includes nine facilities near Hattiesburg that offer a combination of swimming, fishing, boating, picnic areas, nature trails and camping.

The River Cities

HOMOCHITTO NATIONAL FOREST

Natchez   384-5876

Southwest Mississippi's national forest includes 189,000 acres and is a prime spot for deer and turkey. Homochitto is an Indian name that means "big red river." Near Natchez, this forest incorporates Clear Springs and Pipe's Lake, where camping, fishing, nature trails and picnic shelters are available.

The Coast

DESOTO NATIONAL FOREST

(Mid-state to the coast)   928-5291

This forest, which runs across various regions of the state, boasts Airey Lake, which has a bathhouse, primitive camping, fishing and a nature trail. Big Biloxi offers a bathhouse, cabins, developed camping, fishing, a nature trail and picnic shelters. Tuxachanie Trail and Creek has a bathhouse, boat ramp, developed camping, fishing, rentals and swimming.

More than 250 million people flock to U.S. national parks each year. They are indeed our national treasures. Please help take care of them so that future generations can enjoy them too.

Insiders' Tips

The Tale of the Teddy Bear

Interesting things happen in Mississippi. Take the story of the teddy bear, for instance. It unraveled back in 1901 at Onward, a few miles south of Rolling Fork on Highway 61.

Illustration: Mike Lay

Then President Theodore Roosevelt took the advice of friends and journeyed to the Mississippi Delta on a hunting expedition. The hunters were in search of wild game, though it was apparently not too plentiful at that particular time. Finally a member of the hunting party located a bear and decided to save it for the President so he wouldn't be disappointed with a nonproductive hunting trip.

The bear was less than robust and reportedly not much more than a cub, so Roosevelt refused to shoot it. He found it unsporting, so the bear went its merry way, taking with it Teddy Roosevelt's would-be reputation as a great white hunter.

Folks in these parts love good stories, so the story of Roosevelt's refusal to shoot the bear spread far and wide. Once the "teddy bear story" hit the streets of New York City, a smart merchant decided to capitalize by creating a stuffed toy bear to display in his window. The stuffed bear was a tremendous success and resulted in the formation of the Ideal Toy Corporation. So thanks to President Roosevelt's sportsmanship in the Mississippi Delta, millions of children the world over have cuddled and loved their teddy bears.

Big Biloxi and Tuxachanie Trail charge admission. All three sites are near Gulfport.

National Parks

The state's national parks, maintained by the U.S. Department of the Interior, include the beautiful Natchez Trace Parkway, which cuts a scenic trail from the upper northeast corner to the lower southwest corner; the Vicksburg National Military Park; the Natchez National Historical Park (Melrose Plantation); and Gulf Islands National Seashore. Additional information is available through the U.S. Department of the Interior, National Park Service, 3500 Park Road, Ocean Springs 39564, 875-9057.

The Hill Country

NATCHEZ TRACE PARKWAY
680-4025

The beautiful Natchez Trace Parkway begins in Natchez and runs diagonally up to Nashville, Tennessee, cutting a narrow, two-lane route through some of the South's most natural and scenic land. Locals call it simply, "The Trace," and many know it well for the speed limit is a strictly enforced 50 miles per hour. Slow driving encourages you to be observant.

Part of the Trace's prettiness is due to the lack of society's discards, such as Styrofoam containers and paper napkins from the local fast food establishment. There are no fast food establishments, or any establishments, directly on the 440-mile Trace, and park rangers sedulously patrol the area so that litter does not linger. The Trace is one of the nicest things Mississippi has to offer both visitors and locals, and it is well worth a trip.

The River Cities

VICKSBURG NATIONAL MILITARY PARK

3201 Clay St.
Vicksburg   636-0583

Start a visit here at the visitors center for a look at Civil War artifacts from the Siege of Vicksburg and an 18-minute film on the campaign to capture this strategically important city. Then take the 16-mile driving tour through this beautiful, well-preserved battlefield, past monuments and memorials. The tour takes visitors to the Vicksburg National Cemetery, where 17,000 Union soldiers are buried, and to the Cairo Museum, where the gunboat's remains are displayed.

NATCHEZ NATIONAL HISTORICAL PARK

504 S. Canal St.
Natchez   442-7047

This park was created in 1988 and consists of two significant historical elements in the city's history. Melrose Plantation (Montebello Parkway) is a prime example of antebellum life in the days of elegant prosperity. The estate is open daily except Christmas. The William Johnson House, 210 State Street, was home to the free African-American diarist who chronicled life in antebellum Natchez. It is open to the public on a limited basis.

On the site of park headquarters on South Canal a unit will be constructed to commemorate the French outpost, Fort Rosalie, which was built in 1716 overlooking the river.

The Coast

GULF ISLANDS NATIONAL SEASHORE

Park Rd.
Ocean Springs   875-9057

The mainland headquarters of this national park is at 3500 Park Road in Ocean Springs, where visitors can see educational programs presented by rangers, videotapes and exhibits on park resources. The Seashore consists of Davis Bayou, Horn Island, Petit Bois Island and Ship Island. Davis Bayou has activity areas, a bathhouse, a boat ramp, developed and primitive camping, fishing, a nature trail and picnic shelters. Horn, Petit Bois and Ship islands offer primitive camping, swimming, skiing and sailing.

Inside
Daytrips

The attractions and events we've featured in this guide are proof that Mississippi has an abundance of things to do, see, taste, hear and otherwise experience; many are available year round, and some are even open around the clock. One of the state's assets is its enviable location between Louisiana and Alabama, both of which have their own share of treasures to offer. What that means to residents and visitors is easy access to even more things to take in and enjoy.

By sheer geography and the course of history, Mississippi shares much with its neighboring states, but their unique personalities make them great getaways. To the west, across the Mississippi, is Louisiana, with its famous beauty and bounty of natural resources, not to mention a contagious spirit of celebration. To the east, Alabama presents classic Southern charm and history matched by a blend of quiet culture and roaring good times.

Getting from one place to another isn't a problem, whether you're planning a visit of a few hours or days. The highways are good, the traffic's not bad and the opportunities are many. Here are a few of our favorite daytrips to try when you're ready to take in some neighborly hospitality.

Credit: The Sun Herald

Swans grace the water of Bellingrath Garden's Oriental garden near Mobile, Alabama.

From Anywhere in the State

Natchez Trace Parkway

Those 13 million or so people who use the Natchez Trace Parkway each year know it is a little piece of paradise. Called "the Trace" by those who know it best, it is a glorious, two-lane highway that slowly winds its way through some of the prettiest country in the United States. It runs between Natchez, Mississippi, and Nashville, Tennessee, and is unspoiled, uncluttered and noncommercial. It's a great escape, a place to go to when things get crowded — a soothing respite from the real world of phones and faxes. And it's slow and easy, for the speed limit is a strictly enforced 50 miles per hour. The Natchez Trace Parkway is part of the National Park System, managed by the National Park Service, a bureau within the U.S. Department of the Interior.

The Trace has as its southern terminus the lovely old city of Natchez, once the notorious river town where gamblers and wild women congregated "under the hill." It still has its share of notoriety, but today Natchez is known more for its grand antebellum mansions and pure Southern charm. Natchez evokes the old South better than any other place. The town was founded in the early 1700s, but long before that, the Trace was a wilderness trail used by Native American, settlers, soldiers and others who rode the current down the Mississippi River from points north, sold their rafts or boats upon arrival, then headed home inland once their business was conducted. Some never reached home, for the Trace was known to be dangerous in the early days. Danger came from wild animals and other menaces such as roving bands of renegades of one kind or another.

The Trace is indeed historic, and sites along the way are well marked and documented so that travelers can stop to explore. **Mount Locust**, 15 miles northeast of Natchez at milepost 15.5, dates back to about 1780 and was once an inn of sorts, where folks stopped by for the night whether there was room at the inn or not. If it was full, they simply slept under the inn; or in the barn, for during the dangerous days, anything was preferable to the wilderness. Today, Park rangers give informative talks about the history of the old inn, which opens at 8:30 AM daily and closes at 5 PM February through November; grounds are open all year.

On the southern end of the Trace, it's not unusual to see gray moss swinging from the old oak trees or parts of the original trail trodden deep into the soft loose soil. Nor is it unusual to find historic old houses, such as **Springfield Plantation**, 786-3802, just off the Trace near Fayette, where Andrew Jackson reportedly said nuptials with the divorcee Rachel Robards, which shocked proper society of the day. Not far from Springfield is Lorman, just off the Trace, where the **Old Country Store**, 437-3661, has been in continuous operation for more than 100 years. Since you're in the vicinity, don't miss the haunting **Ruins of Windsor**, 23 magnificent towering columns, which are all that remain of the largest antebellum mansion ever built in Mississippi. Windsor was built between 1859 and 1861 and destroyed by fire in 1890. The ruins were featured in the old movie *Raintree County*, starring Elizabeth Taylor and Montgomery Cliff. Windsor is just off the Trace, on Miss. 522 west of Port Gibson, the idyllic little town Union Gen. U.S. Grant said was "too pretty to burn."

Head on toward Jackson, a slight detour off the Trace. While you're in the state's capital city, enjoy its opportunities. Fine museums, art galleries, shopping, and the Ag Museum (see more about it in the Arts and Culture chapter, included as the Jim Buck Ross Agricultural and Aviation Museum) provide interesting forays. Just outside Jackson on the Trace, milepost 102.4, is a good place to stop for traditional Mississippi crafts, from quilts to pottery and jewelry. It's the **Mississippi Crafts Center**, 856-7546, a dogtrot log cabin operated by the Craftsmen's Guild of Mississippi. A few miles north at milepost 122 is the beautiful **Cypress Swamp**, where walkers are invited to see an authentic swamp — and perhaps a reptile or two — from a small wooden bridge. This natural area seems to be a world away from Jackson, yet it's so near.

Your next stop could be **French Camp** at milepost 180.7, where you'll find the site of an old inn built in 1812 by French-Canadian trader Louis LeFleur. The area was first known as Frenchman's Camp and then French Camp. There's also a boarding school named French Camp Academy, a bed and breakfast that's constructed of two adjoining 100-year old log cabins and **Rainwater Observatory**. The observatory is said to be one of the largest in the South; it is open by appointment only. The visitors center at French Camp is housed in an 1840 dogtrot cabin, and from there visitors are directed to other attractions in the area.

Milepost 266 is where you'll find the most information about the Trace, for it is the site of the **Natchez Trace Visitors Center**, 680-4025, 6 miles north of Tupelo. There's a small museum pertaining to the Trace, a 12-minute audiovisual program about the old trail and the new Trace development, a bookstore and a gift shop. Park rangers are available to answer questions and give directions. About 30 miles or so of the Trace wind through the northwest tip of Alabama en route to Tennessee, and the scenery is spectacular here too.

At milepost 327.3, markers indicate the site where a Chickasaw chieftain is said to have charged Andrew Jackson $75,000, in those days a large fortune, to transport his army across the river on a ferry. Look for the site of **Colbert's Ferry** on the Tennessee River. About now you'll be entering the **Tennessee Natchez Trace Corridor**. This is Davy Crockett country, and you'll see the pioneer's name throughout the area, in the **David Crockett State Park**, the **David Crockett Statue** and the **David Crockett Cabin**, all in and around Lawrenceburg, Tennessee. One of our favorite stops here is the **Meriwether Lewis Site**, at milepost 385.9. One can almost imagine seeing Meriwether in this remote area as he must have been when he led the Lewis and Clark expedition to the Pacific Ocean. Lewis, once governor of the Louisiana Territory, died here in 1809 from a gunshot wound thought to have been self-inflicted. He was in his 30s and is buried at the site. A rustic log cabin houses a museum that depicts Lewis' life. Near the Meriwether Lewis site is the small town of **Hohenwald**, a German and Swiss settlement known for its unique resale clothing shops and specialty stores. The Trace ends at Leipers Fork, at milepost 430, near Nashville. If time allows, take Leipers Creek Road to Highway 431, then follow directions to Nashville, one of the South's best cities.

Memphis, Tennessee

You'll always find Mississippians in Memphis. One writer said that the Mississippi Delta begins in the lobby of Memphis' **Peabody Hotel**. It would seem so, for Deltans play and shop in Memphis, usually with the Peabody, 149 Union Avenue, (800) PEABODY, as their base. From the Magnolia State, three major highways, I-55, U.S. 78 and U.S. 61, lead to this big and bustling river city where the Mississippi River reigns supreme. The river runs right beside downtown Memphis, where paddlewheelers keep the water churning and calliopes make known their presence.

Beale Street Blues, Memphis' own music form, competes with rock 'n' roll of the Elvis ilk, though the **Beale Street Historic District**, (901) 526-0110, is the place to hear live music. Nightclubs here are varied, and most have cover charges. Restaurants and gift shops abound. At 130 Beale Street, the **Center for Southern Folklore** is an informal folklife center that showcases the music, people and traditions of the South; films are shown daily. There's also a gift shop that sells books, food, folk art and more.

The **National Civil Rights Museum**, 406 Mulberry Street, is housed in the former Lorraine Motel, site of the Martin Luther King Jr. assassination in 1968. Interpretive exhibits and audiovisual displays help bring the sounds and sights of the Civil Rights movement into this decade. The **Memphis Convention and Visitors Bureau** can provide additional information; call (800) 8-MEMPHIS. Though Mississippi claims Elvis Presley because he was born in Tupelo and lived there until his early teens, Memphis is the place in which he lived as an entertainer. The future king of rock 'n' roll attended Humes High in Memphis, where he was considered odd by his classmates. Elvis wore his hair long and ducktaily while the other boys wore short crew cuts; he wore colorful shirts and pleated slacks while male classmates wore jeans and T-shirts. Not too long after high school, the young man with the guitar, great voice and sultry eyes was making a name for himself as a singer. His unique musical blend of white country and black blues and gospel was as new to the scene as his attire, and he packed the places he played. Soon enough, the swivel of his lissome hips caught the attention of the world, and the poor boy from Tupelo forever changed the music and mores of the world.

Hear and see more about Elvis, perhaps too much more unless you're a die-hard fan, at his home, **Graceland**. It is the big, sturdy but not elaborate, tree-shaded house where the star lived and died. He bought the house when he was 22 years old and commenced to turn it into a fortress shortly thereafter. It still looks as it did in the 1960s and '70s when Elvis and his entourage were in residence. Expect to see lava lamps, deep shag carpet, lots of mirrors and vinyl and other replicas of the age and the man. Graceland is purely commercial, from the tram that transports visitors from the visitors center across to the boulevard, to the guided tours that are ongoing. Droves of fans are there constantly, and they keep coming. Tours consist of a portion of Graceland's interior and exterior offerings, his two airplanes, cars and museum. Graceland is at 3734 Elvis Presley Boulevard. The estate is open for tours from 9 AM to 5 PM daily, with new tours beginning every three to five minutes. The Platinum Tour, which includes all that's available to see, is $17 for adults, $11 for children 5 through 12 and $15.30 for senior adults. The Mansion Tour only is $9 adults, $4.75 children and $8.10 senior adults. For additional information, call (901) 332-3322 or (800) 238-2000. The tours are thoroughly programmed, and there's virtually no time to ask questions or to wander unattended, but serious Elvis fans don't seem to mind.

From Graceland, if you're heading back toward the river to find Mud Island, let the mysterious **Memphis Pyramid** be your guide. It is a bit unusual to find such a structure in this country, for one expects it to be in Egypt, so here's some background. According to sources, Memphis, Tennessee, was named for Memphis, Egypt, because the cities are similar in that they're both located on major rivers. The Tennessee Memphis wanted to honor its Egyptian namesake, which is

what they did when they decided to build a multipurpose center to house major sports events, entertainment, rodeos and more. The Pyramid, on the banks of the Mississippi River at 1 Auction Avenue, is a 32-story stainless steel structure that boasts a 22,500 seat-arena and a base the size of six football fields.

And now on to **Mud Island**, a 52-acre complex where sleek monorails transport visitors to sites and scenes on the island proper, among them the **Mississippi River Museum**, a **River Walk**, and a B-17 bomber — aptly named the *Memphis Belle* — which flew 25 successful missions in World War II. The theme of Mud Island is "Life on the Mississippi River." It is open daily from 10 AM til 11 PM March through November; full admission is $6 adults, $4 seniors and children. The monorail terminal is at 125 Front Street, between Adams and Poplar; call (901) 576-7230.

Culture is not forgotten here, for the outstanding **Memphis Brooks Museum of Art** is the state's oldest and largest museum of fine and decorative arts. Brooks' permanent collection includes an impressive 7,000 pieces of sculpture, prints, textiles, paintings and more, from eight centuries. See the museum at 1934 Poplar Avenue at Overton Park; call (901) 722-3500 for hours and admission.

The **Dixon Gallery & Gardens**, 4339 Park Avenue, (901) 761-5250, is a 17-acre wonderland of gardens and foliage that comes complete with a very interesting art museum. The museum focuses on 18th-century German porcelains and 19th-century paintings. Hours are Tuesday through Saturday 10 AM to 5 PM, Sunday 1 to 5. Admission is $5 adults, $4 senior adults, $3 students and $1 children.

The **Memphis Zoo and Aquarium**, 2000 Galloway Avenue, Overton Park, is home to more than 2,800 animals representing 400 species. This zoo is justly proud of its Cat Country, a new multi-million-dollar, one-of-a-kind exhibit that is home to exotic and endangered wild cats. Avenue of the Animals and Nile River Court are popular exhibits too. The zoo is open daily except for Thanksgiving, Christmas Eve and Christmas Day. Admission is $6 adults, $5 senior adults and $4 children 2 to 11.

Another nice thing to do in Memphis is to take a sightseeing cruise on the mighty Mississippi River. Sunset dinner cruises are available, as well as moonlight music cruises. The Memphis Convention & Visitors Bureau, 47 Union Avenue, (800) 8-MEMPHIS, has brochures. For travel information statewide, contact the Tennessee Department of Tourist Development, (615) 741-2158.

From the Heartland

Birmingham, Alabama

Bold and bright Birmingham is a new Southern city making a name for itself in business and banking, the arts, sports and myriad activities that appeal to visitors. New is a key word here, for when other Southern cities were struggling to cope with the aftermath of the Civil War in the late 1860s, Birmingham did not even exist. It was founded in 1871, and by the turn of the century, the young town had a population of 38,415. Today, Birmingham is a fast-paced and busy city where old-fashioned hospitality and graciousness are not forgotten by the almost 1 million people who call Birmingham home.

Birmingham is attracting an increasing number of visitors, who find a stockpile of accommodations and attractions to hold their interest. Grand old hotels such as **The Tutwiler, The Pickwick** and the **Redmont**, in the downtown area, are favorites of out-of-towners. They are close to good shopping and restaurants, including the shops and eateries at the historic **Five Points**, perhaps the best place to get a real feel for Birmingham. Tree-shaded streets offer interesting shops, superb food and live music. It's the place that locals refer to as the entertainment district.

Shopping is a major experience at **Riverchase Galleria** at the intersection of I-459 and U.S. 31, (205) 985-3020, the largest regional mall in the South. Folks from north Alabama and northeast Mississippi shop the 200-plus stores at Riverchase, just south of Birmingham at Hoover. The arching skylight over the "Main Street" of the Galleria is about a quarter-mile high, with fountains and a selection of restaurants underneath. The highly rated **Wynfrey Hotel**, (205) 987-1600, is at Riverchase Galleria as well.

The big **Birmingham Zoo**, 2630 Chahaba Road, (205) 879-0408, is one of Alabama's top attractions. It's a 100-acre wooded wonderland where 800 rare and exotic animals — including elephants, zebras, giraffes, rhinos and more — have a very nice home. Admission is $5 adults, $2 for children ages 2 through 12 and $2 for seniors.

A tourist attraction that pays homage to the city's industrial heritage is **Sloss Furnaces**, Second Avenue N. and 32nd

Street, (205) 324-1911, a National Historic Landmark and the nation's newest museum of industry and labor. Exhibits, including massive webs of pipe and smokestacks, explain how Sloss pumped out millions of tons of pig iron for Birmingham's mills and foundries for 89 years. In 1971, the two huge blast furnaces ceased operation, and 10 years later, restoration work began for a museum and an anticipated opening date in 1983. Sloss has done well since then, even with the resident ghost. Rumor has it that Sloss is haunted by the spirit of a former foundryman who died a grisly death in one of the furnaces. Sloss Furnaces is the site of fun and festivals, including the eagerly anticipated **Birmingham Jam**, a major fall event. The thousands who attend this three-day festival know they'll hear some of the nation's top performers in jazz, blues and gospel. Sloss Furnaces is also the site for the big **Birmingham Heritage Festival**, said to be the largest ethnic festival in Alabama. It's a popular August event.

Another testament to Birmingham's early rise in industry is the statue of **Vulcan**, Valley Avenue at Old Montgomery Highway, (205) 328-6198, which watches over the city and nearby Appalachian foothills from a perch atop Red Mountain. Vulcan, the Iron Man, at 55-feet tall, is the world's largest cast-iron statue and was initially created as Birmingham's exhibit at the 1904 St. Louis World's Fair. Since 1939, he's held a torch over Birmingham, and a most unusual torch it is. The torch burns green unless there's been a traffic fatality in the city within the past 24 hours, then it burns bright red.

An observation tower in the statue offers a spectacular, panoramic view of Birmingham and vicinity. The **Birmingham Civil Rights Institute,** Six Avenue and 16th Street, (205) 382-9696, provides a compelling look at exhibits depicting the city's darkest days. An outstanding orientation film encourages visitors to mentally re-create a walk on the road to freedom in the era of segregation. The Civil Rights Movement's most memorable moments are replayed in four mini-theatres, and they offer yet another look at a time in our history that seems unreal today. The Institute is more than a museum, for it promotes ongoing research and discourse on human rights issues. It's also the centerpiece for the Civil Right's District in downtown Birmingham, which includes the **Kelly Ingram Park** — where protests and demonstrations were held in the '60s — and the **Sixteenth Street Baptist Church**.

The **Alabama Jazz Hall of Fame**, 1631 Fourth Avenue, (205) 254-2731, just across from the Kelly Ingram Park, is in the Carver Theatre for the Performing Arts. If you don't associate jazz with Birmingham, a trip to the Hall of Fame will change your mind, for you'll see how boogie woogie began with Alabama's own Clarence "Pinetop" Smith. The active **Birmingham Museum of Art**, 2000 Eighth Avenue, 254-2565, is the largest municipally supported arts facility in the Southeast. It proudly houses extensive collections of American, Renaissance, Oriental and African art and hosts traveling exhibits throughout the year. The Museum contains a collection of more than 15,000 works of art, including paintings, sculpture, decorative arts, photography, textiles and the Sculpture Garden.

It appears that any arts function is important in Birmingham, which may be the impetus behind the annual **Birmingham Festival of the Arts,** (205) 252-7652, thought to be the world's oldest continuing arts celebration. The popular festival salutes a different country each year; it calls attention to customs and culture germane to the featured country. Dance, music and fine arts are on the agenda for this April event. Unique to Birmingham is **City Stages**, a major festival that celebrates music and culture during a three-day event in early June. Nationally known performers and local talent join more than 250,000 fans who gather at Linn Park, 20th Street and Park Place N.

Sports fans need not worry about a lack of activity in Birmingham for there's plenty for them to do too. Sportsmen, and apparently most Alabamians, revere former University of Alabama head football coach, the late Paul "Bear" Bryant. Memorabilia relating to Bryant's 25-year career at UA are displayed at the **Alabama Sports Hall of Fame** at the Civic Center, Corner of 22nd Street N. and Civic Center Boulevard, (205) 323-6665. Among other sports legends honored at the Hall of Fame are Joe Louis, Bart Starr, Willie Mays and Jesse Owens. The Birmingham-Jefferson Civic Center is also home to major basketball championships and the **Birmingham Bulls** hockey team. Actually, the Civic Center is an attraction in itself, for this multiuse facility covers almost seven city blocks and welcomes 1.5 million visitors a year.

The **Southern Museum of Flight** at the Birmingham International Airport — the latter of which has invested $47 million in renovation and expansion — houses eight decades of aviation history, including old cropdusters, a 1910 Curtis "Pusher," a Piper J-2 cub, an F-4 Phantom jet and other vestiges of early aviation. Short video clips pertaining to aviation history are available for viewing. The museum shop is a good place to pick up souvenir items.

East of Birmingham just off I-20, near Talladega, the **International Motorsports Hall of Fame and Museum**, (205) 362-5002, is a must-see for auto racing fans. The nonprofit museum opened in 1983 as an entity dedicated to the preservation of the history of motorsports. Allow several hours to walk through and see all the exhibits, including a vast collection of cars and memorabilia from 1902 to the present. The museum sits on 35 acres next to the Talladega Superspeedway. Recent acquisitions include the last ARCA race car driven by Clifford Allison, a 1990 Buick LaSabre; Neil Bonnett's winner, a 1964 Chevrolet Chevelle; and Hermie Sadler's 325 Chevrolet Lumina, which Sadler drove to win NASCARS Busch Series Grand National Division Rookie of the Year title.

For information on any event or attraction mentioned, contact **The Greater Birmingham Convention & Visitors Bureau**, (205) 458-8000 or (800) 458-8085. For general travel information about Alabama, contact the Alabama Bureau of Tourism and Travel in Montgomery, (800) ALABAMA.

From the Coast

When you're situated between two of the South's most historic and hospitable cities, the question often asked about a daytrip from the Mississippi Gulf Coast is, "Which way do I go?"

If you pick west, you'll end up in New Orleans, a city legendary for so many things that after a day's sampling, you'll be looking forward to a return visit. If you choose to travel toward the east, you'll wind up in Mobile, the charming Alabama city that's older (and, some would say, tamer) than New Orleans. Mobile offers good food and good times, with plenty of shopping and sightseeing. Either way, you can't really miss. Let's look at both these daytrip destinations that take the same amount of time to get to from your coastal starting point — about an hour's drive.

Mobile, Alabama

Founded in 1702, Mobile is one of the oldest cities in the country. In fact, its residents have been celebrating Mardi Gras since 1703, longer than New Orleans, whose own version of the carnival season is more famous but a bit "younger" than Mobile's. (Another distinction between the two celebrations is the fact that in Mobile costumed float riders toss Moon Pies, that distinctly Southern treat, along with doubloons and beads to the appreciative crowds.)

This historic city on Mobile Bay is also one of the country's prettiest, filled with majestic live oaks and brilliantly colored flowers found everywhere in public parks and private gardens. Mobile's eventful past is depicted in three interesting museums, a collection of military forts and gracious mansions. The **City Museum**, 355 Government Street, (334) 434-7569, is in a beautifully preserved 1872 townhouse on Government Street that houses an impressive collection of Civil War uniforms, Mardi Gras memorabilia and horse-drawn carriages.

Carlen House on 54 S. Carlen Street, (334) 438-7468, is a restored Creole cottage that is furnished in period pieces and displays 19th-century fashions. The **Phoenix Fire Museum**, 203 S. Claiborne Street, (334) 433-5343, is a restored volunteer fire department in a building constructed in 1859.

History lovers might want to begin their Mobile visit at **Fort Conde**, (334) 438-7304, the city's welcome center at Church and Royal streets. **Fort Gaines** on Dauphin Island is where Admiral Farragut said, "Damn the torpedoes. Full speed ahead!" during the Civil War Battle of Mobile Bay. Fort Morgan at Gulf Shores, built in 1815, is across the bay from Fort Gaines. All are open to the public.

Mobile's historic homes showcase several architectural styles. For example, **Oakleigh Mansion**, 350 Oakleigh Place, is built in the Greek Revival style, and the **Richards-DAR House** (c. 1860) 256 N. Joachim Street, is an Italianate mansion. The Conde-Charlotte Museum House (c. 1822-1824), 104 Theatre Street, was the city's first jail. Next to the Fort Conde Welcome Center, Its individual rooms reflect Mobile's history under five flags. The 20-room, 16-columned **Bragg-Mitchell Mansion**, 1906 Springhill Avenue, built in 1855 with 16 columns, is said to be the most photographed building in town. It combines the Greek Revival and Italianate styles. More fine examples of architecture can be found throughout the city's five historic districts. Walking and driving tours are great ways to take in this aspect of Mobile's history and charm.

Insiders' Tips

The Alabama Theatre for the Performing Arts in Birmingham is a restored movie palace from the 1920s and a popular showplace for film, live theater and musical productions.

Perhaps the best known of Mobile's historic houses is **Bellingrath**, 20 miles south of Mobile, near Theodore, (334) 973-2217, whose gardens and home have long been one of the area's top attractions. In nearby Theodore, Bellingrath has been proclaimed one of the most beautiful gardens in the world. Its 65 acres are filled with plants and flowers, including azaleas, roses, hibiscus, chrysanthemums, salvia, coleus and more. The various blooming seasons make Bellingrath a must-see any time of year. And there's even more to see than the famous gardens. The home is filled with rare art, beautiful china, furniture and glassware, as well as the world's most complete public display of Boehm porcelain sculpture. There's even a bird sanctuary with more than 200 species of permanent residents and migrating birds. You can choose to visit just the gardens or pay an additional fee to tour the home. Bellingrath is open every day of the year from 7 AM to sunset. Admission ranges (for gardens and/or house tour) from $6.50 to $14 for adults.

Other Mobile area attractions include the **Mobile Museum of Art**, 4850 Museum Park Drive, (334) 343-2667, in Langan Park that contains a permanent collection of art and rotating national exhibits. Mobile's **Greyhound Park**, Theodore-Dawes Exit off I-10, (334) 653-5000, southwest of the city, offers top quality dog racing six nights a week, 48 weeks of the year. The **Exploreum/Museum of Discovery**, 1906 Spring Hill Avenue, (334) 476-6873, in a 12-acre Explore Center complex that includes the Bragg-Mitchell Mansion, is a hands-on science museum for kids. The battleship USS *Alabama,* Battleship Parkway off I-10, is a floating, 680-foot piece of World War II history whose crews saw action in the Philippines, Marshall Islands and Ja-

pan. The ship and an adjacent 75-acre park featuring World War II aircraft and a submarine are open daily from 8 AM to dusk.

Dining in Mobile is a pleasant experience. Fresh seafood is on practically every menu, but those in the mood for ethnic dishes can find what they're looking for here.

Shoppers will find plenty of opportunities in the **Bay Area**, especially if you're looking for antiques and bargains. The **Gallery Antique Mall**, (334) 626-0553, in Daphne, east of Mobile, has 60 dealers from across the country all under one roof. It's open daily. The sprawling **Riviera Centre** (334) 934-8888, is a collection of factory stores in Foley. Names such as Liz Claiborne, Bugle Boy, Evan Picone, Coach, Mikasa, Bass, Calvin Klein and Maidenform can be found among the more than 60 stores. And more are being added. It's about 45 miles southeast of Mobile, and it's open seven days a week.

Nearby the city of **Fairhope**, on the Eastern Shore of Mobile Bay, is definitely worth a visit if you're interested in art shows, festivals, theater productions, shopping for antiques and jewelry at specialty stores and much more. The annual **Arts and Crafts Festival** and accompanying **Outdoor Fine Arts Show** held the third weekend in March is a very popular event.

There's plenty to celebrate in and around Mobile, and lots of special events fill the community's calendar. The city is the site of the annual **Senior Bowl** football game and the nationally televised **America's Junior Miss Pageant**. The **Azalea Trail Run and Festival** are held in March.

Fairhope hosts an outstanding arts and crafts festival, and Daphne holds the **Festa Italiana** every October. The **Blakeley Bluegrass Fest** in October in Spanish Fort, a city east of Mobile, and the **National Shrimp Festival** in Gulf Shores both take place in October. The local chambers of commerce can provide exact dates and details, or call the Mobile Tourism and Travel Department at (800) 252-3862.

New Orleans, Louisiana

The name easily conjures up so many sultry images — wrought-iron balconies, jazzy sounds in nightclubs, lively parades and expertly prepared dishes. Try a little bit of everything — food, history, music and fun of the adult and kid variety. Think zoo and aquarium, nightlife, restaurants, museums, historic buildings, the Mississippi River and shops and you'll start to get an idea of how much there is to experience.

The **French Quarter** — To many people, this is New Orleans. And the French Quarter is the Vieux Carre; they're one and the same. Here, you'll discover many of the city's postcard images and some of its best restaurants, bars, art galleries, shops, music, landmarks and attractions. (Remember, New Orleans is no different than any other big city as far as crime is concerned. Be cautious, and stay in well-populated areas of the Quarter and the city in general.)

Go to the **Greater New Orleans Tourist and Convention Commission**'s French Quarter office, 529 St. Ann Street, for tons of free brochures and maps. Stroll through and around Jackson Square, one of the city's most photographed spots that's filled with street musicians, artists, mimes, tarot card readers and other colorful characters. On Chartres Street, visit **St. Louis Cathedral** (504) 525-9585, the **Louisiana State Museum**, (504) 568-6968, including the newly restored Cabildo. Check out the shops and cross over to the **Moon Walk** (a riverfront boardwalk named for a former mayor, Moon Landrieu) for a true Kodak moment, whether you are facing picturesque Jackson Square in one direction or the mighty Mississippi in the other. Stroll down Decatur Street to more shops and the historic **French Market**, where vendors sell fruit, vegetables, jewelry and sugary pralines.

After a visit to the world-class **Aquarium of the Americas**, 1 Canal Street, (504) 861-2537, catch a riverboat to the top-notch **Audubon Zoo**, 6500 Magazine Street, (504) 861-2537. In beautiful City Park you'll find the newly expanded **New Orleans Museum of Art**, (504) 488-2631, 1 Lelong Avenue in City Park, which houses fascinating permanent collections as well as important traveling exhibits. For more art, there are collections of galleries in the French Quarter, along Magazine Street and Julia Street.

Other major sights include three favorites of young visitors — the **Louisiana Children's Museum**, 428 Julia Street, (504) 523-1357, the **Louisiana Nature and Science Center**, Science Read Boulevard at Nature Center Drive, (504) 246-5672, and the **Louisiana Superdome**, Sugar Bowl Drive, (504) 587-3808, home of the New Orleans Saints and the Sugar Bowl.

Shoppers will be pleased with the many specialty shops and major department stores found throughout the city. Antique stores abound in the French Quarter and on Magazine Street.

Music keeps New Orleans moving, and there's always plenty of it to enjoy in clubs and at concerts and festivals. How can you miss when the local talent includes the Nevilles, Pete Fountain, Harry Connick Jr., Irma Thomas, Fats Domino, Wynton Marsalis and The Dixie Cups, among many others. Check the Friday "Lagniappe" insert in *The Times-Picayune* for details on who's playing where.

There's a good chance that there's going to be a great festival or some sort of musical event when you visit. The year-round special events calendar includes the **Tennessee Williams Literary Festival** in March; **Creole Festival** in April; Greek Festival in May; **French Market Tomato Festival** in June; **French Quarter Festival in Spring**; the **Jazz and Heritage Festival** in late April and early May; **Festa d' Italia** in October; and many, many more. Again, check the many guidebooks on New Orleans or the local publications for details.

The ultimate celebration, of course, is **Mardi Gras**. Not for the fainthearted or the claustrophobic, this annual pre-Lenten ritual has to be experienced to be believed. Even locals who don't partake in the madness will usually suggest that newcomers do Mardi Gras at least once.

New Orleans is one of the great food towns in this country, so no one should go hungry on a visit here. Don't even think about dieting; there are just too many good things to taste. At the very least, you must try café au lait and beignets at **Cafe du Monde** just off Jackson Square. And try to pop into **Central Grocery**, just down Decatur Street, to see if you can resist the temptation of the muffuletta, that large crusty, round sandwich of cold cuts topped with salty olive salad that was created at this Italian grocery store. There are a number of signature dishes found on many of the city's menus — gumbo, po' boys and seafood prepared in a variety of glorious methods (or, in the case of oysters, served raw on the half shell). French, Italian, African, Greek, Caribbean and other flavors are served in candlelit elegance at fine dining establishments and at booths in noisy neighborhood spots. Again, the list is endless. Buy a guidebook and take a pick from the restaurant listings.

For more information about New Orleans and all its attractions, contact the **Greater New Orleans Tourist and Convention Commission**, 1520 Sugar Bowl Drive, New Orleans, Louisiana, or call (504) 566-5011. Also, *The Sun Herald's* entertainment guide for the coast, "Marquee," contains information about major special events and music in New Orleans. It's published with the paper's Friday edition.

Inside
Education

When you consider the monumental contributions Mississippians have made to the fields of literature, music, business and medicine, perhaps the state's education system deserves a few accolades. We're proud to say that Mississippi claims several firsts in the field of education. The Parent Teachers Association (PTA) was founded here in 1909. Mississippi was the first state to have a system of junior colleges. The first land grant college for African Americans was Alcorn State University, established in 1871 in Lorman, southwest of Port Gibson.

Since the historic Education Reform Act of 1982, Mississippi has restructured its public education system. New emphasis is placed on early childhood education, with public schools now providing full-day kindergartens and additional staff for early grades. The Legislature also boosted teachers' salaries and dedicated 65 percent of the state's general fund budget to education.

Teacher certification and other classroom quality initiatives, including standards for measuring student achievement, have been made to assure that Mississippians of the future are prepared to thrive in an even more competitive society. Public high schools in Clinton and Tupelo have been recognized by the U.S. De-

Credit: The Sun Herald

The Administration Building on the Hattiesburg (main) campus of the University of Southern Mississippi.

partment of Education for having two of the best high school programs in the nation. Mississippi also established the Mississippi School for Mathematics and Science, one of just five state-supported schools in the nation devoted exclusively to such study at the secondary level. MSMS is in Columbus on the historic campus of Mississippi University for Women, where dorm space is made available for boarding students.

New on the state's agenda for early education is Tech Prep Discovery Courses, a project of the Office of Vocational and Technical Education. With an eye to the future, Tech Prep encourages students in grades 7, 8 and 9 to look at ways to make wise and meaningful occupational and educational choices for life after school. The focus is on four occupational clusters of agricultural and natural resources, business and marketing, engineering and industrial and health and human resources.

For additional information about public education in the state, contact the Mississippi State Department of Education, P.O. Box 771, Jackson 39205, or call 359-3513.

In this chapter we spotlight our four-year colleges and universities, top private colleges, community colleges and highly rated private high schools.

Four-year Colleges and Universities

Colleges and universities in Mississippi consistently garner national recognition for academic excellence. Among them is Millsaps College in Jackson, a private liberal-arts school where entering freshmen have an average ACT score of 24.5. The highly respected Mississippi University for Women in Columbus, the

nation's first state-supported college for women (1884), now co-ed, is a high-ranking national leader in academics as well as leadership programs for women. As a matter of fact, MUW is ranked third in academic reputation among 126 Southern regional liberal arts colleges, according to U.S. News and World Report's 1995 Guide to America's Best Colleges.

The University of Mississippi in Oxford, the state's beloved Ole Miss, has produced the second-highest number of Rhodes Scholars in the South, the sixth-highest in the nation among public universities and the 19th-highest among all U.S. colleges.

The University of Mississippi Medical Center (UMC) occupies a 155-acre site in Jackson and serves as a teaching institution and diagnostic and referral center for the entire state. More than 25,000 inpatients and 122,000 outpatients are treated annually. Along with federal funding for research, private funding is common. The Department of Physiology and Biophysics alone has received in excess of $7.5 million in funding in the past 20 years for continuous research on cardiovascular dynamics. Additionally, UMC is internationally known for its pioneering work in organ transplantation. The world's first heart transplant was performed at UMC in 1964, three years before Dr. Christian Barnard's historic surgery. The world's first lung transplant was performed at UMC too, and today the hospital remains the nation's only active lung transplant facility.

The prestigious University of Mississippi Law School, the fourth-oldest state-supported law school in the country, publishes the world's only legal periodical on air and space law. Ole Miss is also home to the National Center for Physical

Acoustics, the Mississippi Center for Supercomputing Research, the National Center for the Development of Natural Products, the Mississippi Mineral Resources Institute, the Center for Telecommunications and more.

At Mississippi State University in Starkville, grants and funding from industry and private contributors rank among the highest in the nation. Honda Research and Development Company built a $4 million addition to the Raspet Flight Research Lab on the MSU campus. The on-campus Forest Products Research Laboratory is second only to a federal lab in Wisconsin. MSU's Food and Fiber Center is a tremendous asset to the state's ever-increasing agricultural and forest products.

MSU's Mississippi Agriculture and Forestry Experiment Station (MAFES) has branched out to include actual business start-up advice and counseling. The Food and Fiber Center, as a part of the Cooperative Extension Service, does economic and technological feasibility studies for food processors, all of which enhance Mississippi's reputation as one of the best states for food production and processing.

The MSU School of Veterinary Medicine is proud to graduate some of the nation's leading vets and is equally proud of the ongoing research into veterinary sciences.

The University of Southern Mississippi is home to the renowned $20 million Polymer Science center and other research programs. The community enjoys the presentations of USM's fine arts programs. Their arts programs are popular with the community, as is the university's NCAA Division I athletic program.

These are a few of the many attributes at Mississippi's eight public universities and 12 private colleges. Regional state-supported schools, locations and current enrollments are listed below.

The Hill Country

UNIVERSITY OF MISSISSIPPI/OLE MISS

University Ave.
Oxford   232-7226
10,075 students

Since it began operation in 1848, Ole Miss has been a source of pride for most Mississippians. This beautiful, historic campus has as its centerpiece a parklike area known as the Grove. Benches and walkways offer respite for students and visitors who wish to linger under the natural canopy of the old oak trees. Overlooking the Grove are the buildings that comprise Ole Miss, one of which is the Lyceum, built in 1848. The Lyceum is the only survivor of five original buildings. It served as a hospital during the Civil War. Also during the War, the University Greys, a company made up entirely of Ole Miss students and faculty, fought as far north as Gettysburg, though few lived to recount their heroic efforts to save their South from destruction. Ventress Hall, with its towers and turrets, is a Gothic structure that adds architectural interest to the campus; it was built in 1889 for use as a library.

Another unusual building is Barnard Observatory, designed back in 1857 to position Ole Miss as a leader in American science. Now, its claim to fame is that it houses the Center for the Study of Southern Culture, a regional studies program that offers interdisciplinary teaching, research and outreach programs focusing on the American South. The Center is nationally known for its annual week-long Faulkner Conference (studying the work of Oxford native, novelist William Faulkner) and for its extensive research into the music of the Mississippi Delta, the blues. Ole Miss is also home to much more than heritage and happenstance; the Oxford main campus includes the College of Liberal Arts; schools of business administration, education, engineering, pharmacy, law, accountancy and a graduate school. A full-time faculty of more than 400 gives a faculty-student ratio of 1-to-18.

MISSISSIPPI STATE UNIVERSITY
U.S. 82, Miss. 12
Starkville 325-2224
13,162 students

Once known as the state's agricultural college, Mississippi State's focus has expanded considerably, though MSU is still known and respected for its extensive research and development in the area of agriculture and related fields. Mississippi State University-trained engineers are among the nation's best, and many occupy top jobs in their fields. MSU attracts big research grants and private donations because of the quality of its work. Established in 1878, the university today is composed of colleges in agriculture, arts and sciences, business and industry, educa-

tion, engineering and veterinary medicines as well as schools in architecture, forest resources and graduate studies. Eight hundred and forty-three full-time faculty members and 34 part-time faculty make for a faculty-student ratio of 1-to-23.

At MSU's Raspet Flight Research Laboratory, leading flight testing and aerodynamics research has been a viable force for the past 40 years. It is said to be the largest and best-equipped university flight research facility in the country. MSU's High Voltage Laboratory, the largest high voltage testing facility at any university in the United States, researches and tests high voltage electric-field phenomena, electrical insulation, power-system instrumentation and measurement, and power-system hardware and equipment components.

MISSISSIPPI UNIVERSITY FOR WOMEN
College St., Columbus 329-4750
3,020 students

Mississippi University for Women — and smart men too — has been a fixture at the east end of College Street in Columbus since 1884, when it was founded to provide a quality education to young ladies of the South. Affectionately called "The W" by those who know and love it, this fine small college has been co-ed for about a decade, and, indeed, young men who enroll here do have advantages. The W, or MUW, has been the recipient of very favorable national press in the past year. *U.S. News and World Report* said in October of 1994 that among the top 20 percent of Southern regional liberal arts institutions for overall quality, MUW is No. 1 in "best value" for quality education in relation to costs for tuition, room and board and fees.

The average ACT score for entering

freshmen is 23.4. Moreover, the Henry Luce Foundation has awarded support to MUW to establish a Clare Boothe Luce Professorship of Mathematics, one of only 11 such awards in the nation. Among the other universities to receive this honor are Harvard, MIT and Bryn Mawr.

The president of The W is, for the first time in the school's history, a woman, and her influence is seen and felt around the campus, much to the delight of locals and alums. A proud history of achievement is offset by the historical and archi-tectural significance of the W's campus, which includes 24 buildings listed on the National Register of Historic Places. The W focuses on academics, and it was recently named one of "Twenty Model Colleges in America" and one of the 15 best schools in the South. The student-faculty ratio is 18-to-1. Students benefit from small classes, and such attention helps grads of The W land top jobs in their fields. This "little public ivy" is in a league of its own among Mississippi colleges. And since 1920, the W has been among

Credit: The Sun Herald

Administration Building on the campus of 117-year old Jackson State University.

the top-30 universities in the Southeast for the number of women undergraduates who go on to earn doctorates.

The Delta

DELTA STATE UNIVERSITY

Hwy. 8, Cleveland   846-3000
3,790 students

Delta State was created as a teacher's college in 1924 and still has a reputation for training some of the state's best educators, though its School of Business has recently surpassed the School of Education in enrollment. This increase can be attributed to the popular Commercial Aviation program, the only one of its kind in the state. The college offers a degree in aviation management, which leads to jobs as airport managers for some grads. Delta State also does preliminary training for pilots and air traffic controllers. They teach certification in different engines and types of planes. DSU boasts the Roy Lee Wiley Planetarium, which is on the campus and open to the public. While there, visit the art gallery too. A faculty of 168 gives a faculty-student ratio of 1-to-16.

MISSISSIPPI VALLEY STATE UNIVERSITY

U.S. 82 W., Itta Bena   254-9041
2,222 students

This university was established in 1946 primarily to train teachers for rural and elementary schools and to provide vocational training for the region's black students. At first glance, Mississippi Valley State University appears to be a cluster of buildings in the middle of a Delta field, but upon closer inspection, it is indeed a well-manicured campus where strong emphasis is placed on education. This predominantly black four-year school has long provided leadership in education, business and industry. Its graduates are proud of the school's traditions and its new focus on computer sciences and social programs. The faculty-student ratio is 1-to-16. There are 154 full-time teachers.

The Heartland

JACKSON STATE UNIVERSITY

1400 J.R. Lynch St.
Jackson   968-2100
6,079 students

Jackson State University is Mississippi's fourth-largest state-supported university and the nation's eighth-largest historically black institution. This stellar school offers coursework toward master's and doctorate degrees and offers the state's only doctoral programs in environmental science and early childhood education. Additionally, JSU is the only school in the mid-South to offer a bachelor's degree in meteorology. JSU's football team and its marching Tiger band are great local favorites. Originally begun in Natchez in 1877 as a private church school, it was moved to the Jackson site in 1882 and became a teacher's college of the State of Mississippi in 1940. A faculty of 357 gives a teacher-student ratio of 1-to-17.

UNIVERSITY OF MISSISSIPPI MEDICAL CENTER

2500 N. State St.
Jackson   984-1000
1,817 students

The University of Mississippi Medical Center (UMC) is the state's only teaching facility for physicians and dentists. UMC, established in 1955, offers coursework toward degrees in nursing, medicine, dental medicine, medical sciences, cytotechnology, occupational therapy, physical therapy, respiratory care and health records administration, in addition to postgraduate medical education in 25 different areas. The medical school is internationally known for innovative work in hypertension, cardiovascular and high-risk pregnancy research. Additionally, UMC is a pioneer in organ transplant surgery, having performed the world's first human heart transplant. Some of the 400 faculty members at UMC write textbooks in their fields of expertise.

MISSISSIPPI STATE UNIVERSITY/
MERIDIAN CAMPUS

1000 Miss. 19 N.
Meridian   *484-0100*
950 students

MSU's Meridian Campus, established in 1972, boasts a new $5.6 million facility where students can pursue undergraduate and graduate studies or take personal and career enrichment courses. Students can complete their studies to earn degrees in business, education, liberal arts and sociology/social work. A bachelor's in criminal justice is also available. Graduate degrees in a broad range of fields are offered here. Entrepreneurs can benefit from assistance provided to those with established businesses and to those whose ventures are still on the drawing board.

UNIVERSITY OF
SOUTHERN MISSISSIPPI

Hardy St., Hattiesburg   *266-4491*
11,587 students

Mississippi Normal College, now the University of Southern Mississippi, was established in 1910 to train teachers for the state's rural community schools. Today's students are pursuing degrees in a broad range of disciplines at the bachelor's, master's, doctoral and specialist levels. USM is home to the world-class $20 million Polymer Science Research Center as well as other research programs in several disciplines. The renowned deGrummond Children's Literature Collection is housed in the Cook Memorial Library. The university has a strong intercollegiate sports program that includes football, basketball, baseball, tennis, golf, indoor and outdoor track and cross-country. USM's new Payne Center is a top-notch recreation and fitness facility that is among the few of its kind in the nation. It boasts several indoor sports courts, a six-lane indoor pool, an eighth-mile indoor exercise track and a sauna and free-weight room, among other amenities for health-minded students. USM's dramatic and musical groups entertain their fellow students and the community with quality performances throughout the year.

The River Cities

ALCORN STATE UNIVERSITY
Miss. 552, Lorman   *877-6100*
2,742 students

Alcorn, 35 miles north of Natchez, is proud of the fact that it is the oldest predominantly black land grant institution in the United States. Its origins date to 1830 as Oakland College, a Presbyterian college for white males that closed its doors during the Civil War. The Mississippi Legislature created Alcorn in 1871. Alcorn offers a number of degrees, including the associate of science in nursing; bachelor's of arts, science and music education; master's of science in education, agriculture and biology; and a specialist's degree in education. Academic programs include agribusiness management, home economics, computer science, mass communications, accounting, pre-law and sociology. The school also offers four graduate degrees in education, agriculture and science.

A top-notch athletics program features football, basketball, cross-country, track and field and golf. In 1994, quarterback Steve McNair, a football phenomenon, came in a respectable third in voting for the prestigious Heisman Trophy.

ALCORN SCHOOL OF NURSING

15 Campus Dr., Natchez   442-3901

More than 150 students are enrolled at Alcorn's nursing school, which offers an associate's degree and bachelor's of science. A master's program is proposed. This satellite campus also offers some education courses on the undergraduate and graduate levels.

The Coast

UNIVERSITY OF SOUTHERN MISSISSIPPI GULF COAST

730 E. Beach Blvd., Long Beach   865-4500
1,500 students

USM has three locations to serve Coast students. The Gulf Coast Campus is on the site of the former Gulf Park College, which was established in 1921. The beachfront school facility, acquired by USM in 1972, includes the Richard Cox Library, which has a collection of 37,000 books. USM Gulf Coast students also attend classes at Keesler Air Force Base and the Mississippi Gulf Coast Community College in Jackson County. Courses at the bachelor's, master's and specialist levels are offered, and new ones are added to meet the demand. Course offerings include computer science, elementary education, English and nursing. Additionally, USM administers the non-degree granting Gulf Coast Research Laboratory in Ocean Springs, which has a small academic program focusing on marine related research. USM also offers some classes at the Stennis Space Center in Hancock County.

Mississippi's Top Private Colleges

The Heartland

MISSISSIPPI COLLEGE

200 S. Capital, Clinton   925-3000
3,635 students

Mississippi College (MC) is the state's largest private college and the state's oldest institution of higher learning; it was founded in 1831. MC ranked in the top 8 percent of all private colleges in the number of graduates who receive doctorates. This Baptist college, the second-oldest in the country, was recognized by *The New York Times* as one of the "best buys in college educations." Mississippi College offers 31 undergraduate and 14 graduate degrees; it also has the highest percentage of National Merit Scholars among its resident students than any other school in the state. The Mississippi College

---

If you come across a book entitled *Southern Belle*, it might prove to be an interesting read. The author is Mary Craig Kimbrough Sinclair, a Greenwood native who went to New York City as a young woman to study writing. There she met and married writer Upton Sinclair. *Southern Belle* was her only novel and provides a good look at her early life in Mississippi.

Insiders' Tips

School of Law has been under the MC umbrella since the school purchased the Jackson School of Law in 1975. It is now accredited by the American Bar Association and affiliated with the Association of American Law Schools.

MILLSAPS COLLEGE

1700 N. State St., Jackson   974-1000
1,329 students

This prestigious private college has been ranked by the Carnegie Foundation for the Advancement of Teaching as a nationally selective liberal arts college. It is one of only four colleges in the United States to earn a chapter in the liberal arts honorary fraternity, Phi Beta Kappa. Millsaps is also home of the Elks School of Management, one of the country's finest of its kind. Millsaps was founded in 1890 as a Methodist-supported college with a liberal arts curriculum. Today, it offers six degree programs. This school earned professional accreditation for both its undergraduate and graduate business programs by the esteemed American Assembly of Collegiate Schools of Business.

BELHAVEN COLLEGE

1500 Peachtree St., Jackson   968-5928
1,056 students

This small but prestigious liberal arts college places emphasis on the essential education that equips graduates with skills for future life and work. Founded in 1883 by the Presbyterian Church, Belhaven offers 20 majors that lead to four degree programs. Belhaven is most proud of its work in biology, education and business.

REFORMED THEOLOGICAL SEMINARY

5422 Clinton Blvd.
Jackson   922-4988
428 students

Four seminaries and one Bible college are in the Jackson area. Of the four, the largest is Reformed Theological Seminary. It offers master's and doctoral degrees in 14 disciplines. RTS ranked 11th among all seminaries in the United States, according to a recent survey by *Christianity Today*. The seminary serves the community through counseling at a clinic set up for marriage and family problems.

WILLIAM CAREY COLLEGE

498 Tuscan Ave.
Hattiesburg   582-5051, (800) 962-5991
1,076 students

William Carey College is the only private, fully accredited four-year liberal arts college in South Mississippi, and it is the second-largest private college in the state. Founded in 1906, the school is governed by a board of trustees whose members are elected by the Mississippi Baptist Convention. The college offers several undergraduate degree programs, including the arts, business, education, music and nurs-

Insiders' Tips

Author and Laurel native James Street will long be remembered for his novel *Tap Roots*, but one of his best works was a fine short story entitled, "The Biscuit Eater," first published in the *Saturday Evening Post* magazine then released as a book and a film. The story is about an ugly puppy and his two companions — a black boy and a white boy — with all three cast as underdogs. Read it for a treat.

g and a limited graduate-level curricu-
m. In addition to the college's 120-acre
ain campus in Hattiesburg, there is a
-acre beachfront campus in Gulfport
d a nursing program in New Orleans.
illiam Carey students can enjoy the ac-
vities and opportunities provided by the
umerous campus clubs and organiza-
ons.

The Coast

WILLIAM CAREY
COLLEGE ON THE COAST

356 Beach Blvd., Gulfport   865-1500
70 students

The college's coast campus was es-
ablished in Gulfport in 1976 at the site
f the former Gulf Coast Military Acad-
my. Students may choose from 20 aca-
emic areas of study leading to seven un-
ergraduate degrees. The Gulfport cam-
us is the only Carey facility to offer a
achelor's of fine arts. Two graduate level
egrees (in education and business ad-
ninistration) are also available.

Community Colleges

Mississippi boasts the nation's first
planned system of community colleges
and consequently has an outstanding program. Once the second choice for many
tudents, public community colleges and
unior colleges are now viable alternatives
for more than 72,000 students in the state.
Approximately 98 percent of the students
are Mississippi residents; 48 percent are
n academic courses; 22 percent are in
vocational-technical programs; 30 percent
are in continuing education and economic development activities.

Mississippi's 15 community and junior college districts operate 33 centers, including 23 comprehensive campuses and
10 vocational-technical centers. There are
more than 400 different vocational and
technical programs in the junior college
system representing 100 different disciplines. Enrollment figures for colleges
listed below are for the 1993-94 school
year. For additional information, contact
the State Board for Community and Junior Colleges, 3825 Ridgewood Road, Jackson 39211, or call 982-6518.

The Hill Country

EAST MISSISSIPPI COMMUNITY
COLLEGE/GOLDEN TRIANGLE
VOCATIONAL TECHNICAL

P.O. Box 158, Scooba 39358   476-8442
1,055 students
Mayhew Rd., Columbus   243-1900
1,557 students

This community college enjoys an excellent reputation as a vocational training school for area industry. Graduates
successfully find work in their fields of
study, whether it's computer sciences,
welding or any of the 18 courses available
at the Mayhew campus.

ITAWAMBA COMMUNITY COLLEGE

602 W. Hill, Fulton   862-3101
653 Eason Blvd., Tupelo   842-5621
5,384 students Fulton campus; 740 Tupelo

A theater arts department here presents plays and productions that attract
people from throughout north Mississippi. Area businesses benefit from ICC's
teachings and from the many perks it offers as a small business center for the region.

NORTHEAST MISSISSIPPI
COMMUNITY COLLEGE

Cunningham Blvd.
Booneville   728-7751
5,661 students

This two-year college emphasizes
preparation for careers in business and

technology. Students come from surrounding towns to partake of the quality programs offered here.

NORTHWEST MISSISSIPPI COMMUNITY COLLEGE

510 N. Panola St., Senatobia   562-3200
Desoto Center, Southaven   342-1570
Lafayette Yalobusha Center, Oxford 236-2023
Desoto Center, Olive Branch   895-7600
5,694 students, all campuses

NMCC is a multi-campus school that fills a need at each of its four campus locations. Students who aren't ready for a four-year program find a home and a career path at this community college.

The Delta

COAHOMA COMMUNITY COLLEGE
3240 Friars Point Rd.
Clarksdale   627-2571
1,766 students

This small but essential community college serves as a strong foundation for a senior-college program. Students come from several counties for the coursework offered here. It has enjoyed a 29-percent increase in enrollment in one year.

MISSISSIPPI DELTA COMMUNITY COLLEGE
Miss. 3 and Cherry St., Moorehead 246-5631
6,401 students

Mississippi Delta Community College strives to prepare students to meet the challenges of tomorrow in computer sciences, technology and social programs.

Vocational and technical programs her open doors for those who complete th two-year intensive training. A 50-percen increase in enrollment since 1993 is source of pride for educators.

HOLMES COMMUNITY COLLEGE
1 Hill St., Goodman   472-231.
412 W. Ridgeland Ave., Ridgeland 856-540(
1060 Avent Dr., Grenada   226-083(
1,356 students Goodman; 1,034 Ridgeland
695 Grenada

Students at this tri-campus school ca earn a two-year degree or a one-year cer tificate in such high-demand vocationa areas as metal fabrication, which include welding. Students here also receive goo(instruction in computer sciences and busi ness. This school is on the border of th(Delta and the Heartland.

The Heartland

COPIAH-LINCOLN COMMUNITY COLLEGE
Lester Furr Dr., Wesson   643-510(
3,047 students

Co-Lin dates back to 1915 and the establishment of the Copiah-Lincoln Agricultural High School. The junior college was organized in 1928 and today offers associate's of arts and applied associate's of science degrees in a large selection of academic programs of study. These include accounting, computer science, pre-medicine, business education, home economics, history, speech, social work and polymer science. Technical courses

Credit: The Sun Herald

Jefferson College, in Washington is at the gateway to the Natchez Trace (in Natchez). Aaron Burr was arraigned on charges of treason here in 1807. Jefferson Davis was once a student here, and John James Audubon was a drawing teacher.

are divided between the main campus in Wesson, whose vo-tech center is called one of the finest in Mississippi, and the Natchez branch. Technical subjects cover radiography, business and computer technology, welding, drafting, respiratory care technology and hotel-motel/restaurant management, among others. Vocational courses are also available in such fields as automotive mechanics, cosmetology, welding and practical nursing. The sports pro-

gram consists of intercollegiate football, baseball, tennis, track, golf, women's softball and men's and women's basketball.

EAST CENTRAL COMMUNITY COLLEGE
200 Broad St., Decatur 39327   635-2111
2,091 Students

This community college offers 15 different programs in the vocational/technical division, including drafting and metal fabrication. Part of the metal fabrication program includes a one-year certificate in welding. Business and computer sciences are also strong programs.

HINDS COMMUNITY COLLEGE
505 E. Main St., Raymond   857-5261
12,567 students

This big community college boasts seven busy locations in metropolitan Jackson. Students can earn a two-year associate's of arts or associate's of applied sciences degrees. Throughout the state, students from Hinds are gainfully employed.

MERIDIAN COMMUNITY COLLEGE
910 Miss. 19 N., Meridian   483-8241
4,023 students

Founded in 1937, Meridian Community College offers associate's of arts degree programs in health, business and technology. It also provides university transfer programs, one-year career programs, GED test classes, adult literacy tutoring, business development assistance and business incubator and personal enrichment classes. The 64-acre campus has a fitness center and a sports complex for students. The college's Casteel Gallery in the Todd Library houses a permanent collection of 300 works of art, the gift of the former art teacher for whom the gallery is named. MCC's symphony and community band concerts, theater productions and art exhibits are an integral ingredient in the community's arts and culture scene. For those with an interest in sporting events, the college's varsity athletics offerings include basketball, tennis, softball, baseball and golf.

JONES COUNTY JUNIOR COLLEGE
College Dr., Ellisville   477-4000
5,776 students

This junior college offers 36 academic degree programs, nine technical and 10 vocational programs to residents in eight counties. Jones Junior College is the largest single-campus community college in the state, and its football team is always popular with sports fans.

SOUTHWEST MISSISSIPPI COMMUNITY COLLEGE
College Dr., Summit   276-2000
1,833 students

Southwest offers a variety of courses at the two-year lower college level as well as occupational and continuing education courses and community services. The college opened in 1918 as an agricultural high school. The present campus consists of 60 acres with 28 buildings, a stadium, gym and field house. Areas of study include forestry, education, physical therapy and law enforcement technology.

The River Cities

COPIAH-LINCOLN COMMUNITY COLLEGE NATCHEZ CAMPUS
823 U.S. 61 N., Natchez   442-9111
978 students

This branch provides classes and student services at two sites. The former Washington Consolidated school facility on Highway 61 is where academic classes are offered and where you'll find the 20,000-volume library. The 40,000 square-foot vocational-technical center offers seven study programs.

HINDS COMMUNITY COLLEGE VICKSBURG CAMPUS
755 Miss. 27, Vicksburg   638-0606
1,861 students

This local branch offers a two-year associate's degree in addition to technical and vocational courses. It is the largest vocational-technical facility in Mississippi. Students can study child care, auto mechanics, drafting, allied health and other subjects.

The Coast

MISSISSIPPI GULF COAST COMMUNITY COLLEGE

Hwy. 49 S., Perkinston   928-5211
12,798 students (all campuses)

The Mississippi Gulf Coast Community College, established in 1911, is one of the first junior colleges organized in the state. MGCCC has academic, technical and vocational programs as well as continuing education classes offered at campuses and occupational training centers in four counties. Classes are offered at the Jackson County Campus (5,358 students) in Gautier; Jefferson Davis Campus (5,673 students) in Gulfport; the Perkinston Campus (1,131 students); and the West Harrison County Occupational Training Center in Long Beach (160 students); and the George County Occupational Training Center in Lucedale (476 students). The central office is in Perkinston.

PEARL RIVER COMMUNITY COLLEGE

Station A, Poplarville   795-6801
3,475 students

This two-year college considers itself "the pioneer junior college in the state." Pearl River County Agricultural High School opened in 1909, and in 1921 it became the first junior college in Mississippi to offer college credit. Today, PRCC awards a variety of vocational, technical and academic degrees. Two outstanding programs are nursing and state-of-the-art career training. Other study areas include business administration, interior design, music education and computer science. Pearl River's main campus incorporates 30 buildings on 350 acres with a total plant value of $19 million. The library contains 35,000 books, among other holdings. There are numerous clubs and organizations to involve the students, and plenty of action in varsity and intra-mural sports. The band and choral groups are also popular with students and local residents, who take full advantage of the school's theatrical events and football program. In addition to the main campus, there are three allied centers in south Mississippi. Day classes are offered in Hattiesburg, and night classes are held in Bay St. Louis, Columbia and Picayune.

Mississippi's Top Private High Schools

We've included top private high schools in each of the state's geographic areas. Though tuition fees vary, and there are usually discounts for families with more than one child enrolled, the tuition range is from $2,500 to $3,800 per year, payable in monthly increments. Registration fees are separate. For complete information on private schools in Mississippi, contact the Mississippi Private School Association, 5727 County Cork Road, Jackson 39206, or call 956-6872. Enrollment figures are for grades K through 9 unless otherwise specified.

The Hill Country

HERITAGE ACADEMY

625 Magnolia Ln., Columbus   327-5272
659 students

Since 1964, Heritage has offered a viable alternative to public education in Columbus and Lowndes County. The school boasts a complete computer lab that houses 20 IBM computers, and Heritage is pleased to report that 99 percent of graduates enter college and universities throughout the country. The 1993-94 class of 45 seniors had four National Merit semifinalists and one commended student.

STARKVILLE ACADEMY

Academy Rd., Starkville   *323-7814*
882 students

This school is known for excellence and for the fact that about 25 percent of its graduates get academic scholarships. The high ACT ranking (24 average) helps, as do advanced placement courses in calculus, computers and other subjects.

OAK HILL ACADEMY

800 N. Eshman Ave., West Point   *494-5043*
718 students

Students from the town of West Point and the surrounding counties attend Oak Hill, where they benefit from college prep courses and relatively small classes. Sports at this school are important to the students and townspeople.

MARSHALL ACADEMY

100 Academy Dr., Holly Springs   *252-3449*
513 students

Marshall Academy, grades K through 12, offers a full curriculum to city and county students who want less crowded classrooms and a student-teacher ratio more conducive to accelerated learning.

The Delta

PILLOW ACADEMY

Miss. 82 W., Greenwood   *453-1266*
750 students

This school is proud of its academic record and students who receive scholar-ships to such prestigious universities as Harvard. All teachers are certified in their respective fields, and the school offers some foreign languages via a satellite program.

WASHINGTON SCHOOL

1605 E. Reed Rd.
Greenville   *334-4096*
952 students

Students at WS are well prepared for college, and most of them take advantage of their college prep courses by enrolling in top schools throughout the country. Advanced placement studies, teacher certification, small classes and emphasis on academics are a plus here.

The Heartland

JACKSON PREPARATORY SCHOOL

3100 Lakeland Dr., Jackson   *939-8611*
725 students, grades 7 -12

Specializing in secondary education since 1970, Prep has produced 242 National Merit Semifinalists, the state's best record. Students consistently win regional and national awards in language, literature, art, music and drama. Athletically, Prep has had more than 100 students receive college scholarships and leads the conference in overall titles. In 1994, the mean ACT score was 24.4, compared to the state average of 18.7 and the national average of 20.7. In a traditional setting with a small student-faculty ratio of 13-to-1, Prep maintains an atmosphere conducive to intellectual, cultural, social, spiritual and physical development.

MADISON RIDGELAND ACADEMY

7601 Old Canton Rd., Madison   856-4455
912 students

MRA, as this school is called by those who know and love it, was named by Apple Computers as a pilot school for the Jackson Metro area and north Mississippi. MRA is recognized for its work in satellite technology and computer innovations and for its overall academic excellence.

LAMAR HIGH SCHOOL

544 Lindley Rd., Meridian   482-1345
325 students

The middle/senior high school campus is being expanded to incorporate the elementary school during the 1995-96 school year. Lamar offers a college prep curriculum, and approximately 98 percent of its graduates attend college. Lamar opened in 1969. Its sports program consists of football, basketball, softball, baseball, track, tennis, golf and swimming.

HEIDELBERG ACADEMY

Academy Dr., Miss. 528
Heidelberg   787-4589
365 students

This private academy has grades K through 12. A co-ed private college prep school, it has a new computer lab. Students participate in show choir among other activities. The football team is the state champion. Other sports include basketball and baseball.

BROOKHAVEN ACADEMY

Brookway Blvd. Extension
Brookhaven   833-4041
550 students

This co-ed private academy has students from K through 12. The school,

which opened in 1968, employs a staff of 49. Curriculum is college preparatory, and students can take advantage of a new media center and new computer lab with 30 computers. Close to 98 percent of graduates go on to college. The athletic program features all major sports such as football, golf, softball, basketball and tennis.

PARKLANE ACADEMY

1115 Parklane Rd., McComb   684-8113
1,044 students

This large private school has grades K through 12. The college prep courses include foreign languages, and among the fine facilities are labs for computer and science studies. Extracurricular activities feature all sports plus music and band. The Parklane Pioneers recently earned back-to-back state football championships for their District 4-AAA athletic division.

COPIAH ACADEMY

114 E. Gallman Rd., Gallman   892-3770
617 students

Founded in 1967, Copiah Academy is an independent co-ed college preparatory day school between Crystal Springs and Hazlehurst. Teachers here have an average of 12 years classroom experience. Students can get involved in a variety of clubs as well as the show choir, concert and marching bands, student government, community service, yearbook and school paper. The athletics program features football, basketball, baseball, track, golf and tennis.

COLUMBIA ACADEMY

1548 U.S. 98 E., Columbia   736-6418
523 students

Columbia Academy, founded in 1970, is a college prep, co-ed private school that boasts a high number of graduates who attend college and score high on ACT tests. Student athletes participate in tennis, basketball, baseball and football, and the school has an active drill team and cheering program. The staff consists of 50 members.

The River Cities

Adams County Christian School
300 Chinquapin Ln., Natchez   442-1477
910 students

This co-ed Christian school, which opened 20 years ago, recently purchased a neighboring multipurpose facility and uses it for recreation, classrooms, meetings and drama productions. Boys and girls can take some college preparatory courses such as advanced psychology, calculus and English. The staff numbers approximately 60. Grades are pre-kindergarten through 12.

TRINITY EPISCOPAL DAY SCHOOL
321 U.S. 61 S., Natchez   442-5424
400 students

Trinity Episcopal is a college preparatory school whose co-ed students range from 3 year olds in pre-kindergarten through the high school senior level. Typically, all graduates attend college.

The school has a computer lab and a full sports program including football, basketball, baseball, cross-country and tennis.

ALL SAINTS' EPISCOPAL SCHOOL
2717 Confederate Ave.
Vicksburg   636-5266, (800) 748-9957
140 students

All Saints' is a co-ed college prep boarding and day school for students in 8th through 12th grades. Founded in 1908 as a girls' school, the school stresses intellectual and spiritual growth as well as comprehensive physical education. Although All Saints' is owned by the Episcopal Dioceses in Mississippi, Louisiana and Arkansas, it welcomes students of all faiths. Its 40-acre campus is hilly and well landscaped, boasting an Olympic-size pool, rec center, dormitories, music and art studios, among its $6 million facilities. The faculty consists of 25 full-time teachers and administrators.

CHAMBERLAIN-HUNT ACADEMY
124 McComb Ave., Port Gibson   437-4291
148 students

This academy, established in 1879, is a private co-ed boarding and commuter school for grades 4 through 12. The senior high curriculum includes such college prep courses as advanced math and chemistry in addition to foreign languages and computer literacy. Extracurricular activities include student council, honor society, sports, cheerleading, yearbook and newspaper.

Insiders' Tips

Mississippi' State University's largest continuous research project is the Diagnostic Instrumentation and Analysis Laboratory. DIAL has an established program for developing advanced microprocessor-controlled, optical diagnostic instruments to measure thermal and chemical parameters in fossil-fueled combustion systems. The results could benefit power companies and the automobile, rocket and chemical industries.

The Coast

COAST EPISCOPAL MIDDLE/HIGH SCHOOL
22037 Episcopal School Rd.
Pass Christian 452-9442
100 students

Coast Episcopal was founded in 1950 and today is an independent private church school offering college preparatory education to boys and girls in grades 6 through 12. Students can study foreign languages and learn in computer and science lab facilities. More than 98 percent of the school's graduates continue their education at the college level. In addition to academics, Coast Episcopal offers an athletic program including basketball, baseball and soccer.

ST. STANISLAUS SCHOOL
304 S. Beach Blvd., Bay St. Louis 467-9057
640 students

This historic all-boys (6th through 12th grade) day and boarding school run by the Brothers of the Sacred Heart celebrated its 140th anniversary in 1994. It is the largest boys' boarding school in the country and enjoys a reputation for excellence both in education and community service. The college preparatory curriculum includes computer education and advanced foreign language studies. Extracurricular activities include band, athletics and the Key Club. The summer camp for boys ages 10 to 14 mixes fun with academics.

OUR LADY ACADEMY
222 S. Beach Blvd., Bay St. Louis 467-7048
260 students

The all-female student body of OLA shares some of neighboring St. Stanislaus' classroom facilities and extracurricular activities such as band and cheerleading. OLA was founded in 1971 for students in grades 7 through 12. The college preparatory studies include calculus, computer applications, French and Latin. A strong sports program, choral music and campus ministry in a family atmosphere are trademarks of this Catholic school.

MERCY CROSS
390 Crusaders Dr., Biloxi 374-4145
363 students

Mercy Cross is a co-ed Catholic school with grades 7 through 12. Students take college prep classes such as calculus and get involved in community service, drama, band and a comprehensive athletic program. Mercy Cross opened in 1981.

ST. JOHN HIGH SCHOOL
620 Pass Rd., Gulfport 863-8141
400 students

St. John is nearing its 100th anniversary. The Catholic co-ed college prep school, which was founded in 1900, boasts modern labs for the study of computers and science and a computerized research library. The well-rounded offerings feature a full athletic program, campus ministry, service clubs, drama and music.

RESURRECTION SCHOOL
Watts Ave., Pascagoula 762-3353
170 students

Resurrection is the only Catholic school on the Coast that has pre-kindergarten through 12th grade. The middle/high school is co-ed and offers advanced English, foreign languages, advanced physics and math among its curriculum. Sports, community service and campus ministry round out its programs.

For more information about the Catholic Schools of the Diocese of Biloxi, contact the Department of Education, 120 Reynoir Street, Biloxi 39530, or call 374-0440.

Inside
Healthcare

Mississippi is proud of the leadership role its physicians and researchers have taken in healthcare, for they have made significant contributions to the betterment of the human race. We are pleased to talk about such major medical accomplishments as the world's first human lung transplant that occurred at the University of Mississippi Medical Center (UMC) in Jackson in 1963. Even more significant, the first heart transplant in a human took place at UMC in 1964 — three years prior to Dr. Christian Barnard's highly publicized heart transplant.

Jackson, the state capital, is also the state's leader in medical firsts. Along with the firsts above, one of the nation's first artificial kidney units was put in service at the University Medical Center. UMC also houses one of the world's most comprehensive computer models of the cardiovascular system.

Other Jackson hospitals are recognized for firsts too. St. Dominic's was the first in the state to offer nonsurgical treatment for the removal of kidney stones. The Mississippi Methodist Rehabilitation Center has used, since 1985, the nation's first-of-its-kind surgical cabin, which is said to be the most sterile environment for performing surgery. The Methodist Medical Center recently completed a $35 million expansion, which means additional services and

healthcare options for patients. The Mississippi Baptist Medical Center's physicians are nationally known for their gallbladder removal procedure, a unique procedure that is said to reduce certain risks associated with surgery and possibly save the patient time and money.

In this chapter, we've included a selection of hospitals and emergency care clinics for each region. For a complete listing of other fine hospitals in the state, contact the Mississippi Hospital Association, 6425 Lakeover Drive, Jackson, 982-3251. Those who require home care and need referrals, contact the Mississippi Association for Home Care, 362-8987. This Jackson-based group represents 35 Medicaid and Medicare certified home health agencies across the state. The state operates 15 comprehensive Community Mental Health/Mental Retardation Centers under the auspices of the Department of Mental Health, Mississippi Department of Human Services. Mental Health's duties and responsibilities include developing and implementing programs to benefit the mentally ill, emotionally disturbed, alcoholic, drug dependent and mentally retarded persons of the state. For additional information or for a listing of the 15 centers, contact the Mississippi Department of Mental Health, 1101 Robert E. Lee Building, 239 N. Lamar Street, Jackson, 359-1288.

All emergency care clinics listed accept major credit cards.

The Hill Country

Hospitals

BAPTIST MEMORIAL
HOSPITAL GOLDEN TRIANGLE
2520 Fifth St. N.
Columbus   243-1000, (800) 544-8762

Baptist Memorial Hospital-Golden Triangle, a regional referral center for a seven-county area, is dedicated to using the latest medical techniques and equipment, and that dedication includes investing $40 million in a construction project to begin this year. Construction will include an expanded emergency department, relocation of support ancillary services, an expanded surgical and critical care area, a comprehensive cancer center, a new professional office building for the 20 or so new physicians expected in the near future and more. Additionally, BMH-GT was awarded a $3.6 million Certificate of Need (CON) through the Mississippi State Department of Health to establish an open-heart surgery and cardiac catheterization service.

The 328-bed Baptist Memorial Hospital Golden Triangle opened in 1969 as Lowndes General Hospital; its 1989 merger with Columbus Hospital gave the facility 38,000 square feet on 63 acres. The acquisition of the Golden Triangle Regional Hospital by Baptist Memorial Health Care System in 1993 assured a strong commitment to the community for many years to come. BMH-GT also offers a Hospice program, a wellness center, behavioral and mental health services, a large volunteer auxiliary program, participation in the Make a Wish Foundation, among many services. Today, more than 900 employees and 85 physicians cover most areas of medicine and a 24-hour emergency care unit is fully staffed.

NORTH MISSISSIPPI MEDICAL CENTER
830 S. Gloster
Tupelo   841-3000, (800) 843-3375

Since 1937, the 650-bed North Mississippi Medical Center and 190 physicians covering 42 specialties have served the Tupelo vicinity as a regional medical center. The Tupelo-based healthcare system operates four community hospitals in Eupora, West Point, Iuka and Pontotoc as well as 20 Family Medical Centers staffed by primary physicians and nurse practitioners. NMMC also has the distinction of being the nation's largest non-metro hospital, and the city boasts more physicians per capita than any area in the United States except for Rochester, Minnesota, home of the Mayo Clinic. North Mississippi Health Services, the parent company of NMMC, offers mammography services at its Tupelo, West Point and Eupora locations, and now with a Mobile Mammography Unit, screening mammography services are available at sites throughout the northern part of the state. North Mississippi Medical Center has dialysis centers in Tupelo, Oxford, Corinth, Eupora, Holly Springs and Aberdeen as well as home-care offices for eight counties and Hospice services for three. The Cancer Center, NMMC in Tupelo, offers radiation oncologists and outpatient cancer care.

BAPTIST MEMORIAL
HOSPITAL NORTH MISSISSIPPI
2301 S. Lamar, Oxford   232-8100

A part of the Baptist Memorial Health Care System, the Oxford hospital has 150 beds and 60 physicians covering 30 specialties. As part of one of the leading healthcare organizations in the region, BHNM in Oxford offers medical care comparable to that found in metropolitan areas, and innovative special care services are an asset to the community. BHNM offers diagnostic services including certified mammography, MRI, nuclear medicine, rehabilitative services, women's services, cardiac care and support services. Locals say that excellent physicians have chosen Oxford because of its quality of life amenities that enhance healthcare opportunities.

MAGNOLIA HOSPITAL

Alcorn Dr., Corinth   286-6961

Since 1965, Magnolia Hospital has emphasized personal service and quality care. It is a regional medical center that has 146 beds and 32 physicians covering many specialties such as cardiology, gastroenterology, neurology and a 650-member staff of dedicated professionals. Magnolia Hospital boasts a high percentage of nationally certified nurses. The Woman's Center was opened in 1993; it offers an eight-bed maternity suite that encompasses the labor, delivery, recovery and postpartum concept. Emergency-care patients receive care from the only 24-hour physician-staffed emergency department within a 50-mile radius. Superior Home Health and Hospice is another service provided by Magnolia Hospital, which includes nursing care, physical therapy, speech therapy and home health aide services.

Emergency Care Clinics

FAMILY MEDICAL CENTER

1503 Hwy. 45 N.
Columbus   328-9623

Next to McDonald's, this clinic is open seven days a week for the treatment of minor injuries, accidents, flu, infections, physicals and most other non-hospital illnesses. They also have x-ray equipment and a lab. Staff physicians refer emergencies elsewhere if necessary. No appointments are given. Office hours are 8 AM to 8 PM Monday through Saturday and 1 to 8 PM on Sunday.

MED-SERVE

410 Council Cir., Tupelo   844-8822

Just behind the hospital in Tupelo, this clinic is a general medical facility that offers x-rays and some lab work. It treats minor injuries. Colds, flu, infections and other non-life-threatening illnesses can be treated here; no appointment is necessary. Hours are 8 AM to 8 PM Monday through Saturday and 1 to 7 PM Sunday.

The Delta

Hospitals

DELTA REGIONAL MEDICAL CENTER

1400 E. Union
Greenville   378-3783

With 268 beds and more than 70 physicians, Delta Regional Medical Center operates the only burn center in the state.

Patients are flown here from elsewhere in Mississippi for the expert care available. DRMC also features one of Mississippi's few single-room maternity systems, for labor, delivery and postpartum care. Physicians here cover many specialties and provide most services, including a 24-hour physician-staffed emergency room that serves the Delta. DRMC is a regional referral hospital.

GREENWOOD-LEFLORE HOSPITAL
1401 River Rd., Greenwood   459-9751

The Greenwood Leflore Hospital is a city-county medical center with 260 beds. The locally run hospital and its 42 physicians serve surrounding counties in the Delta and offer most every service available in metropolitan hospitals, including an advanced CT scanner, an MRI scanner and a sophisticated mammography machine. Also available are advanced procedures in joint replacement, cataract surgery, cancer treatment and more.

NORTHWEST MISSISSIPPI REGIONAL MEDICAL CENTER
1970 Hospital Dr.
Clarksdale   627-3211

This north-Delta regional medical center is county-owned and serves patients from seven counties. With 174 rooms and 36 physicians, most specialties are offered, as well as a 24-hour emergency treatment center.

Credit: The Sun Herald

The Friendship Oak, located on the Gulf Park Campus of the University of Southern Mississippi in Long Beach, is more than 500 years old. Friends can visit on the deck built among the tree's branches.

Emergency Care Clinics

There are no emergency care clinics in major Delta towns, though the hospitals we've listed offer 24-hour emergency care every day.

The Heartland

Hospitals

UNIVERSITY MEDICAL CENTER
2500 N. State St., Jackson   984-1000

The University Medical Center includes schools of medicine, nursing, dentistry, health-related professions and graduate programs in the life sciences. The University Hospitals and Clinic serve as the teaching laboratories for all educational programs. There are 593 beds in the three hospitals, which are the University, Children's and the Children's Rehabilitation Center. The University of Mississippi School of Medicine is recognized as one of the most prestigious in the country. The 164-acre UMC campus includes the Children's Cancer Clinic, the Verner S. Holmes Learning Resource Center and the 40,000-square-foot University Medical Pavilion, where medical school faculty members see patients. Some of UMC's faculty members are widely acclaimed medical textbook authors and research physicians. Along with the in vitro fertilization program, the medical center services include artificial kidney, coronary, intensive care and stroke units; an MRI center; a CT for brain and body; a hyperbaric oxygen chamber; and a sleep-disorders center. The University Medical Center is especially proud of the heart and kidney transplant units.

MISSISSIPPI BAPTIST MEDICAL CENTER
1225 N. State St., Jackson   968-1000

More than 26,000 inpatients from across the state use this 646-bed facility annually, a far cry — and a far number — from patients who were treated in the eight-room antebellum hospital when MBMC opened its doors in 1911. Today, Baptist Medical Center is one of the largest nonprofit general hospitals in the state and one that offers a full range of healthcare services including a diabetes management program, a sleep disorders clinic and a chemical dependency unit. The Women's Center, provides screening, educational programs, support groups and other areas pertinent to women. Each year, the Cancer Center treats more cancer patients than any other private hospital in Mississippi. Also at Baptist, the Cancer Center/oncology clinic offers a Cancer HelpLink, dial 984-6262.

METHODIST MEDICAL CENTER
1850 Chadwick Dr., Jackson   376-1000

Methodist Medical Center is proud of its $35 million expansion project, completed in February 1995. The expansion added almost 200,000 square feet on the north side of the hospital, enhanced the Ambulatory Care Center and provided a new Emergency Department, a new Surgery Department that includes 13 new operating rooms and a recovery area, a new Labor/Delivery/Recovery areas and a new Neonatal Intensive Care unit and Step-Down Nursery. Methodist Medical Center is an affiliate of Methodist Health Systems, which is a network of 12 hospitals. MMC in Jackson has 473 beds and serves all of Mississippi as an acute-care hospital. Every major physician specialty is represented by the 250 physicians at MMC. It is also known for its comprehensive cancer-care program, where more than 25,000 procedures were performed in 1994. MMC offers a state-of-the-art maternity center, where more than 1,600 babies are delivered each year.

St. Dominic Health Center
969 Lakeland Dr., Jackson   982-0121

This hospital was the Jackson Infirmary until 1946, when the Dominican Sisters of Illinois acquired the title and changed the mission. Today, that mission of combining the spiritual with the physical continues to be the focus at this 571-bed acute-care hospital. The highly respected "St. Dom" boasts a state-of-the-art critical-care wing, the Mississippi Heart Institute, Lithotrispy Institute and the Jackson Mental Health Center. The North Campus boasts an expanded Behavioral Health Program, which includes a chemical dependency unit. The hospital's Hand Management Center specializes in postsurgical therapy for hand and arm problems. Across the street from the main hospital, the 60-bed Doctors Hospital provides medical and surgical services. The new St. Dominic Medical Mall, Inc., a 14-story tower, houses ambulatory services, cardiac catheterization, radiology, surgery services and a pharmacy.

River Oaks Hospital & River Oaks East-Woman's Pavilion
1030 River Oaks Dr., Jackson   932-1030
1026 N. Flowood Dr., Jackson   932-1000

Plans for River Oaks Hospital began in 1978 when 72 physicians pooled efforts to establish a hospital dedicated to patient care and where they could direct the hospital's policies and plans. The hospital officially opened in 1981, with 100 beds and 190 medical staff members. The growth mode was firmly established, for the hospital continued to expand its services to include Outpatient Surgery and an 11-bed, full-amenities unit called The Royal Oaks. In 1994, River Oaks acquired Woman's Hospital and renamed it River Oaks East-Woman's Pavilion. The acquisition helped the hospital offer obstetrics, promote women's health services and provide additional beds — bringing the total to 211 beds. In late 1994, River Oaks opened The Baby Suites, a LDRP (Labor, Delivery, Recovery, Postpartum) unit. Now, River Oaks Hospital & River Oaks East have about 400 physicians representing more than 40 specialties. This hospital also offers one of the state's highest nurse-to-patient ratios, and it is governed by an eight-member board comprised of private practice physicians and staff physicians.

Rankin Medical Center
350 Crossgates Blvd., Brandon   825-2811

Rankin Medical Center has made great strides since it opened in 1969. It is a 90-bed acute-care hospital with a full range of diagnostic capabilities and outpatient services. This popular hospital is relatively small by Jackson standards, though its services are as excellent as any to be found in the nearby capital city. RMC recently underwent a $14 million expansion and renovation, which included an $8.5 million bond issue approved by voters. RMC is proud of the highly regarded Mary Ann Mobley Children's Center and other new and expanded programs devised to assure that the healthcare needs of this fast-growing community are met well into the future. RMC is one of the three area hospitals, along with St. Dominic and Baptist, to form the Mississippi Health Network, a partnership that helps to improve access to primary care and preventive medicine while encouraging cost containment.

MISSISSIPPI METHODIST
REHABILITATION CENTER
1350 E. Woodrow Wilson
Jackson   961-2611, (800) 223-6672

One of the Southeast's largest and the state's only freestanding, comprehensive rehabilitation center, MMRC is a 124-bed facility dedicated to "rebuilding lives" by helping restore patients' independence and self reliance. Rehabilitation programs offered include: brain injury, spinal injury, stroke, arthritis, joint replacement, neurological diseases, pediatric rehabilitation and industrial rehabilitation.

JEFF ANDERSON
REGIONAL MEDICAL CENTER
2124 14th St.
Meridian   483-8811

This comprehensive facility, the largest in the area, has 260 rooms and provides 24-hour emergency-room services in addition to complete cardiac care, same-day surgery, maternity and newborn care

and nutrition-counseling services. The medical center includes Anderson's Institute for Rehabilitative Medicine, 484-5703, the Jeff Anderson Health and Fitness Center, 485-0622, and an 800-car parking complex.

RILEY MEMORIAL HOSPITAL
1102 Constitution Ave., Meridian   693-2511

Riley Memorial offers 24-hour emergency-room services plus surgery, critical care, specialized nursing and pediatric units, radiology, cardiopulmonary services and certified breast-imaging services.

RUSH FOUNDATION HOSPITAL
1314 19th Ave., Meridian   483-0011

Rush Foundation's services include emergency care on a 24-hour basis, occupational health, a family birth center, a wellness center featuring weight training, home health and sports medicine.

FORREST GENERAL HOSPITAL
6051 U.S. 49, Hattiesburg   288-7000

Forrest General is a 537-bed regional medical center that serves a 17-county area with such services as emergency room, rehabilitation, outpatient surgery and psychiatric and chemical dependency. The hospital is undergoing a $20 million expansion, during which 165 new patient rooms will be added. The old rooms will be remodeled for use as diagnostic and support areas. Forrest General is home to Rescue 7, a helicopter ambulance.

METHODIST HOSPITAL

5001 Hardy St., Hattiesburg   268-8000

Methodist is a private facility that has 201 beds and is in west Hattiesburg. Services include emergency room, diagnostic cardiac, new MRI in an expanded radiology department, outpatient surgery, physical therapy, cardiac rehabilitation and home health. The new four-story Wesley Towers houses outpatient services and clinics. Methodist reintroduced maternity services in summer 1995.

Emergency Care Clinics

MEA MEDICAL CLINICS

5606 Old Canton Rd.
Jackson   957-3333

This family medical care facility treats patients with flu, infections and colds and offers occupational medicine, urgent and after-hours care, plus diagnostic, lab, and x-ray equipment. Hours are 9 AM to 9 PM daily, though they prefer that patients arrive no later than 8 PM.

COUNTY LINE FAMILY MEDICAL CENTER

1551 E. County Line Rd.
Jackson   957-2273

Patients of all ages with minor injuries, flu, infections and other non-hospital injuries or sicknesses are treated here, and no appointment is necessary. Staff physicians will refer, when necessary. Hours are 9 AM to 7 PM Monday through Friday and 9 AM to 6 PM on Saturday.

MINOR MED CARE

2860 McDowell Rd., Jackson   372-1117

For minor injuries, x-rays and illnesses, this clinic is open six days a week. No appointment is necessary. Hours are 8 AM to 8 PM Monday through Friday and 8 AM to 3 PM on Saturday.

RUSH FAMILY MEDICAL CENTER

College Park Shopping Center
Meridian   482-2077

Physician Services of Meridian, P.A., provides after-hours care and weekend treatment with no appointments. Hours are 8 AM to 8 PM Monday through Saturday and 1 PM to 8 PM on Sunday.

The River Cities

Hospitals

NATCHEZ COMMUNITY HOSPITAL

129 Jeff Davis Blvd., Natchez   445-6200

A 101-bed general medical/surgical hospital, Natchez Community has approximately 60 physicians on staff. Services include 24-hour emergency with ambulance, outpatient surgery and OB/GYN. During 1995, the emergency room was being expanded and the surgery department was being remodeled.

NATCHEZ REGIONAL MEDICAL CENTER

54 Seargent S. Prentiss Dr.
Natchez   442-2871

This is a public, general medical/surgical facility that has a licensed capacity of 205 beds. There are 49 physicians on staff. The new 24-hour emergency room includes three large trauma rooms. The medical center is undergoing a two-year comprehensive renovation that should be completed in 1997.

PARK VIEW REGIONAL MEDICAL CENTER

100 McAuley Dr., Vicksburg   631-2131

This general medical facility has 240 beds and approximately 85 physicians on staff. The physician-staffed emergency room is open 24 hours a day. This growing hospital has plans for an urgent care center near Pemberton Mall, an outpatient cancer treatment facility and an inpatient psychiatric clinic for the elderly.

VICKSBURG MEDICAL CENTER
1111 N. Frontage Rd., Vicksburg   636-2611

A 154-bed general medical/surgical hospital, Vicksburg Medical Center has a 24-hour physician-staffed emergency service. The staff includes 55 physicians. The hospital offers MRI services as well as full-service OB/GYN including a state-of-the-art nursery.

The Coast

Hospitals

SINGING RIVER HOSPITAL
2809 Denny Ave., Pascagoula   938-5000

This 415-room hospital offers 24-hour physician-staffed emergency care, outpatient surgery, a heart care program that offers open heart surgery and a new full-service cardiac cath lab and a wellness center, among other comprehensive services. The new Regional Cancer Center offers full-service radiology and chemotherapy services. The Singing River Hospital staff includes approximately 85 physicians. Singing River's hospital system encompasses the Ocean Springs Hospital.

MEMORIAL HOSPITAL AT GULFPORT
4500 13th St.
Gulfport   863-1441

Memorial is a 302-bed facility staffed by 200 physicians along with other health professionals. Its services include 24-hour emergency-room care, labor and delivery, cardiology, diabetes care, hyperbaric medicine, outpatient surgery, radiology, oncology and hospice care. Memorial also has the Center for Women's Health, which offers medical services and educational programs.

BILOXI REGIONAL MEDICAL CENTER
150 Reynoir St., Biloxi   432-1571

Biloxi Regional has 153 beds and approximately 135 physicians on staff. It offers 24-hour physician-staffed emergency care, outpatient surgery, ICU/CCU, labor and delivery, MRI, radiation therapy and oncology, mammography and a cardiac and new pulmonary rehabilitation program.

GULF COAST MEDICAL CENTER
180 DeBuys Rd., Biloxi   388-6711

Specialty services here include a 24-hour emergency room staffed by physicians, hyperbaric and wound care, obstetrics and gynecology, outpatient surgery, and respiratory, physical and industrial therapy. The Centre for Breast Care and Center for Sleep Disorders are part of this facility's services. The medical center has 144 beds and 160 physicians.

OCEAN SPRINGS HOSPITAL
3109 Bienville Blvd.
Ocean Springs   872-1111

Ocean Springs Hospital is another member of the Singing River Hospital System. It has 124 beds and 65 staff physicians. Some of the services provided are a 24-hour physician-staffed emergency room, maternal/child-health programs, and outpatient, laparoscopic and laser surgery. A major expansion program will enlarge the ER department and add a new 12-bed ICU, permanent housing for the new MRI and a helipad for air ambulances. The project is scheduled for completion in early 1996.

GARDEN PARK
COMMUNITY HOSPITAL
1520 Broad Ave., Gulfport   864-4210

Garden Park has 120 beds and 155 physicians among its staff members. Services include a 24-hour emergency room and the Gulfport Outpatient Surgical Center, 868-1120. New maternity suites opened in late 1994.

HANCOCK MEDICAL CENTER
149 Drinkwater Blvd.
Bay St. Louis 467-9081

This 60-bed facility completed a major outpatient expansion program in early 1995, upgrading the 24-hour physician-staffed emergency room, outpatient surgery and radiology departments. Other services include ICU, physical and respiratory therapy and OB/GYN and childbirth classes.

KEESLER AIR FORCE BASE MEDICAL CENTER
White Ave., Biloxi 377-6550

Keesler's Medical Clinic serves 39 Air Force, Army and Navy bases in the southeastern United States. It consists of a 350-bed inpatient hospital, 62 outpatient clinics, a clinical research lab and aeromedical facilities. The staff includes more than 1,800 doctors and nurses. The Commission of Accreditation of Hospital and Health Care Organizations has named Keesler Medical Center in the top 10 percent of all civilian and military medical treatment facilities in the country.

VETERANS AFFAIRS MEDICAL CENTER
Pass Rd., Biloxi 388-5541

This acute-care facility offers a number of rehabilitation clinics and programs for veterans including surgery, psychiatry and physical therapy. The medical center has 448 beds, 62 nursing home units and a 252-bed unit for temporary care.

VETERANS AFFAIRS MEDICAL CENTER
200 E. Beach Blvd., Gulfport 863-1972

The VA's Gulfport Division is primarily a psychiatric hospital that provides rehab clinics and related programs for veterans.

Emergency Care Clinics

GULF COAST URGENT CARE CENTER
2771 Pass Rd., Biloxi 388-5144

Open daily 7 AM to 10 PM, this center offers medical treatment for minor ailments and injuries. No appointments are necessary.

WHOLE FAMILY HEALTH CLINIC URGENT CARE CENTER
833 U.S. Hwy. 90 Ste. 1
Bay St. Louis 467-3510

This urgent-care center opened in April 1994 and offers minor emergency treatment from 9 AM to 7 PM Monday through Friday. No appointments are needed.

FAMILY MEDICAL CENTER
2533 Denny Ave., Pascagoula 762-0222

Minor emergencies are handled here, as are general pediatric and adult care, lab work and x-rays. The center is open 8 AM to 8 PM Monday through Friday, 8 AM to 6 PM on Saturday and 1 to 6 PM on Sunday. No appointments are necessary.

Credit: David Purdy, The Sun Herald

Mississippi golf courses are popular with seniors, "snowbirds" from the North, and longtime residents.

Inside
Retirement

Mississippi is attractive to retirees for a multitude of reasons, not the least of which is an affordable lifestyle. And, as more and more new residents are discovering, the state offers a great deal more than affordable housing, food and medical services — even for those on a budget. There are ample opportunities for recreation and entertainment, camaraderie in clubs and associations and the chance to perform volunteer work for many worthwhile social and cultural organizations. Colleges and universities offer special tuition rates to seniors, and some classes are even free.

Mississippi's weather is something to brag about almost year-round, and crime figures are generally lower than average. Retirees also enjoy the spaciousness and easy pace of living that the state has to offer.

There is plenty of housing available in every price range, and there is retirement community living to suit virtually every need and income level.

Mississippi welcomes more and more retirees each year. In fact, state officials work hard to attract new retirees by marketing Mississippi's attributes and creating new ways to make the state more appealing to this group of potential residents. For example, in 1992 the Legislature passed a bill exempting state, federal and private-sector employees from paying state income tax on their retirement benefits.

The Mississippi Department of Human Services' Division of Aging and Adult Services provides services to Mississippi residents who are 60 and older. There are 10 Area Agency on Aging offices serving the state's 82 counties. Programs include home-delivered and congregate meals, senior centers, transportation, homemaker services, nursing home ombudsmen, senior aides and companions and adult daycare. These offices represent valuable sources of information on various issues such as legal and financial matters, health care, housing, insurance and more.

There are many retirement and nursing homes found in each community throughout Mississippi. Here we provide a look at a few of the licensed personal-care homes found in the state. A complete list is available from the Area Agencies on Aging, as is a list of specific agencies that contract with the AAAs to provide a variety of services, such as transportation, meals and senior center operations.

The Hill Country

Columbus and Oxford have been certified by the state as retirement destinations, so indeed, they are up-and-coming retirement communities with many options for retirees. Oxford is a town of 11,000 situated in the lush and lovely hills of north-central Mississippi where wonderful small-town ambiance prevails, yet it's only 75 miles southeast of a major city, Memphis. Those who have already retired in Oxford laud its attributes, one of which is the University of Mississippi (Ole Miss). They say that a combination of youth and cultural opportunities afforded by Ole Miss is an unbeatable perk, and better still, anybody older than the age of 65 can take one college course per year free and for credit. Add 48 lighted tennis courses — and there's always one available — the university's 18-hole golf course that is open to the public, attractive real-estate prices, good health care, outdoor sports, and it's easy to see why Oxford is a top retirement choice. For information about retirement in Oxford, call the Economic Development Foundation, Inc., 234-4651.

Columbus, in Mississippi's Golden Triangle region, is also touting retirement opportunities, with amenities similar to Oxford's but with a larger population. In the works now is a big retirement complex called Plantation Point, once called The Homestead, where patio homes or condos can be bought or leased. The site, east of Columbus, consists of 75 acres and will be home to about 500 residents. It offers independent living for all over age 55, also assisted living will be available. One and two-bedroom apartments will be available, as well, and so will food services and health amenities. For information on Plantation Point in Columbus, call 327-9099.

Columbus is also a college town, and it offers very good hunting and fishing along the Tennessee-Tombigbee Waterway. Golf and tennis are year round options. Retirees in Columbus are as busy as they want to be, for this is a town where volunteers thrive and industry welcomes experienced people who aren't interested in full-time employment. The town is called home by hundreds of military retirees, as Columbus Air Force Base, a pilot-training facility, is here. For more information, call the Chamber of Commerce in Columbus, 328-4491.

The old Henry Clay Hotel in downtown West Point is being renovated and updated to provide 27 independent apartments for the healthy elderly. The hotel was built in the 1930s. It will be a United Methodist Senior Services of Mississippi, Inc. property.

Starkville seeks retirees too, and they've placed retirees on panels and committees to plan activities and events for their age group. Many enjoy performances and classes at Mississippi State University.

TRINITY PLACE
300 Airline Rd.
Columbus   327-6716

Trinity Place, a United Methodist Senior Services of Mississippi, Inc.-sponsored retirement community, provides "independent living with dignity and security" for the healthy elderly and is a recognized leader in elderly care. Trinity Place provides 140 independent living

Insiders' Tips

Visiting during the holidays? Check out the seasonal festivals for some interesting Christmas gifts with Mississippi flavor.

apartments, while Trinity Personal Care offers assisted living 24 hours a day in 52 studio apartments. Construction is scheduled to begin soon for a 60-bed nursing home. There is a waiting list for residency at Trinity Place, as there is with most good retirement properties. Residents enjoy a family atmosphere and discussions, devotionals, exercise and planned activities. Rent is based on income, though $400 to $900 per month is basic rent for independent living. Personal care basic rent is $1,250. The fees are primarily the same for all the Methodist-sponsored retirement properties in Mississippi.

TRACEWAY RETIREMENT COMMUNITY
2800 W. Main
Tupelo   *844-1441*

Traceway Manor was the first of the United Methodist Senior Services ministries, serving the elderly since 1967. The campus includes Traceway Manor and Villas, 133 independent apartments and duplexes, while the Cottages are 35 full-size homes. A 52-unit personal-care facility is available as well as a 130 bed nursing home that provides 17 beds for Alzheimer's patients. Traceway offers a full spectrum of activities for residents as well as meals and a 24-hour staff. Socialization is encouraged, and planned activities are available. There is a waiting list, though it may not be too long a wait. Rent is based on income; see Trinity Place above.

GRAND OAKS
Miss. 7 S. at Hwy. 6, Oxford (800) 541-3881

This retirement complex bills itself as "The South's grand golf course, resort and retirement village," and those who know say that indeed it will be, once completed. The Greg Clark-designed, 18-hole golf course is open now, and as of this writing, the streets are in the process. The latest word for completion is May or June, 1996. On the site will be 108 large wooded lots, 259 small lots for patio homes, 80 to 100 golf villas and golf four-plex villas, a Marriott-managed hotel and conference center, tennis courts, pools and other amenities. Oxford is proud of its designation as one of the best retirement cities in the country, and locals say that Grand Oaks is just the beginning.

The Delta

Hunters and fishermen are familiar with the attributes of parts of the Delta as a retirement choice, for area lakes are known for great fishing opportunities. Golf and tennis are popular year round in this warm Mississippi climate, and the Delta lifestyle is conducive to relaxation. It's as quiet as one wants it to be, though parties are plentiful. As of this writing, scaled-down housing that appeals to retirees is not abundant, but as with most areas of the state, conscientious house hunters reap rewards. Especially in college towns, such as Cleveland, cultural activities offer additional incentives.

FLOWERS MANOR
RETIREMENT COMMUNITY
1251 Lee Dr., Clarksdale   627-2222

Flowers Manor is a United Methodist Senior Services property, and it is a residential retirement home offering 68 independent living apartments and 24 personal care apartments. Several full-size cottages are under construction. Those in personal care benefit from medication monitoring, housekeeping and a complete meal service. A 24-hour staff is in attendance. Flowers Manor offers a secure setting, planned activities and special events in a gracious living setting. Rent is based on income.

MAGNOLIA MANOR

Hwy. 82 E., Greenwood   453-1897

This apartment complex for the elderly is not a nursing home, though it is owned by Golden Age. Residents must be 62 and older and must be able to care for themselves. Residents pay according to income; the lowest possible basic rate is around $200; the highest basic rate is less than $500. Additional services such as meals and housekeeping are not included in basic rates.

The Heartland

Jackson has retirement communities that offer safety and security, plus the city amenities and opportunities to be enjoyed by the elderly. The quality of life is excellent here, and cultural offerings are the best in the state. Public and private golf courses are numerous, and parks offer walking and hiking paths. Medical care is readily available, and the choices are plentiful. Some private retirement complexes prefer not to release detailed information concerning prices unless an entire package is explained and presented, so please call the numbers listed for additional information concerning price structures. Elsewhere in the Heartland, around Meridian, Laurel and Hattiesburg, country acreage is still available, and real estate prices for existing homes in the cities make these areas attractive to retirees. All three of these cities have good healthcare and most medical specialties. Hattiesburg, especially, is known for its state-of-the-art hospitals and healthcare facilities. It is second only to Jackson in hospitals and physicians.

ST. CATHERINE'S VILLAGE

200 Dominican Dr.
Madison   856-0100,(800) 223-0809

This property is Mississippi's only "life care" retirement community, and it offers an idyllic 160-acre setting near a small lake and lovely grounds. Amenities include housekeeping, linen service, maintenance, security, transportation, a library, a hair salon, an exercise area, an indoor swimming pool and enrichment programs. Within minutes are golf and tennis courts for those who live independently. St. Catherine's Village is affiliated with St. Dominic's Hospital, and it accommodates a range of residents — from those who are physically able to live unassisted to those who require assisted living. There are 210 units for gracious independent living, 60 private units for assisted living and 120 beds in the skilled nursing center. Studios and one- and two-bedroom/two bath units are available. St. Catherine's serves all denominations and invites inquiries. Entrance fees and monthly service fees are dependent upon the choice of living unit and services chosen.

THE ORCHARD

600 S. Pear Orchard Rd.
Ridgeland   856-2205

The Orchard enjoys a reputation as an upscale retirement community where gracious living is practiced at all times. In a very good area of north Jackson, The Orchard offers a choice of living units, housekeeping, meals, a beauty/barber shop, planned activities, utmost security, on-site banking, transportation services a 24-hour staff and a nursing staff. All-electric kitchens are available for those in Independent Living who prefer to prepare their own meals, and covered parking is a plus too. The Orchard offers four stages of care, including Independent, TLC, Personal Care and the Rose Garden. The Rose Garden provides a secured home for residents who are in early stages of dementia and/or wanderers. Basic monthly service fees range from $1,300 to $2,150. Call for additional information.

CHATEAU RIDGELAND
745 S. Pear Orchard Rd.
Ridgeland   *956-1331*

This conveniently located retirement complex offers gracious retirement living, plus three nutritious meals per day, weekly housekeeping and linen service, transportation to shopping, security and a resident manager. The price range for apartments, from duplex studio to two-bedroom, is $995 to $1,595 per month; the amenities are included in the monthly rent. A hair salon and barber shop are on the premises, and a family dining room and entertainment lounge are available. The Chateau is near Northpark Mall and I-55, a direct route to nearby Jackson proper.

ALDERSGATE RETIREMENT COMMUNITY
6600 Poplar Springs Dr.
Meridian   *482-5561*

This three-story independent-living facility is owned by United Methodist Senior Services of Mississippi Inc., and it has 120 private, unfurnished apartments plus a few two-bedrooms and studios. Residents get the noon meal six days a week in the dining room and can get all meals and housekeeping services at an extra charge. Transportation to doctors and stores is included, as are activities, exercise classes, use of laundry facilities and utilities, which include cable. Each room has an emergency call button. There is an in-house beauty shop. Sixty of the rooms are rented for market value, and 40 are HUD-subsidized. Cost for a one bedroom, single occupancy is $763 a month, $908 for double occupancy and $994 for two bedroom, double occupancy. Aldersgate opened its personal-care facility in 1995. It offers unfurnished studio and larger apartments, three meals a day and laundry and housekeeping services. It is staffed 24 hours a day.

The River Cities

MAGNOLIA HOUSE
311 Highland Blvd., Natchez   *446-5097*

This assisted-living facility opened in January 1991 and has 30 private rooms, some with double occupancy for couples. There is 24-hour care, with nurses on duty from 7 AM to 3:30 PM five days a week and from 7 AM to 7 PM on weekends; nursing assistants are on duty 24 hours. There is an in-house laundry and beauty shop, and the full-time activity director plans daily activities plus does shopping for residents once a week. Three meals a

Area Agencies on Aging

For additional information on housing or resources concerning senior adults, contact the Division of Aging and Adult Services nearest you. Following is a list of Area Agencies on Aging and the counties they serve.

NORTH DELTA PLANNING AND DEVELOPMENT DISTRICT AAA

P.O. Box 1496
Batesville 38606   563-1281
Coahoma, Desoto, Panola, Quitman, Tallahatchie, Tate and Tunica

SOUTH DELTA PLANNING AND DEVELOPMENT DISTRICT AAA

P.O. Box 1776
Greenville 38701   378-3831
Bolivar, Humphreys, Issaquena, Sharkey, Sunflower and Washington

NORTH CENTRAL AAA

P.O. Box 668, U.S. 51 S.
Winona 38967   283-2675
Attala, Carroll, Holmes, Leflore, Montgomery and Yalobusha

GOLDEN TRIANGLE AAA

P.O. Drawer DN, Mississippi State
Starkville 39762   325-3855
Choctaw, Clay, Lowndes, Noxubee, Oktibbeha, Webster and Winston

THREE RIVERS AAA

72 S. Main St., Pontotoc   489-2415
Calhoun, Chickasaw, Itawamba, Lafayette Lee, Monroe, Pontotoc and Union

NORTHEAST MISSISSIPPI AAA

P.O. Box 6000
Booneville 38829   728-7038
Alcorn, Benton, Marshall, Prentiss, Tippah and Tishomingo

CENTRAL MISSISSIPPI AAA

1170 Lakeland Dr., Jackson   981-1516
Hinds, Madison, Rankin, Copiah, Simpson, Warren and Yazoo

EAST CENTRAL AAA

410 Decatur St., Newton   683-2007
Clarke, Jasper, Kemper, Lauderdale, Leake, Neshoba, Newton, Scott and Smith

AAA OF SOUTHERN MISSISSIPPI

1020 32nd Ave., Gulfport   868-2326
Covington, Forrest, George, Greene, Hancock, Harrison, Jackson, Jefferson Davis, Jones, Lamar, Marion, Pearl River, Perry, Stone and Wayne

---

SOUTHWEST MISSISSIPPI AAA

110 S. Wall St., Natchez   446-6044
Adams, Amite, Claiborne, Franklin, Jefferson, Lawrence, Lincoln, Pike, Walthall and Wilkinson

---

day, including any special diets, are served in the dining room. Snacks are available several times a day. Residents may choose to have a small refrigerator in their rooms for their own snacks.

The dining room doubles as the activity room, and residents are frequently entertained by visiting school groups. Daily exercises done while seated are led by the activity director. Bingo is among the more popular activities. Families are encouraged to visit residents any at reasonable hour, for any length of time and to take patients out for brief outings and weekends.

Rooms are furnished with hospital beds and other fixtures, and residents can decorate or furnish with their belongings. Each room is cable ready and comes with a telephone jack for private phone lines. Rent for a small room is $1,400 a month; larger rooms are $1,950 for a single and $2,500 for double occupancy. There is an additional $10 charge a month for cable if residents want that service.

A new dementia/Alzheimer's wing with 18 beds is scheduled to open in mid-1995.

THE ARLINGTON

2807 Arlington Loop
Hattiesburg   268-9135

This personal-care facility is an extension of Forrest General Hospital. The lobby features a baby grand piano and a glass atrium. The residents' rooms are in two wings off the main lobby; suites are in a separate wing. There is an activity program two times daily, and transpor-

tation to doctor and dentist appointments are provided by a private company. A beauty shop is one of the on-site features. Nurses are on duty 24 hours a day. Three meals a day are served in the beautiful dining room. The cost is $1,500 to $1,800 a month, depending on the size of the room; suites are $2,250 monthly. Payment is made privately.

NORTHVIEW VILLA

625 Northview Dr., Laurel   426-6488

This privately owned one-story facility is for retired and personal care residents. Among the services available are three meals daily in the cafeteria, laundry and daily activities. Cost for a private room (220 square feet) and bath is $1,050 including food, housekeeping, utilities and laundry. For personal care, the cost for a one bedroom furnished or unfurnished apartment is $1,193, for a two bedroom the cost is $1,247. All fees are private pay. Owners plan to expand the facility in 1995.

The Coast

SANTA MARIA DEL MAR
RETIREMENT APARTMENTS

674 Beach Blvd., Biloxi   432-1289

This is one of five retirement apartment complexes owned by the Catholic Diocese of Biloxi. Santa Maria is the largest of the five complexes and has 209 unfurnished one-bedroom and efficiency apartments. Each room has a stove and refrigerator. Tenants pay cable and phone, but not utilities. There is an assembly room, card room and lounge for reading. Coast Transit Authority is readily available for transportation to the grocery store each week. The apartment complex is nonprofit HUD-subsidized, so rent is based on income (30 percent of gross income).

VILLA MARIA
RETIREMENT APARTMENTS
921 Porter Ave., Ocean Springs   875-8811

This 13-story facility has 198 rooms in a one-bedroom or efficiency configuration. The five units on the first floor are for wheelchair users; the remaining rooms are for persons 62 and older. Rent is based on income (30 percent of gross income) and includes all utilities except cable. Each room has a stove, refrigerator, carpet, drapes and an emergency pull cord in the bathroom. There is a laundry, beauty shop and library available to residents. Someone is at the desk 24 hours a day. Transportation to shopping is provided daily by the senior citizen center, including trips there for lunch each day. Also, the Coast Transit Authority trolley passes in front of the apartments on a regular schedule.

THE SAMARITAN HOUSE
642 Jackson Ave.
Ocean Springs   875-1087

Samaritan is a 50-unit, six-story retirement community offering one-bedroom and efficiency accommodations equipped with a stove and refrigerator. There are laundry facilities on-site, and transportation is available through the senior citizens program in Ocean Springs. Rent is based on income. There is someone on call at the desk 24 hours a day. Residents can take part in the regularly scheduled activities such as bingo, parties, dinner functions and church services.

Samaritan House is near shopping centers, banks and historic attractions.

NOTRE DAME DE LA MER
RETIREMENT APARTMENTS
292 U.S. Hwy. 90
Bay St. Louis   467-2885

This retirement community is a four-story high-rise with one-bedroom and efficiency apartments in a location convenient to shopping, banks and churches. Each room is equipped with a stove, refrigerator, drapes, call switch and smoke alarm. Private parking and a central laundry room are also available. On weekdays there is a schedule of activities for residents, and the desk is attended around the clock for security and special needs. Rent is based on income.

GABRIEL MANOR
2321 Atkinson Rd.
Biloxi   388-1013

This retirement community is four stories and has 52 one-bedroom and efficiency apartments with a stove and refrigerator. The desk is staffed 24 hours a day. Transportation is available on request from Coast Transit Authority. Regular planned activities include bingo, cookouts, monthly birthday parties and shopping trips. Rent is based on income.

METHODIST RETIREMENT COMMUNITY
1450 Beach Blvd., Biloxi   435-3861

This independent-living complex consists of Seashore Manor and Gulf Oaks Manor, which have a total of 189 private efficiency, one- and two-bedroom unfurnished apartments on the beach in Biloxi. Seashore Manor, with 125 apartments in a six-story building, is 30 years old. Gulf Oaks, a 65-unit, our-story building adjacent to Seashore Manor, has been open for 10 years. The 2-unit Seashore Personal Care Center opened in November 1994; its residents receive some help with the activities of daily living. The community is owned by United Methodist Senior Services of Mississippi, a not-for-profit agency of the United Methodist Church. Residents must be at least 62 and able to care for themselves. The community is nondenominational.

Conveniences include laundry facilities, a hair salon, some transportation and food services. There is a full-time activity director and maintenance, and the office is staffed around the clock. Rent starts at $226 for efficiencies, $287 for one bedrooms and $363 for two bedrooms. The 65 units in Gulf Oaks are HUD assisted, so the rent is based on income. The Personal Care Center is a private-pay facility that costs $1,400 per month. The fee includes all meals, housekeeping and laundry.

DUNBAR VILLAGE
725 Dunbar Ave., Bay St. Louis 466-3099

This newly remodeled independent-living facility, formerly known as Bay St. Louis Residential Care Center, provides assistance with daily living and health supervision. It has a capacity of 54 residents in private and semiprivate rooms. Three meals a day are provided in the dining room. Residents may decorate or furnish their own rooms. The assistance station is staffed 24 hours a day. The staff includes a consultant registered nurse and registered dietitian. Activities and exercise programs are regularly scheduled, and transportation is available to shopping centers, banks, churches and special events. Optional services include personal transportation and laundry, barber and beauty shop, pharmacy, temporary bedside care and personal telephone. Costs start at $1,075. A 60-bed skilled nursing home adjacent to the residential care center is planned.

Condominiums are popular with retirees, singles, newlyweds and all ages in between.

Inside
Real Estate

With an upbeat economy in Mississippi coupled with attractive interest rates, houses are not as plentiful as Realtors would like them to be, but buyers can still find a home. It's rare to find a spec house, for when a builder builds, it's usually sold long before completion. Doris Hardy, GRI, CIPS, one of the leading real estate agents in Mississippi and the entire Southeast — actually, she ranked third in sales in an 11-state region — says that there's a shortage of houses due to major refinancing and new home material costs. Hardy, with Century 21 in Columbus, adds, "The real estate market is never stagnant. It's ever-changing. Right now, the inventory is low because the interest rate is low, consequently more people are buying existing homes when they find one that meets their needs." And 'finding one that meets buyers' needs' may well be the key this year.

The housing demand is far greater on the Gulf Coast and along the River Cities where casinos are permanently docked. The large number of employees brought in to work the casinos have taken much of the available housing on the Coast and the River Cities. Rental property is difficult to find in casino towns but not impossible. Higher-priced housing, rather than a low to median price range, is more readily available in casino areas.

Commercial development is strong along the Gulf Coast, in metro Jackson and in Vicksburg, where the city is quite proud of its new Southern Cultural Heritage Complex, now in development. Since 1860, the St. Francis Xavier Convent Complex, home to the Sisters of Mercy and St. Francis Xavier School, has been a viable part of Vicksburg. Its renovation as a multiuse cultural center will continue a long tradition of service. This is one of many examples of downtown development that's going on throughout Mississippi. Some towns are actively rejuvenating their downtown areas.

Jackson is a city where old neighborhoods near downtown are still pretty but not as popular a choice as they were a few years back because of increased crime. The trend for higher-income homeowners appears to be to move northeast of the city. Madison and Ridgeland show accelerated activity in new higher-priced house sales. Locals say that Rankin County is still attracting new home building and the market is good. People from Jackson are continuing to move into Brandon, though primarily into Madison and Ridgeland in Madison County, near the Ross Barnett Reservoir. Southwest Jackson is experiencing substantial commercial and residential development, too, and the houses are listing for less than elsewhere in the area.

Throughout the state, there are pockets of new construction. Many areas are actively building; among them are Jackson, Hattiesburg, the Coast, Natchez, Vicksburg, the upper Delta, Oxford and Tupelo. The general consensus is that residential construction in Mississippi is a little better than the national average, and Realtors are hopeful that it will far exceed the national trends. Commercial real estate development is heavier in the areas mentioned above, for residential building follows commercial activity.

For the latest, most accurate information on local real estate markets, contact a local Realtor. Listed below are the Mississippi Association of Realtors board officers in each region and executive offices, if available.

Boards of Realtors

The Hill Country

GOLDEN TRIANGLE ASSOC. OF REALTORS
President Jane Smith
Century 21/Deep South Properties
3499 Bluecutt Rd., Columbus   327-8596
Executive Officer
Jennifer Barden   328-7800

According to Jane Smith, the retail activity that's going on in Columbus has cast an upbeat mood over the real estate market, even though homes are not plentiful. Columbus is a city of diverse neighborhoods with historic homes sprinkled among contemporary dwellings. There's no new housing development on a grand scale except for a proposed retirement community; otherwise, the new homes now being constructed are custom-built, and they are limited. Downtown commercial development is active; new businesses are moving in; old buildings are being converted to offices with living quarters above. Last year set a record for sales, thanks to low interest rates. Price ranges are varied, but for an average house on an average lot, expect to pay about $72,000 to $75,000. There's interest in lots along the Tennessee-Tombigbee Waterway, one of the prettiest sites in the area, and country-home acreage appears to be in demand.

The Starkville Board merged with Columbus earlier to form the Golden Triangle Board, though the markets are not identical. Jan Rhoades with Coldwell Banker in Starkville said that new commercial growth is strong, and residential growth usually follows. Also making a big difference in the university town of Starkville is a planned highway bypass, which will alleviate the traffic congestion in certain areas and open more areas for development. Currently, infrastructure is being done on two new subdivisions, though no spec building is being done. In Starkville, expect an average price of about $85,000.

CORINTH BOARD
President Betty Ann Hauser
Corinth Realty/Better Homes & Gardens
P.O. Box 701, Corinth 38834   287-7653

Corinth still has $100,000-plus houses on the market because a NASA project

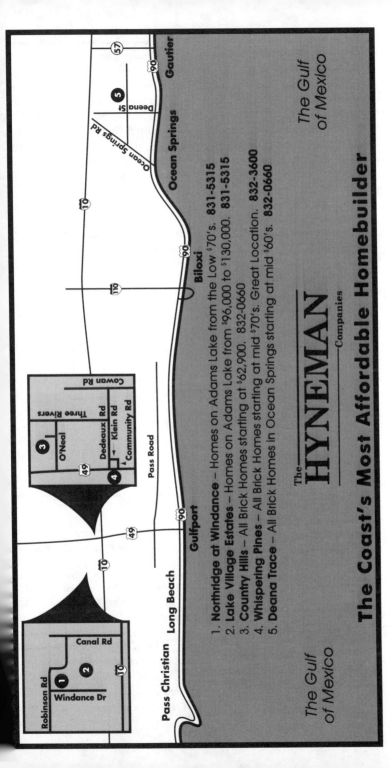

1. **Northridge at Windance** – Homes on Adams Lake from the Low $70's. 831-5315
2. **Lake Village Estates** – Homes on Adams Lake from $96,000 to $130,000. 831-5315
3. **Country Hills** – All Brick Homes starting at $62,900. 832-0660
4. **Whispering Pines** – All Brick Homes starting at mid $70's. Great Location. 832-3600
5. **Deana Trace** – All Brick Homes in Ocean Springs starting at mid $60's. 832-0660

The Gulf of Mexico

The Gulf of Mexico

The ——
HYNEMAN
—— Companies

The Coast's Most Affordable Homebuilder

was abandoned. Locals say that there's a flood of big homes. However, a nice, up-scale three-bedroom home plus amenities can be had for $90,000 to $125,000. Industrial development has increased, so perhaps new houses will follow. Kimberly-Clark is expanding, and there are now four new furniture manufacturers in the area.

NORTH CENTRAL
MISSISSIPPI BOARD (OXFORD)

President Shelby Smith
University Realty
1104 Van Buren Ave., Oxford   234-8888

Oxford is currently one of Mississippi's hottest markets. And according to Shelby Smith, there have been a great deal of residential developments and more are needed. The new growth is attributed to the new VA Hospital, Grand Oaks, a retirement center and golf course and the service businesses that follow such endeavors. A newly built, average-size family home sells for $80,000 to $100,000, while an existing home falls in the $80,000 range. Locals say that Oxford is definitely a seller's market.

NORTHEAST
MISSISSIPPI BOARD (TUPELO)

President Jim Repult
Prudential Magnolia Realty & Assoc.
2436 W. Main, Tupelo   841-1122

The Tupelo sales market remains steady. There's new construction almost continually ongoing, and since the population is the largest in the Hill Country, it's considered a strong market. Though the median price for a three-bedroom two-bath house is about $84,000, there's a strong upscale market considerably over that price. New homes in residential developments are in the $70,000 to $120,000 range. New subdivision lot prices range from $25,000 to $75,000. The market has

ample houses for sale in the $100,000-plus range; few less than that price, and everything moves quickly. Tupelo enjoys active industrial growth, as well, especially with the burgeoning furniture manufacturing market. Now on the drawing board is the $6 million Municipal Complex, which will house the city administration offices. It is scheduled to be completed in 1998.

NORTHWEST MISSISSIPPI BOARD
(SENATOBIA, HERNANDO, BATESVILLE)

President Rozella Harper, Harper Realty
2610 Hwy. 51 S., Hernando   429-9387

In the northwest corner of Mississippi, "It's a real booming market," according to Rozella Harper. The market for house sales is so good because of the influx of nearby casinos and their thousands of employees. New residential development is active, with an average sale price for an average home being $70,000 to $78,000. There are few existing homes available and virtually no rental properties, even though new subdivisions and apartment complexes are being built. The word is that real estate looks very good, indeed, in northwest Mississippi.

The Delta

NORTH DESOTO
COUNTY BOARD (SOUTHAVEN, TUNICA)

President Carol Rickman
Century 21/Wallace Neal Realty
1495 Brookhaven Dr., Southaven   393-5512

This is another very active market. Southaven is a clean and green community just outside of Memphis, Tennessee, which is one reason for the activity and the number of residential developments. Another reason is the burgeoning casino business in nearby Tunica, where 11 casinos are now open and where about

Credit: The Sun Herald

Many condominiums on the Coast are on the water or have a beautiful view of the water.

40 percent of the workers come from out of town and need housing. There is limited rental property, and average houses cost about $80,000, though homes can be found anywhere from $50,000 to $250,000. In 1993, the Multiple Listing Service reported that 528 homes were sold in Southaven and Horn Lake, though the actual total may be closer to 800. Linda White of the North Desoto County Board of Realtors says that substantial new residential development is going on in Southern Trace, Wellington Square, Plantation Lakes, Hickory Forest, Poplar Forest Estates of Lake Forest, and more. Consequently, new houses are plentiful in these new areas. "People want to live in our area because of less crime and a great school system," said White. New commercial development includes a new Sam's Club and Wal-Mart and Kmart superstores. Also of note in this bustling market are four new hotels under construction that will help accommodate the 50,000 to 75,000 people who come to the Tunica casinos daily.

CLARKSDALE BOARD

President Peter Vincent
C.F. "Peter" Vincent, Real Estate
Appraiser/Sales
223 Sharkey Ave.
Clarksdale   624-8282

Pete Vincent says that the market is tight. Some influx from the casinos was seen last year but not much now. No new subdivisions are being built and not many existing homes are on the market. Even lake property, which was a stagnant market for a long time, is tight now. Industry is good, and those who find the home they want are paying more than $100,000 for the upper market, while a median range is around $70,000.

CLEVELAND BOARD

President Lynn Pace
Lynn Pace General Appraiser, Realtor
703 N. Davis Ave., Cleveland   843-6680

This Delta town is holding steady with not a lot of new development and not too many available houses. Higher income buyers have a better chance of finding houses for more homes in the $100,000-

plus range are available. Cleveland's median price range for existing, average-size homes is less than $65,000.

GREENVILLE AREA BOARD
President Lanier Sykes Bogen
Coldwell Banker
Lanier Sykes Bogen Realty, Inc.
157 Reed Rd., Greenville   334-1450

This is a busy market. Colorado River Oaks residential development offers houses in the $75,000 to $80,000 range, while West Manor houses sell for $100,000 to about $129,000. New construction is occurring in additional phases of these two areas. Greenville is definitely a seller's market. Lanier Bogen says, "We have a very good market, however, there is a shortage of housing in certain price ranges. The market is very active with lots of qualified buyers." So if a house is found, the word is to act quickly; it may not be available long.

GRENADA BOARD
President Bonnie Hankins
Magnolia Realty of Grenada
P.O. Box 1516, Grenada 38901   226-7325

In the town of Grenada where the median price range for existing homes is $75,000 to $90,000 and new homes begin at about $85,000, it is advised that buyers act quickly if a home is found. According to Bonnie Hankins, "We have a good supply of people moving into Grenada but a limited number of homes available for sale." Hankins adds that commercial development is substantial, though residential development is scarce. As in most places in Mississippi, it is a seller's market at the present time.

GREENWOOD BOARD
President Ron Dubard
ERA Dubard Realty
P.O. Box 1063
Greenwood 38930   455-5885

Ron Dubard says that they sell everything they list and that 1994 was his agency's best year. Three new spec houses have been built and sold within the past few months, all in the $90,000s. Though the average selling price is in the $70,000s, there are also homes in the $200,000 to $400,000 range in the lovely area along Grand Boulevard. There's not much new building going on in the city, though it is needed. Greenwood is in line with national averages in that it's a seller's market. There are a few prime residential areas where schools are very good, which means that houses in these areas are higher, between $80,000 and $95,000. In outer areas, the same size house sells for $65,000 to $75,000. The area east of Greenwood, toward Carrollton, is developing nicely, though there are still lovely homes and homesites in Greenwood proper.

The Heartland

JACKSON ASSOCIATION
President Katie Godfrey
P.O. Box 1047, Jackson 39215   948-1332

There's always something good going on in Jackson. Growth and development is positive; people are positive, and overall, that's why so many Mississippians from elsewhere in the state choose to move and call Jackson home. The top area where residential activity is strong, dollar-wise, is around the reservoir and Madison/Ridgeland area, northeast of Jackson. New subdivisions are going from planning to development at a fast pace. The average sales price of existing homes around Jackson, average meaning 1,800 to 2,000 square feet, is around $99,000. New homes of the same size sell for an average of $152,000. Homes south of Jackson sell for less, and substantial new development is ongoing there. Throughout the city, empty-nesters appear to be scaling down and buying property around golf clubs northeast of the city. The number of houses on the market has declined in the last couple of years, but housing is still available in all areas of the city and in all price ranges, according to the Jackson Association of Realtors.

MERIDIAN BOARD
President Tony Winstead   483-4563
Board Executive Director Barbara Bosarge
P.O. Box 336, Meridian 39303   485-7113
In Meridian, the market remains active, particularly on the residential side. There are approximately eight new subdivisions being developed in the city and county. There is also a good deal of renovation of older properties taking place in the city.

Meridian is home to a number of large medical facilities serving the region, and some of those facilities are expanding. Among some of the plans on the drawing boards is a new mall proposed for the city. The military presence in Meridian brings in people who need housing.

According to statistics provided by the Meridian Board of Realtors, the average

price of a residential property inside the city limits in 1994 was approximately $70,000 in the city and $91,500 in the county. During 1994, there were 458 homes sold.

HATTIESBURG BOARD
President Sue Gallaspy, Remax   544-1995
Executive Officer Trudy Bounds
6158 U.S. 49, Hattiesburg   582-0099
The real estate market in Hattiesburg is booming, thanks to new housing and commercial developments. The new Turtle Creek Mall is now open and already into its first expansion phase, which will add a JCPenney, Sears and smaller specialty shops.

The older Cloverleaf Mall has expanded with Stein Mart and Hudson's opening there. A new convention center is being constructed, among other developments, and this has caused an increase in demand for rental properties, which are almost nonexistent. The city actively courts retirees to move into the community, and their efforts are paying off. All of this means more jobs and new people moving in, limiting the housing inventory. The average selling price is in the mid to high $70,000s.

LAUREL BOARD
President Ed Boone, Boone Real Estate
P.O. Box 422, Laurel 39441   426-9847
Realtors in Laurel still need listings badly and are waiting for new construction to help meet the great demand for houses. Most building is taking place outside the city limits because there is no available land inside Laurel, according to Ed Boone of the local Realtors group. The average price of a three-bedroom, two-bath ranch is around $70,000. There are some in the $200,000 range, but not a great many.

The local economy has improved and, although not booming, it is expected to continue its upward swing. Not much new industry is moving in, but established industries, including Masonite and Howard Industries, continue to expand their operations, which means additional employment.

The River Cities

NATCHEZ BOARD
President Janet Gay
Stedman and Associates
193 Sergeant Prentiss, Natchez   442-2286

The big news from the current real estate market in Natchez is the Wal Mart Super Store now under construction. A fall 1995 opening for the store is planned.

In the residential market, there are fewer homes for rent and sale than in some time, but, according to Janet Gay of the local Realtors board, there is still an adequate supply. An average single-family home went for $74,000, with a median price tag of $60,500, according to the local MLS figures. From listing to closing, homes sold in an average of 122 days, and they went for 91 percent of the list price.

Gay said the local market was good and strong and that Natchez Realtors are excited about the future.

VICKSBURG-WARREN CO. BOARD
President Lawrence Koestler, P.L. Hennessey
1204 Mission Park Dr.
Vicksburg   634-1921

In Vicksburg, Board President Koestler described the residential real estate market as "fair" but said that there were some homes available in all price ranges. The average selling price of a house was $68,000. All the action seems to be in the commercial market, which Koestler characterized as "hot." That's because several new restaurant chains are being built, others are newly open, and a new retail outlet mall was set to open in 1995.

Local casinos last year filled the apartments in Warren County to capacity, forcing some employees to look as far away as Jackson for rental housing. The current situation is similar. The rental market is really tight; one 60-unit complex was recently constructed. Rent has increased because of the heavy demand. Some increases have been as high as $100 a month, but most have increased by $50 to $75. Average rent for a two-bedroom unit is approximately $450.

The Coast

WEST GULF COAST ASSOCIATION
President Earline Sawyer, Sawyer Realty
P.O. Drawer 490
Gulfport 39502   863-0232
Executive Officer Betty Stokes   896-3122

BILOXI/OCEAN SPRINGS
BOARD OF REALTORS
2355-A Pass Rd., Biloxi
President Carolyn Catchot   388-7700
Century 21 Bay South
Jackson County Board of Realtors
Sandra Morgan

The real estate market on the Coast has been very active for the last two years, thanks to the influx of new residents working at the newly opened casinos. The large military presence also has a major impact on Coast real estate, as does a favorable interest rate.

Several apartment complexes are under construction, and others are expanding to handle the demand, particularly in Harrison County around Gulfport and Biloxi.

The residential market has slowed somewhat in the past year but is described as very active compared to three years ago

In 1994 the average cost of a home was $83,621, and 2,366 houses were sold that year, according to the West Gulf Coast Board of Realtors.

According to Biloxi/Ocean Springs Board of Realtors President Carolyn Catchot of Century 21 Bay South, the market on the eastern end of the Coast is improving. Things had slowed during the previous year because the casino market leveled off. The impact of the military is still good, she said. There are two large apartment complexes being built in Biloxi, and several subdivisions are constructing new phases of development.

Construction of casinos has all but ceased after a whirlwind period marked by round-the-clock construction to meet opening day deadlines. The big news now is the construction of hotels adjacent to the casinos in Biloxi and Gulfport.

Construction

The Hill Country

In the north Mississippi Hill Country, Tupelo leads the region in construction. Three new apartment complexes will be completed in 1995, providing 350 apartments for the people who are coming here with the furniture industry, banking, medicine and other categories of employment. Spring Lake Ranch is developing a 650-family residential community, with lots now being sold. Elsewhere in the Hill Country, there's construction on a couple of retirement communities, some speculative buildings for industrial clients, a major hospital expansion in Columbus and industrial expansions. There are many fine construction companies in the area, though we have listed a few well-established firms.

W.L. "BILL" FURR CONSTRUCTION
Tupelo   844-7341

TAYLOR CONSTRUCTION
Tupelo   841-0003

CHEROKEE CONSTRUCTION
P.O. Box 7620
Columbus   329-2342

LARRY BUTTS CONSTRUCTION
2612 Jackson Ave.
Oxford   234-5940

KENNETH ASH CONSTRUCTION
2590 Jackson Ave. W.
Oxford   234-3644

The Delta

The upper Delta is experiencing un-precedented building. Webster Franklin, executive director of the Tunica County Chamber of Commerce, reports that four new hotels are under construction as of this writing, and plans are in the works for other tourist-related businesses, such as golf courses and perhaps a theme park. Greenville is enjoying growth, as well, and as in Tunica, much of it is associated with casinos.

W.G. YATES & SON CONSTRUCTION CO.
P.O. Box 129
Tunica, 38676   363-2365

REEVES WILLIAMS BUILDERS
P.O. Box 167
Southaven, 38671   393-4250

WHITE CONSTRUCTION CO.
P.O. Box 656
Clarksdale, 38614   627-4705

The Heartland

Jackson and the northeast sections of the area show great growth and move-ment, consequently commercial and resi-dential building is active. Madison, par-ticularly, is attracting new citizens who come for the small-town atmosphere

found here. Whisper Lake appears to be especially appealing to Jacksonians who want scenic surroundings. Commercial building is strong city-wide, with the Greater Jackson Business and Industrial Center, I-55 at Byram, south of Jackson, boasting 20 firms that employ about 1,200 people. More than $230 million has been invested in the park since 1992. To the north, Madison County's top 10 commer-cial building permits of the 1990s show more than $41 million invested in such diverse entities as Levi Strauss Distribu-tion Center's expansion, apartment com-plexes, St. Andrew's School dining hall, Hederman Printing's commercial print-ing building, Kroger, office buildings and more.

BURTON BUILDERS
805 East River Pl., Jackson   354-4151

DREW CONSTRUCTION CO.
780 Dixon Rd., Jackson   922-1090

LANDMARK BUILDERS
6779 Siwell Rd., Jackson   372-3723

RIVES CONSTRUCTION CO.
15 Santa Clara Ct., Madison   856-8040

River Cities

In Natchez, there are a number of sig-nificant commercial activities under con-struction, according to Henry Watts, president of the local home builders as-sociation. The projects include a Super

Insiders' Tips

A house will show better and sell quicker if it's freshly painted and free of clutter, including "refrigerator art." Eliminating clutter creates a sense of spaciousness.

Wal-Mart store, a $13 million hospital addition, a new dormitory at Alcorn's nursing school and major additions to the Copiah-Lincoln Community College's Natchez campus. Across the river in Louisiana, a new Fruit of the Loom plant is under construction. On the residential side, Watts' company is constructing a new single-family subdivision in Natchez.

Here are a couple of the construction companies in Natchez:

HENRY WATTS AND CO. INC.
333 Lower Woodville Rd.
Natchez   445-2021

PAUL GREEN & ASSOCIATES
301 U.S. 61 S.
Natchez   442-2768

The Coast

Construction activity on the Coast has been strong, due to a large number of major projects, not the least of which are some major casino hotels. Builders called 1994 a banner year, and they feel optimistically about the near future. Already some hotels have opened, others were renovated, large supermarkets were recently finished and several restaurant chains have opened.

Among the major projects under construction are the first phase (200,000 square feet) of the Prime Retail Outlet Mall near I-10 in Gulfport that should be completed before the 1995 Christmas season. Developers plan to eventually add two 100,000-square-foot additions.

The Isle of Capri's 370-room, $45 million Crowne Plaza Resort hotel is expected to open in summer of 1995. The Grand Casino plans an October 1995 completion for its Gulfport hotels, six months after the Grand's Biloxi hotel opened for business. Between them, the hotels represent 900 rooms and a capital investment of $75 million.

On the drawing board are a 60,000-square-foot Postal Service distribution center in Harrison County, the $120 million Imperial Palace casino, a golf course at Casino Magic's Bay St. Louis site and expansion at Edgewater Mall in Biloxi.

On the residential side of the equation, activity is about the same as the previous year, local builders and Realtors say. Most notable are several large apartment complexes being built or expanded in the Biloxi area. A newly announced development will mean 80 townhomes near Biloxi's Back Bay. Southwind Townhome Estates, at Southwind Country Club, will have two-bedroom townhomes complete with marble fireplaces and Jacuzzis. The starting price is $119,000. The developer is Jack Tiblier of Tiblier Construction in D'Iberville.

Naturally, there are many construction companies in the Coast area. Here are a few:

J.O. COLLINS CONTRACTOR INC.
206 Iberville Dr.
Biloxi   374-5314

GEORGE HOPKINS INC.
520 34th St.
Gulfport   863-8614

J.W. PUCKETT & CO. INC.
1899 28th St.
Gulfport   864-6201

HAMILTON & LOVELESS INC.
9524 Creosote Rd.
Gulfport   863-0133

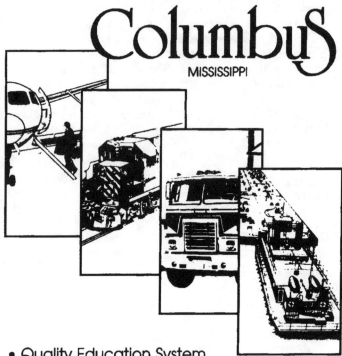 

Inside
Business and Industry

Mississippi is home to many a business success story, ranging in scope from the neighborhood mom-and-pop ventures to *Fortune 500* companies.

Mississippi enjoys a thriving business community, and its workers are the foundation on which it is built. Mississippians work hard, and their dedication to the task at hand helps to perpetuate a strong work ethic that companies here say is hard to match. An example is found in the state's turnover rates (less than 5 percent) and absentee rates (below 3 percent), which are among the lowest in the country.

Besides a reputation for productivity, the state has other attributes that attract top industry, including a strategic location (within a day's drive of more than 55 percent of the U.S. population), a good transportation network, competitive labor costs, low taxes and incentive programs. Mississippi is a right-to-work state, and less than 8 percent of its workers belong to unions. That compares to 20 percent nationally. Customized training programs are available through the state's community colleges.

Many Mississippians are recognized in the business world for their successful endeavors as they sell their Mississippi-made products to national and international markets. Many of them set industry standards.

Peavey Electronics in Meridian is a world leader in the sound equipment industry. Delta Pride Catfish in the Mississippi Delta is billed as the world's largest freshwater fish processing plant. On the Coast, Ingalls Shipbuilding has been designing and building vessels for the U.S. Navy for decades. Mississippians ably produce upholstered furniture for La-Z-Boy, tires for Cooper Tire and Rubber, wire harnesses for Chrysler and Ford, wood products for Georgia-Pacific, piano cabinets for Baldwin and they print *National Geographic* magazines at the Ringier America printing company.

Mississippi's largest private employers are: Litton Industries/Ingalls Shipbuilding, with 15,044 workers; Mohasco Corporation, 4,145 employees; B.C. Rogers Inc., 3,434 employees; Sara Lee Corp., 3,400 employees; General Motors Corp., 3,397 employees; International Paper, 3,386 employees; Georgia Pacific, 3,379 workers; and McCarty Farms Inc., 3,369 employees.

The state is ready to assist new and existing businesses by providing some innovative types of assistance. For example, the Mississippi Resource Center helps companies find the best possible location by giving managers a high-tech interactive video "look" at sites from around the state without having to visit every one.

Businesses can benefit from

Mississippi's top flight research capabilities, including the Polymer Science Department at the University of Southern Mississippi, the National Center for Physical Acoustics at the University of Mississippi and the High Voltage Laboratory at Mississippi State University. To emphasize the level of research available in the state, officials point out that one-fourth of the nation's supercomputing capabilities is located here.

Capable workers, state-backed incentives, prime location — these and other factors combine to give Mississippi an impressive track record in commerce. And things are looking up. Recently, *U.S. News & World Report* named Mississippi as the first state in the nation to recover economically from the recession in the early '90s.

Forestry and Wood Products

Mississippi's abundant resources are responsible for forestry and wood products being vitally important to the state's economy. Of a total land area of 30.2 million acres, almost 17 million, or 56 percent, are classified as commercial timberlands. Among the industry's major private employers are Georgia Pacific, International Paper, and Weyerhaeuser. Newsprint South is up and running with its new $350 million mill in Grenada; it is a subsidiary of Mississippi Chemical Corporation in Yazoo City. North Mississippi is home to a relatively new industry in the state that is somewhat dependent upon forestry and wood products, and that is furniture manufacturing. What began with a few plants in the 1960s now includes more than 250 manufacturing plants. Mississippi now enjoys the position of being America's largest manufacturer of upholstered furniture, with annual factory sales an estimated

$1.2 billion, or about 6 percent of the nation's total of $20 billion. It is home to half of the nation's top-10 motion furniture and recliner manufacturers, among them La-Z-Boy, Benchcraft, and Mohasco. The furniture industry in Mississippi employs more than 27,000 workers, and now hosts a furniture market that is gaining national prominence and is the fastest growing furniture market in the country. The furniture market is located in Tupelo, and the two markets are getting bigger and better each year. During markets, products from more than 35 states are showcased in Tupelo.

The state does its part to provide ancillary services to the furniture industry. Mississippi State University has a Forest Products Utilization Laboratory— the second largest facility of its kind in the country— that meets the industry's technical needs in wood protection, wood chemistry, adhesives and resins, and wood processing. Also on the premises is a Furniture Research unit. Additionally, other research and support organizations are located here. The Southern Forest Experiment Station in Starkville, an affiliate of the U.S. Department of Agriculture, and the Mississippi Agricultural and Forestry Experiment Station are tremendous assets to the furniture industry.

Shipbuilding

The craft of building ships has long been practiced in the coastal area of Mississippi, but shipbuilding on a major commercial scale dates back to the late 1930s when Robert Ingalls took over a shipyard in Pascagoula. Ingalls embarked on a commercial venture that would ultimately evolve into Ingalls Shipbuilding, a company that today is the largest employer in all of Mississippi. Its workload consists of designing and construction of advance surface combat ships. The company has an annual payroll of more than $4 million.

In the 1990s, shipbuilding and ship repair make up a significant segment of the Coast's and state's economy.

Seafood

The fish, shrimp and oysters harvested from Gulf waters fed the early coastal settlers, and seafood grew into an industry that supported many coastal families. Biloxi especially benefited from a growing demand for seafood and was known as the "seafood capitol of the world." The city's Maritime and Seafood Industry Museum depicts the historic influence of this once thriving enterprise.

While the number of seafood processing plants has dropped over recent years, seafood is still big business in Mississippi. Direct and indirect employment statewide was approximately 14,000, most of which was on the Coast. Of all the domestic fisheries, the Gulf shrimp is the most valuable; some 220 million pounds are caught each year.

Aquaculture

Gracing plates in world restaurants and homes is a proud Mississippi product: catfish. The state's 270 catfish farmers provide more than 70 percent of the catfish produced in the United States. Thanks to the emergence of the aquacul-

ture industry, Mississippi now produces a large percentage of the catfish consumed worldwide. Delta Pride Catfish is an industry leader and an American success story. As a cooperative entity owned by the farmers who grow catfish, the company employs nearly 2,000 workers at plants in the Delta towns of Indianola, Inverness and Belzoni.

The aquaculture industry encompasses about 92,500 acres of channel catfish production, 300 producers, six feed mills and 13 commercial fish processing plants. More than 4,000 Mississippians work in the catfish industry.

Agriculture

Mississippi's contributions to the world of agribusiness are legion, and upon close examination, it is clear that Mississippi State University is at least partially responsible for success in farming. As a land grant institution, MSU's research has been a boon to the state's farmers. Mississippi Agricultural & Forestry Experiment Station (MAFES) conducts invaluable on-going experiments. MSU also provides assistance to farmers and cattlemen through the Dairy Research Center, the Animal Research Center, and the School of Veterinary Medicine. In the Delta, the USDA/MSU Research Facility at Stoneville, near Greenville, is the largest of its kind east of the Mississippi. It has been called "the Silicon Valley of Agriculture," and for good reason; the area also attracts private research farms of Fortune 500 companies. It is a most

Credit: The Sun Herald

Chiquita Brands celebrated its 20th anniversary at the state port in Gulfport by extending its lease until the year 2008. They import 8,000 tons of tropical fruit through the Gulfport Harbor each week.

impressive complex, and visitors are welcome.

Food Producers

Mississippi's research facilities are gearing up to assist food producers, and such companies as Sara Lee, Bryan Foods, Frito-Lay, Borden, Tyson Foods, Uncle Ben's, McCarty Farms, Marshall Durbin and Sanderson Farms are taking note and expanding their operations in the state. With the instate location of these and other food processors and distributors, service and support firms flourish too.

Poultry

With new emphasis on low-fat diets, Mississippi is on the cutting edge with heart-healthy catfish and poultry production. The state ranks fifth nationwide in broiler chicken production. Unique to the area is the South Central Poultry Research Laboratory at Mississippi State University. The lab provides poultry and egg research through its affiliation with the U.S. Department of Agriculture.

Telecommunications

Mississippi's telecommunications industry is already home to several national companies, among them Mobile Telecommunication Technology Corporation (Mtel), a paging provider; LDDS, a long distance telephone carrier; and Mobile Comm, another paging company. Peavey Electronics, a manufacturer of amplifiers, speakers and other music equipment, is also based in Mississippi. The burgeoning high-tech industry is enhanced by additional research at the University of Mississippi's Center for Telecommunications, where expertise in technology and the legal and business end of telecommunications is readily available.

Chemicals and Plastics

Chemicals and plastics find the state's economy and environment attractive too, and this category is represented by such major corporations as E.I. Dupont De Nemours and Co., Inc., Chevron U.S.A., Pacific-Dunlop, Kerr-McGee and Hercules, Inc. Trained workers and research efforts are supplied by the University of Southern Mississippi's polymer science programs and the Mississippi Polymer Science Institute in Hattiesburg.

Transportation

Mississippi has an excellent transportation infrastructure, from the inland ports on the Mississippi River and the Tennessee-Tombigbee Waterway, to good access to rail and interstate highways. The state is proud of its 800 miles of commercially navigable waterways and the major international connections through deep water ports on the Gulf of Mexico. As a result of the state's port facilities, Mississippi is the nation's second-largest import/export center for tropical fruit. Five U.S. Customs offices and two foreign trade zones enhance international trade opportunities. The state's highway system, recently ranked fourth-best in the nation and the best in the South, includes six interstates and 14 federal highways.

Tourism

The business of tourism is a viable industry in Mississippi. Tourism/recreation accounted for approximately 62,500 direct jobs and a statewide income of $3.3 billion, taking the total linkage multiplier into account. Sources vary on the exact ratio, but tourism is either the second- or third-largest industry in the state. It's the world's largest industry, and it now boasts an economic impact of more than $328

Credit: Mississippi Department of Economicand Community Development

A fisherman sorts his catch from the Gulf in Biloxi.

billion worldwide. In this country, we spend more money on travel than on clothes, jewelry, accessories and personal care items combined.

Taxes from tourism go toward local projects and services, and the benefit to Mississippi communities is monumental. Tourism is clean, it requires little infrastructure enhancements, and it shows off with great pride Mississippi's best and brightest. The wonderful state parks, the historic homes and sites, the great beaches, the mini-mountains of the northeast and the vast and mysterious Delta attract visitors year after year. More than 2.9 million visitors registered at the 10 Mississippi Welcome Centers in 1994. Welcome Center staffs welcomed 4,701 motorcoaches with 106,447 passengers, an increase of 124

percent over 1993. The tourism toll-free phone number (800) WARMEST experienced a 120 percent increase in visitors inquiries, and the divsion responded to 95,211 mail inquiries and 57,137 telephone requests for information. Indeed, visitors are interested in Mississippi.

Casinos

Casino gaming is bringing in loads of visitors, and the impact is tremendous. Total gaming tax revenue in 1994 was $85.4 million. Additionally, the gaming industry is responsible for more than 22,000 direct jobs and 15,400 indirect jobs, mainly in construction and infrastructure improvements. The numbers keep growing. Las Vegas-style casinos are on the Gulf Coast, along the Mississippi River in the towns of Natchez, Vicksburg, Greenville, Tunica and an inland casino is open and thriving on the Choctaw Indian Reservation near Philadelphia.

For more information ...

Companies interested in Mississippi as a location site may want to know of the variety of financial packages, incentive programs and tax credits available. For additional information concerning business and industry, contact the Mississippi Department of Economic and Community Development in Jackson, 359-3449, or local economic development entities such as CLEDA (Columbus-Lowndes Economic Development Association) in North Mississippi, 328-8369, and the Harrison County Development Commission, 863-3807, on the Coast.

Inside
U.S. Military and NASA

Mississippi is home to six major federal government installations that have a tremendous impact on the state's economy and population. The Air Force has bases in Columbus and Biloxi, while the Navy has an air station in Meridian and a homeport and Seabee base on the Coast. The Navy is also the largest element at NASA's John C. Stennis Space Center, a multi-agency facility that tests rocket engines, among its other missions.

Government bases mean employment to these areas. For example, on the Coast four of the major employers are government related: Ingalls Shipbuilding (the state's largest employer), Keesler Air Force Base, Naval Construction Battalion Center and Stennis Space Center. Their combined local employment is approximately 25,000; the local annual payroll totals more than $1 billion.

These military facilities and their employees also have a major influence on the quality of life in their respective communities through participation in United Way campaigns, blood drives and other good-neighbor programs. Additional employment opportunities for residents is provided by other government facilities that support the military personnel. For example, there are two Veterans

Technicians at Keesler Air Force Base in Biloxi practice their skills in tracking and providing ground troops with vital information. Keesler is the electronic, computer and weather training site for the U.S. Air Force.

Credit: David Purdy, The Sun Herald

Administration hospitals and the U.S. NavalHome on the Coast.

Many of the military personnel assigned to Mississippi bases choose to remain after their tours of duty, and others return after retirement to make the state their permanent home. These individuals add to the diversity of the state's population and are some of their adopted state's biggest boosters.

Military Bases

The Hill Country

COLUMBUS AIR FORCE BASE
Hwy. 45, Columbus   *434-7322*

Columbus is proud to be an Air Force town and very pleased to welcome some of the nation's best and brightest for a temporary tour of duty at Columbus Air Force Base, home of the 14th Flying Training Wing of Air Education and Training Command. The wing's primary mission is undergraduate pilot training, a demanding 52-week program that teaches basic aircraft handling, navigation and instrument and formation flying. To earn Air Force wings, each student flies nearly 200 hours in T-37 primary and T-38 advanced jet trainers and completes 300 hours of flight-related classroom instruction. About 19 percent of pilots trained at Columbus are from the air forces of U.S. international allies. Introduction to fighter fundamentals training is also conducted here for Air Force pilots who will fly fighter aircraft. This six-week course in the AT-38 teaches basic fighter maneuvers, air-to-surface attack and low-level and formation flying.

Seeing those training jets zip around the skies over north Mississippi evokes a great sense of pride among area residents. And zip they do, for this is a very busy base. CAFB flies an average of 250 sorties a day with about 1,000 aerial events taking place on its three parallel runways. The base handles more than 250,000 military, commercial and private air operations annually in more than 4,000 square miles of air space through its state-of-the-art air traffic control facility. A former Strategic Air Command base, CAFB is known for its outstanding support capabilities, including a 2-mile-long runway that was instrumental in the base being chosen as a reception base for NASA's space shuttle on its return journey from Edwards AFB, California, to the Kennedy Space Center in Florida. Additionally, NASA astronauts use the flight simulators here for annual emergency procedures training. In addition to flight training, the base's combat support mission keeps about 250 Air Force people ready for deployment at all times. At any one time several dozen CAFB members are likely to be deployed around the world supporting national defense and U.S. security objectives.

Not only does CAFB introduce outstanding military personnel to the community, the base also pumps $4.1 million a week — more than $214 million annually — into the local economy, and Air force officials expect the base to grow. CAFB's 1,581 military and 1,346 civilian personnel have a combined annual payroll of almost $78 million. Nearly 3,000 military retirees who have made Columbus their home add an additional $41 million. Construction and services expenditures account for $24 million and other purchases for an additional $25 million. CAFB was a recent recipient of the prestigious Air Force Outstanding Unit Award, and it is home to the best civil engineer squadron, public affairs office and communications squadron in the Air Force.

The Heartland

NAVAL AIR STATION MERIDIAN
Lizelia Rd., Meridian 679-2211
The Navy station in Meridian trains about half of the jet aviators in the Navy and Marine Corps. The main base is a little more than 8,000 acres; an outlying training field and facility cover about 4,400 additional acres. Employment is around 3,000, and the payroll is approximately $47 million. Total payroll generated directly and indirectly by the base is nearly $69 million.

NAS Meridian was commissioned in 1961. With 520 housing units and 97 other buildings, its current value is estimated to be $314 million.

The Coast

KEESLER AIR FORCE BASE
White Ave., off U.S. 90
Biloxi 377-1110
Keesler Air Force Base, one of the largest technical training centers in the Air Force, is the electronics, computer and weather training center of the Air Force. The base, located on a 3,600-acre tract of land inside the Biloxi city limits, has been a major military training center since World War II when 142,000 aircraft mechanics and 336,000 recruits were trained there.

Today's students get high-tech training

Credit: Stennis Space Center

Real space hardware, like this solid rocket booster, is on display at NASA's Stennis Space Center.

mainly in electronics specialties such as computer systems programming and air traffic control. More than 1,000 instructors teach 4,000 students in 250 classes a day. Keesler graduates number nearly 2 million. Keesler's primary mission is and always has been training, but it is also home to two units whose mission is flying. One squadron is the famous hurricane hunters who fly huge C-130 aircraft into storms and relay weather data to the National Hurricane Center in Miami.

Keesler's 26,000 population includes 9,000 military, 4,000 civilians and 13,000 dependents. Its military payroll is more than $200 million; civilian income is around $81 million. The Air Force estimates that Keesler's economic impact on the Gulf Coast is more than $378 million.

NAVAL STATION PASCAGOULA

Singing River Island, Pascagoula   761-2140

Naval Station Pascagoula is a new arrival to the Coast's military family. The station, on Singing River Island 10 miles from the Gulf of Mexico, was formally dedicated on July 4, 1992.

The Naval Station's mission is to support the U.S. Atlantic Fleet ships. This small station is home to six Perry class guided missile frigates that are tied up to a 680-foot double-deck pier.

Naval Station Pascagoula consists of a medical/dental facility, weapons facility, enlisted dining facility, bachelor enlisted quarters, Navy exchange and gymnasium. Approximately 1,600 sailors are assigned there, and employment is 200. Annual payroll is approximately $30 million. Its economic impact is estimated to be $55 million.

NAVAL CONSTRUCTION
BATTALION CENTER GULFPORT

Broad Ave. and 25th St.
Gulfport   871-2121

The Seabees are the construction arm

of the Navy whose history began with the civilian construction workers who supported the Navy in the Pacific Theater and in Europe during World War II. Seabees have been a part of the Coast community for more than 50 years, starting with the establishment of the Advanced Base Depot in Gulfport in 1942. During the war years the center changed from a receiving station to a naval training center and then to a storehouse. In 1952 the Naval Construction Battalion Center was established, and in the 1960s the long-inactive training center began to grow. Today this Naval Station is called home of the Atlantic Fleet Seabees and houses and supports several units of the Naval Construction Force.

Base population of 4,400 includes 3,500 military and 800 civilians. Economic impact is estimated to be $194 million.

Seabees have made their mark on the coast community by building parks and ball fields as part of their training to provide invaluable assistance in the wake of devastating hurricanes.

NASA

The Coast

JOHN C. STENNIS SPACE CENTER
Hwy. 607, Hancock County   688-2211

NASA's arrival on the Mississippi Gulf Coast in the early 1960s brought the nation's race to the moon close to home for residents of rural Hancock County. A tract of 125,000 acres of sparsely populated land was selected as the site to test-fire the large rocket boosters that would propel *Apollo* astronauts to the moon. Several small communities gave way to thick concrete-walled office buildings and other

Credit: John Fitzhugh, The Sun Herald

An unidentified airman walks a C-141B "starlifter" jet from
the Mississippi Air Guard.

structures. Large concrete-and-steel towers were constructed to hold the rockets
down while they were "hot fired" in tests
that shook homes and rattled windows for
miles around. These so-called ground tests
were designed to show engineers if the rockets would work properly during an actual
launch.

When the Apollo test program ended
in the early '70s, the complexion of the test
site began to change. Other agencies took
up residence in the vacant buildings and
carried out their own work unrelated to
the space program. Some longtime tenants include the Environmental Protection
Agency and the U.S. Geological Survey.

The era of the Space Shuttle got the
facility back into the engine testing business, and today the center is still used to fire
the shuttle's main engines. Personnel also
test engines for the aerospace industry.

Still, the presence of other government
agencies at this NASA site is prominent.
In addition to the Navy, other agencies
include the National Data Buoy Center,
which operates offshore data collection
stations for weather forecasts and research,
and the National Marine Fisheries Service, which studies the marine resources
in the Gulf of Mexico, Caribbean Sea and
South Atlantic Ocean.

The economic impact of the 22 agencies and eight contractors located at Stennis
Space Center is $374 million. Employment
is 3,575.

Even though the Stennis Space Center
is technically a NASA facility, the Navy is
the largest agency to reside at the Hancock
County site. There are four major Navy
divisions located there. The Commander,
Naval Meteorology and Oceanographic
Command directs a worldwide operation
that consists of approximately 3,000 military and civilian personnel. Their duty is to
assist every ship in the Navy's fleet by providing mapping and weather information.
The Commander is the only active duty
admiral in the state of Mississippi. The
Command's largest subordinate activity is
the Naval Oceanographic Office, a worldwide operation that employs 1,000 civilian
and military personnel who collect, ana-
lyze and distribute information relating to
the world's oceans. The oceanographic information is gathered from ships and aircraft and is provided to the Navy's fleet and
commercial interests around the clock. The
Naval Oceanography Command Facility
manages the training and equipment for
the Naval Oceanography Command.

In addition to these groups, the space
center is also home to Naval Research
Laboratory, the Navy's principal lab for
studying the impact of the ocean environment and atmosphere on Navy systems. These agencies are said to make up
the world's largest collection of oceanographic expertise.

Inside
Historic Places
of Worship

Settlers began coming into Mississippi in increasing numbers after the Mississippi Territory was organized in 1798. From then until the outbreak of the Civil War, organized religion in the State was in a growth mode; changes in doctrine were common, and ministers were often scarce. Clergymen had arrangements with several churches to minister to each, thus they "rode the circuit" from community to community. In the process, the missionary movement developed, as did the "Sunday School" concept, where families met on the Sabbath to study and learn.

The Mississippi Baptist Association was formed in 1806; the first Baptist State Convention was organized at Clear Creek Church in Washington, near Natchez. This was a difficult time for a denomination whose individual churches had previously run their own affairs. There were more Baptist churches than any other, therefore more dissension.

In 1826, the American Home Missionary Society was organized to enable churchmen to promote the work of God among Native Americans and the lawless frontier. The Methodists, too, did

Credit: Herb Welch, The Sun Herald

Trinity Episcopal Church in Pass Christian, shown here five years after its 1971 consecration, is similar to the old structure. In 1969 Hurricane Camille destroyed the church's 120 year-old chapel along with two other buildings on the grounds. Through the years members have worked to replace the structures.

missionary work among the Indians. In fact, Alexander Talley, a Methodist minister, held offices around 1828 in the home of Choctaw Chieftan Greenwood Leflore, who was half French (LeFleur). By 1860, the Methodists were larger in number of churches, though the Baptists had more members.

The Presbyterians also worked with Indians and once had a school called the Bell Indian Mission, at Cotton Gin Port on the Tombigbee River in Monroe County. They also organized the Synod of Mississippi in 1835, though a split in the church resulted in the organization of Cumberland Presbyterian. New Englanders became involved in Presbyterian mission work, and they too formed missions, eight in all, including the Mayhew Mission near Columbus.

The Church of England was represented in early Mississippi as well. The Rev. Adam Cloud was in Natchez during the days of Spanish rule and later returned. In 1820 he organized Christ Episcopal Church at Church Hill, near Natchez, and later held a convention there to establish a diocese. The state's first Episcopal bishop was the Rt. Rev. William Mercer Green.

It was also in Natchez that the Catholics first became organized. The Catholic parishioners were initially supervised by the Bishop of Baltimore. The Diocese of Natchez was organized in 1841; priests were on call in Natchez and Vicksburg, but there were as yet no parishes. Shortly thereafter, Catholic churches sprang up in the river towns, along the Coast, in Jackson, Yazoo City and Columbus; a monastery was located at Paulding in Jasper County.

The issue of slavery created problems for Mississippi churches once abolitionist activity in the north accelerated. Consequently, the Methodist Episcopal Church South and the Southern Baptist Convention were formed.

Today, the predominant churches in most Mississippi towns are Baptist, Methodist and Presbyterian, in that order. The Gulf Coast has more Catholics than any other region; most towns, except Jackson, where you'll find more options, have one Catholic church, one or two Episcopal churches, one or two Lutheran churches and one Church of Christ. You'll usually find a Jewish synagogue in larger towns. Nondenominational, charismatic churches seem to be growing in number. See below for more information on historically significant churches in the five geographic regions. A complete listing of churches in each town is available at chambers of commerce.

The Hill Country

Aberdeen and Monroe County boast 18 churches, one of which has a few unanswered questions associated with it. **St. John's Episcopal**, 402 Commerce, was built between 1851 and 1853. Its first rector was well-known novelist Joseph Holt Ingraham. Perhaps through his connections, a group of New York merchants in 1853 sent a bell made of nickel, which

Insiders' Tips

It's always a pleasant surprise to drive through the Mississippi countryside and find a beautifully tended, small white church nestled in a grove of trees.

still sits atop the church. No one knows for sure why the merchants sent the bell.

The **First Methodist Church**, 300 College Place, boasts stained glass and chandeliers attributed to Louis Comfort Tiffany.

Columbus and Lowndes County have 118 churches serving many denominations, though Baptist churches are greatest in number. **St. Paul's Episcopal Church**, 618 College Street, was built as a frame church in 1839; the still-in-use Gothic brick edifice was completed in 1860 and boasts a signed Tiffany stained-glass window. Playwright Tennessee Williams, a Columbus native, claimed the adjoining rectory as his first home. His grandfather was the rector. The lovely Victorian rectory that once sat next to the church has now been moved to a new location on Main Street, at River Hill, and it serves as the Mississippi Welcome Center, Columbus.

The First Methodists built their first building in 1831 and their second in 1844. The First Baptists organized in 1832 and built in 1838. During the Civil War, the churches of Columbus housed and tended the wounded from nearby battlefields. According to legend, the elegant carpet in the **First Baptist Church**, Seventh Street N., was taken up and cut into squares to serve as blankets for the soldiers.

Bethel Presbyterian Church in south Lowndes County was founded in 1834. An original record still in the church lists founding members who agreed to pay for construction. Members and historians spent from 1986 to 1994 restoring and preserving this National Register of Historic Places church. It's 12 miles from Columbus, with turns off various gravel roads. The Columbus CVB has directions; call 329-1191.

Corinth and Alcorn County have a total of 107 churches; most denominations are represented. **The Christian Church**, Van Dorn and Randolph streets, a brick structure built in 1858, was torn down by Union troops during the Civil War so that they could use its bricks to make an oven for baking. In the early 1900s, the U.S. Government compensated Corinth churches for damages sustained during the Civil War.

College Hill Presbyterian Church, 8 miles northwest of Oxford on College Hill Road, is said to have housed Union Gen. William T. Sherman's horses when his troops occupied College Hill in 1862. It's also the church where novelist William Faulkner was married in 1929.

The Gothic-style **Christ Episcopal Church** in Holly Springs was consecrated in 1858, complete with a slave gallery. The popular priest/novelist Joseph Holt Ingraham, formerly of the Aberdeen parish, was rector at the time. Two years later, Ingraham shot himself in the church, though the suggestion of suicide was silenced. The Romanesque Revival **First Presbyterian Church**, Memphis Street, was occupied by Federal troops during its construction.

The Delta

Greenville and Washington County have more than 150 churches, and Greenville is proud to be one of the five cities in the state to have a synagogue at the **Hebrew Union Temple**, 504 S. Main. **St. Joseph Catholic Church**, 412 Main, is listed on the National Register of Historic Places, and its original construction cost was said to have been paid by the parish priest. It boasts exquisite Emil Frei stained glass. **Sacred Heart Roman Catholic Church**, 422 E. Gloster, was

Credit: David Purdy, The Sun Herald

Max gets a handshake from Rev. Jack Biggers at a blessing of the animals at the Church of the Redeemer on U.S. 90 in Biloxi.

once the United States' only seminary for black priests. Today, although no longer a seminary it is an active church. It is a Romanesque Revival structure.

The Heartland

In the capital city, expect to find a deep and abiding faith among Jacksonians, for they wholly and enthusiastically support more than 400 churches. Some are proud to say that Jackson is the buckle of the Bible belt. It's a big Baptist town, where some of the congregations number in the thousands. **First Baptist Church** and **Broadmoor** are among the biggest.

The beautiful Cathedral of **St. Peter the Apostle**, 123 N. West Street, c. 1897, replaces the first building, which was burned by Federal troops in 1863. An outstanding example of Gothic Revival architecture is the 1903 **St. Andrews Episcopal Cathedral**, 305 E. Capitol Street. **Beth Israel Temple**, 5315 Old Canton Road, is one of five synagogues in the state.

The Episcopal **Chapel of the Cross in Madison**, Highway 463 at Mannsdale

Road, was built in 1850. The Gothic-style chapel boasts original rafters that were carved from huge trees that grew on the plantations of founding members. **Canton's Grace Episcopal Church**, 161 E. Peace, is a rare example of Southern Gothic architecture. It was completed in 1853 and is the oldest church in Canton.

Meridian has more than 150 churches representing 30 denominations. Several historic churches played a key role in the city's African-American heritage, including those that follow.

Founded in 1868, **New Hope Baptist Church**, 2614 13th Street, is Meridian's oldest Black Baptist Church. The original church structure served as a public school from 1892 to 1894. Between 1896 and 1902, the basement was the site of classes for the Meridian Baptist Seminary. **First Union Baptist Church**, 610 38th Avenue, was founded in 1902. This church was the site of many of the organizational meetings of the Civil Rights movement during the 1960s. **St. John Baptist Church**, 2600 18th Avenue, was organized in 1884 and was moved to its present location in 1912. The structure was remodeled in 1946 and again in 1951.

St. Paul's United Methodist Church, 2702 13th Street, was organized in 1866 by Rev. Gilbert Brooks. The church was instrumental in the establishment of two local schools for African Americans, the Freedman's Bureau School and the Meridian Academy.

Good Shepherd Lutheran Church, 3101 12th Street, is the only remaining structure left from the Lincoln Academy School for Negroes. The academy was one of several private schools opened for the education of blacks starting around 1867. Two German missionary orders, the Society of the Divine Word and the Sister Servants of the Holy Spirit, established **St. Joseph Catholic Church**, 1918 18th Avenue, in 1910. A coed school founded by the sisters was also located here.

The River Cities

Natchez, Vicksburg and Port Gibson have a number of churches, including many of historical significance.

In Natchez, the **B'Nai Israel Temple**, Commerce at Washington streets, was dedicated in 1905, replacing a temple built in 1872 that was destroyed by fire. The original structure was built following approval in 1848 from the Mississippi Legislature. **Jefferson Street Methodist Church**, Jefferson at Union streets, was built in 1872 to replace the church that burned. The first church on this site was built in 1807. **First Presbyterian Church**, Pearl at High Street, was the second church built in Natchez; its cornerstone was laid in 1812, and construction was completed in 1819. This downtown church is considered a landmark in the city. **Kingston Methodist Church**, Highway 61 S. at Kingston Road, was built in 1856 to replace a brick one that was destroyed by a tornado in 1840. That church replaced a building for the first Protestant congregation in Mississippi that was organized in 1773. **Pine Ridge Presbyterian Church**, Martin Luther King Road, is Mississippi's oldest Presbyterian congregation. It celebrated its 185th anniversary in 1992.

St. Mary's Cathedral, 105 S. Union, is the oldest Catholic building still in use in the state. The original barn structure dates back to 1843. Noteworthy features include stained glass from Germany, Italian marble altars, a painting of the Crucifixion and fine carved woodwork. Also in Natchez, **Holy Family Catholic Church**, St. Catherine at Orange Avenue, was originally a small frame building on Beaumont Street in 1890 and moved in 1894 to the present building. It was the first black Catholic parish in Mississippi.

Trinity Episcopal Church, Commerce at Washington Street, is the oldest church structure in Natchez, and its congregation, founded in 1822, is the second-oldest Episcopal congregation in the state. Originally, the church had a gilded dome, which was removed during an 1888 remodeling. Its distinct features include interior arches and a slave gallery. **Rose Hill Baptist Church**, 607 Madison Street, was Mississippi's first African-American Baptist church, dating back to the 1830s. The Romanesque Revival building was constructed in 1908, replacing the original church that burned.

Washington Methodist Church, Highway 61 N., is where Methodism was born in Mississippi back in 1799, across the road from Jefferson Military College. The church is handmade of sun-dried bricks, heavy doors and wavy glass windows. **Zion Chapel African Methodist Episcopal Church**, Martin Luther King Drive at Jefferson Street, was founded in

1858. Its minister became the first black man to serve in Congress when he fulfilled the unexpired Senate term of Jefferson Davis in 1870.

In Vicksburg, **Christ Episcopal Church**, 1119 Main Street, is noted as being the city's oldest building used for public assemblies. Its cornerstone was laid in 1839 by Bishop Leonidas Polk, who later served as a lieutenant general in the Confederate Army. During the siege of Vicksburg in 1863, daily services were conducted in the church. Today there are regular weekly worship services held in the church, which contains many of its original furnishings. Next door, the mid-19th-century house is still used as the rector's residence.

Port Gibson calls itself a "city of churches," and there are eight on Church Street alone, including the **First Presbyterian Church**, organized in 1807. This church is widely known for the gilded hand on the steeple pointing upward. It is 145 feet high from the ground to the tip of the finger and measures slightly more than 10 feet from the base of the wrist to the fingertip. The chandeliers are from the steamboat *Robert E. Lee*. Other Church Street churches include **St. Joseph's Catholic Church**. Founded in 1849, this is the oldest surviving church building in Port Gibson. Significant features include carvings by local craftsman Daniel Foley.

The Coast

In the three coastal counties, there are literally hundreds of churches representing most denominations. The largest denomination is Catholic, followed by Baptists and United Methodists. What follows is a look at some of the historic churches on the Coast.

In Bay St. Louis, **Our Lady of the Gulf Church**, 228 S. Beach, was erected in 1850 and was destroyed by fire in 1907. The cornerstone for the present church was laid in 1908. Adjacent to the church is the outdoor Shrine of Our Lady of the Woods. The statue was brought from France by a young priest in 1860.

St. Mark's Episcopal Church, 123 Church Street, in Gulfport is the oldest Episcopal Church organized on the Mississippi Gulf Coast (1846). At one time, Jefferson Davis was a member. The church was moved to its present site in 1924.

Biloxi's **Nativity of the Blessed Virgin Mary Cathedral**, 870 Howard Avenue, was constructed around 1902 in the Gothic style. This Catholic cathedral contains beautiful German-made art glass windows. Also in Biloxi is the **Church of the Redeemer-Episcopal**, 610 Water Street. Its congregation included Confederate President Jefferson Davis, whose his pew has been preserved. The Gothic Revival church was built in 1873 and 1874. The present structure is the older of two buildings that predates Hurricane Camille, which destroyed much of the Coast in 1969. The bell tower from the 1894 church is the only surviving part of that building.

St. Michael's Catholic Church, 177 First Street, in Biloxi was organized in 1870; the present church was built in 1965. Unique features include stained-glass windows showing the apostles as fishermen.

Resources

For additional information about places of worship, contact the organizations listed below. If a denomination is not listed, ask a local clergyman of that faith to provide a list of the denomination's churches in the area of your choice.

MISSISSIPPI BAPTIST CONVENTION BOARD
Mississippi Baptist Building
515 Mississippi St.
Jackson   *968-3800*

BAPTIST CONVENTION PRAYER LINE
Jackson   *969-7729*

CATHOLIC DIOCESE OF JACKSON
(Serves central and north Mississippi)
237 E. Amite St., Jackson   *969-1880*

CATHOLIC DIOCESE OF BILOXI
(Serves south Mississippi)
120 Reynoir St., Biloxi   *374-0220*

EPISCOPAL DIOCESE OF MISSISSIPPI
St. Andrews Cathedral
305 E. Capitol St., Jackson   *354-1535*

UNITED METHODIST MISSISSIPPI CONFERENCE
Office of the Bishop
666 North St., Jackson   *948-4561*

SYNOD OF ST. ANDREW
(Presbyterian, North Mississippi)
P.O. Box 1176, Oxford 38655   *234-6069*

LUTHERAN, MISSOURI SYNOD DISTRICT HEADQUARTERS
Southern District
P.O. Box 8396
New Orleans, La. 70182   *(504) 282-2632*

CHURCH OF GOD STATE OFFICE
4655 Terry Rd., Jackson   *372-2714*

ASSEMBLIES OF GOD STATE HEADQUARTERS
P.O. Box 7439
Jackson 39282   *373-1943*

UNITARIAN UNIVERSALIST CHURCH
4872 N. State St., Jackson   *982-5919*

NONDENOMINATIONAL
Storehouse Church
Hwy. 98 W., Hattiesburg   *268-6300*

There is an informal coalition of non-denominational churches that meets regularly in different cities. For more information, contact David Taylor, pastor, Storehouse Church, Hattiesburg.

Inside
Media

Put it before them briefly so they will read it, clearly so they will appreciate it, picturesquely so they will remember it and, above all, accurately so they will be guided by its light.

— Joseph Pulitzer on communicating through the media.

Apparently many Mississippians ascribe to Pulitzer's statement, for many have won prestigious Pulitzer Prizes in journalism. Hodding Carter of the Greenville *Delta Democrat Times* won the Pulitzer for editorial writing in 1946. So did Ira B. Harkey Jr., of the *Pascagoula Chronicle* in 1963, as well as Hazel Brannon Smith of the *Lexington Advertiser* in 1964. There have been other winners in other categories that are too numerous to list. Here's something else to brag about: Knight-Ridder, *The Sun Herald's* group, has won 61 Pulitzers, the most of any newspaper chain.

Indeed, Mississippians have long been proud of their reputations as producers of good print and broadcast journalists. One favorite editor, the late J.W. West of the *Laurel Leader Call*, believed that discord of the day must be reported responsibly and ethically, regardless of the circumstances. During the early days of the Civil Rights movement, his pressroom

Credit: The Sun Herald

A Mississippi minister records a message for radio listeners.

was bombed because someone took issue with his editorials. Yet, he continued to write editorials and print the news by using pressroom facilities in a neighboring town.

Today, the commitment to good journalism continues in small weeklies and large dailies throughout Mississippi. It is a pleasure to see the quality of writing that appears in some of our local papers, and more than a few local newscasts are as good as any in major markets. The media in Mississippi is also notable for its willingness to serve the community through public service space and time. Newspapers and radio and TV stations do more than is required here in the Magnolia State, and they appear to do it gladly.

The newspapers in the state with the highest circulation are, in this order: *The Clarion-Ledger*, Jackson (Gannett); *The Sun Herald*, Biloxi/Gulfport (Knight-Ridder); *Northeast Mississippi Daily Journal*, Tupelo (Independent); and the *Hattiesburg American* (Gannett). Among the largest television stations in areas of dominant influence are: WLOX (ABC), Biloxi; WDAM (NBC), Hattiesburg/Laurel; WLBT (NBC), Jackson; WTVA (NBC), Tupelo; and WCBI (CBS), Columbus. The following listings reflect the largest media entities in each region. If you require additional information, contact the Mississippi Press Association, 981-3060, or the Mississippi Association of Broadcasters, 957-9121.

The state is also home to several good magazines and periodicals. We've included them under their respective regions.

The Hill Country

Daily Newspapers

COMMERCIAL DISPATCH
516 Main St., Columbus   328-2424
Sun. through Fri., PM
Circulation: 14,792 daily, 15,958 Sun.

THE DAILY CORINTHIAN
1607 S. Harper Rd.
Corinth   287-6111
Mon. through Fri., PM
Circulation: 8,655

OXFORD EAGLE
916 Jackson Ave., Oxford   234-4331
Mon. through Fri., PM
Circulation: 5,094

STARKVILLE DAILY NEWS
316 University Dr., Starkville   323-6586
Mon. through Sun., AM
Circulation: 6,500

NORTHEAST MISSISSIPPI DAILY JOURNAL
1655 Green St., Tupelo   842-2611
Mon. through Sun., AM
Circulation: 38,491 daily; 36,559 Sun.

DAILY TIMES LEADER
227 Court St., West Point   494-1422
Tues. through Fri., AM; circulation "not reported," Gale Directory of Publications, 1995

The *Today in Mississippi* tabloid is a cooperative monthly publication of the Electric Power Associates of Mississippi. It reaches more than 325,000 homes served by rural electric power.

Insiders' Tips

Magazines

THE OXFORD AMERICAN
"A MAGAZINE FROM THE SOUTH"
114A S. Lamar, Oxford   236-1836

RECKON
"THE MAGAZINE
OF SOUTHERN CULTURE"
301 Hill Hall, Univ. of Miss. Campus
Oxford   232-5742

LIVING BLUES
301 Hill Hall, Univ. of Miss. Campus
Oxford   232-5742

KUDZU AND YOU
312 Fifth Ave. S., Armory   256-9562

Radio

WMAE-89.5 FM
Booneville
Public Radio in Mississippi (PRM) 3825
Ridgewood Rd. Jackson   982-6565

WMAV-90.3 FM
Oxford-University
PRM
3825 Ridgewood Rd.
Jackson   982-6565

WMAB-89.9 FM
Starkville-Mississippi State
PRM
3825 Ridgewood Rd.
Jackson   982-6565

WCKO-FM-94.0
Oldies
University Mall, Columbus   327-9410

WACR-AM-1050/FM-103.9
Inspirational, Black/Urban
1910 14th Ave. N.
Columbus   328-1050

WJWF-AM-1400
WMBC-FM-103.1
Religious, Country, News
702 Second Ave. N.
Columbus   329-1030

WVOM-AM-1270
WFXO-FM-104.9
Country
311 Eastport St., Iuka   423-6059

WQLJ-FM-93.7
Adult Contemporary
307 S. Lamar, Oxford   234-5107

WOXD-FM-95.5
Oldies ('50s, '60s, '70s)
2211 S. Lamar, Oxford   234-9631

WWMS-FM-97.5 "MISS 98"
Country 2017 University E., Oxford 234-6881

WKOR-AM-980/FM-94.9
News/Talk, Hot Country
201 W. Lampkin St.
Starkville   323-4980

WMXU-FM-106.1
Contemporary Hits
608 Yellowjacket Dr., Starkville   323-1230

WSSO-AM-1230
Simulcast, Classic rock
608 Yellow Jacket Dr., Starkville   323-1230

WWKZ-FM-103.5
Contemporary Hits
3200 W. Main, Tupelo   844-2887

WELO-AM-580
WZLQ-FM-98.5
Oldies, Classic Rock
P.O. Box 410, Tupelo 38802   842-7658

WFTA-FM-101.9
Adult Contemporary
855 Cliff Gookin Blvd., Tupelo   842-7625

WSYE-FM-93.3

Adult Contemp.,Oldies
1705 S. Gloster, Tupelo   844-9793

WROB-AM-1450
WKBB-FM-100.9

Easy Listening, R&B, Talk
413 Forrest St., West Point   494-1450

Television

WCBI-TV 4 (CBS)

201 Fifth St. S., Columbus   327-4444

WTVA-TV 9 (NBC)

Beech Springs Rd., Tupelo   842-7620

WLOV-TV 27 (FOX)

West Point location, c/o WTVA
P.O. Box 350
Tupelo 38801   494-8327, 842-7620

The Delta

Daily Newspapers

PRESS REGISTER

123 Second St., Clarksdale   627-2201
Mon. through Fri., PM, Sun. AM
Circulation: 7,113 daily; 7,277 weekend

BOLIVAR COMMERCIAL

821 N. Chrisman
Cleveland   843-4241
Mon. through Fri., PM
Circulation: 7,621

DELTA DEMOCRAT TIMES

Mon. through Fri., PM, Sun. AM
988 N. Broadway
Greenville   335-1155
Daily, PM
Circulation: 12,565 daily, 13,686 Sun.

COMMONWEALTH

329 Hwy. 82 W., Greenwood   453-5312
Mon. through Fri., PM, Sun AM
Circulation: 8,805 daily, 9,099 Sun.

THE DAILY SENTINEL-STAR

158 S. Green St., Grenada   226-4321
Mon. through Fri., PM
Circulation: 4,500

Magazines

DELTA WILDLIFE MAGAZINE

P.O. Box 276
Stoneville 38776   686-4062

DELTA FARM PRESS

Farm Press Publications
14920 U.S. Hwy. 61, Clarksdale   624-8503

Radio

WMAO-90.9 FM

Greenwood
PRM
3825 Ridgewood Rd.
Jackson   982-6565

WCLD-AM-1490/FM-103.9

Oldies, Urban Contemporary
1101 S. Davis Ave., Cleveland   843-4091

WBAQ-FM-97.9

Easy Listening
136 S. Broadway, Greenville   335-3383

WGVM-AM-1260
WDMS-FM-100.7

Talk, Contemporary Country
1383 Pickett St., Greenville   334-4559

WKXG-AM-1540
WYMX-FM-99.1

Urban   Contemporary/Gospel,   Adult
Contemporary
Browning Rd., Greenwood   453-2174

WJNS-FM-92.1

Christian
Hwy. 49 E., Yazoo City   746-5921

Television

WXVT TV (CBS)
3015 W. Reed Rd., Greenville   334-1500

WABG TV (ABC)
P.O. Drawer 720, Greenwood 38930   453-4001

The Heartland

Daily Newspapers

THE CLARION-LEDGER
311 E. Pearl St.
Jackson   961-7000
Mon. through Sun., AM
Circulation: 111,794 daily, 130,345 Sun.

THE MERIDIAN STAR
814 22nd Ave., Meridian   693-1551
Mon. through Fri., PM; Sun. AM
Circulation: 21,896 daily, 24,085 Sunday

HATTIESBURG AMERICAN
825 N. Main St., Hattiesburg   582-4321
Mon. through Fri., PM; Sat. - Sun., AM
Circulation: 26,622 daily, 29,936 Sunday

McCOMB ENTERPRISE -JOURNAL
Oliver Emmerich Dr.
McComb   684-2421
Mon. through Fri., midday; Sun. AM
Circulation: 12,173 daily, 12,511 Sunday

THE DAILY LEADER
P.O. Box 551
Brookhaven 39601   833-6961
Mon. through Fri., PM
Circulation: 7, 581 daily

LEADER-CALL
130 Beacon St., Laurel   428-0551
Mon. through Fri., PM, Sat. AM
Circulation: 9,896 daily, 10,000 Sunday

Magazines

MISSISSIPPI MAGAZINE
Downhome Publications
P.O. Box 16445
Jackson 39236   982-8418

MISSISSIPPI TRAVEL GUIDE
(ALSO 55 & FINE MAGAZINE)
P.O. Box 13929
Jackson 39236   981-0933

MISSISSIPPI BUSINESS JOURNAL
P.O. Box 4566
Jackson 39296   352-9035

JACKSON BUSINESS JOURNAL
P.O. Box 12727
Jackson 39236   956-0756

Radio

WMPN-91.3 FM
PRM
3825 Ridgewood Rd.
Jackson   982-6565

WKXI-AM-1300
WTYX-FM-94.7
Black Adult Contemporary-Blues
222 Beasley Rd., Jackson   957-1300

WSLI-AM-930
WJDX-FM-96.3
Talk, Adult Contemporary
811 E. River Pl., Jackson   925-3458

Insiders' Tips

During the Jimmy Carter Presidency in 1978, the late President Jefferson Davis, Confederate States of America, had his U.S. citizenship restored.

WZRX-AM-1590
WSTZ-FM-106.7

Big Band-Nostalgia
4500 I-55 N., Highland Village
Jackson   982-1067

WQST-AM-850
WQST-FM-92.5

News/Talk, Country
U.S. 80 E., Forest   469-3701

WFCA-FM-107.9

Southern Gospel
Rt. 1 - Box 12, French Camp   547-6414

WKOZ-AM-1340
WBKJ-FM-105.1

Contemporary, Country
Golfcourse Rd., Kosciusko   289-1340

WALT-910 AM
WOKK-97.1 FM

Urban AM, Country FM
Hwy. 45 N., Meridian   693-2661

WTUX-102.1 FM

'70s, '80s and '90s hits
Hwy. 45 N., Meridian   693-2661

WJDQ-101.3 FM

Top-40
4307 Hwy. 39 N., Meridian   693-2381

WZMP-95.1 FM

Hot Country
4307 Hwy. 39 N., Meridian   693-2381

WMER-1390 AM

Praise
208 Fifth Ave., Meridian   693-1414

WMOX-1010 AM

Country/Talk
Hwy. 80 E., Meridian   693-1891

WNBN-1290 AM

Gospel (day), R&B/Oldies after 5 PM
1290 Hawkins Crossing
Meridian   483-3401

WMAW-88.1 FM

Public Radio in Mississippi (PRM)
3825 Ridgewood Rd.
Jackson   982-6398

Television

WAPT TV 16 (ABC)

Channel 16 Way and Maddox Rd.
Jackson   922-1607

WDBD TV 40 (IND., FOX)

Channel 16 Way
Jackson   922-1234

WJTV TV 12 (CBS)

1820 TV Rd., Jackson   372-6311

WLBT TV 3 (NBC)

715 S. Jefferson St., Jackson   948-3333

WTOK-TV, ABC

Ninth St. and 23rd. Ave.
Meridian   693-1441

WGBC-TV, NBC

4608 Skyland Dr.
Meridian   693-3030

The River Cities

Newspapers

NATCHEZ DEMOCRAT

503 N. Canal, Natchez   442-9101
Tues. through Sun., AM
Circulation: 13,500

VICKSBURG EVENING POST

920 South St., Vicksburg   636-4545
Mon. through Fri., PM; Sat. and Sun AM
Circulation: 14,594 daily, 14,876 Sunday

PORT GIBSON REVEILLE

708 Main St., Port Gibson   437-5103
Weekly
Circulation: 2,206

Radio

KAIN-1040 AM
News/Talk
Beltline Hwy., Natchez   446-8803

WMIS-1240 AM
Gospel
20 E. Franklin, Natchez   442-2522

WTYJ-97.7 FM
Urban contemporary
20 E. Franklin St., Natchez   442-2522

WQNZ-95.1 FM
Country
No. 2 O'Ferrall St., Natchez   442-4895

WTRC-97.3 FM
Adult Contemporary
No. 2 O'Ferrall St., Natchez   446-9730

WBBV-101.1 FM
Country
899 Hwy. 61 N., Vicksburg   638-0101

WQBC-1420 AM
Adult Contemporary/Urban Gospel
3190 Porters Chapel Rd.
Vicksburg   636-1108

WKPG-1320 AM
Gospel/R&B/Blues
615 Market St., Port Gibson   437-8413

The Coast

Newspapers

THE SUN HERALD
205 DeBuys Rd., Gulfport   896-2100
Daily, AM
Circulation: 49,868 daily, 54,691 Sunday

MISSISSIPPI PRESS REGISTER

405 Delmas Ave.
Pascagoula   762-1111
Mon. through Fri. PM, Sun. AM
Circulation: 22,209 daily, 23,062 Sunday

Magazines

COAST MAGAZINE
Regional magazine
934A 33rd Ave.
Gulfport   868-1182
Circulation: 25,000

COAST BUSINESS
934A 33rd Ave.
Gulfport   868-1182
Circulation: 8,000

PASS CHRISTIAN REVIEW
Local coverage of events and people
116 Davis Ave.
Pass Christian   452-3358

Radio

WKNN-99.1 FM
Modern Country
10536 Auto Mall Pkwy., Biloxi   392-7100

WVMI-570 AM
WMJY-93.7 FM
Country AM, Adult Contemporary FM
10536 Auto Mall Pkwy., Biloxi   392-7110

WXLS-107.1 FM
Adult Contemporary
212 DeBuys Rd., Biloxi   388-1490

WXBD-1490 AM
Big Band
212 DeBuys Rd., Biloxi   388-1490

WXRG-96.7 FM
Classic Rock
212 DeBuys Rd., Biloxi   388-1490

WXYK 105.9

Contemporary
212 DeBuys Rd., Biloxi   388-1490

WROA-1390 AM
WZKX-107.9 FM

Easy Listening AM, Country FM
11737 Klein Rd., Gulfport   832-5111

WGCM-1240 AM, 102.3 FM

Oldies
11737 Klein Rd., Gulfport   832-5111

WOSM-103.1 FM

Gospel
4720 Radio Rd., Ocean Springs   875-9031

WZZJ-1580 AM

Contemporary Christian
5115 Telephone Rd.
Pascagoula   762-5683

WBSL-1190 AM

Jazz and Blues
1000 Blue Meadow Rd.
Bay St. Louis   467-1190

WMAH-90.3 FM

Public Radio in Mississippi (PRM)
3825 Ridgewood Rd.
Jackson 39211   982-6398

WXOR-92.5 FM

Christian Contemporary
212 DeBuys Rd., Biloxi   388-1490

Television

WLOX-TV 13, ABC

DeBuys Rd., Biloxi   896-1313

WXXV-Channel 25, Fox

Hwy. 49 N., Gulfport   832-2525

Credit: Division of Tourism, Mississippi Department of Economic Development

*This monument in the Vicksburg National Military Park
honors a Rhode Island Infantry.*

Inside
Service Directory

This entire book contains information a visitor or newcomer will find useful, whether you need to locate accommodations or zero-in on the nearest zoo. Our Service Directory is devoted exclusively to services — the kinds of things folks want to know when they arrive in a new place for a visit or to stay.

Money is a most important item, so we've listed automated teller machines (ATMs) in key Mississippi cities. Western Union may be essential on occasion, and just in case, its toll-free number is (800) 325-6000.

Most cities and towns in the state use the emergency number **911**. In times of emergency or crisis, no matter the location, dial 911. If that number is not operational in the area, the call will go directly to a telephone operator who can connect the caller with emergency personnel.

We've also listed chambers of commerce, for they have very good information on the towns in which they are located. For those who want to know what's going on and when, we've included phone numbers and addresses for convention and visitors bureaus (CVBs) and tourist councils. For more detailed information on the entire state, stop in at any of the welcome centers listed in this chapter.

Pet lovers often need kennels, so we've included some in each region. If you do not find a kennel listed in the area in which you're interested, ask a local veterinarian. Some of the vets in Mississippi also board, or they know of those who do. The listings in this chapter do not attempt to be all inclusive. We're certain there are many excellent ATM locations, chambers or kennels that we haven't mentioned.

The Hill Country

ATMs

DEPOSIT GUARANTY BANK
2114 Hwy. 45 N., Columbus

Hwy. 182 W. and Gardner Blvd., Columbus

1324 Military Rd., Columbus

Hwy. 45 and 72, Corinth

300 University Dr., Starkville

101 Russell St., Starkville

Mississippi State University
Colvard Student Union, Starkville

934 S. Gloster, Tupelo

212 S. Thomas, Tupelo

TRUSTMARK BANK
207 Alabama St., Columbus

1404 Old Aberdeen Rd., Columbus

3600 BlueCutt Rd., Columbus

970 Holly Spring St., Hernando

2475 Goodman Rd. W., Horn Lake

9039 Pigeon Roost Ave., Olive Branch

Ole Miss Union, Grove Cir., Oxford

1401 W. Jackson, Oxford

500 Stateline Rd. W.
Southaven MSU Union, Starkville

Hwy. 12, Starkville

2402 W. Main, Tupelo

963 S. Gloster, Tupelo

3929 N. Gloster, Tupelo

Kennels

ANIMAL MEDICAL CENTER, PA
Hwy. 69 S., Columbus   328-8395

BOSWELL'S ANIMAL CLINIC
5405 Hwy. 45 N., Columbus   328-6432

CREATURE COMFORTS
1122 B Military Rd., Columbus   328-8699

STARKVILLE VETERINARY HOSPITAL
Hwy. 25 S., Starkville   323-7078

HANKINS SMALL ANIMAL CLINIC
2604 W. Jackson, Tupelo   842-1118

KLAUSER ANIMAL HOSPITAL
2826 Cliff Gookin, Tupelo   842-8707

COLLEGE HILL KENNELS
Rt. 3, Box 22, Oxford   234-3865

SMALL ANIMAL CLINIC OF OXFORD
2008 Harris, Oxford   234-8022

Chambers of Commerce

ABERDEEN/SOUTH MONROE
COUNTY CHAMBER OF COMMERCE
The Magnolias
Commerce St./Hwy. 45 N.
Aberdeen   969-0022

ECONOMIC DEVELOPMENT
PARTNERSHIP OF MONROE COUNTY (EDP)
601 Second Ave., Amory   256-7194

BATESVILLE CHAMBER OF COMMERCE
402 Hwy. 51 N.,Batesville   563-3126

BOONEVILLE/PRENTISS CO.
DEVELOPMENT ASSOC.
P.O. Box 672, Booneville 38829   728-3505

CLAY COUNTY ECONOMIC
DEVELOPMENT CORP.
P.O. Box 177, West Point 39773   494-5121

COLUMBUS/LOWNDES
CHAMBER OF COMMERCE
318 Seventh St. N., P.O. Box 1016
Columbus 39703   328-4491

COLUMBUS/LOWNDES ECONOMIC
DEVELOPMENT ASSOCIATION (CLEDA)
618 Second Ave. S., P.O. Box 1805
Columbus 39703   328-8369

CORINTH/ALCORN
CHAMBER OF COMMERCE
810 Tate St., Corinth 39060   287-5269

HOLLY SPRINGS
CHAMBER OF COMMERCE
154 S. Memphis
Holly Springs 38636   252-2943

MACON CHAMBER OF COMMERCE
503 S. Washington
Macon   726-4456, 726-4080

OLIVE BRANCH
CHAMBER OF COMMERCE
6820 Cockrum St.
Olive Branch   895-2600

OXFORD CHAMBER OF COMMERCE
299 W. Jackson, Oxford   234-4651

PONTOTOC CHAMBER OF COMMERCE
81 S. Main, Pontotoc   489-5042

SOUTHAVEN   CHAMBER
OF COMMERCE
210 Goodman Rd.
Southaven   349-2545

STARKVILLE CHAMBER OF COMMERCE
P.O. Box 2720
Starkville 39759   323-5783

TUPELO COMMUNITY
DEVELOPMENT FOUNDATION
Drawer A
Tupelo   842-4521

Convention and
Visitors Bureaus (CVBs)

COLUMBUS-LOWNDES
CONVENTION & VISITORS BUREAU
321 Seventh St. N.
P.O. Box 789   329-1191
Columbus 39703   (800) 327-2686

CORINTH TOURISM
PROMOTION COUNCIL
810 Tate St.
P.O. Box 1089   287-5269
Corinth 38834   (800) 748-9048

OXFORD TOURISM COUNCIL
299 Jackson Ave.
P.O. Box 965   234-4651
Oxford 38655   (800) 880-6967

STARKVILLE VISITORS
& CONVENTION COUNCIL
P.O. 2720
Starkville 39759   323-3322

TUPELO CONVENTION
& VISITORS BUREAU
399 E. Main
P.O. Box 1485   841-6521
Tupelo 38802   (800) 533-0611

Mississippi Welcome Centers

COLUMBUS (LOWNDES COUNTY)
Main St./Hwy. 82   329-1191
The new state welcome center for this region is now at home in the old Victorian former home of playwright Tennessee Williams. Once the rectory for St. Paul's Episcopal Church (where Williams' grandfather was rector), the two-story home has been moved to a new location on the west end of Main Street, which is also Hwy. 82. Plan to stop by to see the historic home and pick up brochures and info about the area.

For an update on annual festivals in Mississippi, contact any of the Chambers of Commerce or Convention and Visitors Bureaus listed in this chapter, or call the state tourism information line, (800) WARMEST.

Insiders' Tips

HERNANDO (DeSoto County)

I-55   429-9969

This Mississippi Welcome Center is the first one in the state as you enter from Tennessee. On I-55 south of Hernando, it's well-marked, and contains good information.

TREMONT (ITAWAMBA COUNTY)

Hwy. 78   652-3330

You'll find this welcome center as you come into the state from Alabama. It's just east of Tremont. You'll gather ample information on the region here.

The Delta

ATMs

CITIZENS BANK & TRUST

202 Jackson St.
Belzoni 210 E. Broadway, Yazoo City

BANK OF MISSISSIPPI

1997 S. Commerce, Grenada

PLANTER'S BANK & TRUST

Hwy. 82, Indianola

SUNBURST BANK

Delta State University Union Bldg., Cleveland

700 Park Ave.
Greenwood Hwy. I S., Greenville

TRUSTMARK BANK

1637 Hwy. I S. Mall
Greenville Park Ave.

938 Hwy. 82 Bypass, Greenwood

Kennels

DINGUS DELTA KENNEL

104 E. 2nd St., Leland   686-4614

GREENWOOD ANIMAL HOSPITAL

506 I1 St. S., Greenwood   453-7672

WESTSIDE ANIMAL CLINIC

Hwy. 8 W., Grenada   226-7200

Chambers of Commerce

BELZONI/HUMPHREYS COUNTY CHAMBER OF COMMERCE

111 Magnolia St.
Belzoni   247-4838

CLARKSDALE CHAMBER OF COMMERCE

1540 DeSoto St. Clarksdale   627-7337

CLEVELAND/BOLIVAR CO. CHAMBER OF COMMERCE

P.O. Box 490, Cleveland 38732   843-2718

GREENVILLE AREA CHAMBER OF COMMERCE

915 Washington Ave.
Greenville   378-3141

GREENWOOD/LEFLORE COUNTY CHAMBER OF COMMERCE

Hwy. 82 Bypass and Sycamore
Greenwood   453-8003

GRENADA CHAMBER OF COMMERCE

P.O.Box 628 Grenada 38902   226-2571
Grenada 38901   226-2571

INDIANOLA CHAMBER OF COMMERCE

104 E. Percy St., Indianola   887-4454

LELAND CHAMBER OF COMMERCE

S. Deer Creek Dr., Leland   686-2687

YAZOO CITY/COUNTY CHAMBER OF COMMERCE

212 E. Broadway, Yazoo City   746-1273

Convention and Visitors Bureaus (CVBs)

GREENVILLE/WASHINGTON CO. CONVENTION AND VISITORS BUREAU
410 Washington Ave.
P.O. Box 5217   334-2711
Greenville   (800) 467-3582

GREENWOOD CONVENTION AND VISITORS BUREAU
1902 Leflore Ave.
P.O. Box 739   453-9197
Greenwood 38930   (800) 748-9064

YAZOO CONVENTION & VISITORS BUREAU
332 N. Main
P.O. Box 186   746-1815
Yazoo City 39194   (800) 381-0662

CLARKSDALE/COAHOMA CO. TOURISM COMMISSION
1540 DeSoto St.
Clarksdale   627-7337, (800) 626-3764

Mississippi Welcome Center

GREENVILLE (WASHINGTON COUNTY)
Hwy. 82   332-2378
It's hard to miss this unique and interesting welcome center. It's just west of town on Highway 82, and it is a replica of a riverboat, which ties in with Greenville's Mississippi River history. Once inside, find great information and a friendly staff.

The Heartland

ATMs

BANK OF MISSISSIPPI
1451 Canton Mart Rd., Jackson

2866 McDowell Rd., Jackson

758 Pear Orchard Rd., Jackson

DEPOSIT GUARANTY BANK
1675 Lakeland Dr., Jackson

One Deposit Guaranty Plaza
Downtown Jackson
Northpark Mall
1240 E. County Line Rd.

Jackson Medical Center, 2727 N. State, Jackson

947 N. State St., Jackson

TRUSTMARK BANK
Main Office, 248 E. Capitol St., Jackson

Northpark Branch
1108 E. County Line Rd.   Jackson

Highland Village
1351 E. Northside Dr., Jackson

Westland Plaza
2516 Robinson Rd., Jackson

4801 Hwy. 18 W., Jackson

205 Meadowbrook Rd., Jackson

Woodland Hills
3100 Old Canton Rd., Jackson

The Mississippi Library Commission offers a marvelous outreach program, including Talking Books and Braille Services. For information, call 354-7208 in Jackson.

Insiders' Tips

2945 Terry Rd., Jackson

UMS Medical Center
2500 N. State St., Jackson

Deville Plaza
1440 Canton Mart, Jackson

St. Dominic
969 Lakeland Dr., Jackson

Metro Branch
3635 Hwy. 80 W., Jackson

Castlewoods
6189 Lakeland Dr., Brandon

Crossgates Branch
101 Office Park Dr., Brandon

150 Liberty Rd., Canton

203 Clinton Blvd., Clinton

Mississippi College Student Center, Clinton

2425 Hwy. 80 E.
Pearl Hwy. 49 S. at Harper Rd., Richland

426 Hwy. 51 S., Ridgeland

Hwy. 39 and 45 Bypass, Meridian

4921 Poplar Springs Dr., Meridian

Village Fair Branch (inside the mall), Meridian

CITIZENS NATIONAL BANK
705 Sawmill Rd., Laurel

23rd Ave. at 11th St., Meridian

22nd Ave. S, Meridian

Broadmoor Mart Shopping Center, Meridian

College Park Shopping Center, Meridian

Miss. 39 and 45 Bypass, Meridian

4921 Poplar Springs Dr., Meridian

Village Fair Branch (inside the mall), Meridian
22nd Ave., Meridian

Kennels

FOREST HILL ANIMAL HOSPITAL
248 Maddox Rd., Jackson   922-8393

**NORTH STATE
ANIMAL & BIRD HOSPITAL**
5208 N. State, Jackson   982-8261

ANIMAL LOVERS' PET SERVICE
542 Post Oak Pl., Madison   853-4185

BLUE RIBBON KENNELS
3821 Faulk Blvd., Jackson   981-0183

BRIARWOOD PET SHOP & KENNELS
1461 Canton Mart Rd.
Jackson   956-5102

PAMPERED PETS
7706 Old Eighth St. Rd., Meridian 483-6502

PET PRIORITY BOARDING KENNEL
Dees Rd., Meridian   483-4001

BOBBY'S PROFESSIONAL GROOMING
3316 20th St., Meridian   483-8699

Insiders' Tips

Newcomers to Mississippi have 30 days after entering the
state to purchase a Mississippi automobile tag.

Chambers of Commerce

BRANDON/RANKIN
COUNTY CHAMBER OF COMMERCE
101 Service Dr.
Brandon   825-2268

CANTON/MADISON COUNTY
CHAMBER OF COMMERCE (LIBERTY)
3348 N. Liberty St.
Canton   859-1606

CLINTON CHAMBER OF COMMERCE
100 E. Leake
Clinton   924-5912

METRO JACKSON
CHAMBER OF COMMERCE
201 S. President, Jackson   948-7575

MADISON CHAMBER OF COMMERCE
180 Main St.
Madison   856-7060

KOSCIUSKO/ATTALA
COUNTY CHAMBER OF COMMERCE
301 E. Jefferson, Kosciusko   289-2981

PHILADELPHIA/NESHOBA
COUNTY CHAMBER OF COMMERCE
410 Poplar Ave., Philadelphia   656-1742

MERIDIAN/LAUDERDALE
COUNTY PARTNERSHIP
721 Front St. Ext., Acme Plaza   693-1306
Meridian   (800) 748-9970

JONES COUNTY
CHAMBER OF COMMERCE
153 Base Dr., Ste. 3
Laurel   428-0574

PIKE COUNTY CHAMBER OF COMMERCE
AND ECONOMIC DEVELOPMENT DISTRICT
202 Third St.
McComb   684-2291

BROOKHAVEN-LINCOLN
COUNTY CHAMBER OF COMMERCE
230 S. Whitworth Ave.
Brookhaven   833-1411

Convention and Visitors Bureaus

METRO JACKSON
CONVENTION & VISITORS BUREAU
921 N. President St.
Jackson   960-1891, (800) 354-7695

CANTON
CONVENTION & VISITORS BUREAU
226 E. Peace
Canton   859-1307, (800) 844-3369

KOSCIUSKO TOURIST
PROMOTION COUNCIL
301 E. Jefferson
Kosciusko   289-2981

HATTIESBURG
CONVENTION & VISITORS BUREAU
6443 U.S. 49
Hattiesburg   268-3220

Mississippi Welcome Centers

MERIDIAN (LAUDERDALE CO.)
I-20/I-55   632-1142
Enter from Alabama, and find all the information available about tourist destinations in Mississippi.

PIKE COUNTY WELCOME CENTER
P.O. Box 168
Magnolia 39652   783-5068
This Mississippi Welcome Center is located on I-55, 43 miles south of Hammond, Louisiana. It's a beautiful mansion with white columns and a porch and is well lighted at night. Of course, there's lots of information and hospitality available inside.

The River Cities

ATMs

DEPOSIT GUARANTY BANK
Mission 66 Branch
3051 Mission 66, Vicksburg

DEPOSIT GUARANTY BANK
Main Office, 825 Crawford St., Vicksburg

FIRST NATIONAL
BANK OF VICKSBURG
Main Office, 1301 Washington St.
Vicksburg

FIRST NATIONAL
BANK OF VICKSBURG
Pemberton Square Mall, Vicksburg

MERCHANTS BANK
Clay Street Branch
Clay St. and Mission 66, Vicksburg

Kennels

VICKSBURG ANIMAL HOSPITAL
Baldwin Ferry Rd., Vicksburg   636-8112

ANIMAL MEDICAL CENTER
201 John R. Junkin Dr., Natchez   442-7407

BLUFF CITY VETERINARY SERVICES
429 Hwy. 61 N.
Natchez   446-5899

NATCHEZ VETERINARY CLINIC
404 Liberty Rd.
Natchez   445-5271

Convention and
Visitors Bureaus

VICKSBURG CONVENTION
AND VISITORS BUREAU
Clay St. and Old Hwy. 27   636-9421
Vicksburg 39181   (800) 221-3536

NATCHEZ CONVENTION
AND VISITOR BUREAU
422 Main St.
U.S. 61   446-6345
Natchez 39121   (800) 647-6724

NATCHEZ-ADAMS COUNTY
CHAMBER OF COMMERCE
205 N. Canal St.
Natchez   445-4611

Chambers of Commerce

PORT GIBSON/CLAIBORNE
COUNTY CHAMBER OF COMMERCE
P.O. Box 491
Port Gibson 39150   437-4351

Mississippi Welcome Centers

VICKSBURG (WARREN COUNTY)
I-20   638-4269
  This Mississippi Welcome Center, the first stop over the river bridge from Louisiana, is a big plus because one can view the river from the front porch. It is truly lovely.

ADAMS COUNTY WELCOME CENTER
370 Seargent S. Prentiss Dr.
Natchez   442-5849
  This is one of two state welcome centers not located on an interstate (Greenville is the other one). Just follow the blue signs past the truck scales on the 61 Bypass. It's set on a hill. Camper, be aware: the center does not have a circular driveway.

The Coast

ATMs

BANK OF MISSISSIPPI
All branches including:

Edgewater Plaza, U.S. 90   Biloxi
1414 25th Ave.   Gulfport

U.S. 90 and Washington Ave.   *Ocean Springs*
524 Courthouse Rd.   *Gulfport*

HANCOCK BANK
All branches including:
601 U.S. 90
Bay St. Louis

1430 25th Ave.,Gulfport

FUEL SERVICES
I-10 at Menge Ave.   *Pass Christian*

Edgewater Mall U.S. 90, Biloxi   868-4754

Kennels

BUTLER'S KENNEL
2030 Pass Rd., Biloxi   388-4093

LAMAY'S KENNEL
10118 Choctaw Dr., Bay St. Louis 467-5281

PET HAVEN VETERINARY CLINIC
2016 Benigno Dr., Bay St. Louis 467-3910

PINE BARK KENNEL
U.S. 90 E., Ocean Springs   875-1771

Chambers of Commerce

HANCOCK COUNTY
CHAMBER OF COMMERCE
U.S. 90, Bay St. Louis   467-9048

MISSISSIPPI GULF COAST
CHAMBER OF COMMERCE
U.S. 90, Gulfport   863-2933

OCEAN SPRINGS
CHAMBER OF COMMERCE
Washington Ave.   875-4424

JACKSON COUNTY
CHAMBER OF COMMERCE
U.S. 90, Pascagoula   762-3391

Mississippi Welcome Centers

HANCOCK COUNTY
WELCOME CENTER
I-10
Bay St. Louis 39520   533-5554

Take Exit 2 off I-10 for a visit to this beautiful welcome center filled with furniture dating back to the 1800s. Look for the signs. The center is slightly off the interstate exit, but it's still visible from the interstate. It's well worth a stop to enjoy this center's beauty.

JACKSON COUNTY WELCOME CENTER
I-10, Moss Point   475-3384

A two-story Colonial-style home with columns out front welcomes visitors traveling I-10 east 3 miles from the Alabama state line. Visitors can enjoy the beautiful grounds and take advantage of the dozen picnic pavilions.

PEARL RIVER COUNTY
WELCOME CENTER
I-59 N., Nicholson   798-8184

This welcome center is a brick building easily found by following the interstate signs. Inside, the friendly staff provides information and serves beverages to visitors.

Index of Advertisers

Index

Z

ORDER FORM
Fast and Simple!

Mail to:	Or:
Insiders Guides®, Inc.	**for VISA or**
P.O. Drawer 2057	**Mastercard orders call**
Manteo, NC 27954	**1-800-765-BOOK**

Name _____

Address _____

City/State/Zip _____

Qty.	Title/Price	Shipping	Amount
	Insiders' Guide to Richmond/$14.95	$3.00	
	Insiders' Guide to Williamsburg/$12.95	$3.00	
	Insiders' Guide to Virginia's Blue Ridge/$14.95	$3.00	
	Insiders' Guide to Virginia's Chesapeake Bay/$14.95	$3.00	
	Insiders' Guide to Washington, DC/$14.95	$3.00	
	Insiders' Guide to North Carolina's Outer Banks/$14.95	$3.00	
	Insiders' Guide to Wilmington, NC/$14.95	$3.00	
	Insiders' Guide to North Carolina's Crystal Coast/$12.95	$3.00	
	Insiders' Guide to Charleston, SC/$12.95	$3.00	
	Insiders' Guide to Myrtle Beach/$14.95	$3.00	
	Insiders' Guide to Mississippi/$14.95	$3.00	
	Insiders' Guide to Boca Raton & the Palm Beaches/$14.95 (8/95)	$3.00	
	Insiders' Guide to Sarasota/Bradenton/$12.95	$3.00	
	Insiders' Guide to Northwest Florida/$14.95	$3.00	
	Insiders' Guide to Lexington, KY/$14.95	$3.00	
	Insiders' Guide to Louisville/$12.95	$3.00	
	Insiders' Guide to the Twin Cities/$12.95	$3.00	
	Insiders' Guide to Boulder/$12.95	$3.00	
	Insiders' Guide to Denver/$12.95	$3.00	
	Insiders' Guide to The Civil War (Eastern Theater)/$14.95	$3.00	
	Insiders' Guide to North Carolina's Mountains/$14.95	$3.00	
	Insiders' Guide to Atlanta/$14.95	$3.00	
	Insiders' Guide to Branson/$14.95 (12/95)	$3.00	
	Insiders' Guide to Cincinnati/$14.95 (9/95)	$3.00	
	Insiders' Guide to Tampa/St. Petersburg/$14.95 (12/95)	$3.00	

Payment in full (check or money order) must
accompany this order form.
Please allow 2 weeks for delivery.

N.C. residents add 6% sales tax _____

Total _____